The Chamberlain Letters

A SELECTION OF THE LETTERS OF

JOHN CHAMBERLAIN CONCERNING LIFE

IN ENGLAND FROM 1597 TO 1626

EDITED BY

Elizabeth McClure Thomson

WITH A PREFACE BY

A. L. Rowse

CAPRICORN BOOKS

For D. M. McC.

CAPRICORN BOOKS EDITION 1966

Library of Congress Catalogue
Card Number 65-20691

Contents

PREFACE by A. L. Rowse   vii

INTRODUCTION   xi

  I. ELIZABETHAN CHRONICLE   1

  II. GAZETTE, 1599-1612   27

  III. PRIVATE LIVES AND PUBLIC SERVICE, 1600-1610   44
      Carleton's Diplomatic Apprenticeship and the Gunpowder Treason

  IV. PRINCE HENRY AND PRINCESS ELIZABETH, 1612-1613   67

  V. PRIVATE LIVES AND PUBLIC SERVICE, 1611-1614   79
      The Death of Robert Cecil, Earl of Salisbury, and After

  VI. THE HOWARDS AND ROBERT CARR, EARL OF SOMERSET   111

  VII. GAZETTE, 1612-1619   124

  VIII. PRIVATE LIVES AND PUBLIC SERVICE, 1614-1617   155
      Mr. Secretary Winwood

  IX. SIR WALTER RALEIGH   192

  X. TRADE AND EMPIRE   204

  XI. PRIVATE LIVES AND PUBLIC SERVICE, 1617-1624   228
      War in Bohemia, Parliamentary Heroes and Scapegoats

  XII. GAZETTE, 1619-1624   270

  XIII. THE SPANISH MARRIAGE   299

  XIV. LAST LETTERS   319

POSTSCRIPT   361

INDEX   363

THE HOWARD CONNECTIONS

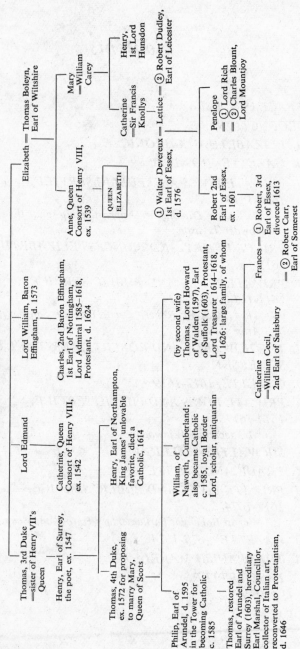

Thomas Howard, 2nd Duke of Norfolk
Victor of Flodden, d. 1524, father of
11 sons and at least 6 daughters, of whom:

Thomas, 3rd Duke
=sister of Henry VII's
Queen

Henry, Earl of Surrey,
the poet, ex. 1547

Lord Edmund

Catherine, Queen
Consort of Henry VIII,
ex. 1542

Elizabeth = Thomas Boleyn,
Earl of Wiltshire

Anne, Queen
Consort of Henry VIII,
ex. 1539

QUEEN
ELIZABETH

Mary
=William
Carey

Catherine
=Sir Francis
Knollys

Henry,
1st Lord
Hunsdon

Lord William, Baron
Effingham, d. 1573

Charles, 2nd Baron Effingham,
1st Earl of Nottingham,
Lord Admiral 1585-1618,
Protestant, d. 1624

Henry, Earl of Northampton,
King James' unlovable
favorite, died a
Catholic, 1614

Thomas, 4th Duke,
ex. 1572 for proposing
to marry Mary,
Queen of Scots

Philip, Earl of
Arundel, d. 1595
in the Tower for
becoming Catholic
c. 1585

Thomas, restored
Earl of Arundel and
Surrey (1603), hereditary
Earl Marshal, Councillor,
collector of Italian art,
reconverted to Protestantism,
d. 1646

William, of
Naworth,
Cumberland;
also became Catholic
c. 1585, loyal Border
Lord, scholar, antiquarian

(by second wife)
Thomas, Lord Howard
of Walden (1597), Earl
of Suffolk (1603), Protestant,
Lord Treasurer 1614-1618,
d. 1626: large family, of whom

Catherine
=William Cecil,
2nd Earl of Salisbury

Frances = ① Robert, 3rd
Earl of Essex,
divorced 1613
② Robert Carr,
Earl of Somerset

① Walter Devereux = Lettice = ② Robert Dudley,
1st Earl of Essex,   Earl of Leicester
d. 1576

Robert 2nd
Earl of Essex,
ex. 1601

Penelope
= ① Lord Rich
= ② Charles Blount,
Lord Mounjoy

iv]

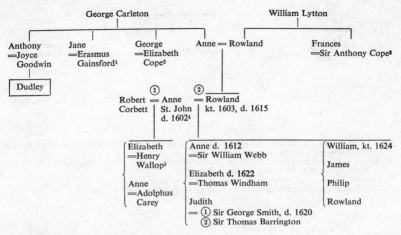

1. Sir Henry Wotton's great-uncle.
2. Widow of Edward Cope, father of Sir Anthony and Sir Edward.
3. Brother of Sir Edward, Carleton's chief means of access to Salisbury, 1605–1610.
4. Anne, daughter of Oliver, 1st Lord St. John of Bletsoe. Her sister was wife of William, 3rd Lord Howard of Effingham, eldest son of Charles Howard, Earl of Nottingham, Lord Admiral. Her sister Judith was wife of Sir John Pelham.
5. Cf. Letter 1, n. 7: it is Henry Wallop's sister Winifred whom Chamberlain calls "my wife" in the early letters.

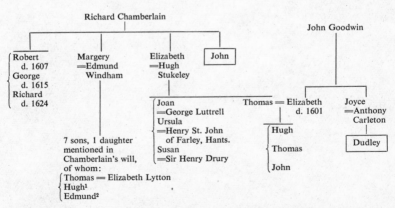

1. Chamberlain's housekeeper 1625–1628, and his principal heir; knighted 1641; Master, Ironmongers, 1638, 1642.
2. His wife Christobella was nurse to Prince Charles, afterwards Charles II.

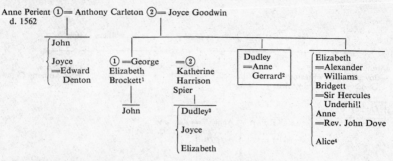

1. Daughter of Sir John Brockett; her sister Frances married Dudley, 3rd Lord North, her sister Mary, Robert Dormer of Dorney, Bucks.
2. Daughter of George Gerrard of Dorney, Bucks, widow of Sir Walter Tredway, stepdaughter of Sir Henry Savile, Provost of Eton; married 1607.
3. Carleton's successor as Ambassador at The Hague, and his heir.
4. Chamberlain's favorite, a frequent correspondent, warmly remembered in his will.

PREFACE BY

A. L. Rowse

JOHN CHAMBERLAIN has long been known as the best letter writer of his time, the Jacobean age—in effect, the first quarter of the seventeenth century—of which his letters, much relied on and used by historians, offer a discriminating portrait, with their own interest and charm. This selection of them, from the standard two-volume edition edited by N. E. McClure, is admirably representative and from it we may draw our own portrait of the age. The letters have a double value, as history and as literature, and should therefore have a dual appeal.

But there is also the quiet delight that grows upon one in reading them, in savoring the character of the writer, for he was clearly a delightful character, a good man, considerate and kind. In that brilliant and brutal age, uneasy, on edge, vulgar and ostentatious—the age of the full flowering of Shakespeare's genius, of the poetry of Donne and Lancelot Andrewes' sermons, of the career and fall of Bacon, the execution of Raleigh, the sordid murder of Sir Thomas Overbury, of Gunpowder Plot and the planting of Virginia—John Chamberlain represents another side, quieter and without panache, soberly bourgeois, sincere and generous, a constant friend, without a touch of the *Schadenfreude* that the toppling down of the great so often elicited.

For all that he lived a private life, without business or office or even a house of his own, Chamberlain knew very well what was going on in the world. In fact he made that the business of his life, to be a spectator, an onlooker, a reporter. To do that well requires a particular combination of gifts, perhaps a peculiar disposition. In the first place, he wanted nothing for himself, except his own ease and comfort of mind; like the confirmed bachelor he was, he hugged his own retiredness, taking none of the risks of life. As he confesses— and his knowledge of himself was as candid and entire as his knowledge of others: "It hath pleased God still so to deal with me and so to temper my fortune that, as I did never abound, so I was never in want. . . . I am past all ambition, and wish nor seek nothing but how to live *suaviter* and in plenty."

This was a prime qualification for a professional letter writer: it meant that he was not *engaged,* but singularly disinterested. Then, too, he was a conscientious man, very careful to get his facts right, to check his information before handing it on to his correspondent. The moderation of his temperament helped: he was not carried away by anything, he saw through everybody's shams, particularly those of the great, of the Court. Even of his friend, the puritanically inclined Sir Ralph Winwood, Secretary of State, he wrote, "well-conceited of himself and of his own sufficiency": you could not tell him anything.

Professor Notestein pays Chamberlain a tribute, with a compliment to the people of whom he was a good representative: "He had an engaging English frankness, at least with his intimates. Something else he had that was English: a way of explaining a situation with a considered moderation." Though without illusions and disliking all pretenses, there was nothing cynical about him, but "a personal generosity" as well as "a certain generosity of outlook." An inveterate Londoner, Chamberlain lived nearly all his life within a stone's throw of Old St. Paul's, making it his business to walk every day in Paul's Walk—up and down the nave and aisles of the cathedral, which in those days served as a general exchange and mart, humming with activity and news—and collecting information for his young friend Carleton, serving his diplomatic apprenticeship abroad. Chamberlain must have had a passion for news, been a perfect old gossip— no wonder he was such a sought-after guest among his friends in the country. What better qualification could there be for a letter writer? Chamberlain's personality radiated trust and confidence; this is why historians have reposed confidence in him in return and relied so much upon him for the Jacobean scene.

Of course, one has to attune one's ear to the overtones and hints. Chamberlain was frank and free in speech for his time, when one could trust few in speaking of politics and the affairs of the great. Today, when human communication is all noise, exaggeration and overemphasis, and one wearies of the relentless assault upon ear and eye, it is refreshing to turn to Chamberlain's "still and quiet course"; it makes for good practice in underemphasis and irony, too, a more subtle mode in manners and speech. One had to be careful what one said about kings. Reading between the lines, one sees that Chamberlain had no very high opinion of James I: "He forgets not business, but he hath found the art of frustrating men's expectations and holding them in suspense." Nor had he much liking for those great rivals, the glittering Lord Chancellor Bacon and the avaricious, self-seeking Attorney General Coke. Chamberlain liked quieter, more sincere people.

He was very well placed in his friends, and had a most interesting circle of acquaintance. A middle-class man himself, with his father a substantial London ironmonger, Master of the Company, who left his son a competence for life, Chamberlain's friends were drawn from that middle rank of society, city burgess folk allied to the lesser country gentry, who were the most representative and ultimately the prevailing element in the nation, backbone of its history. There was Secretary Winwood, and young Carleton himself to become Secretary of State one day; there were Sir Henry Wotton and Sir Thomas Bodley, both scholars and diplomats, the former an excellent writer, the latter founder of the great Library. Chamberlain counted among his friends such men as Lancelot Andrewes, who valued his letters and asked for more, Camden the historian, William Gilbert the scientist, in whose house Chamberlain lodged; among the country gentry with whom he hobnobbed and regularly stayed, Lyttons and Fanshawes in Hertfordshire, Dormers in Oxfordshire, Wallops in Hampshire.

It was an admirable spread of sail from which to catch wind of all that was going forward. Hence it is that Chamberlain, and this selection of his letters in turn, give us so full a portrait of the age. Stroke by stroke a telling portrait of James is built up, and of his favorites, of Carr and his odious Countess, the resplendent Buckingham. We hear of the doings of people we want to know about, John Donne, Robert Cecil, Essex and Bacon. Chamberlain is a source of information for us about Raleigh and Shakespeare's patron, Southampton, who became a leading figure in the Virginia Company, in which Chamberlain was a stockholder, disappointed by the difficulties of the colony and its long-deferred success. We watch soberly the exciting events of the time—the Essex rebellion and the death of the Queen, James's accession, the Gunpowder Plot; the fall of the Somersets and the rise of Buckingham; the farce of the Spanish match, the decline from the heroic Elizabethan age to the doubts and disputes of the Stuart period that led to the Civil War.

Then there is the literary appeal of the letters, the charm of their writing, when the language was young and fresh, the quietude of life expressed in even tones with their own sober poetry, for there was the natural rhythm of speech so apt to be lost in modern use (or abuse) of the language. Chamberlain "delighted in particular circumstances": nothing could be more propitious for a good style or for the veracity that is the heart of history.

Most of the letters were written for the benefit of young Carleton, in whom and whose career Chamberlain felt an affectionate interest as if Dudley were the son he might have had if he had not fixed upon the bachelor state. In youth Chamberlain had been delicate; hence his dedication to quiet, abjuring the risks of an active career. He went to Cambridge, but left without taking a degree; he traveled a little in France, and later spent a year with Carleton in Venice.

Was there no woman in his life? Did he never contemplate changing his state?

Apparently there was, and he had considered it. For by his will he bequeathed the bulk of his modest fortune to Carleton's favorite sister, Alice; and there is the telltale explanation: "This I do, in regard of the sincere goodwill and honest affection I bear her, and of the true and long-continued friendship between us, and for a testimony of that further good I had intended to her, if God had given me means."

Introduction

THIS selection of the letters of John Chamberlain is taken from the complete edition of Chamberlain's *Letters,* edited by N. E. McClure and published by the American Philosophical Society, Philadelphia, Pennsylvania, in 1939, recently reprinted. Those two large volumes are used by all who undertake scholarly study of the period between 1597 and 1626. I hope that this compact Chamberlain will travel with many more explorers of Shakespeare's London and the paradoxical world of James I.

Most of the sections of this edition are designed to be read as well separately as in sequence; the arrangement throughout has been planned for the convenience of the non-expert, the student, and the interested general reader. The sections called "Gazette" try to capture the flavor of everyday events, the talk of the man in the street, the news and comment that require no special knowledge or further analysis. It is significant that more and more political matters seem to come naturally into the scope of the Gazette toward the end of the reign of James I, as debate about foreign policy, and about parliamentary control over both policy and finance, spread beyond Whitehall and Westminster to absorb more and more of the public's attention.

Chamberlain comments frequently, remarkably so for a home-loving Londoner, on news of trade and exploration. From these casual reports emerges a picture of the economic activity of a nation which, after a generation of dashing adventures, was less glamorously laying the foundations of empire.

The sections called "Private Lives and Public Service," which do form a consecutive chronicle, focus naturally on Chamberlain's friends, especially Dudley Carleton, to whom most of the letters were written. His long apprenticeship, his suits for promotion, and his difficulties in pursuing loyally the unpredictable policies of the King are a principal concern of the letters. Carleton's chosen career, diplomacy, was a comparatively new one; it illustrates beautifully the trials of transition from medieval to modern machinery of government. The mutual friends of Chamberlain and Carleton include a further interesting group of those public servants who thought of themselves as professional men rather than as courtiers. Their choice and pursuit of careers, their family connections and ultimate loyalties all throw interesting light on the government of James I. Secretary of State Winwood, whom few people knew as well as Chamberlain did, emerges as a figure worthy of further study.

The great men of the period appear in the context of these friendships. There are revealing glimpses of Robert Cecil's pervasive influence on public affairs, the "world of suitors"—Carleton among them—taking their toll of him, and the startling change his reputation suffered immediately following his death. Chamberlain foresaw that the irresponsible prodigality of Cecil's cousin, Francis Bacon, would cause him trouble long before that great man was in a position to accept the gifts that ruined him. Cecil's niece, Lady Hatton, contentious second wife of Sir Edward Coke, was a friend of Carleton's father-in-law; Chamberlain closely followed Coke's tribulations, professional and domestic, and his final triumph as a parliamentarian. The power of the Howards and the rise of Buckingham concerned this group of friends, both personally as they sought promotion, and professionally as reflected in the policies they had to defend.

A concluding selection of complete letters aims, perhaps too little and too late, to restore what the fragments cannot retain of the flavor of Chamberlain's correspondence: the tempo of his long chronicle, its sometimes artful, sometimes ingenuous combination of serious and trivial, public and private, of careful reporting and brisk editorial comment.

The numbering of the letters in the complete edition is retained here for easy reference. The only textual changes are modernized spelling (in the case of proper names, the Dictionary of National Biography spellings and, for any not appearing there, their most familiar form, as they appear in McClure's footnotes), and enough revision in punctuation to make it as unobtrusive as possible—an unfortunately subjective exercise. Chamberlain's juxtapositions of private affairs and public policy lose some of their animation when marshaled into paragraphs, but this visual concession is one the twentieth-century eye demands.

The problem of dating, which always vexes these years, is solved by using the new style—starting the new year on January 1 instead of on March 25—except where actually transcribing Chamberlain's address. The fact that the days of the month in England were still ten days ahead of the continent's new Gregorian calendar appears only occasionally in the text, for example Letter 428, where the Spanish Ambassador was "to set out thence the first of their May, or rather, as the Spanish Ambassador here gives out, the tenth."

The editor of Chamberlain's complete *Letters* found him a sympathetic subject. Norman McClure, a dedicated teacher and an admirable if reluctant administrator, would never have allowed himself to live so simply "*suaviter* and in plenty"; but he and Chamberlain observed the world with the same perceptive mixture of amusement and asperity, the same balanced judgment of personality and probability. One would guess that they had much the same influence on their close friends, being themselves so uncompromisingly honest and constructively kind. I hope that this selection of the *Letters* may widen their circle of friends, in affectionate memory of both of them.

Selected bibliography:

A number of outstanding books on the period have appeared in the past ten years which use Chamberlain's *Letters* extensively and add enormously to the enjoyment of both the letters and the period. See especially:

Akrigg, G. P. V., *Jacobean Pageant,* Harvard, 1963.
Bowen, C. D., *The Lion and the Throne, Life of Sir Edward Coke,* Boston, 1956.
    Francis Bacon, the Temper of a Man, Boston, 1963.
Handover, P. M., *The Second Cecil, 1563-1604,* London, 1959.
Willson, D. H., *King James VI and I,* London, 1956.

Garret Mattingley's *Renaissance Diplomacy,* London, 1955, is a masterful introduction to the problems of Carleton's profession.

Wallace Notestein, in *Four Worthies,* London, 1956, devotes nearly half of the book to Chamberlain. And a strange, not-unscholarly book by T. Longueville (who calls himself only "the author of *A Life of Sir Kenelm Digby*"), entitled *Policy and Paint, Some Incidents in the Lives of Dudley Carleton and Peter Paul Rubens,* London, 1913, describes an aspect of Carleton's career with which Chamberlain had little to do.

I. Elizabethan Chronicle

JOHN CHAMBERLAIN *had come to terms with himself before his correspondence with Dudley Carleton began, when he was forty-three and Carleton was a recent graduate of Oxford. During the years 1597-1603, while Carleton was serving a difficult apprenticeship, Chamberlain already played the part of undemanding friend. If he had once considered marrying Carleton's "best-esteemed sister" Alice (and one can imagine the enthusiastic support this idea must have had from the rest of the Carletons and the Lyttons), the decision to remain a bachelor at the service of his friends had been deliberately taken long since. Even to the style of his letters, Chamberlain is uncannily constant throughout.*

In 1597 Chamberlain was living at the home of Dr. William Gilbert, whom he may well have met at Cambridge. Gilbert's appointment as personal physician to Queen Elizabeth in 1601 caused "the dissolution of our society" and Chamberlain's removal, first to Dr. Mark Ridley, a colleague of Gilbert, then to his brother Richard's home in Aldermanbury, all within a few hundred yards of St. Paul's Cathedral.

St. Paul's was the center of Chamberlain's London life and the key to his professional usefulness to Carleton.

Francis Osborne (1593-1656) describes the ritual of Paul's-walking as it must have been in Chamberlain's day:

> *It was the fashion of those times, and did so continue till these . . . for the principal gentry, lords, courtiers, and men of all professions not merely mechanic, to meet in Paul's Church by eleven and walk in the middle aisle till twelve, and after dinner from three to six, during which times some discoursed on business, others of news. Now in regard of the universal commerce there happened little that did not first or last arrive here. . . . And those news-mongers, as they called them, did not only take the boldness to weigh the public but most intrinsic actions of the state, which some courtier or other did betray to this society. Amongst whom divers being very rich had great sums owing them by such as stood next the throne, who by*

*this means were rendered in a manner their pensioners. So as I have
found little reason to question the truth of which I heard then, but
much to confirm me in it.*[1]

Chamberlain spent "term time," the three annual sessions of the
law courts, in London, as did his professional friends like Sir Henry
Fanshawe, Remembrancer of the Exchequer, and Alexander Williams
of the Office of the Pipe Rolls. They all followed the example of the
Court, visiting homes and friends in the country at Christmas, Easter,
and late summer. Many of Chamberlain's pleasantest associations,
and many of Carleton's hopeful connections, revolved around "your
cousin Lytton" and his wife, energetic parents of a large family.
Rowland Lytton took an active part in county affairs and moved in
the orbit of the Cecils, but never sought the jobs that took his friends
and relatives—Copes, Norths, Pelhams, Wallops—to Ireland or the
Low Countries or to Court. Chamberlain always records Lytton's
whirlwind plans with affectionate amusement, but he found the house-
ful of small children at Knebworth a disheartening place after their
mother's death in 1602.

Carleton spent these years first in travel, then as military aide to
Sir Edward Norris, Governor of Ostend. His first diplomatic job in
1601, as one of several Secretaries to Sir Thomas Parry, Ambassador
in Paris, turned out unhappily, and he joined the ill-fated household
of Henry Percy, ninth Earl of Northumberland, soon after Queen
Elizabeth's death.

The pattern of power at Court during this period was shaped by
the rivalry of the younger generation of leaders as they maneuvered
to inherit the power exercised by William Cecil, Lord Burghley, and
to influence the choice of the Queen's successor. Burghley's generous
household had sheltered at times both his young ward Robert Devereux, second Earl of Essex, and Francis Bacon, his second wife's
nephew. Robert Cecil, the clever, hunchbacked son of that second
marriage, trusted neither of them to become the sort of selfless servant
of the crown that his father had tutored him to be. Then, too, there
was Raleigh, brilliant, unpopular, unpredictably ambitious; and the
Howards—Lord Admiral Charles, the Queen's long-lived contemporary, and "good Thomas" had thrived, but evil, fawning Henry
wanted to ensure better success in the next reign. How weary the old

---

[1] *Works* (1689, 9th ed.), pp. 449-451; cf. Notestein, *Four Worthies*, London,
1959, p. 31, n. 2.

Queen must have become of them all as she outlived more and more of the friends and servants of her own generation. And with what magnificent dignity did she manage her own demise and the nomination of her successor.

The lingering war with Spain dictated the shape of foreign policy and of internal measures concerning security and religion. The cautionary ports, Flushing, Brill and Rammekens, held as security for large loans in support of the Dutch war of independence, kept England involved in the Low Countries. Catholic revolt in Ireland smoldered and continued to flare up as long as Spanish help seemed likely. The royal budget remained remarkably low; money was found ad hoc for any official undertaking. Less officially, many English soldiers went off to seek their fortune against Spain in Holland, and many West Country families sent their sons and ships as privateers against Spanish shipping and the annual treasure fleet, while other sons tried to carve themselves estates and keep the peace in Ireland, a heartbreaking task. But both sides were weary of all this; Philip III was as ready as Robert Cecil to talk about peace and commerce.

Day in, day out, fleets and ministers and the private letters of John Chamberlain had to wait for favorable winds. Mysterious illness and sudden death visited grand and lowly with equal familiarity; the will of God was equally real and inscrutable to Anglican, Puritan and Catholic. It follows that the business of daily life was to savor the day's adventure, be it a ripe melon, a trial for treason, a baby safely delivered, a letter from a friend, or a treaty of peace, and to hope for one's friends and oneself a good end.

[1] June 11, 1597: We have great preparation here for a sea voyage, which troubles our discoursers how or where it shall be employed. The common sort talk of Calais, others of the islands of Tercera; but the most likely, in mine opinion, is to set upon the King of Spain's navy wheresoever they can find it, or to meet with the Indian fleet. Their whole number consists of fifteen of the Queen's ships, besides the two Spanish ships that were taken the last year (which he new-fashioned after the English manner), and of two-and-twenty men-of-war of Holland, and some four-and-twenty flyboats and hoys that serve for carriage of men and victuals. They have with them 4000 pressed men and 1200 musketeers that come with Sir Fra. Vere out

of the Low Countries; the voluntaries are thought will rise towards 2000.

The Earl of Essex is General both at sea and land, the Lord Thomas Vice-Admiral, Sir Walter Raleigh Rear Admiral,[2] who is newly restored to the executing his place in Court of Captain of the Guard. The Earl of Southampton, the Lord Mountjoy, and the Lord Rich go as adventurers. . . .

The press of gentlemen will be very great, but I will not stand to set down any but one or two of your acquaintance, that is your cousin Michael Dormer, whom I can by no means yet dissuade, and Hugh Beeston, that stands to be treasurer of the journey, though I doubt he shall not be troubled with much receipt. For I am half of our Doctor's opinion that warrants him, if he have it, that a well-saddled rat may carry all his accounts. But his true errand is to be knighted asoon—or before Sir Peter Evers; neither doth he dissemble it greatly to his friends, but says merrily he hath been a scabbed squire a great while and could now be content to be a paltry knight the rest of his time.[3]

[2] May 4, 1598: Master Secretary[4] returned the first of this month somewhat crased[5] with his posting journey: the report of his father's dangerous estate gave him wings, but for aught I can learn the old man's case is not so desperate but he may hold out another year well enough.

Most of his followers shipped themselves at Nantes and came away by long seas, and were well coursed and almost taken by four

---

[2] Essex felt that the triumphant sack of Cadiz, 1596, should be followed up by a final crippling blow to the Spanish fleet, with himself as hero. This "Islands Voyage" turned into a fiasco. Lord Thomas Howard of Walden (given his peerage 1597 and created Earl of Suffolk by King James, 1603) was a hero of the Armada's defeat. Essex never forgave Raleigh, who led the only successful maneuver of the expedition.

[3] Hugh Beeston was in fact knighted, as was Peter Evers, in 1603, in the euphoric first year of his reign during which King James made 838 new knights. When Queen Elizabeth died "hardly a shire in England could muster enough knights to make a jury" (Akrigg, *Jacobean Pageant,* 232-33).

[4] Sir Robert Cecil, with John Herbert, Master of Requests, had been on a fruitless mission to persuade Henry IV of France not to make separate peace with Spain. William Cecil, Lord Burghley, and his old enemy Philip II of Spain both died later this same summer.

[5] Ill.

or five Spanish ships off Bluet, but yet arrived safely at Sandwich. Himself came overland to Caen and so to Portsmouth. Dr. Herbert and his train are not yet come to town, but I hear they be in England. The success of this journey is not fully known but thus far, that it hath stayed the French King from going through with Spain and made him pause at least.

The States offer to maintain him 4000 men in Picardy, which with little other help will continue the war there now that he hath nothing to do elsewhere. They have likewise offered the Queen that, whensoever it shall please her to make an invasive journey into Spain, to assist her with great store of shipping at their own charge, some say to the number of 150 sail.

Yet for all this it is still in deliberation whether we shall join with France in a peace and leave the Low Countries, or stick to the Low Countries and hold out the war. And the balance sways not yet on either side, at leastwise that can be discerned.

Matters in Ireland are farther out of square than ever, so that there is no other way but to provide the sharper sword. Here is speech of forces to be sent thither, but they cannot yet resolve upon a Deputy; for Sir Walter Raleigh, Sir Rob. Sidney, and Sir Christopher Blount (as I hear) have refused it.

Here be certain apprehended for a conspiracy against the Queen's person and my Lord of Essex's, whereof one should be a Scottishman or somewhat that way. Much buzzing hath been about it, but either the matter is not ripe or there is somewhat else in it, for it is kept very secret.[6]

Alabaster[7] that was clapped up for Popery hath broken prison and got away. Snelling, the ruffian that had the brabble with Charles Chester,[8] had not so good luck, for on Monday morning he went

[6] "One Valentine Thomas, a man most distained with foul facts, and being now to be condemned of theft . . . accused the King of Scots of ill affection towards the Queen. She was so far from harkening to those that whispered these things in her ears that she detested this man as a dishonest backbiter and maliciously suborned by others to work trouble to her and the King of Scots. . . . And she thought not good to have the man put to death lest any aspersion should be laid upon the King's reputation." Camden, *Annales*, p. 499; McClure, i, 34, n. 8.

[7] William Alabaster had accompanied Essex to Cadiz as chaplain, turned Catholic, later recanted; he was caught in Rochelle and sent back (Letter 23).

[8] Charles Chester was "a perpetual talker and made a noise like a drum in a room. So one time at a tavern Sir. W[alter] R[aleigh] beats him and seals up his mouth (i.e. his upper and nether beard) with hard wax." Aubrey, *Brief Lives;* McClure, i, 34, n. 10.

a-Maying to Tyburn and was hanged there for a robbery committed about Highgate the Tuesday before.

I hear that Justice Beaumont and Sergeant Drew that rode the northern circuit are both dead, upon some infection of the jail as is most like. . . .

The merchants have news that the Emperor of Muscovy died in January last, and that his wife's brother that was elected after him should be murdered before his coronation, whereupon there is great confusion in those parts.

[6] August 30, 1598: I came out of Oxfordshire on Saturday last, and on Monday came posting to London with your cousin Lytton to be a beholder of the solemn funeral,[9] wherein he and your brother Carleton were actors. They are gone down together this day since dinner, and have left me to convey their letters and to write you such refuse news as peradventure might scape them. But the worst is I hear your boat goes away the next tide, so that I am forced to make huddling haste which of all things I love not, and that causes me to tarry behind them for two or three days, for I am no friend to sudden motions, but of a settled constitution and naturally loath to remove.

The Lord Treasurer's funeral was performed yesterday with all the rites that belong to so great a personage. The number of mourners one and other were above 500, whereof there were many noble men and among the rest the Earl of Essex, who (whether it were upon consideration of the present occasion, or for his own disfavors) methought carried the heaviest countenance of the company.[10] Presently after dinner he retired to Wansted where they say he means to settle, seeing he cannot be received in Court, though he have relented much and sought by diverse means to recover his hold; but the Queen says he hath played long enough upon her, and that she means to play upon him, and to stand as much upon her greatness as he hath done upon stomach.

The Lord Treasurer hath left the Queen's coffers so bare that there is but £20,000 to be found, and the Queen is fain to demand

---

[9] Of William Cecil, Lord Burghley.

[10] Essex had just been banished from Court after the famous quarrel during which he had turned his back on the Queen, laid his hand on his sword, and had his ears boxed.

in loan of the City £40,000, whereof they can presently furnish her but with the one half.

Of his private wealth there is but £11,000 come to light, and that all in silver. . . . And his lands seem not so great as was thought, for Master Secretary[11] says his own part will not rise to £1600 a year upon the rack. It is much labored to make him Lord Treasurer, wherein if he fail it is assuredly thought he shall be Master of the Wards; for of necessity there must be one, by opinion of all the lawyers. . . .

The States are gone away well contented, in that they think they have tied us fast by offering to pay our men of war, garrisons and all, and to reimburse £30,000 yearly to the Queen till the whole debt be run out. Yet for all this it is thought we shall treat—marry, so that the States must be included with their own conditions. . . .

We have lately received a great blow in Ireland. Sir Henry Bagnal, the Marshal, went with 3500 foot complete and 300 horse to relieve the fort of Blackwater distressed by Tyrone, and being come within two mile of it, in a pace or wood where the enemy had strongly entrenched himself, was so furiously set upon that himself was there slain with 16 other captains and above 700 soldiers. The rest retired to Armagh (having lost to the enemy seventeen ensigns) not knowing how to tarry there or remove thence in safety, the enemy being between eight and ten thousand strong. But news came yesterday that they had made their appointment, and that Tyrone out of his merciless bounty had granted them leave to bury their dead and to go away with all they had, so that the fort might be delivered him; to the Governor whereof, Captain Williams, and his soldiers he would give no better conditions than to depart in their doublets and hose only, with rapier and dagger.

This is the greatest loss and dishonor the Queen hath had in her time, and yet it seems we are not moved with it; which whether it proceed more of courage than of wit I know not, but I fear it is rather a careless and insensible dullness. . . .

The Lord Cobham[12] was installed Lord Warden of the Cinque Ports on Bartholomew Day at Canterbury, at which ceremonious solemnity were assembled almost 4000 horse. And he kept the feast

---

[11] Sir Robert Cecil, son of Lord Burghley.
[12] Henry Brooke, Lord Cobham, brother-in-law of Robert Cecil, succeeded his father as Lord Warden. He is chiefly remembered for his part in the inept plotting that undid Raleigh.

very magnificently and spent 26 oxen with all other provision suitable. . . .

Our merchants have lost two or three ships going to Muscovy and one is missing that should come from thence.

Mistress Vernon is from the Court and lies in Essex House.[13] Some say she hath taken a venue under the girdle and swells upon it. Yet she complains not of foul play, but says the Earl of Southampton will justify it. And it is bruited underhand that he was lately here four days in great secret of purpose to marry her, and effected it accordingly.

[9] October 20, 1598: The voice ran all this week with Sir John Fortescue to be Lord Treasurer, but now it is come about again to the Lord Buckhurst,[14] and so every three or four days it is tossed from the one side of the Court to the other. The next new Counsellors are thought shall be the Lord Mountjoy and the Lord Chief Justice,[15] who hath played rex of late among whores and bawds and persecutes poor pretty wenches out of all pity and mercy.

The Court of Wards sits not, for want of a master, and though the Earl of Essex be alone in election yet there is still some rub in his way that he comes not on. Some say the Queen means to dissolve that Court and instead thereof to raise a yearly contribution out of all lands *in capite* or knight service, which would be more for her profit and less grievance to the subject, but that is too good to be true. Others say he may have it if he will, but because there is a course spoken of somewhat to geld and curtail it, he refuseth to accept it unless he may have it whole and unmaimed.

[11] November 22, 1598: This long and permanent abode of westerly winds brings us no news but such as we least desire to hear of.

---

[13] Essex did not improve his standing by promoting this elopement of Elizabeth Vernon, Maid of Honor to the Queen. The beautiful Henry Wriothesley, 3rd Earl of Southampton, one of the candidates for Shakespeare's W. H., made an honest woman of her; they had a daughter in November, "and to mend her portion the Earl her father hath lately lost 18,000 crowns at tennis in Paris." (Letter 10.)

[14] Chancellor of the Exchequer, the Queen's cousin.

[15] Sir John Popham.

I mean out of Ireland, whence messengers come daily (like Job's servants) laden with ill tidings of new troubles and revolts. The English of Munster are much blamed for making no better proof of themselves, and giving so easy way to the rebels. . . .

The day that we looked for Stanley's[16] arraignment, he came not himself but sent his forerunner, one Squire, that had been an under-purveyer of the Stable, who being in Spain was dealt withal by one Walpole, a Jesuit, to poison the Queen and the Earl of Essex, and accordingly came prepared into England, and went with the Earl in his own ship the last journey, and poisoned the arms of handles of the chair he used to sit in with a confection he had received of the Jesuit, as likewise he had done the pommel of the Queen's saddle not past five days before his going to sea; but because nothing suc-ceeded of it, the priest thinking he had either changed his purpose or bewrayed it, gave Stanley instructions to accuse him, thereby to get him more credit and to be revenged of Squire for breaking promise. The fellow confessed the whole practice and as it seemed died very penitent.

The seventh of this month the Queen's Attorney[17] married the Lady Hatton, to the great admiration of all men, that after so many large and likely offers she should decline to a man of his quality, and the world will not believe that it was without a mystery. . . .

The Queen came to Whitehall the last week, being received a mile out of town by the Lord Mayor and his brethren accompanied with 400 velvet coats and chains of gold. Her day[18] passed without any extraordinary matter more than running and ringing.

[13] December 20, 1598: From Tuesday last till Sunday it held fast and firm that the Earl of Essex was to go [into Ireland] and all things were accordingly settled and set down; but a sudden altera-tion came on Sunday night, the reason whereof is yet kept secret. Some say the Queen had promised to forgive him twelve thousand pound debt due by his father and £20,000 he owed her himself

---

[16] John Stanley had arrived from Spain in September, claiming that he had been employed by the King to kill Queen Elizabeth.

[17] Sir Edward Coke. He married Elizabeth Cecil, niece of Sir Robert, and widow of Sir William Hatton who was the son of Queen Elizabeth's old favorite, Sir Christopher.

[18] The anniversary of her accession.

. . . which belike was mistaken, for the Queen says she meant but the forbearance of it and that it should not be called upon in his absence. But whether it were this or some other matter, all is turned upside down, and he and Master Secretary have so good leisure that they ply the tables hard in the Presence Chamber, and play so round game as if Ireland were to be recovered at Irish.[19] . . .

The loan of £150,000 makes many of our citizens shrink and pull in their horns, but yet it goes forward and they must furnish it, and some whispering there is that when that is done we shall hear of a benevolence. If we be driven to these shifts already, God knows how we shall hold hereafter; and I marvel that they which knew these wants did harken no more after the peace when they might have had it with good conditions.

You see how confidently I write to you of all things. But I hope you keep it to yourself, and then there is no danger. And I am so used to a liberty and freedom of speech when I converse or write to my friends that I cannot easily leave it.

[15] January 17, 1599: The Queen on Twelfth Day to close up the holy days and do the Danish Ambassador honor, danced with the Earl of Essex very richly and freshly attired. Since, there fell out a great unkindness twixt the Earl and the Lord Admiral,[20] and some high words passed. . . .

The Earl's journey for Ireland is somewhat prolonged, for his victualers that had order to make their provisions for February are now put over till March. He shall carry a great troop of gallants with him, if all go that are spoken of. . . . But it is said the Earl gives few places nor bestows offices to any as yet, because he will hold his followers in heart till he have them there. Many that wish well to the journey have no great conceit of it, seeing so many raw youths press for the greatest charges. Here was speech that the Earl of Kildare and the Lord of Delvin began to stand upon terms and to give doubtful answers, and that the chief rebels in Munster began to put water in their wine and to proceed with more temper. . . .

The Queen is very angry with Sir Thomas Gerrard for the escape of one Blackwell, an archpriest, out of the Marshalsea.

---

[19] An old game resembling backgammon.
[20] Charles Howard, Earl of Nottingham.

There was a plot laid by certain Jesuits and priests to murder or poison the Scottish king, as it is confessed by some that are taken.

Here be many Englishmen come out of Spain, that were delivered at the young King's coming to the crown. They say that the King had a sore bruise with the fall of an horse in running at the ring, for the which he was let blood four times. It is said likewise (how truly I know not) that the very same day his Queen was so scared with a fire that took in the house where she lay at Milan that she was driven to run into the street in her petticoat.

The news comes now very hot that Sebastian, the King of Portugal that was said to be slain in the battle in Barbary,[21] is at Venice, and hath made so good trial of himself that the Venetians allow him, and maintain almost fourscore persons about him at their charge. They say he tells very strange stories, how he with fourteen more escaped from the battle and got up into the mountains and so by many adventures he went and he went till he came into Ethiopia, or Prester John's land, meaning from thence to have gone into the East Indies; but understanding that they were yielded and sworn to the King of Spain, durst not proceed, but turned back again, and *per tot discrimina*[22] in this long pilgrimage (wherein he hath been taken, bought and sold twelve or thirteen times) got at last to Venice, where he tells them all that was negotiated twixt him and them, whether by letters or ambassadors, since he was of any good remembrance, and that with so many particulars as are thought infallible testimonies. Besides it is said that his confessor is come out of Portugal, and upon conference with him avoucheth all to be true that he saith touching what passed between them in confession, both at other times and specially the day before the battle. We run away with all, as though all were our own, and are easily persuaded to believe that we would have. What will come of it God knows, but it were a happy turn for Christendom if it were true and so believed; but it will by no means sink down with me, but that still I fear he will be cozened and trussed up in the end. The King of

---

[21] King Sebastian (1554-1578), grandson of Emperor Charles V, was a quixotic mystic whose passionate aim was to drive the Moors out of North Africa. He was killed and his army annihilated at Kasr el Kebir, August 4, 1578. Like King Arthur, he became a legend and figurehead of a patriotic cult who awaited his miraculous return. Four pretenders impersonated him, of which this last, a Calabrian named Marco Tullio, knew no Portuguese and was ultimately exposed and executed.

[22] Through all perils.

Spain is said to be going into Portugal with a 1000 horse and 3000 foot upon this rumor, but I rather think it is to be received there and crowned.

[16] January 31, 1599: I received your letters of the first and ninth of this present very lately, and marvel you had not heard of your skipper before that time. I pray God all be well with him, and that he have not miscarried, for you had a rich adventure in him of *Thesaurus Geographicus,*[23] sent by your cousin Lytton, who is now in town and commends him to you. . . .

The Earl of Essex's commission for Ireland is at length after many difficulties agreed on, though not yet signed. He hath the name of Lieutenant, may return at pleasure, make barons, and dispose of such lands as shall be won from the rebels at his good liking; and many other such points are spoken of, but how truly *viderit successus.*[24] He makes great provision for horses, and many are presented him. They talk likewise of carrying over two or three hundred mastiffs to werry[25] the Irish, or rather (as I take it) their cattle. The press of his followers will be much abated by reason the Queen countermands many. . . . The unkindness twixt him and others is not yet reconciled, which no doubt will much hinder this action that had need of all furtherance. . . .

Here is a great and curious present going to the great Turk, which no doubt will be much talked of, and be very scandalous among other nations, specially the Germans.

Upon the Duke of Florence's embargo and complaint of our piracies, here is order taken upon pain of death that no prizes be taken in the Levant seas.

We are like enough to fall at some odds with the French King about his traffic into Spain, for of late (meaning to set his people on work and make them industrious) he hath forbidden all manner of wrought silks to be brought into his dominions, or any work made of woolen (which is contrary to our former contracts of intercourse), and doth withal encourage his people all he can to build and buy ships, thereby to get the whole trade of Spain; wherein if

---

[23] The famous work by the cartographer Abraham Ortelius.
[24] The result will show.
[25] "To kill or injure by biting or shaking" (OED).

he be not prevented, he will soon beggar both the Hollanders and us, and hereafter we shall have more ado with him and his than ever we had with the Spaniard. Here hath been much contesting about it with his ambassador, and that hotly enough, but we have the wolf by the ears and know not how to hold him nor how to let him go.

The Queen's want of money is not yet so fully supplied but that they are fain to descend to mean men and pick it up here and there as they can get it, and you must think they were near driven when they found out me as a fit man to lend money, but I think I answered them sufficiently, that where nothing is to be had the Queen must lose her right. There is a sale in hand of £3000 of the Queen's land, which is thought will help well to stop a gap. . . . Sir William Hervey's marriage with the old Countess of Southampton[26] that hath lain smothering so long comes now to be published.

[22] August 9, 1599: Though here be little happened since I wrote last, but only scambling provisions and preparations for war, yet because I cannot tell when I shall write again if any sudden alarm call us away, I think it not amiss to let you understand what was and is intended to be done. The news increasing daily of the Spaniards' coming, and advertisements concurring from all parts of their design for London (whereof the Adelantado himself gave out proud speeches) and the day of their departure from the Groin being said to be appointed at the uttermost as Sunday last, order was given for a camp to be raised, whereof the Lord Admiral to be General, the Lord Mountjoy Lieutenant, Sir Fra. Vere Marshal, the Earl of Northumberland General of the Horse, the Earl of Sussex Colonel General of the Infantry, Sir Will. Russell his Lieutenant (but he refused), Sir Tho. Wilford Sergeant Major, Sir Ed. Wotton Treasurer, and Master Maynard Secretary. The rendezvous for Hertfordshire men was to be at Tottenham, the 12 of this month, and so forward to Tilbury or somewhither else as should be enjoined them. Your cousin Lytton hath the leading of 300 men and came up to make his provisions, whom I mean to accompany, and (though I were never professed soldier) to offer myself in defense of my country, which is the best service I can do it.

---

[26] Hereupon hangs A. L. Rowse's identification of Shakespeare's W.H.

Twelve or thirteen of the Queen's ships are preparing in all haste, whereof the Lord Tho. Howard to be Admiral, Sir Wal. Raleigh Vice-Admiral, Fulke Greville Rear-Admiral. Sir Thomas Gerrard was appointed Colonel of the Londoners, but for an old grudge since the last Parliament they would none of him, whereupon the Earl of Cumberland was given them to have charge of them and the River, which he undertook with great confidence, meaning to make a bridge somewhat on this side of Gravesend, after an apish imitation of that of Antwerp, and to that end got together all the lighters, boats, western barges, cables and anchors that were to be found, giving out that with 1500 musketeers he would defend that bridge or lose his life upon it (but God forbid he should have been put to it). But whether upon trial they find it not feasible, as bearing another manner of breadth and billow than the river of Antwerp, or upon what other reason I know not, yesterday after much turmoil and great charges bestowed, it was quite given over, and now they have an imagination of sinking certain hulks in the channel if need should be.

Upon Monday toward evening came news (yet false) that the Spaniards were landed in the Isle of Wight, which bred such a fear and consternation in this town as I would little have looked for, with such a cry of women, chaining of streets and shutting of the gates as though the enemy had been at Blackwall.[27] I am sorry and ashamed that this weakness and nakedness of ours on all sides should show itself so apparently as to be carried far and near to our disgrace both with friends and foes.

Great provision is made for horse, as being the best advantage we are like to have if the enemy come, and the noblemen about Court have rated themselves at round proportions: as the Lord Admiral a 100, the Earl of Shrewsbury 100, the Earl of Pembroke 200, the Earl of Worcester 100, the Earl of Northumberland 100, Master Secretary 100, the Archbishop 100, Sir William Russell 50, and the rest, both Court and country, according to their ability.

But now after all this noise and blustering, methinks the weather begins to clear somewhat, for our preparations begin to slack and go not on so headlong as they did, so that there may be hope all shall be well; and our rendezvous at Tottenham is put off for five days.

Out of Ireland we have uncertain reports of diverse feats done, as that the Lord Cromwell hath overthrown 6000 of Tyrone's company,

---

[27] On the Thames, below Greenwich.

but I cannot learn when nor where; that the Earl of Essex hath likewise defeated 1500 in Offaly, laying 240 of them along and bringing away 1000 cows and more.

[23] August 23, 1599: The world is well amended here since I wrote last, and the storm that seemed to look so black almost blown over. Yet our Navy is gone to sea prettily strong and in good plight, for so short warning, containing 23 ships and pinnaces of the Queen's, 12 good merchant ships provided by the City, and six more hired by Her Majesty, with 14 hoys well furnished with ordnance and made for fight. Our land forces are daily discharged little and little, and this day I think will be quite dissolved; the Hertfordshire men were sent home first, and so by degrees one after another, yet they all received pay more or less, some for four, some five days, and some for a whole week. On Friday there mustered 1600 horse by St. James's, and the next day 400 for the Clergy in St. George's field. Yet none of the noblemen have showed their troops, which together with other voluntaries are thought would double that number. If occasion had been to draw forces to a head or into camp, it is thought the first proportion would have risen to 27,000 foot and 3000 horse. I assure you they were very well provided, for the most part of horse, armor, and apparel, and wanted not their setting forth with feathers, scarves, and such other light wear.

The Lord General with all the great officers of the field came in great bravery to Paul's Cross on Sunday was sevennight and dined with the Lord Mayor; and then was the alarm at hottest that the Spaniards were at Brest, which was as likely and fell out as true as all the rest.

The vulgar sort cannot be persuaded but that there was some great mystery in the assembling of these forces, and because they cannot find the reason of it, make many wild conjectures, and cast beyond the moon: as sometimes that the Queen was dangerously sick; otherwhile that it was to show to some that are absent, that others can be followed as well as they, and that if occasion be, military services can be as well and readily ordered and directed as if they were present; with many other as vain and frivolous imaginations as these.

The forces in the West Country are not yet dismissed, for there if anywhere may be some doubt of danger. Sir William Russell was sent thither to be General and to take order for all things as he thought best.

And now in the midst of all this hurly-burly is a sudden sound of peace, and that certain fellows are come from Brussels with commission from Spain. . . .

The Earl of Essex hath made many new knights, but I cannot as yet come by the beadroll; marry for a taste you shall have as many as I well remember, as first Sir Henry Lindley, Sir Harry Cary (that was Sir Fra. Vere's Lieutenant), two Lovelaces, Sir Ajax Harington, Sir Jack Heydon, Sir Dick Morrison, *cum multis aliis* English and Irish, to the number of 59 in the whole, since his first arrival. It is much marvelled that this humor should so possess him, that not content with his first dozens and scores, he should thus fall to huddle them up by half hundreds; and it is noted as a strange thing that a subject, in the space of seven or eight years (not having been six months together in any one action) should upon so little service and small desert make more knights than are in all the realm besides; and it is doubted that if he continue this course he will shortly bring in tag and rag, cut and longtail, and so draw the Order into contempt. . . .

Your brother Carleton hath been almost this sevennight in town to offer his service with two horses to Master Secretary, but yet could never find him at leisure, so that I doubt he will come too late when the play is done.

This is all we have, unless I should tell you that last week at a puppet play in St. John's Street the house fell and hurt between thirty and forty persons and slew five outright, whereof two (they say) were good handsome whores.

[36] February 3, 1601; We have great speech of building twelve galleys, four by the Queen, two by this City, two by Essex, Suffolk, Norfolk and Lincolnshire, two by Kent, Surrey, Sussex and Hampshire, the rest by Somerset, Devonshire and Cornwall; for the speech is that the Spaniards are to bring more galleys along with them into the Low Countries, and we must learn to fight with them after their own fence. It was reported awhile that they were severed by tempest and twelve or fifteen sail of them cast away on the coast of Ireland, but there is no great credit given to it. But we hear for certain that

two Spanish frigates arrived at Sligo with powder, munition, and money to furnish the rebels. . . .

The new fort at Plymouth was lately defaced and blown up with powder. The Dunkirkers are very busy all along that coast and take prizes even in the very harbor. They stay thereabout to convoy the Spaniards that are coming for the Low Countries.

[37] February 24, 1601: Yours of the 14 of this present found so ready passage that I marvel how ours at other times stay so long by the way. This is my fourth letter since the middle of January[28] that I came from Knebworth, besides one I sent at my going thither, and it is strange to me that our ill news should fly so fast as to overtake you in five days, when our ordinary letters cannot find the way in five weeks. I was out of the way when your letter came, and when the messenger gave warning of his sudden departure; for the covey is now dispersed, and we are driven to seek our feeding farther off, our Doctor being already settled in Court, and I ready to go to Ascott, and there and in suchlike places to lead a country life, so that you must take a short pittance, sith I am so shortened in time.

I wrote you in my last as well as I then could, the beginning and progress of our troubles and as many particulars as I could bethink me of in such huddling haste. No doubt you have many relations there by this time of all that happened, and you must excuse me if I do not engulf myself into a long narration without a constant settled wind to carry me through. I do not well remember whether I sent you word of Tom Lee's traitorous enterprise to possess himself of the Privy Chamber, which he communicated to Sir Henry Neville that married my Lord Treasurer's daughter, and to Sir Rob. Cross, who revealed him both at once; and he being apprehended confessed his meaning was but to have gotten the Queen to have signed a warrant for the noblemen's delivery, wherein if he had found difficulty he knew not what would have followed, and those should have been guilty of any harm might come to her that had hindered his attempt; but at his arraignment, though he were confronted by Sir Rob. Cross and the rest, yet he stood to the denial, affirming his intent to be only

---

[28] Only one of these, February 3, survives; the account of "the beginning and progress of our troubles"—Essex's rebellion—is lost.

to have angered her for one half hour, that she might have lived the merrier all her life after; and in this tune died the 17 of this present at Tyburn, very resolutely and to seeming religiously.

The 19 hereof the Earls of Essex and Southampton were arraigned at Westminster, before the Lord Treasurer—Lord High Steward of England for that day, and 25 of their peers, whereof were 9 earls and 16 barons. The only matters objected were his practice to surprise the Court, his coming in arms into London to raise rebellion, and the defending his house against the Queen's forces. To the two latter he answered that he was driven for safety of his life, to the former that it was a matter only in consultation and not resolved upon, and if it had taken effect it was only to prostrate himself at her Majesty's feet, and there manifest such matters against his enemies as should make them odious and remove them from about her person, and recall him to her former favor.

This was the sum of his answer, but delivered with such bravery and so many words, that a man might easily perceive that, as he had ever lived popularly, so his chief care was to leave a good opinion in the people's minds now at parting. But the worst of all was his many and loud protestations of his faith and loyalty to the Queen and State, which no doubt caught and carried away a great part of the hearers, but I cannot be so easily led to believe protestations (though never so deep) against manifest proof. Yet I must needs say that one thing sticks much in many men's minds: that whereas diverse preachers were commanded the Sunday before to deliver to the people, among his other treasons, that he had complotted with Tyrone, and was reconciled to the Pope; and whereas Master Attorney at Tom Lee's arraignment averred the same combining with Tyrone, and that he had practiced by the means of seminary priests with the Pope and the King of Spain to be King of England, there was no such matter mentioned at his arraignment, and yet there was time enough for it, from nine o'clock in the morning till almost seven at night.

At his coming to the bar his countenance was somewhat unsettled, but after he was once in, I assure you I never saw any go through with such boldness and show of resolution and contempt of death; but whether this courage were borrowed and put on for the time, or natural, it were hard to judge. But I hear he begins to relent and among other faults to acknowledge and be sorry for his arrogant, or rather (as Master Secretary well termed it to his face), his impudent behavior at his arraignment; and, which is more, to lay open the whole plot, and to appeach diverse not yet called in question. His execution was expected Saturday, then yesterday, now tomorrow or on Thursday. Most of the Council have been with him these three or four days together.

The Earl of Southampton spake very well (but methought somewhat too much as well as the other), and as a man that would fain live, pleaded hard to acquit himself, but all in vain for it could not be; whereupon he descended to entreaty, and moved great commiseration, and though he were generally well liked, yet methought he was somewhat too low and submiss, and seemed too loath to die before a proud enemy.

Here have yet no more been brought to trial, save nine the next day to the King's Bench bar, but six of them were carried back again without trial, and only Sir Ed. Bainham, John Littleton of Worcestershire, and one Cap. Orwell were condemned, but not yet executed; for it is thought my Lord himself shall lead the way, and then they shall follow thick and threefold. Yet the general opinion is there will be no great executions, for the Queen is very gracious and inclines much to mercy. . . .

Your cousin Lytton is here with his trained band of 300 and other captains with some 2000 men of the neighbor shires hereabout, and we have continual watch and ward day and night in arms through the city, and these strangers at Court and places ajoining.

[42] October 31, 1601: The last I wrote you was from Knebworth, whence I came eight days since, and brought nothing with me but rheums and toothaches, and to mend the matter find nothing here but subsidies and payments to Ostend and such other odd reckonings. Our Parliament began on Tuesday, whither the Queen went with ordinary solemnity. . . .

I make no doubt but your ears ring with the report of the Spaniards' landing in Ireland. They are between three and four thousand under the conduct of Don Juan d'Aquila (that was in Britain). They fortify at Kinsale a haven within ten or twelve miles of Cork. The Lord Deputy[29] is not far from them with 6000 men, and here be 4000 foot and 300 horse going with all possible haste to reinforce him; besides six of the Queen's ships and as many merchants to keep them

---

[29] Charles Blount, Lord Mountjoy.

in at sea. In the meantime Tyrone, with 4000 foot and 700 horse, gallops the Pale and burns and spoils where he list. Many of our discoursers give the Spaniards for lost, and make it a matter of ease to defeat them by sickness, famine or the sword. For mine own part I see not that Spain is so overladen with people, nor think not so meanly of their wit, that they would willfully cast them away, or not provide for so open and ordinary inconveniences.

Sir Robert Mansell and Sir Amias Preston have brought in six Easterlings into the river that came out of Spain laden with spices and some bullion, which we pretend should belong to certain Portugals. It comes well to pass if it fall out so in the end, but many doubt they will scant prove good prize.

[43] November 14, 1601: We have not a word out of Ireland, the wind stands so full in their teeth, which I hope hath carried our ships thither by this time, unless they loiter too much at Plymouth.

The Duke of Lennox,[30] after twice or thrice putting off, was at Court on Wednesday.

The Parliament handles no high matters, only they have had a cast at Osborne's office, to correct and amend it at least, but there is no great hope of success. The alpha and omega is concluded already: I mean the grant of four subsidies and eight fifteens.[31]

[51] October 2, 1602: I know you think it long till you hear from me, and I am in your debt for two letters at least, which I received whiles I was at Knebworth, wherein you served two pigeons with one bean, and they could not come where they should find better welcome, for we were all alone, and the first brought with it much good company of pictures and discourses that entertained a good part of the time that otherwise would have been very tedious, for I cannot well

---

[30] Ludovic Stuart, 2nd Duke of Lennox, King James's great friend.

[31] A subsidy could be expected to produce £100,000; a fifteen, or a tenth-and-fifteenth, varied from two to four shillings per pound on land and goods and produced perhaps £30,000. But as there was only local machinery for both assessment and collection, assessment was a largely arbitrary exercise in self-discipline and collection depended on the voluntary cooperation of the gentry. Cf. A. L. Rowse, *The England of Elizabeth,* pp. 336-38.

digest the solitariness of that house[32] that was wont to be so stirring and cheerful.

The commencement at Oxford was very famous: for plenty of Doctors, that were fifteen, twelve divines and three lawyers; for store of venison whereof Doctor King had 27 bucks for his part; for royal cheer and an excellent *concio ad clerum,*[33] wherein your cousin Dr. Goodwin bare the bell; for the exceeding assembly of gentles; but specially for the great confluence of cutpurses, whereof ensued many losses and shrewd turns, as first Master Bodley lost his clock, Sir Richard Lee two jewels of 200 Marks, which Sir Harry Lee and he meant to have bestowed on the bride, Master Tanfield's daughter; and diverse other lost good sums of five, eight, and fourteen pounds, besides petty detriments of scarves, fans, gloves; and one mad knave, whether of malice or merriment, took the advantage to pull off a gentlewoman's shoe and made the goose go home barefoot. . . .

The Queen's progress went not far, first to Chiswick to Sir William Russell's; then to Ambrose Coppinger's, who, because he had been a Master of Art, entertained her himself with a Latin oration; then to Harefield to the Lord Keeper's; so to Sir Will. Clarke's at Burnham, who so behaved himself that he pleased nobody, but gave occasion to have his misery and vanity spread far and wide; then to Oatlands, where she continues till the seventh of this month that she comes to Richmond. The causes that withheld her from the Earl of Hertford's and the Lord Chief Justice's were the foul weather, and a general infection of the smallpox spread over all the country. The Lord Hume came this way home and had audience at Court on Sunday; the Queen was very pleasant with him and well disposed. . . .

Sir Fra. Vere is said to be well recovered of his hurt, but is thought shall have an impediment in his tongue, which some think to be no great harm. We hear that Grave Maurice hath been dangerously sick of the plague, and that the sore is burst out in his neck. This summer's work with such an army and such a noise hath lost them a great part of mine opinion of their soldiership: to make such a perambulation to no purpose, and not to dare to follow any part of their first project.

Sir Rob. Mansell and the Vice-Admiral of Flushing met with six of Spinola's galleys, and have stemmed or overrun two of them and, they say, spoiled the rest so that they be unprofitable: whereof one is run on ground at Calais. The reports of the manner of the fight are

---

[32] Because of the recent death of Rowland Lytton's wife.
[33] Sermon.

so uncertain and contrarious that I know not how to set it down, but will leave it to time to discover.

Out of Ireland we hear nothing but that Tyrone runs up and down distressed, and offers to come in upon any conditions with life.

[62] March 30, 1603: I have not written since I received yours of the 8th of this present, after your style, for we were held in suspense and know not how nor what to write, the passages being stopped, and all conveyance so dangerous and suspicious.[34] I make no question but you have heard of our great loss before this come at you; and no doubt but you shall hear her Majesty's sickness and manner of death diversely related, for even here the papists do tell strange stories, as utterly void of truth as of all civil honesty or humanity.

I had a good means to understand how the world went, and find her disease to be nothing but a settled and unremovable melancholy, insomuch that she could not be won or persuaded, neither by the Council, divines, physicians, nor the women about her, once to taste or touch any physic; though ten or twelve physicians that were continually about her did assure her with all manner of asseverations of perfect and easy recovery if she would follow their advice. So that it cannot be said of her as it was of the Emperor Adrian that *turba medicorum occidit regem,*[35] for they say she died only for lack of physic.

Here was some whispering that her brain was somewhat distempered, but there was no such matter, only she held an obstinate silence for the most part; and because she had a persuasion that if she once lay down she should never rise, could not be gotten to bed in a whole week till three days before her death. So that after three weeks' languishing, she departed the 24 of this present, being Our Lady's eve, between two and three in the morning. . . .

The Archbishop of Canterbury,[36] the Bishop of London,[37] the Almoner,[38] and other her chaplains and divines had access to her in her sickness diverse times, to whom she gave good testimony of her

---

[34] On account of Queen Elizabeth's death on March 24.
[35] The multitude of doctors killed the king.
[36] John Whitgift.
[37] Richard Bancroft.
[38] Anthony Watson.

faith by word, but specially towards her end by signs when she was speechless, and would not suffer the Archbishop to depart as long as she had sense, but held him twice or thrice when he was going and could no longer endure, both by reason of his own weakness and compassion of hers.

She made no will, nor gave anything away, so that they which come after shall find a well-stored jewel house and a rich wardrobe of more than 2000 gowns with all things else answerable.

The nobility and Council came from Richmond that morning, and before ten o'clock had proclaimed King James at Whitehall, Temple Bar, and so forward in Cheapside and other places. Sir Rob. Carey was the first that of his own motion carried news of her death into Scotland. The next day the Lords sent Sir Charles Percy and Thomas Somerset, with the proclamation and letters to the King; and yesterday Master Carew, a Master of the Chancery, and Master Lake[39] were dispatched about other business. There is much posting that way and many run thither of their own errand, as if it were nothing else but first come first served, or that preferment were a goal to be got by footmanship. . . .

We attend him here with great devotion and begin to think long till we have him. The Lords have sent to know his pleasure whether he will come by land or sea, for which purpose there be eight or ten ships ready that were going for the coast of Spain but do now tarry to keep the Narrow Seas. Surely the Council dealt very providently and beyond that that was to be expected or hoped for in so sudden an accident; and no doubt but God did direct them, seeing all things passed so quietly and in good order.

During the Queen's sickness some principal papists were made sure, and some dangerous companions clapped up, among whom Sir Edmund Bainham was committed to the Marshalsea for some desperate speeches (they say) against the King; but it should seem there was no great matter, for I hear he is now at liberty again. Here was a rumor two days since that the Lord Beauchamp[40] stood out and gathered forces, but it was a false alarm, for word is come since that his father was one of the foremost in his country to proclaim the King.

The Council went on Saturday to Richmond, and that night late brought the corpse with an honorable attendance to Whitehall, where

[39] Thomas Lake, who became a Secretary of State.
[40] Edward, son of Edward Seymour, Earl of Hertford; through his mother, Lady Catherine Grey, he was a possible candidate for the throne.

the household remains; the body was not opened but wrapped up in cerecloths and other preservatives.

Sir Henry Danvers was dispatched on Sunday to carry the proclamation into Ireland, whence we have heard nothing a good while. . . .

We hear the Archduke hath great store of men, shipping, and galleys at Sluse; and, because it is known that Spinola hath been covertly in Zeeland and taken view and measure of their dikes, it is supposed that he hath some design to cut their sea walls and drown the whole island. The Dunkirkers have been very busy with us of late, and between Quinborough and Lee took three pinks coming from Flushing, whereof one was better worth than ten thousand pound. We hear that the King of Denmark's brother that married the Muscovite's daughter the last year is dead, whereof our merchants are nothing sorry. The King of Denmark is daily looked for in Scotland, and if he come before the King get thence it is thought he will come along with him. . . .

The Lord Cobham is even now taking post to go toward the King and do his wonted good offices; but the Lords do so little like his going that I think his errand will be there before him, or soon overtake him. This alteration hath reculed [41] Master Winwood's employment till the King's coming or some commission from him.

I know not whether you have seen the King's book[42] but I sent it at all adventures, for it is new here. The other book will serve when you have leisure to laugh, for both in the matter and manner of setting it down you shall find pretty knavery. Your friends are all in good health, and so wishing to you, I commit you to God's holy protection.

[63] April 12, 1603: Since my last of the thirtieth of March, all things continue here in the same quiet course, only here was a proclamation to retain the Council and all other officers in their old places, and to restrain the concourse of idle and unnecessary posters into Scotland, the number whereof grew to be a great burthen to the country and brought all things out of order. The Lord Henry Howard was sent thither to possess the King's ear and countermine the Lord Cobham. Your old friend Tobie Matthew was sent with a letter from

---

[41] Delayed. Winwood was Chargé d'Affaires in Paris.
[42] *Basilicon Doron.*

Master Bacon, but I doubt neither the message nor messenger were greatly welcome.

The King uses all very graciously and hath made Sir Rob. Carey of his Bedchamber and Groom of the Stole. John Davies is sworn his man and Neville is restored (as he writes himself) to all his titles and fortunes. The tenth of this month the Earl of Southampton and Sir Henry Neville were delivered out of the Tower by a warrant from the King.

These bountiful beginnings raise all men's spirits and put them in great hopes, insomuch that not only protestants but papists and puritans, and the very poets with their idle pamphlets, promise themselves great part in his favor: so that to satisfy or please all, *hic labor hoc opus est*,[43] and would be more than a man's work. The last that were sent were Sir Harry Neville and Sir Harry Lennard with five thousand pound in gold and one in silver, saving your cousin Mompesson that carried him six geldings and a coach with four horse, and other officers that are daily sent away to provide and execute their charge.

Here have come diverse from the King, as Roger Aston, Foules, Hamilton, and now last one Bruce, whom they call Lord or Abbot of Kinloss and is thought shall be incorporated into our Council. We have no certainty where the King is. They that come last say he is appointed to be at Berwick the seventh of this month, and think he is now on the way to York, where he will make no long stay, but come to Worksop, a house of the Earl of Shrewsbury's, so to Belvoir Castle, thence to Burley, then to Oliver Cromwell's by Huntington, to Sir Thomas Sadler's in Hertfordshire, to Hertford Castle, to Theobalds, to the Charterhouse or Howard House, and so to the Tower, till his coronation. I cannot hear that the Queen or any of the princes come with him, only they talk of the Duke of Lennox, two marquises, and the Earl of Mar (whose brother, Sir Thomas Erskine, they say is made Captain of the Guard), and two hundred other nobles and gentles. Though you had no greater business, yet methinks you might make an errand to see these sights, for there will be arches and pageants great plenty.

The Queen's funeral is appointed the 28th of this present with as much solemnity as hath been used to any former prince, and that by the King's own direction. It shall be kept at Westminster, and the Lady Arabella is to be chief mourner, accompanied with two marquises, 16 countesses and 30 baronesses with all their train, besides

---

[43] Drudgery is the result.

the greatest part of the nobility, all the Council, and officers of Household.

Sir George Carew, President of Munster, came out of Ireland a fortnight since, and yesterday came Sir Oliver St. John with news that Tyrone hath yielded and submitted himself to the Lord Deputy, who hath brought him to Dublin; so that it appeareth the Queen's good fortune followed her after her death, for they had no notice of it when he came away, the winds having been so contrary that none could get over.

Here is common bruit that the Earl of Clanrickard hath married the Lady of Essex,[44] wherewith many that wished her well are nothing pleased; and the speech goes that the King hath taken order and sent her word that her son shall be brought up with the young Prince.

When I came from Paris I brought thence the best satin that ever I wore, whereupon I have a little suit to you, that when you come, if you have either money or means, and that the carriage be not too cumbersome, you would provide me five ells and a half or thereabout of the best black satin you can choose, for those we have here are both dear and naught; and so with my best wishes I commit you to God.

---

[44] Frances, daughter of Sir Francis Walsingham, and widow of Sir Philip Sidney and Robert Devereux, 2nd Earl of Essex.

II. Gazette, 1599-1612

[20] June 28, 1599: On Monday was sevennight Tom Compton and MacWilliams went into the field upon an old quarrel, where Mac-Williams was left dead in the place and Compton came away sore hurt. The Lady Cheke and her friends follow the matter with great extremity and will not be persuaded but that he had help, which for aught I hear will not be proved. The same day in Nottinghamshire John Stanhope assaulted Sir Charles Cavendish very foully, the whole manner whereof I have here sent you as I had it from my Lord of Shrewsbury.

Enclosure: About nine o'clock in the morning Sir Charles Cavendish, being at his new building, which is some quarter of a mile from his little house where he and his Lady do lie, and going from thence to a brick kiln, as far distant from that building as that is from his house, being attended by these three persons only, Henry Ogle, Launcelot Ogle, his page, and one horsekeeper, he discerned to the number of about 20 horse on the side of a hill, which he thought to be Sir John Byron with company hunting. But suddenly, they all galloping apace toward him, he perceived he was betrayed, whereupon, being upon a little nag, he put spurs to him, thinking to recover the new building, but the tit fell with him, and before he could recover out of the stirrup he was overtaken; and before he could draw his sword, two pistols were discharged upon him, and one of them with a round bullet hit him in the inner side of the thigh but missed the bone, and lies yet in the flesh near the point of his buttock. He hath also diverse small shot in several parts of his thigh and body thereabouts, which are thought came out of the same pistol.

Notwithstanding, so strong was the hand of God with him as, after this wound received, he and his two poor men and boy unhorsed six of them and killed two in the place. A third fell down in the forest and is thought dead also, and the fourth was left behind in the same place so sore hurt as it is not thought he can recover, and lieth in the village ajoining. Upon this some of the workmen came towards them, being without weapons. John Stanhope, who was the hindmost during all the fight, was now the foremost in running away, carrying all the rest of his hirelings with him.

Sir Charles is hurt also in the head and in the hand, but these two are but small hurts, and the surgeons do assuredly hope that there is no great danger in the other wounds with the pistol, though by incision they intend to take out the bullet, which is within an inch and a half of the skin. Sir Charles and his three had rapiers and daggers only.

They left behind them six good geldings, whereof some are worth twenty pounds apiece, two or three cloaks, two rapiers, two pistols, one sword and dagger, and some of their hats, all which are safely kept by Sir Charles. All this company did all the morning before lie in the forest, seeming as though they had been ahunting. One of them that were killed was a keeper, whom Stanhope that morning took with him as he found him in his park, without boots or weapon but a pike-staff which he had, and, as the fellow confessed before he died, he know not thither he was carried, or what to do, until he came to the hillside where they stayed so long.

This is the truth of that accident.

[**32**] October 10, 1600: One Ben. Wood, an adventurer that hath been out these four years and had taken great riches in the South Sea to the value of two millions and better, in his return homeward was driven to that want that they were fain to eat one another, and forced at last to put into Puerto Rico, where all that were left are taken and their wealth lost. . . .

A piece of the south battlements of Paul's fell down lately and killed a carman's horse without doing more harm. Here were five or six soldiers hanged the last week in diverse quarters of this town for running from their captains.

[**33**] October 15, 1600: The Muscovy ambassador went yesterday to Court. I cannot learn yet what passed, but the hall and chambers were very richly hanged, and great preparation made to receive him royally.

The Barbarians[1] take their leave sometime this week to go home-

---

[1] Muly Hamet Xarife and his embassy from the King of Barbary, a minion of the Turkish Sultan.

ward, for our merchants nor mariners will not carry them into Turkey, because they think it a matter odious and scandalous to the world to be too friendly or familiar with infidels. But yet it is no small honor to us that nations so far remote and every way different should meet here to admire the glory and magnificence of our Queen of Sheba.

[35] December 22, 1600: The French King kept the solemnity of his marriage at Lyons the 23 of the last, and saw not the Great Duchess nor the Duchess of Mantua who went into Lorraine another way because they espied his humor, that he lingered at the camp for the nonce only to avoid charges and give them no presents. His miserie[2] and ambition is much misliked of all, and the clergy will in no wise be well persuaded of him. He was so desirous and hasty to see his Queen that he went disguised as a private gentleman with others (that he had appointed) to see her dine, and caused a letter from himself to be delivered her in his presence, unknown yet, which she received with such humbleness that it was praised of everybody and pleased him not a little. He could not tarry the solemnity, but went that night to her unknown, and one of his minions demanding what he meant; told him he went to do that he never did in his life, to lie that night with an honest woman. But would you think that precedence or place is as much esteemed by women in France as in England, and that Madame de Fresné and Madame de Chambourg, two great ladies, at their first interview before the Queen, fought for it and scratched each other cruelly?

[36] February 3, 1601: Upon Twelfth Day the Queen feasted the Muscovy ambassador, who hath been since invited to diverse other places and taken his pleasure abroad in hunting. During the holidays here was the Duke of Bracciano, chief of the family of the Orsini by Rome, that came into France with the new Queen,[3] his cousin-german. The Queen entertained him very graciously, and to show that she is not so old as some would have her, danced both measures and galliards in his presence. He was feasted by the Lord Burleigh for some

---

[2] Miserliness.
[3] Marie de Médicis.

favor showed to Will Cecil or his other sons at their being in Italy; and should have been by the Lord Treasurer, and by Gray's Inn that made preparation of shows to entertain him, but he made such haste away that they were disappointed. The Queen at his parting sent him a cup of gold of sixscore pound and a jewel, for the which he gave the bringer, Michael Stanhope, a chain of fourscore pound. He went hence to visit the Archduke and Infanta,[4] leaving behind him a general report of a very courtlike and complete gentleman.

Somewhat more than three weeks since, the Lord Grey and Earl of Southampton had a little bickering in the Strand on horseback, for the which the Lord Grey was committed to the Fleet and hath lain there till yesterday that he was released, notwithstanding all the friends he could make. During his restraint the old Countess of Bedford died, and left him not above £300. The greatest part of her wealth she bequeathed to young Norris, and yet the world says by that he hath discharged her funerals and other legacies there will not be £3000 left for his share. . . .

I remember nothing else but that the Cross in Cheap is going up, for all your Vice-Chancellor of Oxford and some other odd divines there have set down their censure against it.[5] We have daily here many new experiments made, as the last week one came hopping from Charing Cross into Paul's bound in a sack, and this morning another carried up a horse and rode upon him on the top of Paul's steeple: with diverse other such wagers, and among the rest Green, that was lately your cousin Lytton's man, hath set up a printed paper and doth challenge all comers at wrestling.

[**45**] April 26, 1602: Here were three seminary priests hanged and quartered the last week, but what is that among so many?

[**47**] May 17, 1602: This last week one Pye, an utter barrister of the Inner Temple, stood on the pillory before the Temple Gate and lost

---

[4] Albert of Austria and his wife, the Infanta Isabella.

[5] A cross in Cheapside, one of several set up by Edward I in 1290. It was partly demolished by citizens in 1581. In 1600 the Bishop of London proposed to rebuild it; the Puritans objected, but the Queen and the Council supported him.

both his ears for contriving and plotting the death of one of his fellow lawyers by the way of justice. Sir Thomas Throckmorton, a knight of Gloucestershire, was likewise fined in the Star Chamber at 2000 marks, imprisonment during pleasure, and disabled from bearing any office in the Commonwealth, for diverse foul matters and extortions committed in his country.

[49] June 27, 1602: The Council have lately spied a great inconvenience of the increase of housing within and without London, by building over stables, in gardens and other odd corners, whereupon they have taken order to have them pulled down, and this week they have begun almost in every parish to light on the unluckiest, here and there one, which God knows is far from removing the mischief.

[53] October 15, 1602: Gommershall, the Mercer of Temple Bar with the fair wife, hath laid the key under the door and is become bankrupt; his wife was prettily well furnished when, among her inventory, thirty of her smocks were priced at threescore pound.

[54] November 4, 1602: Now coming so fresh from reading your letters and discourses of Biron, I cannot go on without touching a point or two *en passant*. Let the French twattle what they list of his dying *en soldat,* I cannot perceive by aught I have seen or heard but that he died very timorously and childishly, which shows that his valor was rather a French fury than true fortitude. . . .

We hear out of Spain that O'Donnell,[6] riding toward the Court at Valladolid, died suddenly by the way, and being opened there was found in him a serpent (as some call it) or rather a worm, with two heads, of eight foot long. . . .

We have much talk of an apparition in Wales not far from Chester of great troops of horse and foot in battle array, seen upon a mountain by sixteen or eighteen persons of credit, but, when they came to discover what they were, suddenly vanished.

We have here four youths come from Muscovy to learn our lan-

---

[6] Hugh Roe O'Donnell, an Irish rebel in exile.

guage and Latin, and are to be dispersed to diverse schools at Winchester, Eton, Cambridge, and Oxford. . . .

This is all, unless I should tell you that a prentice, pursued by his master to be beaten, leaped out of a garret by Holborn Bridge and fell upon a porter's neck and got away without harm.

[55] November 19, 1602: We had lately a proclamation against the Jesuits and the priests their adherents, that they are to avoid the realm within thirty days upon their peril; and the secular priests before the beginning of February at the farthest, unless they will submit themselves to the Queen's mercy and make profession of their loyalty, in which case further order shall be taken with them: and what a vain thing it was in them or any other to dream of a toleration, whereas her Majesty had never any such meaning nor any of her Council durst ever make such a motion. This was the effect of it. Now what effect it will work, or how they are affected with it, we shall see hereafter. I fear it comes very late, yet better late than never. . . .

I must not forget to tell you of a cozening prank of one Vennar of Lincoln's Inn that gave out bills of a famous play on Saturday was sevennight on the Bankside,[7] to be acted only by certain gentlemen and gentlewomen of account. The price at coming in was two shillings or eighteen pence at least, and when he had gotten most part of the money into his hands, he would have showed them a fair pair of heels. But he was not so nimble to get up on horseback, but that he was fain to forsake that course and betake himself to the water, where he was pursued and taken and brought before the Lord Chief Justice,[8] who would make nothing of it but a jest and a merriment, and bound him over in five pound to appear at the Sessions. In the meantime the common people, when they saw themselves deluded, revenged themselves upon the hangings, curtains, chairs, stools, walls and whatsoever came in their way very outrageously, and made great spoil. There was great store of good company and many noblemen.

[57] December 23, 1602: The Lord Admiral's[9] feasting the Queen had nothing extraordinary, neither were his presents so precious as

---

[7] At the Swan Theatre.
[8] Sir John Popham.
[9] Charles Howard, Earl of Nottingham.

was expected, being only a whole suit of apparel, whereas it was thought he would have bestowed his rich hangings of all the fights with the Spanish Armada in eighty-eight. These feastings have had their effect to stay the Court here this Christmas, though most of the carriages were well onward on their way to Richmond.

[58] January 17, 1603: The world hath not been altogether so dull and dead this Christmas as was suspected, but rather the Court hath flourished more than ordinary, whether it be that the new Comptroller[10] hath put new life into it by his example (being always freshly attired and for the most part all in white, *cap à pied*), or that the humors of themselves grow more gallant: for besides much dancing, bear-baiting, and many plays, there hath been great golden play, wherein Master Secretary[11] lost better than £800 in one night and as much more at other times, the greatest part whereof came to Edward Stanley's and Sir John Lee's share.

[60] February 11, 1603: A Spanish ship, laden with wools, wine and oils, wrecked at Dover in a mist on Sunday last. A Hollander coming from the East Indies was driven to that extremity for want of victual that they ate one another, and were grown so feeble that in a small storm they were seen by an English ship to sink not far from our coast.

Mowbray the Scot, seeking to break prison and escape out of the castle of Edinburgh (as I take it), his sheets, ropes, and other provisions were so short that he fell down and bruised himself so sore that he lived not past two hours after. On Monday last here was a great prize and challenge performed at the Swan between two fencers, Dun and Turner, wherein Dun had so ill luck that the other ran him into the eye with a foil, and so far into the head that he fell down stark dead, and never spake word nor once moved. The case is and will be much argued by Lawyers, whether it will prove chance medley, manslaughter, or murder, by reason of malice and many challenges passed between them before.

---

[10] Sir Edward Wotton.
[11] Sir Robert Cecil.

[61] February 28, 1603: The twelfth of this present one Richardson, a priest, was taken in Clement's Inn and executed at Tyburn the sixteenth. The last Star Chamber day one Darling, a youth of Merton College (that pretended heretofore to be dispossessed of a devil by Darrel), was censured to be whipped and lose his ears, for libelling against the Vice-Chancellor of Oxford and diverse of the Council. He had part of his punishment the last week in Cheapside; the rest is or shall be performed at Oxford. . . .

Here is fresh news out of Spain of one Newport, a seaman, that with two ships hath taken five frigates laden with treasure coming from Carthagena and Nombre de Dios towards the Havana; if all be true that is reported, it will prove the greatest prize that ever I heard of, for they that are most modest talk of two millions at least. The King of Spain hath sent out eight men-of-war to waylay and intercept him if he chance to touch at the Terceras or thereabout; and some are coming to the coast of England.

One Griffith, a Welsh pirate, is lately taken at Cork in Ireland, and his lands, which some give out to be £500 a year, given to the Lord Grey to hold him up a while longer.

[67] December 18, 1604: The tragedy of Gowrie[12] with all the action and actors hath been twice represented by the King's players, with exceeding concourse of all sorts of people. But whether the matter or manner be not well handled, or that it be thought unfit that princes should be played on the stage in their lifetime, I hear that some great Councillors are much displeased with it, and so is thought shall be forbidden.

[69] January 26, 1605: The King went to Royston two days after Twelfthtide where and thereabout he hath continued ever since, and finds such felicity in that hunting life that he hath written to the

---

[12] On August 5, 1600, at Gowrie House in Perth, and under highly mysterious circumstances, King James had escaped assassination—according to his account —at the hands of the Master of Ruthven and his brother the Earl of Gowrie. August 5 was made a day of national thanksgiving forever after, and a special sermon was preached at Court every Tuesday to commemorate James's escape. The play mentioned by Chamberlain is lost.

Council that it is the only means to maintain his health, which being the health and welfare of us all, he desires them to undertake the charge and burden of affairs and foresee that he be not interrupted nor troubled with too much business. He continues still his wonted bounty. . . .

You have heard of the putting off the Parliament till October, the reason whereof I cannot understand nor reach unto, unless it be that they would have all the privy seals paid in, and that they would have these matters of the Church thoroughly settled, wherein it is hard to say what course were best to take, for that more show themselves opposite than was suspected. And the bishops themselves are loath to proceed too rigorously in casting out and depriving so many well reputed of for life and learning: only the King is constant to have all come to conformity.

Though he seek to be very private and retired where he is, yet he is much importuned with petitions in their behalf, and with foolish prophecies of dangers to ensue. And great speech we have of a strange apparition lately at Berwick of two armies that fought a long time with horse, foot, and ordnance.

[70] February 16, 1605: Our Puritans go down on all sides, and though our new Bishop of London[13] proceed but slowly, yet at last he hath deprived, silenced, or suspended all that continue disobedient, in which course he hath won himself great commendation of gravity, wisdom, learning, mildness and temperance, even among that faction, and indeed is held every way the most sufficient man of that coat. Yet those that are deprived wrangle and will not be put down, but appeal to the Parliament and seek prohibitions by law; but the Judges have all given their opinions that the proceedings against them are lawful. . . .

But now to make all even, and that the Papists should not take heart upon the depressing of the Puritans, or that indeed they did so and flattered themselves with a vain hope of toleration, or that it were cunningly imposed upon them by the contrary part: upon Sunday last the King made a long and vehement apology for himself in the Council Chamber, that he never had any such intention, that if he thought his sons would condescend to any such course he could

---

[13] Richard Vaughan, Bancroft having become Archbishop of Canterbury.

wish the kingdom translated to his daughter, that the mitigation of their payments was in consideration that not any one of them had lift up his hand against his coming in and so he gave them a year of probation to conform themselves; which, seeing it had wrought none effect, he had fortified all the laws that were against them and made them stronger (saving for blood, from which he had a natural aversion), and commanded they should be put in execution to the uttermost.

[71] April 30, 1605: For news here is none, but only of matches, marriages, christenings, creations, knightings and suchlike, as if this world would last ever . . . only I cannot omit three pulpit-occurrents that happened on Sunday last. First, that Dean Gordon,[14] preaching before the King, is come so far about the matter of ceremonies that, out of Ezekiel and other places of the prophets, and by certain Hebrew characters and other cabalistical collections, he hath found out and approved the use of the cross, cap and surplice, etc. Then Haydock of New College,[15] the sleeping preacher so much followed and admired in Oxford and everywhere, being sent for to the Court and there playing his prises,[16] was discovered and confessed himself an impostor. Lastly, Doctor Milward,[17] preaching at Paul's Cross, in the midst of the sermon, a cuckoo came flying over the pulpit (a thing I never saw nor heard of before) and very lewdly called and cried out with open mouth. You see what petty reckonings I am fain to pick out to make up a sum.

[74] October 24, 1605: Yesterday a goldsmith in Cheapside was fined in the Star Chamber for arresting the Countess of Rutland upon an execution, and it was thoroughly argued how far noblemen and women are privileged in their persons from arrests. The week before there was a purveyor censured for misdemeanor in his place, to ride with his face to the horse's tail, wherein one of his judges dissented

---

[14] John Gordon, Dean of Salisbury.

[15] Richard Haydock, physician, of Salisbury, preached sermons while pretending to be asleep.

[16] Playing his game.

[17] John Milward, chaplain to King James.

from the rest and would rather have it upon an ass, and that for two reasons: first it would be more wonderment and gather more boys about him, and secondly the slow pace of the ass would prolong his punishment. . . .

The King finds such variety of sports that he cannot easily leave Royston and those quarters. He is now fallen into a great humor of catching larks, and takes as much delight in it, or more, than in hunting.

[78] March 27, 1606: Garnet[18] is to be arraigned this day at Guild Hall with great concourse. I doubt he will deceive their expectation for I am of opinion he will say little. . . . He hath been very indulgent to himself, both in the Gatehouse and in the Tower, and daily drunk sack so liberally as if he meant to drown sorrow.

[79] April 2, 1606: Garnet's arraignment . . . lasted from eight in the morning till seven at night. The King was there privately and held out all day, besides many courtiers and ladies. . . .

The sum of all was that Garnet, coming into England in '86, hath had his finger in every treason since that time, and not long before the Queen's death had two breves sent him from the Pope, directed to the nobility and clergy of England, to provide that *Quandocunque contigerit miseram illam faeminam ea hac vita excedere,*[19] they should . . . make choice of such a one as either were Catholic or would tolerate Catholic religion. Which breves he kept by him till he saw the King duly settled, and then burned them.

The declaration of the foresaid treasons was a long work, and when all was done he was not to be touched for them, having gotten the King's general pardon the first year of his reign.

But touching this late hellish conspiracy, he was proved to be privy to it two several ways at least, both by Catesby[20] and by Tesmond or Greenway.[21] To which he answered that from Catesby he had it

---

[18] Henry Garnet, Superior of the Jesuits in England, accused of complicity in the Gunpowder Plot.

[19] At whatever time it should befall that miserable woman to depart this life.

[20] Robert Catesby, who planned the Gunpowder Plot.

[21] Oswald Greenway, alias Tesmond.

only in general terms, and from Tesmond *sub sigillo confessionis*,[22] and that he did not only dissuade but pray against it; which, though it were no sufficient answer, yet it was further replied that Catesby having imparted to him the particulars of the same plot to be executed in Queen Elizabeth's time, it is not likely he would conceal them from him now. And having continual intercourse with the chief actors, and sending letters both by Winter into Spain, by Fawkes and Wright to the Archduke, and by Sir Edmund Bainham (captain of the damned crew) to the Pope, it would not be but that he was acquainted with all their secrets. Besides, the very next day after the plot should have been performed, he was at the rendezvous in Warwickshire.

But to show what credit was to be given to his or any of their denials or speeches, the Earl of Salisbury . . . declared that, by reason of their impudent slanders and reports, we are kept in such awe that we dare not proceed against them by such means as they do in other countries to get out the truth, but are fain to flatter and pamper them; . . . so that this man, by the cunning of his Keeper, was brought into a fool's paradise and had diverse conferences with Hall which were overheard by spials set of purpose: whereof being examined, he utterly denied any such interlocution. But being urged further, and some light given him that they understood somewhat, he denied it still with greater asseveration and protestation upon his soul. And being now asked in all this audience how he could do it, answered boldly that, so long as he thought they had no proof of it, he was not bound to accuse himself; but when he saw they had proof, he stood not long in it. . . .

It were to no end to trouble you further, only I will tell you how my Lord Admiral nicked it in saying to him, "Garnet, thou hast done more good in that pulpit this day" (for he stood in a pew by himself) "than in all the pulpits thou ever camest in in thy life."

In conclusion, he was found guilty and had judgment. But it is thought he shall not die yet, if at all, for they hope to win much out of him, and used him with all respect and good words. And he carried himself very gravely and temperately.

[80] April 5, 1606: That false alarm of the King's loss[23] . . . spread far and near and could not be countermanded in the country in three

---

[22] Under the seal of confession.

[23] He had been reported assassinated at Woking, March 22.

or four days, insomuch there was fain to be a proclamation to restrain assemblies and seditious rumors.

At his coming to town the same day, the whole Court went to meet him, the Parliament sent Sir Maurice Berkeley with four knights more to welcome him, the Speaker with his mace went beyond the Park corner to bring him in, and the Lord Mayor with his brethren went to him after supper to congratulate his safety. To all which he made several harangues, as likewise to the people's acclamations the next day when he went to the sermon, telling them that he took these demonstrations more kindly than if they had won a battle for him; that a better king they might have, but a more loving and careful for their good they could not; and that these signs were the more welcome to him for that foreign ambassadors might see the vanity of those reports that were spread abroad in other countries of mislikes and distastes twixt him and his people.

But amongst all these mutual rejoicings, Sir Lewis Lewknor had the most feeling comfort, being presented by the Spanish Ambassador with a chain of sixscore pound, for bringing the good news.[24]

[83] July 16, 1606: At our Sessions the last week there were two Spanish cutpurses condemned, the one to be pressed, the other hanged. But they are both yet reprieved, whereat our common people repine and say our own cannot find such favor. One Franc. Dormer, an ordinary youth, hanged himself on Sunday not far from our lodging upon shame that he was beastly drunk the day before. Derrick the hangman (to the great rejoicing of all the boys in town) was well whipped at Bridewell for burning a fellow in the hand with a cold iron. . . .

Sir Henry Cary is come out of the Low Countries so Spanish in attire as if he were in love with the nation.

[84] October 5, 1606: The Jesuits here have a new Superior, and all the priests that were lately shipped over and banished are said to be returned and to have brought others worse than themselves. The Pope hath lately made eight new Cardinals, all Italians, so that it seems they will tie the Holy Ghost to choose a vicar of that nation.

---

[24] He first informed the Court of the King's safety.

[90] February 6, 1607: I hear the King hath undertaken the debts of the Lord Hay, the Viscount Haddington, and the Earl of Montgomery to the value of four and forty thousand pounds, saying that he will this once set them free and then let them shift for themselves. In the meantime his own debts are stalled, to be paid the one half in May come two years, the residue in May following.

[93] September 27, 1607: The greatest news of this country is of an ingenious fellow that in Berkshire sailed or went over a high steeple in a boat all of his own making, and, without other help than himself in her, conveyed her above twenty miles by land over hills and dales to the river and so down to London.

[96] January 8, 1608: Above Westminster the Thames is quite frozen over and the Archbishop came from Lambeth on Twelfthday over the ice to the Court. Many fantastical experiments are daily put in practice, as certain youths burnt a gallon of wine upon the ice and made all the passengers partakers. But the best is of an honest woman (they say) that had a great longing to have her husband get her with child upon the Thames.

[98] July 7, 1608: Here is a ship newly come from Virginia that hath been long missing. She went out the last year in consort with Captain Newport, and after much wandering found the port three or four days after his departure for England. I hear not of any novelties or other commodities she hath brought more than sweet wood. . . .

The progress holds on toward Northamptonshire, as unwelcome to those parts as rain in harvest, so as the great ones begin to *remuer mesnage*[25] and to dislodge, the Lord Spencer to his daughter Fane in Kent, and diverse other gentlemen devise errands other ways. . . .

The new bourse[26] at Durham House goes up apace, whereat the

---

[25] To break up housekeeping.
[26] The Bourse built by Robert Cecil, Earl of Salisbury, on the site of the present Adelphi, worried the merchants of the Royal Exchange.

citizens, and specially the Exchange men, begin to grumble, foreseeing that it will be very prejudicial and mar their market; and thereupon have made a petition to the Lord Mayor to provide *ne quid detrimenti Respublica capiat*.[27] This petition with the reasons being sent to his Lordship doth nothing please him, but all the answer he makes yet is that, Westminster being the place where he was born and of his abode, he sees not but that he may seek to benefit and beautify it by all the means he can.

[99] July 15, 1608: The desperate planet hangs over us still, for on Monday one Captain Ludlow was stabbed in the White Hind, a tavern without Cripplegate. Our bill [28] is shrewdly risen this week to 162, whereof 26 of the plague. On Monday a gentleman won a great wager for riding five measured miles (between Brainford and Kensington) twenty times over in less than five hours.

[105] December 9, 1608: The King is at Thetford where he was received by three cormorants that had planted themselves upon the church and would not be removed either by ringing of bells, shouting of the people, or shooting of pieces at them, till after much levelling one of them was taken down with a bullet, and then his fellows flew away.

[113] March 3, 1609: The Earl of Dorset died on Monday night, leaving a heavy widow, God wot, and his son, seeing him past hope, the Saturday before married the Lady Anne Clifford (with whom he had been in speech in his grandfather's time), and so prevented [29] the Duke of Lennox and others that made earnest means for his wardship. But howsoever he hath done a true part, and pleased himself, yet the matter might have been better handled, and he eased himself of a burthen he may peradventure feel hereafter.

---

[27] That the public good suffer no damage (Caesar).
[28] Total deaths during the week.
[29] Forestalled.

[119] May 2, 1610: Our Parliament is at a stand and knows not (as they say) *de quel bois faire flèches*.[30] Their offer of £100,000 yearly for wards and tenures is neither refused nor accepted. But withal they were given to understand by the Lord Treasurer that the King, besides that, must have two hundred thousand pounds more of yearly support, which makes them pull in their horns and know not what to say; for the realm grows poor, and traffic decays apace, insomuch that the customs of London are fallen this year £14,000, and fewer ships arrived by 360. So that this proposition breeds much discontent already, and I am sorry to see us in this, as in all the rest, to grow so fast into the French fashion of loud-speaking and base suffering.

[120] May 24, 1610: The solemnity of creating the Prince of Wales is appointed the 4th of the next month, when there shall be 24 new knights of the Bath made, whereof there is like to be better choice than heretofore, for none shall be admitted but nobly descended. . . .

Touching Parliament matters, I know not what to write, seeing they have sit now fourteen weeks to so little purpose. Of late there have been some tempests raised about their meddling with impositions, which by a message from the King they were forbidden to deal in; but because the message came not *modo et forma*,[31] nor immediately (as they took it) from the King, they did in a sort refuse to take notice of it. Whereupon grew more messages and much contestation. But in the end, they saw that *motus praestat componere fluctus*,[32] and with a moderate answer pacified his Majesty; so that the 21th of this present he made another speech to both the Houses, but so little to their satisfaction that I hear it bred generally much discomfort: to see our monarchical power and regal prerogative strained so high and made so transcendent every way that, if the practice should follow the positions, we are not like to leave to our successors that freedom we received from our forefathers, nor make account of anything we have, longer than they list that govern.

Many bold passages have been since in the Lower House, and among the rest a wish that this speech might never come in print. But

---

[30] From which wood to make arrows.
[31] In due form and manner.
[32] It is better to calm the passion of the waves (Virgil).

what this business now in hand will come unto, God knows; for besides his Majesty, some great persons are engaged in this matter of impositions, and no doubt will maintain their doings, knowing that, though men storm never so much, yet *vanae sine viribus irae*.[33]

[129] December 18, 1611: Some few days since, two gentlemen shooting the Bridge were drowned, at least one of them, brother to Sir George Clifford, and the two watermen; the other, Fitzhughes, was taken up at the Tower and with much ado saved.

Rich Sutton[34] is dead at last, the 12th of this month. I cannot yet learn many particulars of his will, but thus much hath been told me from the mouth of Auditor Sutton,[35] one of the executors: that he hath given twenty thousand pounds ready money to charitable uses, to be disposed by the Archbishop of Canterbury, the Bishop of Ely, and the Bishop of London. He hath left eight thousand pound land a year to his college or hospital at the Charterhouse (which is not bestowed on the Prince, as was given out) to the maintenance of eightscore soldiers, sober men who are to have pensions according to their degrees, as they have borne places of captains, lieutenants, or ancients and the like. There is a school likewise for eightscore scholars, with a £100 stipend for the schoolmaster, and other provision for ushers, with a 100 marks a year wages for a gardener to keep the orchard and gardens in good order. . . . I cannot learn of much that he hath given to his poor kindred, not above the value of £400 a year.

---

[33] Rage is useless without power.

[34] Thomas Sutton, reckoned to be the richest commoner in England, made a fortune from the coal on lands he leased around Durham; he also married a rich wife, Elizabeth, widow of John Dudley. His death had been rumored as early as October.

[35] Richard Sutton, auditor of the Exchequer.

III. Private Lives and Public Service, 1600-1610

CARLETON'S DIPLOMATIC APPRENTICESHIP AND THE GUNPOWDER TREASON

JOHN CHAMBERLAIN *must have written at least one long letter almost every day of his life. His weekly or fortnightly letters to Carleton were the most continuous series, thanks to Carleton's long periods of residence abroad, but a series just as complete apparently went to Sir Ralph Winwood during his long embassy at The Hague. Chamberlain also seems to have kept up a regular correspondence with his friend William Gent in Oxford. There were less regular, more topical communications with William Camden and Lancelot Andrewes; and he probably treated Lady Fanshawe at Ware Park and Lady Winwood at Ditton with the sort of letters he wrote to Alice Carleton. When he was not gathering news and writing letters, he was delivering both; or else he was busy with a world of errands for his friends, or was helping one family set off for the country while entertaining another on their visits to London.*

Carleton, who hated working for the unimpressive Ambassador Sir Thomas Parry, evidently used Northumberland's official visit to Paris in 1602 to solicit a job as secretary in his household. Henry Percy, ninth Earl of Northumberland, must have been stimulating company, but he was a dangerous patron, especially for someone who hoped to seek diplomatic employment. One errand secretary Carleton performed for his employer shadowed his career for nearly a decade: he arranged that a house belonging to one Mrs. Susan Whynyard should be let to Thomas Percy, a cousin of the Earl. The fact that the house was next to the Houses of Parliament did not concern Carleton until he found himself under suspicion of treason following the Gunpowder Plot.

In 1604 a "coolness" between himself and Percy prompted him to change his position. He still sat as Member of Parliament for St. Mawes, a pocket borough in Cornwall. In 1605 he accompanied Lord

Norris on Lord Admiral Nottingham's peace-making mission to Madrid. While Norris lay seriously ill in Paris on their return journey, Carleton was recalled to explain his connections with the Percies and the fatal house in Westminster. He spent a miserable Christmas in 1605 imprisoned in the house of a bailiff, though by February was "airing myself on the Chiltern Hills in order to take away the scent of Powder." But he waited nearly five years for Cecil to find him another post abroad, and was not allowed even to resume his seat in Parliament.

During most of this time Carleton rusticated, banking rather heavily on Chamberlain's good nature to run his errands for him. He courted and won Anne, stepdaughter of Sir Henry Savile, Provost of Eton, and helped his father-in-law with his "Greek letters," the great edition of St. Chrysostom. Moreover, it must have been all the more vexing to watch his remote cousins Sir Walter Cope and Sir Henry Wotton prosper—the one Cecil's faithful servant, but not very clever; the other clever indeed, but of uneven judgment.

[34] October 21, 1600: Good Master Carleton, I had answered your letter this morning but for your cousin Lytton, who, being to go out of town, not only trifled out the time himself but made me such a trifler that I doubt I shall come short of your messenger. Your cousin will be here again on Monday, and brings his son William to see my Lord Mayor's pageant, and these uncouth ambassadors. The Barbarians[1] were yesterday at Court to take their leave, and will be gone shortly; but the eldest of them (which was a kind of priest or prophet) hath taken his leave of the world and is gone to prophesy *apud inferos*[2] and to seek out Mahound [*sic*], their mediator.

Here is no foreign news at all, but a saying that Ostend should be besieged and two forts built upon the water to take away the haven, and that the Grave Maurice should give great words that he will visit Flanders once more and venture to relieve it; but the time of year, besides other circumstances, make it unprobable. The world says Sir Ed. Norris[3] foresaw these tempests, and like a wise pilot provided to keep

---

[1] An embassy from the King of Barbary: cf. Gazette, Letter 33.

[2] Among the shades.

[3] Governor of Ostend, 1590-1599; Carleton had returned from his service there between August 1599 and February 1600.

himself and his in safe harbor, for as the matter is used, the town is now held scant tenable.

Sir Henry Neville[4] is urged to return into France, but he makes many excuses and so resolute resistance that he pretends he will not back again unless he be sent *pieds et poings liez*.[5]

[36] February 3, 1601: Sir Gerrard Harvey with his Lady, mother, and sisters, kept their Christmas at Knebworth,[6] where I had much good company of his brother John, and ran over many old stories of you and Ostend. Your cousin Lytton is in town and tarries all or most part of the term. Your brother Carleton came yesterday. And your cousin Acton is looked for within two or three days to come and sojourn in Little Britain. . . .

The Queen hath made choice [of our] Doctor[7] for her physician, but he is not yet sworn. I doubt our college[8] will be dissolved, and some of us sent to seek our fortune. . . .

When I was now bidding you farewell your brother Carleton comes in and prays me to put in his commendations, and to tell you that your place in Oxford[9] will tarry for you one year more. Vive vale.

[38] May 27, 1601: Your friends have not been unmindful of you, for upon the first bruit that Master Cecil[10] should go ambassador lieger into France, your cousin Lytton was with him to make your way. But both he, Master Bodley, Sir Rob. Sidney, Sir Ed. Wotton, Sir Tho. Parry, Sir Ant. Mildmay and some others that were named in that place having flatly refused or avoided, as yet *sub judice lis est*[11] which of them, or whether any at all, is to be sent. In the meantime Master Winwood supplies the place and hath the Queen's letters to the French King for his credence.

---

[4] Ambassador to France. He had returned to England earlier in the year complaining of deafness. A friend of Essex, he may have known even this early of the plot that culminated in the February uprising.

[5] Tied hand and foot.

[6] Rowland Lytton's home in Hertfordshire.

[7] William Gilbert, with whom Chamberlain lived.

[8] Household.

[9] His fellowship at Christ Church.

[10] Presumably Edward Cecil, third son of Thomas, 2nd Lord Burghley.

[11] The case is before the judge (Horace).

Sir Henry Neville is in the Tower, which at first made many men think he should come to his answer, but this whole term having passed without any arraignment makes me think there shall be no more blood drawn in that cause.[12]

[41] September 19, 1601, from Knebworth:

MASTER CARLETON,

I answered your letter of the 24th of July from Ascott, where I since received another of yours of the fifth of August at my return from my Hampshire progress; the progress whereof is not worth the writing, save only that I came to the churching of my Lady Wallop, who is not a little proud of her little boy, and visited mine old wife[13] at her new home, where she plays the housewife out of cry, but will have much ado to bring that riotous and disordered house into any order; yet her virtue will shine the more if she can bring light out of darkness, or alter the frame of that confusion into any reasonable government. Once the place and state of that living is worthy of her travail, and I do not greatly despair of the success, having so kind and tractable a husband towards her, and one that makes very much of her, whereof I take no small comfort, and the more for that it is thought she is prettily forward with child, though I need not brag nor boast of it. I visited likewise my niece St. John,[14] newly brought abed, and my niece Stukeley[15] that looks very shortly, and now I am come hither to Knebworth where your cousin Lytton is ready to lie down and looks hourly, so that this hath been a gossiping journey, and full of increase.

The Queen is now in progress as far as Basing, a house of the Lord Marquis's, where she entertained your Frenchmen with all favor and gracious usage. I cannot tell you the particulars, for I was nothing near. Our friend the Sheriff of Berkshire was almost out of heart at the first news of the Queen's coming into the country, because he was altogether unacquainted with courting, but yet he performed it very

---

[12] Essex's rebellion.

[13] A nickname Chamberlain employs in several letters for Winifred, the young daughter of his friend Sir Henry Wallop.

[14] Ursula, wife of Henry St. John and daughter of Chamberlain's sister Elizabeth and Hugh Stukeley.

[15] Elizabeth, wife of Thomas Stukeley, the son of Elizabeth and Hugh Stukeley. She and her newborn son died shortly after childbirth.

well and sufficiently, being exceedingly well horsed and attended, which won him commendation on all sides.

The Queen's first remove from Windsor was to Master Ward's, then to Reading. During her abode there, she went one day to dinner to Master Comptroller's[16] at Caversham. Master Greene, Sheriff of Oxfordshire, met her at the bridge very well accompanied. Master Comptroller made great cheer and entertained her with many devices of singing, dancing, and playing wenches, and suchlike. At her going thence she made three knights, your cousin Sir Fra. Goodwin, Sir Edmund Fettiplace, and Sir Richard Ward. But what need I trouble you with these things when your brother was there in person, who can relate all at large, *et quorum pars parva fuit;*[17] for I imagine his small troop was half drowned in the sea of such shows as the Oxfordshire men made, when Sir Ant. Cope, Sir Richard Wenman and the rest set up all their sails, and Master Dormer for his part came with ten or twelve men well mounted.

Two or three days after, the Queen dined with Sir Edward Norris at Englefield, where I heard of no wonders, but that she knighted Sir Read Stafford and his Lady's father. . . .

[Postscript by Rowland Lytton] I have not fraught for a coal lading and therefore I will embark my commendations in this vessel, adding only for news that since the beginning of this letter my state is mended by the worth of one daughter more which my wife hath brought; and so with the best wishes of an assured friend and loving kinsman, I commit you to God.

> Yours ever so,
> R. Lytton

[**43**] November 14, 1601: I wrote to Master Winwood[18] the last week and sent him such poor occurrents as the time affords. I meant to have saluted you likewise and given you thanks for yours of the 24th of the last, which came to my hands that week, but I could neither find time nor place, unless I should have crept into some scrivener's shop, for Master Lytton whiles he is here hath so much company and so much to do that he possesseth every corner; so that I am driven to a narrow shift to write now.

---

[16] Sir William Knollys.
[17] And in which his part was small.
[18] Ralph Winwood was then Chargé d'Affaires in Paris.

He hath brought up his son William and placed him at Westminster, and himself stays the longer in town about a troublesome business to get his horse (that he sent for Ireland and is returned from Bristol as unsufficient) to be seen and allowed. There were certain commissioners appointed to receive and ship them, who were so curious and dainty that of 50 horse sent by the Clergy they returned 28, and of 10 sent out of Hertfordshire refused six, and so of other countries, with very uncivil and untrue certificates; whereupon the Clergy have so followed the cause that (for all the difficulty of discountenancing commissioners) they have their horses reviewed here and sent back upon their charges that refused them; and Master Lytton hopes for the like conquest, for he stands much upon his reputation in these points.

[45] April 26, 1602: I went to Knebworth some four or five days after your departure, where we found a sad and sorrowful house,[19] and I led a mournful life; but by the help of the books you left with me, I made shift to convert a good part of my melancholy into devotion. Your cousin Lytton did all he could to bend himself, and to put on sometimes a philosophical, sometimes a Christian, resolution. Yet his patience was not of proof to bear out such a trial, but that many times it failed him when he had most need. We found him very much dejected, and altogether out of taste with any comfort that could be afforded him. Yet many wholesome cordials went down without relish at unawares that have since had good operation, and I doubt not but the approved medicine of time will work as well with him as with others.

The funeral was performed very orderly and with good solemnity, and the more by Master Clarenceux's[20] friendly presence, who came from the burial of the Lady Barrington unlooked-for and unrequested, but went not empty away as he pretended and would needs have done.

[48] June 17, 1602: The Lord Ambassador[21] goes not yet these eight or ten days, and . . . his Lady goes not at all. I perceive he

---

[19] Anne, wife of Rowland Lytton, died February 28, 1602.
[20] William Camden, the antiquary, Clarenceux King-of-Arms.
[21] Sir Thomas Parry. His mission to Paris was getting off to a reluctant start.

begins to see his error, and shakes off his followers as fast as he took them. He hath already dismissed Davison, and some say Gosnoll, but all is one, for his vanity and overweening will shortly dismiss itself, for I hear he gives it out and is plotting already to be left Agent when his Lord comes away.

I doubt we are not like to have Master Winwood so soon as he and we would, for there is no such great opinion of his[22] sufficiency that is to succeed, but that it is resolved he must stay longer to tutle and direct him till he be thoroughly acquainted with those courses. I would have written so much to him, but that I know it will not be welcome, and I am loath to discourage my friends, and therefore I pray you impart it when you see fit time, as likewise that it is for the good conceit of him and his service which Master Secretary[23] is not sparing to publish upon any occasion or mention of him.

[52]　October 2, 1602:

GOOD MASTER CARLETON,

Now I have dispatched the ordinary occurrents,[24] it will not be amiss to inform you of some private matters apart, which course you may hold with me (if you please) in whatsoever you would have kept close or reserved; for both you and I have so many good friends here in common, that if they hear of any post or packet, they think themselves wronged if they see not the original, whereof I assure you I am not so liberal but that they see it comes *invita Minerva*[25] and not at first call.

Upon my first coming to town Master Cope inquired when I heard from you, and told me of two papers he had delivered you, of the genealogies and matches of the great houses of France, which he desired you to continue and draw out till this time; I gave no great care to him then, but upon a second and third summons I told him what other employments and business withheld you that you could not attend such trinkets. His answer was that you might get some expert

---

[22] Parry's.
[23] Sir Robert Cecil.
[24] This letter was enclosed with Letter 51. Carleton, unhappy over his treatment in Paris as secretary to Ambassador Sir Thomas Parry, had inquired about a post under "Master Secretary" Robert Cecil.
[25] Against (my) better judgment (Horace).

Frenchman to do it for you according to those copies, or at leastwise send him back his own papers which he had out of his old Lord's[26] memorials. Though I hold him neither apt nor greatly able to do any friend he hath good, yet must we sometimes hold a candle before the devil, and do as the people of Calcutta, that worship him not so much for any help they look for at his hands, as because he should do them no harm. I use him somewhat after that kind, and though for some inward respects I malign him as much as any old friend he hath, yet I comply thus far with him as to serve his humor now and then when it comes upon me; as this other day, expostulating with me why I did not present Master Secretary with some toys to keep me in his remembrance: I delivered him some of those pictures and verses you sent me, in your hand, which I presume Master Secretary knows—at leastwise I told Wat Cope I had them from you—and he says Master Secretary chose the last picture and the last verses you sent, so that if it do me no good it can do you no harm.

If you did not know me so well as you do, methinks you might guess I aim at somewhat, but I vow and swear unto you by our love and friendship (which is a sound oath) that I am past all ambition, and wish nor seek nothing but how to live *suaviter* and in plenty. To which end and to your own good, if you sometimes furnish me with such toys as you think fit it will not be amiss, and withal any pamphlets of the Jesuits or such like: specially *La verité Defendue,* so often alleged by Arnault in his *Franc Discours,* whereof Dr. Andrewes[27] is very desirous, and I have promised it him if it be to be had. You see how bold a beggar I am, but it is upon confidence you will always use me as boldly, if ever it come to my turn to stand you in stead.

Your cousin Lytton and I have conferred upon your letter and are not very hasty to follow that course you speak of, for though Willis[28] be removed (only upon his insolent and harsh behavior towards his master, as both Wat Cope and Hugh Beeston have told me in confession) yet the places are full and supplied by Bruerton and Levinus; and if you were once in his service, what usage soever you found, there is no starting but that you are lodged. Whereas now it is *integrum*[29] to you to take what way you list, and that may serve for *ultimum refugium;*[30] and I hope for better at your hands than a bare service.

---

[26] William Cecil, first Lord Burghley.
[27] Lancelot Andrewes, Dean of Westminster.
[28] Simon Willis, secretary to Sir Robert Cecil.
[29] Open.
[30] Last refuge.

The place you are in will make you known, and there will be always means to further you to his favor. If there be not extreme cause to the contrary, I would wish you to continue a while as you are, for I assure you, both Court and country take notice of you and give you your due. Therefore you must not *succumbere oneri*,[31] but go on cheerfully to the journey's end.

Touching the little gentlewoman without Cripplegate,[32] she continues still wavering and ready to slide upon every occasion. Yet it may be but a natural inconstancy, and that she will not fall downright, but loves to hold her friends in suspense; unless the coming of your fair niece and your sister Faringdon (who are shortly looked for) alter the case. Mistress Faringdon sent her your monitory letter with advice not to neglect the counsel of so careful and loving a brother: marry, for her part, she would not intermeddle in such matters, but wished her to follow her conscience—with diverse other clauses that pulled down as fast as she set up, which show that she herself is far gone. And indeed I hear she is fully perverted. The little gentlewoman tore the letter in the midst and sent her back half, and sent it back with this answer: that seeing it most concerned her, she thought it reason to keep her part. Wherewith the other was not so well satisfied but that it made a little pique.

All that I have gotten by meddling in these matters is (which I always suspected and looked for) to be traduced and tossed like a tennis ball among the faction, so far forth that Valentine sought out Master Gent at Oxford and told him how far he had prevailed and that she was fully resolved [33] had not I reclaimed her, and withal told him many lying and ridiculous reasons that I had used to that purpose; whereas I never spake with him past once in my life, and then had not many words neither. But I perceive cogging[34] and gross lying is a great part of their profession.

Your sister Williams hath had pretty doings in her new house for so small a time; first in burying out of it one Master Gifford, whom they took in of kind heart when he was past all recovery, to season it and die there; then in a christening of her son; and now shortly in a marriage of one of her maids.

---

[31] Sink under the burden.
[32] One of Carleton's sisters, oversympathetic with Roman Catholicism.
[33] To become a Roman Catholic.
[34] Deceit.

You see I am willing you should know all, and more peradventure than I shall have thanks for. *Vive vale,*

Yours,
J. C.

[Marginal note] A friend sent me *La Verité Defendue* this morning as I was closing up this letter.

To your own good self, Master Carleton.

[57] December 23, 1602: I am little beholding to the post that brought Master Winwood's letters and yours of the 23rd of the last and 7th of this present, for he kept them a whole week in his hand after his arrival, so that I had scant leisure to run over the enclosed discourse, for that your brother was to go that day homeward, and Sir Edward Norris went away not past two days before. A third, of the 12 of this present, I received three days since.

In answer to all which I can say little for the present, being full fraught with spleen and indignation of such unworthy usage; and he were a wise man could tell what were best to be done in the case. But at all adventures, I would you had set at six and seven in the instant and left him[35] in the lurch; whereas now *lupum auribus tenes,*[36] and it is alike difficult and dangerous to hold or let go. I understand Master Winwood is to come shortly away, but I doubt his absence will not remove the mischief, for there is some further matter of degenerate jealousy that will not endure your sun should dim his torch. Howsoever . . . what course soever you take shall have my voice, for I know it will be grounded upon reason and judgment, and no man can give you better advice than yourself. . . .

I am going tomorrow to keep Christmas at Knebworth, whither I am so vehemently urged that it were no good manner to forsake them now in their solitariness, having always had so great part of their pleasure and plenty. I mean not to stay there long, and whatsoever we can hammer out there together you shall hear by my next. I make full account that when your honorable friend [37] shall understand the whole

---

[35] Sir Thomas Parry.
[36] You hold the wolf by the ears.
[37] Sir Edward Norris.

matter, he will not be quiet till he see you better provided, and that this disgrace will double his care and kindness towards you.

I have pacified Wat Cope in showing him what you write touching his papers. Master Secretary did him a very extraordinary favor to admit him a partner in his entertainment to the Queen, and to permit him to present her with some toys in his house, for the which he had many fair words, but as yet cannot get into the Privy Chamber, though he expect it daily. . . .

Here is a buzz already that the Lord of Northumberland [38] shall go to the christening of your Fille de France. If it so fall out, you may bethink yourself what use might be made of it. . . .

The little gentlewoman without Cripplegate sends you word that her mother marvels she cannot hear of you. I have sent you here an almanac, that you may see how our year passeth away, which I wish as happy to you as I wish to myself; and so, being ready to horseback, I commit you to God.

[60] February 11, 1603: Master Winwood was the more welcome for bringing your letters, which were so long wanting that I began to suspect all was not well on our side, and did sometimes call myself to account to see wherein I had failed; but finding nothing, I easily concluded that either your leisure or the place you hold would not permit often writing, or else that some whispering and schooling monitor (either here or there) had counselled you to the contrary. It was never my desire nor meaning to encroach upon news or secrets, specially as long as Paul's is so furnished that it affords whatsoever is stirring in France, and I can gather there at first hand to serve my turn sufficiently (saving for certain particulars), so that I shall not need to put you to trouble or pains, but only to understand your estate, *ut vales, ut memor es nostri*,[39] and such other complements of kindness and friendship.

Master Winwood hath been but once with Master Secretary, but makes account to go with him to Court tomorrow. I have brought your cousin Lytton, your brother Carleton, Master Edmondes and

---

[38] Henry Percy, ninth Earl of Northumberland. (See introductory notes to this section.)

[39] That you are well, that you remember us.

him together, and have had some speech of your business, but, to tell you truly, methinks we are like physicians that consult of a patient without feeling any part of his pain, and finding the disease somewhat difficult, apply no other remedy but good words and good wishes, and make him believe that time and good diet will cure it alone. Indeed patience and time must be your best medicine till we see what Master Winwood's absence from thence and his presence here will effect. You still forget Master Cope, whom I could wish you had at this time remembered. . . .

Yesternight Master Edmondes, Master Winwood, your brother, Master Gent and myself supped at the Mermaid, where your health was often remembered, and better provided for *inter pocula*[40] than our own, for I have been distempered ever since.

[61] February 28, 1603: I shall not need to write you what favorable access and audience Master Winwood found at her Majesty's hands, nor anything else concerning him, sith he is best able to relate it himself, and is now dispatching letters by a messenger of Master Savile's towards you. Mine only errand is to thank you for yours of the 23th of this present, with the Jesuitical apology, wherein (for so much as I have read) I find little but that I have seen in other their pamphlets before, so that it seems they are fain to feed us with crambe[41] for want of better provision. You make mention of another little discourse to be interpreted to the little gentlewoman, but either it is shrunk in the carriage or you forgot to send it.

[63] April 12, 1603: It may be you have not heard of Sir Edward Norris his sickness, whereof though I can send you no certainty (I mean touching the danger or hope of recovery), yet I thought it good to give you this notice as a matter that nearly concerns you and that would require your presence if you may be spared. And of that mind are your other friends, who have likewise to confer with you about another business wherein I can say little, but only of a foolish

---

[40] In the course of our drinking.
[41] Cabbage.

prejudicate fancy of mine own,[42] and therefore will leave it to your own discussing. I confess all likelihoods and presumptions run on their side, so that I cannot nor have not so much as made show of contradiction, but must suffer vain apprehensions to be overruled by sound reasons.

[**64**] July 10, 1603: I returned out of Hertfordshire on Monday, and meant to have tarried here till the coronation, but seeing it will be so private, and the sickness increaseth so fast upon us, I wish myself there again, and will make all the haste I can out of town, for it grows hot here. I hope to be gone about Thursday or Friday toward Knebworth, and after I have been there some fortnight to go forward to Ascott. Among other tedious inconveniences this will not be the least wearisome, not to know how to hear of our friends when I am there; yet if you will now and then cast off a loose letter to your cousin Lytton's or Master Dormer's, they cannot be lost.

Master Winwood was married on Tuesday with much thunder, lightning, and rain; the ominous weather and dismal day put together might have made a superstitious man startle, but he turned all to the best, and so may it prove. There was nobody at the wedding but myself and Master Serle. I hear he went away yesterday with bag and baggage, and is by this time embarked at Gravesend, for by good hap he met with a ship that will deliver him at Rotterdam, which will save him a great deal of trouble and cost, and me a journey to the seaside, which I avoided by that means, and the bringing them to Gravesend by this foul weather. I parted with him on Thursday in Paul's, and one of his greatest regrets was that he should not see you before he went.

I long to hear what you have concluded at Henley. I found the little gentlewoman[43] at my coming to town much distressed, and had almost wept out her eyes for cursed heart, and upon a suspicious imagination that we had all conspired to cozen her; but I soon pacified her, and brought her to that pass that she condemned herself and all she had done. I thank you for your letter by our James.

---

[42] *Editor's Note:* This murky passage is included on the assumption that Chamberlain's "prejudicate fancy" concerned the enmity between Northumberland, Carleton's prospective employer, and Robert Cecil over King James's accession, of which there must have been echoes in Paul's Walk.

[43] One of Carleton's sisters. See Letter 52.

Here is nothing in the world to requite you, unless peradventure you have not heard of a ship of Alderman Hampson's fired by mischance at Blackwall the day you went hence, and came driving with the tide up to Greenwich and there set an outhouse or twain on fire and put the whole town in danger.

Paul's grows very thin, for every man shrinks away, and I am half ashamed to see myself left alone. Our pageants are prettily forward, but most of them are such small-timbered gentlemen that they cannot last long, and I doubt if the plague cease not the sooner they will rot and sink where they stand.[44]

[74] October 24, 1605: I assure you the sight of your letter was never less welcome, fearing it had brought the confirmation of that which was generally bruited[45] . . . so that your letter lay by me an hour or twain unlooked on, and longer perhaps had it lain had not your brother sent to me to learn more particulars, having presently sent his own to the Lady Norris. . . . I was with Sir Walter Cope to learn what construction was made of your provident care herein. He says all is very well taken, neither can it be otherwise.

[75] November 7, 1605: Though I looked for you before this time, and have often wished you here among your old schoolfellows that are almost all come up to the Parliament, yet as matters are lately fallen out about your Lord, I am well content you be absent.

Not that your Lord (as I hope) can be any way touched with this devilish conspiracy;[46] but that nearness of name, blood, long and inward dependence, and familiarity, cannot but leave some aspersion that will not easily or lightly be washed off without time: in which consideration I hear he is rather wished than willed to keep his house.

I cannot but remember what you have diverse times told me touch-

---

[44] A state entry into London was planned to follow the coronation of King James on July 25, 1603, but because of the plague the ceremony was postponed until March 15, 1604.

[45] Francis, second Lord Norris, with whom Carleton was travelling, was reportedly desperately ill in Paris.

[46] The Gunpowder Plot, implicating by association Carleton's former employer, the Earl of Northumberland.

ing Thomas Percy,[47] that you suspected him to be a subtle, flattering, dangerous knave. He hath not only verified your judgment but exceeded all degrees of comparison and gone beyond Nero and Caligula, that wished all Rome but one head that they might cut it off at a stroke; for he at one blow would have ruined the whole realm.

He had hired the house or lodging next to the Parliament, together with the cellar or vault under the Upper House, into which by the means of one Johnson,[48] his man—a superstitious papist, or rather a priest as is thought—he hath conveyed any time this twelvemonth as much powder in satchels, as four or five and thirty barrels, hogsheads and firkins could contain, with intent the first day of the Parliament, when the King should be in his speech, to blow them all up; and had so cunningly covered them with billets, faggots, and such trash that without long search they could not be discovered. And but that God blinded him or some of his to send this enclosed,[49] without name or date, to the Lord Monteagle, it was very like to take effect.

But the carrying it to the Lord of Salisbury and so to the King, it gave such light that, watch being set, the fellow was taken making his trains at midnight with a blind lantern and presently confessed the plot, yet with such show of resolution that he seemed to be chiefly grieved that it had wanted success. The next day he was carried to the Tower, but what Sir William Waad (that is Lieutenant) and other examiners have wrang out of him I cannot learn. Only I hear Sir Edward Bainham, come lately out of the Low Countries, is sought for, and some five or six Jesuits and priests taken in a privy search.

Percy, coming up on a sleeveless errand, and before he was looked for, to your Lord, durst not tarry to see the event but went away that night that his man was taken. . . .

On Tuesday at night we had great ringing and as great store of bonfires as ever I think was seen. . . .

Monsieur Beaumont, the French Ambassador, went homeward the first of this month, and hath blotted his former reputation with very mechanical tricks at parting. For having 2000 ounces of plate given him, he cavilled for 500 more, as having seen a precedent of the like;

---

[47] An active participant in the plot, cousin of Northumberland.
[48] Guy Fawkes insisted that his name was John Johnson for several days after his arrest.
[49] A copy of the anonymous warning sent to Lord Monteagle on October 26.

which being granted him, he begged two horses more by name of the King, besides pictures great and small, with jewels at his own appointment; and not a nobleman or other of his near acquaintance but he got horses, geldings, or somewhat of him; and the impost of 60 tun of wine of the Lord Treasurer, which he sold to French merchants for threescore pound, with diverse other such petty larcenies, as if he made no conscience to rob the Egyptians.

We hear that Master Winwood hath a son, and that the States and the Lady Conway were his gossips.

[76] March 5, 1606: Seeing you mean to be here so soon,[50] I will only tell you that I heard not of your letters till Monday night late, and yesterday delivered the enclosed to Sir Walter Cope, who, Councillor-like, gave me audience at a little table, and after the reading delivered this oracle, that he would show it to my Lord of Salisbury. I told him how much you relied upon him both for advice and furtherance. His answer was very laconical, that he thought you took the best course, and that he could do no more but show your letter to my Lord of Salisbury.

I wished you with us on Thursday, that you might have done your young lady mistress, his daughter, some knight-service at a play, where your presence might have excused me of much trouble and some cost, for I was fain all alone to squire her and Sir Rowland's huswives,[51] till I was as weary as they wanton. All the comfort I had was that my Lady Cope said she would not commit her daughter to any man's care but mine, which was enough to make some man proud to have the charge of such a jewel, though he were ne'er the richer nor the wiser for it.

I inquired of my Lady Cope of my Lord Norris's[52] coming; she told me she would be as glad to hear of it as anybody, and the sooner the more welcome, and this is all the certainty I can send you.

---

[50] Carleton was "airing himself on the Chiltern Hills in order to take away the scent of Powder" after his confinement for suspected complicity in the Gunpowder Plot.

[51] The young daughters of Sir Rowland Lytton.

[52] Francis, 2nd Lord Norris, whose serious illness in Paris had suspiciously delayed him when the Council summoned him home to explain his activities as Secretary to Northumberland.

[77] March 12, 1606: On Saturday I went to Sir Walter Cope to
know the success of your letter, which he had not yet showed to
the great Lord,[53] but promised to do it without fail with the next
opportunity. I told him by way of speech it was not enough to show
a bare letter, unless he did second it with some good affection, and
that I doubted he did not use to reply and urge.

"Yes," quoth he, "as familiarly as I do now with you, unless it be
a matter where I see him directly bent to the contrary."

On Monday I was at him again, but he had not yet delivered it,
but wished me to come again the next morning, which I did; and
then he told me how he had moved my Lord in good terms for your
travel, which he would in no wise hear of till your Lord's causes were
ended.[54] Then he spake of your coming to the Parliament, because
you were weary of idleness and doing nothing; but neither would that
be granted.

"Why," said Sir Walter, "his fellow Francis comes."

"Do you make their cases alike," quoth my Lord, "when he is
accused by two witnesses to be privy to the hiring of the house for
the main blow?"

Sir Walter answered you stood so much on your innocency that
you did not believe there could be any such witness produced.

"Nay, but I assure you there are," said my Lord, "and he hath
been favorably dealt with that the matter hath been no further looked
into."

So that I see you must bear of this storm as well as you may, and
ride it out at anchor till the weather grow more calm.

[83] July 16, 1606: I have been once or twice to seek the oracle in
the Strand,[55] as you wished me, but seeing what cold comfort you
found at his hands, I am not sorry I missed him, for I had rather
receive such an answer at second hand than from himself. Yet if I
can light on him this day or tomorrow I mean to have a bout with
him to see if I can find him in a better humor, for I understand he

---

[53] Robert Cecil.

[54] Northumberland, though not directly involved in the plot, was sentenced to
imprisonment for life and lived in the Tower until released in 1623.

[55] Sir Walter Cope, to whom Carleton had applied for help in obtaining employment.

hath cause enough to be pleased, having lately obtained a grant of the King of a hundred pound a year in Chantry lands or parsonages, wherein you may easily have audience if you can furnish him with any particulars to fill up his book.

[84] October 5, 1606: Will Lytton is become as it were young Cranborne's mignon, and hath followed him in a long hunting progress out into Stafford, Lancashire, and I know not whither, his father half *nolens volens,*[56] being fain to furnish him with new clothes, two men to attend him, two geldings for his own saddle, and all things else answerable. It is thought strange that so wise a father as the Earl of Salisbury should so far humor his son (yet a child) as to let him run these wild courses, and to have all his will; but some that seem to know somewhat make answer that he means to give him his fill, and, when he hath taken a surfeit of these pleasures, to recall him to better matters, as though it were not ordinarily seen that men fall from one vanity to another.

There is a meaning that after a year he shall travel, and Will Lytton is like to accompany him, whereupon Sir Rowland casts about that it were a convenient course for you to be their conductor. I do not know how you will taste it, but methinks it would not be amiss if it may be compassed with good conditions; but howsoever, keep it to yourself.

[85] October 15, 1606, from Ware Park: Here is a new kennel of hounds setting up, and store of hawks more than partridges. And such a coil about gardening that a man cannot be idle though he do but look on—nor greatly well occupied, it goes so slowly forward; and yet here have been every day since my coming above forty men at work, for the new garden is wholly translated, new levelled, and in a manner transplanted, because most of the first trees were dead with being set too deep. And in the midst of it, instead of a knot, he is making a fort in perfect proportion, with his ramparts, bulwarks, counterscarps, and all other appurtenances, so that when it is finished it is like to prove an invincible piece of work.

---

[56] Willy-nilly.

[87] November 11, 1606: I see God and fortune provides better for us both than we ourselves, for where you seem to seek advice and help out of so barren a soil as my brain, Sir Rowland Lytton hath supplied that turn, and out of his large and fertile fields hath furnished all your wants with a double harvest—unless perhaps it be but a transcript of his former letter, as indeed the cover was the very copy of that I had, almost word for word. But howsoever it be, I will not with Phormio take upon me to read a lecture to Hannibal.

Only I will wish you to follow your own genius and let your heart guide your head without overmuch curiosity, for whatsoever is feelingly spoken is commonly feelingly heard. Neither would I have you fail yourself or give over till you had touched some string or found some tune that would sound well in those ears. . . .[57]

Your brother Williams hath gotten a piece of a tale by the end, that the Earl of Northumberland should be offended with his Lady and you for complotting to wring a manor from him, whereby you may see how oddly things will spread.[58]

[89] December 21, 1606, from Ware Park: Unless I should tell you of paling or ditching, plashing of hedges, stocking of trees, catching of moles, or such other kind of husbandry, that is all our country exercise; for *madame de céans* is not yet delivered, though she look hourly and is past her reckoning ten or twelve days, insomuch that her sister Fanshawe that came down with us to hold her back, weary of waiting the good hour, is returned home yesterday to provide for her Christmas guests.

This week the King lay two or three days in an inn at Ware with his hawks, but was so little pleased either with the sport or weather that it is hoped he will take no great liking to the place. . . .

---

[57] Lytton urged Carleton to write to Salisbury, which he did on November 16, hoping that as his innocence had been established, he might be restored to his place in Parliament, and that, having been trained for public life and fitted for no other, he might find favor.

[58] On August 14, Carleton had written to Northumberland saying that as the Court was closed to all connected with his Lordship, could he please make Carleton one of his country farmers. Northumberland replied firmly that Court was the place for Carleton and offered him a small pension so that he would not think of "turning clown." Carleton, fearing deeper involvement, refused the pension.

I am setting forward tomorrow towards Knebworth, where I am become a kind of implement of household for the Christmas time; but if I may have mine own will hereafter, I will make as few winter journeys as I can.

[91] February 13, 1607: The Parliament is begun and your school fellows ply it hard, but do rather yet con their old lessons than venture upon new.

[93] September 27, 1607, from Ascott: The Lord Norris was here on Thursday and tarried all night. He told me he understood by your brother that you were in physic, but he says it is only idleness and because you have nothing else to do, for he never knew you sick when you had any other business.

[95] January 5, 1608: I am sorry to hear Sir Rowland Lytton is so craisie.[59] I pray you tell him I wrote the last week to Farleigh by the persuasion of my cousin Stukeley, who would needs have me try that dry-handed knight for a doe, against our funeral the 13th of this present.[60] I am much busied and troubled about it with Clarenceux and otherwise, but if I might have had my will there should have been less ado, for of all things I love not show nor ostentation. But there be so many precedents of very fresh date of his equals and inferiors that it could not be well avoided. But the worst is the charge will be very great and riseth above a thousand marks, which is too much for a private man. I do every day more and more commend my good fortune rather than my judgment in refusing the executorship, which is such a labyrinth that I doubt I should never have found the way out.

---

[59] Ill.

[60] Chamberlain's brother Robert had died late in December. He had been Master of the Worshipful Company of Ironmongers in 1594.

[98] July 7, 1608: On Tuesday I went with the Lady Fanshawe and other good company to visit Cope Castle at Kensington,[61] and calling in at the Strand we took the Lady, Little Betty, and the Infanta Norris along with us. We had the honor to see all but touch nothing, not so much as a cherry, which are charily preserved for the Queen's coming.

I took my leave of him yesterday, and upon some mention of you he made this short reply, that your books[62] were very well accepted, and that he would overslip no opportunity to do you good. He grows more and more into the great Lord, and it is conceived that if any place should fall whereof Sir Caesar[63] were capable, he should presently step into his room and bear the greatest burthen of the Chequer business.

[103] November 8, 1608: I have neither been idle nor greatly well occupied about your business with Master,[64] and yet I have made three or four errands to find him at leisure but all in vain, so that I was fain to take him by snatches and gather up his curtal[65] answers by piecemeal. The effect is that there is no sign of removing those that are now employed, but that matters stand at a stay. . . .

On Thursday his Lady was invited by the Lady Fanshawe to see her daughters dance, upon speech of entertaining Rawlins to teach Mistress Betty; but her censure was partial on her own side, and thought her daughter did best, when God knows she rather hopped like jackdaw than showed any decent or graceful carriage.

[105] December 9, 1608: I went to the idle oracle of the Strand on Saturday to see what was become of your letter,[66] who told me it

---

[61] Cope's new house, which has been known as Holland House since 1624, when Sir Henry Rich, who married Cope's daughter Isobel, was created Earl of Holland.

[62] Carleton had sent Robert Cecil, Earl of Salisbury, some Spanish books specially bound.

[63] Sir Julius Caesar, Chancellor of the Exchequer.

[64] Sir Walter Cope.

[65] Brief, curt.

[66] Carleton had written Sir Walter Cope, enclosing a letter to Salisbury.

was not yet delivered. . . . Whereupon seeing me discontented he brake out into this protestation, "God is my judge, I am as careful of it as yourself," and so we parted. But as I was going his Lady got a glimpse of me and called after me, to whom I complained that friends were to look for little at his hands that in three weeks or a month's space could not find means to deliver a poor letter. She seemed to marvel at it too, but in the end fell to excuse him with age, want of memory, and multiplicity of business; but if you would now and then call upon her with two or three pretty lines, she would continually put him in mind and become your true solicitor. For which favor I complimented with her after my fashion, and so leave it to your discretion how far you will make use of it.

[106] December 16, 1608: I have not been in the Strand since I wrote last, for I doubt the very sight of me doth vex his little heart, and I would be loath to haunt him like a sprite; and when all is done the answer and protestation he made admits no reply but to leave him to himself. And yet time must not be neglected, for if this next summer (as the report goes) Sir Rafe Winwood leave the Low Countries, Sir Thomas Edmondes go for France, and Sir Henry Wotton for Spain, you must *omnem movere lapidem* [67] to step in upon these removes.

[107] December 23, 1608: I met Sir Walter Cope on Wednesday in Paul's churchyard in his coach, and he did us the favor to stay, for my brother was with me with whom he had conference about money matters. . . . I moved a word to him about you. His answer was that he had you in remembrance to the Lord for Venice, the Archduke's,[68] or the Low Countries, but answer was made it were too great a leap, and that it were more fit you should be first sent on some message.

---

[67] Leave no stone unturned.
[68] Brussels. Cope had recommended Carleton to Lord Salisbury for one of these posts.

[109] January 10, 1609: Having lost some labor in going to the Strand, yet it was my hap to light on him yesterday. . . . One thing I observe, that though our conference be neither often nor long, yet commonly at the end he comes in with your unlucky dependence,[69] at which straw he still stumbles as if it were a great block.

[110] January 23, 1609: On Friday I had an errand into the Strand from Sir Rowland Lytton, when I took occasion to make some little mention of you, which was soon answered, for it seems there hath been nothing more done nor said of late. I found him *occupatissimo,* unless perhaps (with Chaucer's lawyer) he would seem more busy than he was; and yet of late he hath been much employed about state matters and new projects in the Petty Council, which hath reference and makes relation every Saturday of their proceedings to the Council table.

[112] February 21, 1609: I had some speech with Sir Harry Wallop concerning Ireland, who sayth that the Senior Secretary's place, by reason of the Privy Seal, always in his custody, and other perquisites belonging to his office, may be worth 400 marks a year, but the Second Secretary hath small doings, and must in a manner feed altogether upon hope. This he learned from such as profess to understand the secrets of that place. Now consider whether you will stoop to so poor a prey; at least I could wish you should make account of it as *ultimum refugium,* and the last anchor.[70]

---

[69] The service of Northumberland.

[70] A week later Carleton wrote to Chamberlain that he had decided to decline the post in Ireland because the remuneration was too poor. He spent some time with his new father-in-law at Eton, but took a house in London when his wife became pregnant. Carleton was finally appointed Ambassador to Venice, and received his knighthood on June 25, 1610. He arrived in Venice on December 1. Chamberlain, who went with him, stayed until August, 1611. With regard to this trip, Carleton wrote Winwood: "You may quarrel with me for taking John Chamberlain from hence, whose letters gave you extraordinary satisfaction; but you shall know that Sir Thomas Bodley, Sir Rowland Lytton, and Mr. Gent, as well in my respect as his own, to put new life into him, were all persuaders to this journey."

IV. Prince Henry and Princess Elizabeth, 1612-1613

BEFORE *he came to the throne of England, King James had written for his infant son the sober book of advice,* Basilicon Doron. *By 1612, eighteen-year-old Prince Henry was taking seriously his role as heir to the throne. His interest in warlike sports and the Navy, and his outspoken Protestantism, made him tremendously popular with his future subjects. His friends included Sir Walter Raleigh, Phineas Pett, the naval architect, and Chapman, the translator of Homer. He pleased his father with his scholarship, and displeased him by interfering in matters of Household administration and even of policy.*

The Prince ran his own Household, modelled on the King's after he became Prince of Wales in 1610, with an efficiency and economy that contrasted blatantly with James's lax prodigality and which must have bolstered Henry's considerable self-confidence to almost dangerous heights. There were notes of self-righteousness too: for every oath uttered in his presence, fines were collected for the use of the poor, which could not have amused his profane parent.

A difficult decade obviously lay ahead for father and son, a quite different future for England. But 1612 robbed James of his heir as well as of his Treasurer and Principal Secretary, Lord Salisbury. The ship of state never quite got under way again.

James had not decided whether to marry Prince Henry to a German Protestant princess, or to the daughter of the rich Duke of Savoy, or to young Christine, second sister of Louis XIII of France. However, as leader of the Protestant Union, he had quite properly decided to give his lovely daughter Elizabeth to the young Protestant Count Frederick, Elector Palatine of the Rhine. Elizabeth, two years younger than Henry and only survivor of the three daughters Queen Anne bore her husband, had been sensibly and affectionately raised away from Court by Lord and Lady Harington at Combe Abbey in Warwickshire. Her French was excellent, her reading wide, her spirit gay, her virtue apparently untouched by the prevailing smut at Court, which she joined in 1608, still under the supervision of her kindly guardians.

*Princess Elizabeth spent the autumn of 1612 getting acquainted
with her fiancé; but she was denied the pleasure of engagement parties
because of her brother's death. Despite the Queen's desire for a
Catholic son-in-law, Count Frederick was a success. The marriage took
place on Valentine's Day, 1613, as soon as was decently possible
after Prince Henry's funeral.*

*Chamberlain had found Frederick very adequate "if he were a
king's son as she is a King's daughter." Elizabeth evidently thought
so too; in the autumn of 1619, she made the decisive remark that she
would rather eat sauerkraut as wife of a king than roast meat as wife
of an Elector. Frederick accepted the crown of Bohemia from Protestant nobles there who hoped he would bring a strong English
alliance against the new Emperor Ferdinand.*

*Less than two years later, Elizabeth and Frederick arrived in The
Hague without a furrow of land left to support them. There Elizabeth
charmed Ambassador Carleton and together they did their best to
raise money for the expenses of her large family. She lived most of the
remainder of her life in exile, but when her grandson, George of Han-
over, came to England in 1714 it was as King George I.*

[150] October 22, 1612: The King came from Theobalds on Saturday, having notice of the Count Palatine's arrival at Gravesend the
night before. He had a very speedy and prosperous passage, for,
coming from The Hague on Thursday at eleven o'clock, he embarked
that evening at Maesland Sluice, and the next night about ten o'clock
landed at Gravesend, where he continued all Saturday. And on Sunday
morning, the Duke of Lennox and some other noblemen and courtiers
were sent to conduct him to the Court, where he arrived about five
o'clock and was met at the water gate by the Duke of York, attended
by the Earls of Shrewsbury, Worcester, and others, and so brought
through the hall and along the terrace to the new great chamber where
the King expected him. The Prince[1] stirred not a foot, which was much
noted.

He had a great peal of ordnance as he passed by the Tower, and
came with some disadvantage into such a presence, having been so
long on the water in the coldest day that came this winter. And yet

---

[1] Prince Henry.

he carried himself with that assurance, and so well and gracefully, both toward King, Queen, Prince, and specially his mistress, that he won much love and commendation. The King is much pleased in him, and carried him presently into his bedchamber and there bestowed a ring of the value of £1800 upon him.

From thence he was conveyed through the privy lodgings and galleries to the water, and so to Essex House where he yet remains, but is every day at Court and plies his mistress hard, and takes no delight in running at ring, nor tennis, nor riding with the Prince (as Count Henry, his uncle, and others of his company do), but only in her conversation.

On Tuesday she sent to invite him as he sat at supper to a play of her own servants in the Cockpit, and yesterday they were all day together at Somerset House, which is much beautified within this year or two. He hath a train of very sober and well-fashioned gentlemen. . . .

I hear a whispering that the match with Savoy[2] cools, so that unless Fabritio and suchlike blow the coal to warm themselves, it may in good time be quite quenched.

[153] November 12, 1612: When I was closing up my letter to you the last week, I understood more of the Prince's sickness than I was willing to impart, for I knew it could be no welcome news anywhere, and I was in hope the world might amend. But going the next morning, the fifth of November, to hear the Bishop of Ely preach at Court (upon the 22 verse of the third chapter of the Lamentations), I found by the King and Queen's absence from the sermon and by his manner of praying for him how the case stood, and that he was *plane deploratus;* [3] for I cannot learn that he had either speech or perfect memory after Wednesday night, but lay as it were drawing on till Friday between eight and nine o'clock in the evening, that he departed. . . .

It is verily thought that the disease was none other than this ordinary ague that hath reigned and raged almost all over England since the latter end of summer, which by observation is found must have his ordinary course, and the less physic the better, but only sweating

---

[2] For Prince Henry with a daughter of that wealthy duke. "Fabritio" refers to Sir Henry Wotton.
[3] Quite beyond hope.

and an orderly course of keeping and government. The extremity of the disease seemed to lie in his head, for remedy whereof they shaved him and applied warm cocks and pigeons newly killed, but with no success. It was generally feared he had met with ill measure, and there wanted not suspicion of poison; but upon the opening of him the next day toward night, there was nothing found. . . .

The King when he saw no hope left went away on Friday morning to Theobalds, and the Queen removed the same day to Somerset House. His death was exceeding grievous to them both, but specially to the King, who takes it with more impatience than was expected. And yet, somewhat to comfort him, there is an observation made that he is the seventh Prince since the conquest that had been taken from us at man's estate. The King on Monday came from Theobalds to Kensington, to Sir Walter Cope's. . . .

The Lady Elizabeth is much afflicted with this loss, and not without good cause, for he did extraordinarily affect her, and during his sickness inquired still after her; and the last words he spake in good sense, they say, were, "Where is my dear sister?" She was as desirous to visit him, and went once or twice in the evening disguised for that purpose, but could not be admitted because his disease was doubted to be contagious.

[154] November 19, 1612: We look now shortly for some resolution, by reason the greatest differences in Court are compounded very lately, and the rumors from abroad do somewhat quicken and awake our fatal security; but specially the Prince's death hath taken away the means of helping ourselves by his marriage and stopping the gap of our wants for the present by that way, so that we must of necessity have recourse to a Parliament. . . . The *candidati* for every place ply their canvass and will not *demordre*,[4] specially Sir Thomas Lake and Sir Fra. Bacon. . . .

The King was quickly weary of Kensington because he said the wind blew through the walls that he could not lie warm in his bed. He came to Whitehall yesterday was sevennight, and went away on Tuesday last to Theobalds and is this day for Royston. He carried the Count Palatine along with him, whose marriage by this late acci-

---

⁴ Give up.

dent is retarded, because it would be thought absurd that foreign ambassadors, coming to condole the Prince's death, should find us feasting and dancing; so that it is deferred till May Day, and the mourning for the Prince to continue but till the 24th of March. But the fiancing is appointed the 27th of December, and his Councillors hope and do their best to advance the marriage soon after. But the King is earnest to have him send away his train, saving some four or five and twenty.

The Prince's . . . papers showed him to have many strange and vast conceits and projects.

The same day sevennight he died, there fell out a very ridiculous accident. A very handsome young fellow, much about his age and not altogether unlike him, came stark naked to St. James's whiles they were at supper, saying he was the Prince's ghost come from heaven with a message to the King. But by no manner of examination or threatening could they get any more out of him, or who set him awork. Some say he is simple, others mad. He belongs to one of the Chancery. All the penance they gave him was two or three lashes, which he endured as it seemed without sense, and keeping him naked as he was all night and the next day in the Porter's lodge, where thousands came to see him. The King sent to have him dismissed without more ado or enquiry.

[155] November 26, 1612: The King begins to digest his late loss, and seems to have no more feeling of so rude a blow, but gives order that the young Prince be kept within a stricter compass than the former, and not to exceed his ordinary in diet or followers or any other course of show or charge.

[157] December 31, 1612: Sir Thomas Lake on Sunday last outstripped his competitors[5] by one step, by reading the contract twixt the Palsgrave and the Lady Elizabeth, which is the part of a Principal Secretary. . . . But they say he had translated the words of our Communion Book into French so badly, and pronounced them worse, that

---

[5] For the office of Principal Secretary of State, left vacant by the death of Robert Cecil, 1st Earl of Salisbury.

it moved an unseasonable laughter as well in the Contractors as in the standers-by, which was soon silenced by the Archbishop's grave interposing himself, and with an audible voice using these very words, "The God of Abraham, Isaac and Jacob bless these nuptials and make them prosperous to these kingdoms and to his church."

[159] January 9, 1613: The Prince Palatine (for so he is now styled and since this contract is usually prayed for in the church among the King's children) was very royal in his presents this New Year's tide, giving to the Lord and Lady Harington in golden and gilt plate to the value of £2000, to their servants £400, to all the women about the Lady Elizabeth £100 apiece and a medaglia with his picture, . . . to the Prince a rapier and pair of spurs set with diamonds, to the King a bottle of one entire agate containing two quarts, esteemed a very rare and rich jewel, to the Queen a very fair cup of agate and a jewel, and lastly, to his mistress, a rich chain of diamonds, a tiara for her head all of diamonds, two very rich pendant diamonds for her ears, and above all, two pearls for bigness, fashion and beauty esteemed the rarest that are to be found in Christendom.

[163] February 4, 1613, to Alice Carleton in Venice: Here is extraordinary preparation for fireworks and fights upon the water, with three castles built upon western barges, and one great castle upon the land over against the Court. One or two of the King's pinnaces are come already from Rochester, and diverse other vessels to the number of six and thirty are provided . . . and above five hundred watermen already pressed, and a thousand musketeers of the trained bands in the Shires hereabout made ready for this service. . . .

On Tuesday I took occasion to go to Court because I had never seen the Palsgrave, nor the Lady Elizabeth near hand of a long time. I had my full view of them both, but will not tell you all I think but only this, that he owes his mistress nothing, if he were a king's son as she is a King's daughter. The worst is, methinks, he is much too young and small-timbered to undertake such a task.

[165] February 11, 1613: The marriage draws near and all things are ready. On Sunday was their last time of asking openly in the chapel. The Queen grows every day more favorable, and there is hope she will grace it with her presence.

Here is a band of 500 musketeers made ready by the City to guard the Court during these triumphs, and we have extraordinary watches of substantial householders every night, and an alderman in person to oversee them. . . .

The preparations for fireworks and fights upon the water are very great, and have already consumed £6000. . . . I believe there was never such a fleet seen above the Bridge. . . . The tides fall out very fit, as being both spring tides, and the water at the best height from three to six; so that if the weather serve as well, they can wish no more, for they have the whole river at liberty, being shut up both above and beneath with a huge number of lighters and long masts that no boats can come to trouble them. Sir Robert Mansell is chief commander, who takes great pains.

[166] February 18, 1613, to Alice Carleton: On Thursday night the fireworks were reasonably well performed, all save the last castle of five, which bred most expectation and had most devices, but when it came to execution had worst success. On Saturday likewise, the fight upon the water came short of that show and brags had been made of it . . . but the King and indeed all the company took so little delight to see no other activity but shooting and potting of guns that it is quite given over and the navy unrigged and the castle pulled down, the rather for that there were diverse hurt in the former fight (as one lost both his eyes, another both his hands, another one hand, with diverse others maimed and hurt), so that to avoid further harm it was thought best to let it alone. . . .

On Sunday I was fetched from Paul's (where I was set at the sermon) to see the bride go to church, and though it were past ten o'clock before we came there, yet we found a whole window reserved in the jewel-house, which was over against her coming down a pair stairs out of the gallery in the preaching place to a long stage or gallery made along the court into the hall, so that we had as much view as a short passage could give. But the excess of bravery and the continued succession of new company did so dazzle me that I could not observe the tenth part of that I wished.

The bridegroom and bride were both in a suit of cloth of silver, richly embroidered with silver, her train carried up by thirteen young Ladies (or Lord's daughters at least) besides five or six more that could not come near it; these were all in the same livery with the bride, though not so rich. The bride was married in her hair that hung down long, with an exceeding rich coronet on her head which the King valued the next day at a million of crowns. Her two bridemen were the young Prince and the Earl of Northampton.

The King and Queen both followed, the Queen all in white but not very rich saving in jewels. The King methought was somewhat strangely attired in a cap and a feather, with a Spanish cape and a long stocking. . . .

It was done all in English, and the Prince Palatine had learned as much as concerned his part reasonable perfectly. . . .

The next morning the King went to visit these young turtles that were coupled on St. Valentine's day, and did strictly examine him whether he were his true son-in-law, and was sufficiently assured.

That afternoon the King, Prince, Count Palatine, with diverse others, ran at the ring, and when that was ended and the King and Prince gone, the Palsgrave mounted upon a high-bounding horse which he managed so like a horseman that he was exceedingly commended and had many shouts and acclamations of the beholders, and indeed I never saw any of his age come near him in that exercise.

It were long and tedious to tell you all the particularities of the excessive bravery both of men and women, but you may conceive the rest by one or two. The Lady Wotton had a gown that cost fifty pound a yard the embroidering . . . and the Lord Montague (that hath paid reasonably well for recusancy) bestowed fifteen hundred pound in apparel for his two daughters. . . . But this extreme of cost and riches makes us all poor.

On Monday night was the Middle Temple and Lincoln's Inn masque, presented in the Hall at Court. . . . It went from the Rolls all up Fleet Street and the Strand, and made such a gallant and glorious show that it is highly commended. They had forty gentlemen of best choice out of both houses rode before them in their best array, upon the King's horses. And the twelve maskers with their torch-bearers and pages rode likewise upon horses exceedingly well trapped and furnished, besides a dozen little boys dressed like baboons that served for an antimasque (and they say performed it exceedingly well when they came to it), and three open chariots drawn with four horses apiece that carried their musicians and other personages that had parts to speak. All which, together with their trumpeters and other attendants, were so well set out that it is generally held for the best show that hath been seen many a day. . . .

On Tuesday it came to Gray's Inn and the Inner Temple's turn to come with their masque, whereof Sir Fra. Bacon was the chief contriver. And because the former came on horseback and open chariots, they made choice to come by water from Winchester Place in Southwark, which suited well enough with their device, which was the marriage of the river of Thames to the Rhine; and their show by water was very gallant by reason of infinite store of lights very curiously set and placed, and many boats and barges with devices of light and lamps, with three peals of ordnance: one at their taking water, another in the Temple garden, and the last at their landing; which passage by water cost them better than three hundred pound.

They were received at the privy stairs, and great expectation there was that they should every way exceed their competitors that went before them both in device, daintiness of apparel, and above all in dancing. . . . But by what ill planet it fell out I know not, they came home as they went without doing anything, the reason whereof I cannot yet learn thoroughly, but only that the Hall was so full that it was not possible to avoid it or make room for them, besides that most of the ladies were in the galleries to see them land and could not get in. But the worst of all was that the King was so wearied and sleepy with sitting up almost two whole nights before that he had no edge to it. Whereupon Sir Fra. Bacon adventured to entreat his Majesty that by this disgrace he would not, as it were, bury them quick. And I hear the King should answer that then they must bury him quick, for he could last no longer; but withal gave them very good words and appointed them to come again on Saturday. But the grace of their masque is quite gone when their apparel hath been already showed and their devices vented, so that how it will fall out God knows, for they are much discouraged and out of countenance, and the world says it comes to pass after the old proverb: the properer men, the worse luck.

One thing I had almost forgotten for haste, that all this time there was a course taken and so notified, that no Lady or gentlewoman should be admitted to any of these sights with a farthingale, which was to gain the more room, and I hope may serve to make them quite left off in time. And yet there were more scaffolds and more provision made for room than ever I saw, both in the Hall and Banqueting Room, besides a new room built to dine, sup, and dance in.

[168] February 25, 1613: Our Gray's Inn men and the Inner Templers were nothing discouraged for all the first dodge, but on Saturday last performed their parts exceeding well and with great applause and approbation both from the King and all the company. The next night the King invited the maskers with their assistants to the number of forty to a solemn supper in the new marriage room, where they were well treated and much graced, with kissing his Majesty's hand and every one having a particular *accogliènza*[6] from him. The King husbanded the matter so well that this feast was not at his own cost, but he and his company won it upon a wager of running at the ring of the Prince and his nine followers, who paid thirty pound a man. The King, Queen, Prince, Palatine, and Lady Elizabeth sat at a table by themselves, and the great Lords and Ladies with the maskers (above fourscore in all) sat at another long table, so that there was no room for them that made the feast, but they were fain to be lookers-on, which the young Lady Rich took no great pleasure in, to see her husband (who was one that paid) not so much as drink for his money.

[170] March 11, 1613: We are now preparing for the Lady Elizabeth's departure. I am of opinion her train will not be so great by many degrees as was expected, for we devise all the means we can to cut off expense, and not without cause, being come *ad fundum*[7] and to the very lees of our best liquor: else should not the Palsgrave's house have been so abruptly broken up, and the most part of the company dissolved and sent away so suddenly, presently after the King's going to Newmarket, which the Lady Elizabeth took very grievously and to heart; but necessity hath no law. . . .

Upon Tuesday was sevennight, the Prince and the Palsgrave went from Newmarket to Cambridge, where I hear they found great enter-

---

[6] Welcome.
[7] To the bottom.

tainment and had two very commendable acts in divinity and philosophy, besides two excellent comedies, but they marred them with length
and made them grow tedious, the one of them lasting between seven
and eight hours.

[171] March 25, 1613: The King is very angry and out of love with
our Cambridge men for their questions at the Palsgrave's being there,
specially whether *electio* or *successio* were to be preferred in kingdoms, and is out of patience that it should be so much as argued in
schools. . . .

Here is a general stay of all shipping, that none may go forth till
the Lady Elizabeth be gone, which shows a great penury and decay of
navigation, that they cannot provide 2500 mariners to furnish eight or
nine of the King's ships without all this ado and noise.

[172] April 29, 1613: I cannot yet send you any certainty of the
Prince Palatine's and the Lady Elizabeth's passage, for the winds have
been so cross and contrary that they cannot get away, unless they have
taken the benefit of a southerly wind that lasted all Tuesday night and
yesterday till the afternoon. They have been shipped once or twice,
but fain to come on shore again. Methinks she goes very meanly
and slenderly accompanied of Ladies, having only besides her own
women the Countess of Arundel (who goes upon another errand of
her own) and the Lady Harington.

The King and Queen brought them no further than Rochester, and
there took their leave. The Prince went with them to Canterbury and
there stayed with them, meaning to see them shipped, but was sent for
away to St. George's feast. . . .

The King brought the Queen on Saturday to Hampton Court, onward on her way to the Bath. On Monday she went to Windsor, the
next day to Caversham, a house of the Lord Knollys, where she was
gallantly entertained with revels and a masque performed by the Lord
Chamberlain's four sons, the Earl of Dorset, the Lord North, Sir
Harry Carey, and Sir Harry Rich. . . . She makes account to stay
at the Bath not above ten days, and yet this journey is thought will
stand her in £30,000.

Prince Henry: A Postscript

[251] November 9, 1616:[8] The King came to town on Allhallow Eve and stood on the gallery stairs at Whitehall to see the Prince come along from Richmond, attended by the Lord Mayor and all the Companies of London in their barges in very good order and made a goodly show. The Queen would not be present at the creation, lest she should renew her grief by the memory of the last Prince, who runs still so much in some men's mind that on Tuesday I heard the Bishop of Ely, preaching at Court upon the third verse of the 37th of Isaiah (*venerunt filii ad partum et non erant vires parientii*) [9] pray solemnly for Prince Henry without recalling himself.

---

[8] *Editor's Note:* This excerpt from a later letter, describing the ceremony of creating Prince Charles the Prince of Wales, has been included here for obvious reasons.

[9] The children are come to the birth, and there is not strength to bring forth.

V. Private Lives and Public Service, 1611-1614

THE DEATH OF ROBERT CECIL, EARL OF SALISBURY, AND AFTER

DUDLEY CARLETON'S *chosen profession was a comparatively new one. Within the medieval concept of the Christian Commonwealth, a resident ambassador could only be considered a contradiction in terms. When all governments had the same ostensible ends—peace, dynastic marriages and successions according to traditional rule, and the service of a universal religion—diplomatic missions were either ceremonial, to attend a wedding or mourn a death, or* ad hoc, *to sign a specific treaty or demand a specific right. In either case, the grander the courtier and the gifts he bore, the greater the honor to both parties. To propose a permanent embassy was to imply that some continuing difference of interests existed between the court who sent and the court who received the "lieger"; or to suppose that continuing intelligence of another government's plans and policies was necessary to the safety of one's own—to support, in short, a nest of spies if not of saboteurs.*

By 1600 Europe was clearly a collection of nation-states with territorial ambitions that were not simply dynastic, with religion differentiated beyond the hope of reunification, with trade developing profitably, and an interesting race for empire posing new problems on national lines. Obviously a continuing difference of interests did exist; just as obviously, a less expensive alternative to permanent warfare was the exchange of resident diplomatic missions.

This exchange had become habitual among the Italian states, and Spain supported a corps of professional diplomats throughout the sixteenth century. But Queen Elizabeth's Protestant ambassadors had found life hard in Catholic capitals. Except to The Hague and to Paris, they continued to go "extraordinary." Peace with Spain brought English agents to Venice and to the Archduke Albert and his Infanta in Brussels, as well as to Philip III at Madrid. The prospects of trade promoted interest in agents or ambassadors resident in Moscow and Constantinople.

For the decade during which Robert Cecil was Secretary of State, before he took over the Lord Treasurership in 1608, the administration of foreign affairs and the appointment of resident diplomats had a hope of early rationalization under a Principal Secretary for Foreign Affairs. But at Cecil's death, the office of Secretary of State was still distracted by responsibility for all sorts of domestic affairs as well. Moreover, James fancied his own expertise in foreign affairs, while allowing patronage even in the most professional offices to be dispensed to one favorite or another. Lacking clear administrative leadership in foreign affairs, the diplomats found their problems of job hunting multiplied, while hopes of dependable remuneration faded. In 1602, when Parry was sent so reluctantly to Paris, none of the prospective ambassadors had wanted to leave Court while the Queen's succession was in doubt and a new round of job hunting seemed imminent. In 1613 and 1617 and 1624, it was just as necessary to come to Court to press claims and give gifts in order to realize the most reasonable hope of promotion. And a courtier was always likely to be sent off over the heads of the professionals.

Still King James's ambassadors stuck to the public service. A century earlier, Winwood, Edmondes, Carleton and Wotton would probably have become churchmen. Now they dared to serve the fickle national state, and trained their secretaries to follow them.

[122] September 3, 1611, from Augsburg, to Carleton in Venice: It were too long a piece of work to give you a particular account of our hard and tedious journey, being indeed the hardest task that ever I undertook, by reason of the suspicion of sickness in diverse places where we were to pass, so that we were forced to seek byways and ride sometimes all night through dark and dangerous passages. But the worst of all was that when we thought ourselves past danger then we were nearest, being stayed upon the borders of Bavaria and not suffered to pass through any town nor so much as a village, but were fain to seek unknown ways and travel over the fields till both we and our horses were utterly tired. And yet

with all these difficulties I thank God we came to this town the second of this present in reasonable health but well wearied; and now when I hoped to find rest, I have been all this day tired with seeing of sights, which are here many worth the seeing; and tomorrow morning, God willing, are to go hence towards Frankfort. . . . Hoeschelius[1] is keeper of the library, and withal keeps a school. He dined with me this day, and found better entertainment every way with the Dutch than I could give him for lack of Latin.

[123] October 5, 1611, from The Hague: My journey from Frankfort was suitable to the rest, very foul and rainy till we came to Cologne, which took away the pleasure that the beauty of the river (planted all the way with vines on both sides) had otherwise yielded. I wished my Lady some of our excellent salmons, which we bought commonly two a day and were all our food in the boat. From Cologne we came to Arnheim and so to Utrecht, where I parted from my company and left Amsterdam unseen, because I was loath to travel these cold nights by water in open boats. Coming by Leyden, I found them enlarging the town at both ends, beginning first with the fortifications and then with the buildings. The weather is extraordinary cold and tempestuous, which hath detained me here these ten days, and I do still attend the good time, the wind being high west, and they terrifying me with lying four or five days twixt Rotterdam and Flushing, and likely enough to be driven back.

[124] November 6, 1611: I would describe the adventures of my journey from The Hague, whence I parted the 12th of October in hope after so continual foul weather to have found a fair passage. I was two days and two nights twixt Rotterdam and Arnheim. I stayed one night at Middleburgh, and the next morning went to Flushing. At Rotterdam I lighted upon Calandrini,[2] whom I met at Frankfort, and we hired our cabins and made provision together to pass for England. We embarked the next day in a pink with a

---

[1] David Hoeschel or Hoeschelius, Rector of the College of St. Anne at Augsburg.

[2] Caesar Calandrini, later preacher of the Italian church in London.

southeast wind, and went away in company of three men-of-war and four passage boats, with great shooting and sound of drums and trumpets. We sailed well till toward midnight, when there arose a sore tempest that lasted about two hours and brought the wind to the west full against us, so that after much striving we were forced to turn back the next day and came home not far from Ostend, so that we could well discern the town. We had the honor to come in last of all the company, much about the same hour we set out the day before.

That night came in an English ship to Flushing that set out from Dunkirk for England and, meeting with this storm, had her mainmast and foremast blown down and cut overboard, and so with one little sail was driven before the wind to Flushing. In this ship was Hugh Richardson, Master Howard's man, being sent by his master from Augsburg into England with letters, and had order to meet him at Paris; but he was fain to stay with us a fortnight at Flushing for wind. For though some made shift to get over to Sluse and so overland to Calais, yet considering it was six or seven hours' sailing, a dangerous passage as the wind lay, foul ways and unsafe by land, and then another passage by sea and land, I thought it better to adventure ten or twelve hours longer sailing if the wind came anything fair than to run into certain difficulties and charges which might be better avoided.

And indeed if I had had no other business than mine own I would rather have lain a month for a settled wind than undertaken such a voyage, being very well lodged and treated at Flushing, specially by the Lieutenant Governor, Sir John Throckmorton, upon no recommendation nor former acquaintance, insomuch that he would not suffer me at any time to be two days together absent from his table, but would either come or send to fetch me, being in my judgment a very sober and sufficient gentleman, and no way inferior to his predecessor Sir William Browne.

We put to sea once or twice more, but after we had been out an hour or twain we were forced to turn about and recover our haven whence we came. Lastly, upon Simon's and Jude's day,[3] we embarked ourselves in the English ship that had new trimmed herself, and in company of four pinks more set sail, having threescore passengers aboard and three pilots, one of Dover, one of Sandwich, and another that came with a ship from Hamburg to Amsterdam. We

[3] October 28.

made reasonable way all that night, but the next morning, when we were between Dunkirk and Calais, the wind came strongly against us, and so laboring all that day, about evening we had a sore tempest that continued all that night and the next day and drove us up as high as Yarmouth, where, offering to enter into the haven, the tide being spent, we struck upon the bar, where if we had stuck we had been all lost. But it pleased God we got over, and with full sails beat upon the head or piles, so as if the ship had not been new and strong she had been spilt or beaten in pieces.

In this fear and confusion, some adventured to leap upon the piles when she came close, for she struck upon them four times. Some few made shift to scramble up, but four of our company leapt short, whereof three were drowned in our sight and one beaten against the piles all to pieces; we got them all taken up afterwards and buried. In the meantime some boats came from the shore but would not approach us without order given to take in but three or four at once. The seas were very high, and it was dangerous landing, so that till I had seen the success of four boats, one after another, I would not stir, and as it pleased God I had the best passage, most of the rest being washed over head and ears, or overtumbled in the landing.

Many other adventures and particularities there were which were too long to relate, so that I will only tell you that, tarrying that night at Yarmouth, we went the next day to Norwich and so toward London. And the first night our guide lost his way on Newmarket heath, so that we wandered up and down in rain and blustering weather and extreme dark till after eleven o'clock, whereas we might have been at our lodging anon after seven. And so finally, the third of this present, we came safe to this town. . . .

I am now late to my lodging from attending to deliver your letter to the Lord Treasurer, where I have waited now three days and cannot get access, and yet have I all the furtherance that Sir Walter Cope, Master Kirkham, and Master Finet can afford. . . .

Sir W. Cope and Master Finet both told me of the scandal was like to be laid upon you, but my Lord dealt therein very nobly,[4] they tell me, and hath dispersed those clouds and made the weather clear again. I understand for certain that my Lord of Northumberland himself hath done you this wrong.

---

[4] A disgruntled servant of Northumberland, Timothy Elks, in August, 1611, had tried to make his fortune by reasserting Northumberland's foreknowledge of the Gunpowder Plot. Carleton's name was again raised, but the cautious Salisbury was loyal to his officials, once chosen.

One thing I will not omit whiles I think of it: that I would wish when you write hereafter to Sir Wa. Cope to be brief and seek out some quick conceit to spur up his dull spirits, for I see it is a pain to him to read a long letter, and makes so many pauses as if he were tired and labored up a hill.

[125] November 13, 1611: Since my last of the 6th of this present, I received yours of the 18th of October: and the next day after my writing delivered your letter to the Lord Treasurer, having attended four days before I could come to his presence . . . till at last an honest doorkeeper offered me the courtesy to bring me to my Lord's presence, and I think performed it. My audience was short and sweet, with inquiry after your health and my Lady's, and remembrance of acquaintance, and that we were both grown gray, and that he would confer with me at more leisure and so forth. There is a world of suitors continually attending, so that you may see the tide of affairs runs still strongly that way. . . .

During my waiting at my Lord Treasurer's, Signor Fabritio[5] was there among other suitors. There passed but short salutations between us, neither was he willing to talk single.

[127] November 27, 1611: Three or four days since, finding Master Harriot[6] at great leisure in Paul's, I accosted him to see what I could learn of his great Lord. He told me that he had some enlargement and that any of his servants or friends might have access to him, that this last tempest was already blown over, that Elks and his accusations began to vanish; only there was some doubt that his fine of £30,000 would be called upon.

And for the matter wherein you were mentioned, it fell out thus, that the Lord being urged about a letter that should be written for Percy's lodging, firmly denied it; but his man Rowliffe, debating the

---

[5] Carleton and Chamberlain's special name for Sir Henry Wotton, who had preceded Carleton as Ambassador to Venice.

[6] Thomas Harriot, celebrated mathematician and astronomer, pensioner of Northumberland.

matter with him, wished him not to stand too stiffly in it because he remembered that Percy went up and down the house inquiring after you, and told him it was for such a purpose. Whereupon the Lord, at his next examination, though this point were no more in question, of his own motion told them that he could not call to mind any such letter, but if there were it was without any ill intent; and it was likely you had written it.

This was taken hold of, and *pro concesso*,[7] whereas he spoke it doubtfully and by way of caution. But Hippesley utterly denied all this and said his Lord had forgotten and wronged himself, for that there was no letter written, but himself was employed by Percy to Whynyard [8] in his Lord's name by word of mouth.

[128] December 4, 1611: The Dorcas arrived within the river the latter end of the last week, and somewhat ado there hath been, both with the Customers and those of the glasshouse to let all pass, and some little difficulty there was about partition, by reason that the writing and superscriptions were worn off. My Lady Hatton laid claim to all the drinking glasses, but I remembered there was a chest for the Lady Cope, and a looking glass, the greatest save one. She looked out your letter and sent a note of the particulars, and I think all was divided yesterday according to your intent.

I complained to her of the slow payment of your money, which she seemed to marvel at, and said no doubt Sir Walter knew not of it, for he would take order it should be no more so, seeing it turned so much to your prejudice and loss as I made it appear unto her. But I am persuaded that neither he nor she can further the matter nor advance the payment one whit. I have heard that my Lord Treasurer was not pleased with your bill of charges of transportation and stormed a little at it, and I was desirous to learn what I could of her; but I perceive she knows nothing, only she told me she heard the journey stood you in a just hundred pound, whereby you may see what good intelligence she hath, and how capable she is of it. I assured her it was not the fifth part of your charge.

---

[7] As established fact.
[8] Owner of the plotters' house in Westminster; Hippesley, long in Northumberland's service, was a friend of Buckingham's, knighted in 1617.

[129] December 18, 1611: I wrote not since the fourth of December, having ever since kept house and not once stirred abroad, by reason of a lingering disease that hath hung upon me almost this month, proceeding as I take it of a confirmed cold that would not be worn out nor wrestled withal any longer, so that I was driven to physic in an unseasonable time and sore against my will. . . . I made account my body had been well emptied and cleared at sea, but they say that melancholy was so settled in the veins that it would not be removed but by purging and sweating.

But for charge of carriage, I would have sent you a letter of Master Gent's from Oxford, wherein he rails upon this course and dilates at large, and with many reasons, that it cannot proceed of melancholy.

[130] December 31, 1611: Many old folks of my acquaintance drop away this winter, which hitherto hath been hard and pinching enough. . . .

Cottington, that was Secretary to Sir Charles Cornwallis[9] and left by him in Spain, was sent away thither the last week with commission to be consul at Seville and thereabout for the merchants, with allowance of ten shillings in the hundred of all English goods that come thither or go thence, which is like to rise to a good sum and to take away much of the Ambassador's business and benefit; who I hear is very weary there already and spends all his means and more, having a very disorderly company, and Rossingham his steward as unruly as the rest. His Lady being with child went thither unprovided of midwife or nurse, and it is thought she miscarried and not without some danger, but her waiting woman and one of her chambermaids discharged themselves of their burthen with more ease. All this and much more to like purpose was told me under benedicite, and so I pray you let it continue.

[132] January 29, 1612: If you have not heard it, Pory's employment into France was to carry a treatise of the Bishop of Ely's and Casaubon's to the Cardinal Perron in answer of a certain letter of his sent to the King; and withal, good part of Queen Elizabeth's life, col-

---

 [9] Resident Ambassador to Spain, 1605-1609.

lected with the help of Sir Robert Cotton and written by Clarenceux, for a present to Thaunus,[10] to be inserted into his works: which, if it so prove, Camden hath taken a deal of pain to small purpose and is like to lose the honor and fruit of his labors, to see them drowned and swallowed up in such a gulf.

[133] February 12, 1612: The King is expected here on Friday. His book[11] was finished the last week, but not published till this day, and that only in French, the Latin and English copies being yet in the press. An hundred of them were sent away with all speed on Saturday to Sir Rafe Winwood, by whose means I could wish you had one. Otherwise I would have adventured it, though it be with the biggest for a packet. His Majesty doth Sir Rafe all right and favor, as well in setting down his propositions and letters, as in giving allowance to his proceedings. . . .

This is the last day of the term, and yet your brother Williams cannot get your money, which drives him into dumps sometimes and makes him say it is a strange world; but I doubt we are not yet at the worst.

[135] March 11, 1612: I will begin with the best news first: that the Lord Treasurer is so well recovered that he walks daily in his garden, and it is thought will shortly remove to Kensington. He forsook the Court to be more private at home, but he cannot avoid the perpetual visits that still follow him. The King and Prince were with him on Sunday and the Queen every second day the last week. His disease proves nothing so dangerous as was suspected, being now discovered to be but the scorbut, or (as we term it) the scurvy, which is of easy and ordinary cure if it be not too far overpast.

His sickness drowned all other news. Every man's care or curiosity ran that way, insomuch that it seems he was never so well beloved as

---

[10] William Camden, Clarenceux King-of-arms; and the French historian James Augustus de Thou.

[11] *His Majesty's Declaration concerning his Proceedings in the Cause of D. C. Vorstius.* Vorstius had succeeded Arminius as Professor of Theology at Leyden in 1609, and James, through Winwood, had been demanding his removal ever since for holding views repugnant to Calvinist theology.

now when they thought him so near lost. He begins to embrace business again, which found a great want of him, and no doubt will cross some of their courses that were so forward to part the bear's skin. You will not think what a number of competitors stood or were named, nor what manner of men, for the place of Secretary, but most speech ran upon Sir Thomas Lake and Sir Henry Neville, who protests it was not so much as in his thought (as Master told me yesterday when I found him with him); but they that look more narrowly into my Lord's inclination are more afraid of Fabritio, to whom in that regard I lent a charity that may chance stand in some stead. . . .

The Duke of Bouillon is expected here shortly, who is thought to have a double errand, as well from the Palatine of Rhine as from the Queen Regent. His coming hastens Sir Henry Wotton away,[12] whose company of note is a son of the Lord William Howard's, two sons of Sir Charles Cavendish, one Yorke, and Sir Robert Rich tarries for him in France. The presents he carries are ten light ambling geldings, with variety of saddles and rich furniture. They went away yesterday, conducted by Sir Charles Saltonstall, one of the King's escuriers. There is likewise a rich sword with the hilt, pommel, handle, and chap of gold set full of fair diamonds, to the value of sixteen thousand pound; certain selected, sworn jewellers have so valued it. . . .

The last week I sent your sister a note of such things as I had shipped for you in the Elizabeth-and-John, whose Master is Henry Beale. I could not prevent my Lady Cope's kindness (neither had I your letter in time), but they say she would needs send you three fair cases of knives, which I think were presents made to herself and Sir Walter and so put them to the less cost but me to the more trouble, and Sir Walter, because they came when the box was gone and I was driven to break it open again.

There is a little treatise of the northwest [sic] passage, written by Sir D. Digges,[13] but I may say *beatus qui intelligit*,[14] specially the first period—which is but a bad beginning, to stumble at the threshold. Some of his good friends say he had been better have given five

---

[12] Wotton was bound for Turin as Ambassador to the Duke of Savoy, whom he had visited on his way home from Venice in January, 1611. The Duke was hoping grandly for a double marriage alliance with Princess Elizabeth and Prince Henry.

[13] *Fata mihi totum mea sunt agitanda per orbum*, 1611, published anonymously, or *Of the circumference of the earth, or a treatise of the north-east passage*, 1612.

[14] Blessed is he who can make it out.

hundred pound than published such a pamphlet. But he is wonderfully possessed with the opinion and hopes of that passage.

Sir Richard Cooke, your Irish colleague, is here very fresh, and desires to be recommended unto you. Master Finet is likewise very desirous to understand whether a letter to you with an enclosed to Tintoretto[15] came safely to your hands, and what answer he may expect from him.

[136] March 25, 1612: Within this fortnight my Lord's[16] disease hath varied (at leastwise in name or opinion) twice or thrice, for first it was held the scorbut, then the dropsy, and now it hath got another Greek name that I have forgotten, but it imports as much as *malus habitus*,[17] wherein he hath found most good from the physicians and surgeons of the hospital, and specially of Fenton.[18] . . .

Sir Henry Wotton went away this day sevennight with the rich sword, which by good chance he kept better than his own that was stolen out of his chamber the night before he went, with full assurance (as it should seem) that it was the right.

[137] April 29, 1612: Tomorrow is the great marriage at Kensington twixt Sir Harry Rich and Betty Cope, and on Friday Sir Walter goes after the Lord Treasurer and will overtake him before he come at the Bath; of whose well-doing and recovery I wish I could send you better assurance, but as far as I can learn there is more cause of fear than hope . . . and the only vigor of his mind maintains his weak body. . . . Speeches go that he was very ill by the way yesterday and was almost gone once or twice. . . . The physicians themselves have no great opinion of doing good at the Bath, for it is no way proper for the disease, but it was my Lord's own desire, as being the last anchor, and perhaps he thought it the best place to be at peace. He had long speech with the King once or twice before his going, and on Tuesday

---

[15] First indication of Carleton's dealings in art, which became extensive both in Venice and in The Hague.

[16] Salisbury's.

[17] I.e., "illness."

[18] Joseph Fenton, a colleague of Dr. William Harvey at St. Bartholomew's Hospital.

and Saturday last spake each time two hours together (as they say) at the Council table, whereby you may see how strong his spirits are. He travels with a coach, a litter, and a portative chair. He is already much lamented, and every man says what a miss there would be of him, and indeed is much prayed for.

[**139**] May 27, 1612: I am sorry I have no better subject to write of at this time than the loss of such a friend as I know the late Lord Treasurer was to you, though his long, languishing sickness gave cause enough to any that depended on him to prepare and provide for the worst. . . . He found so little good in the Bath that he made all the haste he could out of that suffocating, sulphurous air, as he called it, though others think he hastened the faster homeward to countermine his underminers and, as he termed it, to cast dust in their eyes. As the case stands, it was best that he gave over the world, for they say his friends fell from him apace, and some near about him; and howsoever he had fared with his health, it is verily thought he would never have been himself again in power and credit. I never knew so great a man so soon and so generally censured, for men's tongues walk very liberally and freely, but how truly I cannot judge.

He died on Sunday last, the 24th of this present, at Marleborough in the parsonage house between one and two in the afternoon, as he was coming hitherward, and had his memory perfect to the last gasp, and prepared himself for it; but yet he looked not to have gone so suddenly nor at the instant that he did. . . .

I was yesterday with Sir Walter Cope who came to town with the young Earl. He told me that he was enjoined by the late Lord, together with the Lord Chamberlain,[19] to overlook his papers, which since his coming he had done, and finding certain letters of yours (which he showed me), willed me to tell you that you should take no care of them for that they were in safe keeping, and read me some part of them of latest date. He wished me likewise to persuade you to cast away a letter (as he called it) now and then on the Lord of Northampton,[20] as likewise to insinuate with the Lord of Rochester,[21] and send

---

[19] Thomas Howard, first Earl of Suffolk.
[20] Henry Howard, who hoped to step into Salisbury's shoes.
[21] Robert Carr, the King's favorite, newly made Councillor.

him some pretty advertisements; and for the first time you might do it by his means and so he would make your way—or rather, peradventure, his own. But if I might advise, I would you could rather devise how to grow in with the Prince, and not without need, if all be true I have heard which I take to proceed from your old friend Fabritio, who is thought to be much in his favor.

[140] June 11, 1612: [The King] is much troubled with the multitude of competitors for the Secretaryship . . . but . . . in this distraction makes no haste to nominate any, but says he is prettily skilled in the craft himself, and till he be thoroughly weary will execute it in person.

[141] June 17, 1612: Sir Walter Cope wishes you should write now and then to Master Chancellor,[22] for he may stand you in great stead. I inquired of him both before my going out of town and now since my coming back whether there had been any meaning to recall you and for what intent. He told me that my late Lord Treasurer said not long before he died that some about my Lord of Rochester had gone about such a matter, belike to serve their own turn, and put in some of their own creatures. How likely this is you may judge, but it doth not sound with me, and so I told him; for Sir Thomas Overbury, for aught that ever I knew, doth not wish you ill, and Sir Robert Killigrew, who is one of his next favorites, is your fast friend. And I heard but yesterday that Master Packer, your old friend, is become his secretary. But the surest card of all, Sir Henry Neville, will never see you wronged where he may help. If he had not been strongly oppugned every way, he had been settled before this in the Secretaryship;[23] but it is said too much soliciting hath hindered him, and the flocking of Parliament men about him . . . hath done him nor them no good, for the King says he will not have a Secretary imposed upon him by Parliament.

---

[22] Sir Julius Caesar, Chancellor of the Exchequer.
[23] I.e., the office of Secretary of State, which Salisbury had filled in addition to being Lord Treasurer.

[142] June 25, 1612: The outrageous speeches against the deceased Lord continue still, and there be fresh libels come out every day; and I doubt his actions will be hardly censured in the next Parliament if the King be not the more gracious to repress them.

In his last letter to the King, wherein he recommended Sir Harry Wotton, among other things he vowed that he was worse by £100,000 than when he entered into the Treasurership. . . .

Sir Rafe Winwood arrived here yesternight, being sent for by a letter of the King's own hand, but to what purpose God knows.

[143] July 2, 1612: The memory of the late Lord Treasurer grows daily worse and worse, and more libels come as it were continually, whether it be that practices and jugglings come more and more to light, or that men love to follow the sway of the multitude. But it is certain that they who may best maintain it have not forborn to say that he juggled with religion, with the King, Queen, their children, with no-bility, Parliament, with friends, foes, and generally with all. Some of his chaplains have been heard to oppose themselves what they could in pulpit against these scandalous speeches, but with little fruit. . . .

I came this morning from Sir Rafe Winwood, who sent for me to have gone with him to Greenwich, whither he went to do his duty to the Queen. At the first flight of his, this day sevennight, in the Court at Wansted, he was looked upon like an apparition, for nobody knew of his coming but the King, and it was imagined he should presently be Secretary. But it hangs yet in suspense, and the King says nothing to him of that matter, but employs him in writing letters, which breeds much discourse about him *pro et contra*, and sets envy awork how to prevent him, and to kill him with lies (after the Irish proverb). In the meantime, he makes them all afraid, and for my part, though I am not usually confident in such cases, yet I think verily he will carry it in the end, if his own impatience to lie thus between wind and water do not hurt him. Some say the King hath made a promise to the Queen not to dispose of the place till the return of Sir Harry Wotton, which is the cause of this delay.

[145] July 15, 1612: Sir Walter Cope hath made an apology for the late Lord Treasurer and delivered it to the King when he was last week at Kensington, wherein besides his answer and defense for all or most of that objected against him, he insinuates himself and his own sufficiency, as having much experience and many secrets that may be for the King's service, and so would fain be set on work.

[148] August 11, 1612: Your letters of the 16th of the last met me here, just at my return out of Oxfordshire, where I made no long stay, being sorry to see so much representation of ruin in a place where I had heretofore taken so much delight, for they have in a manner cut down all the trees about Ascott, and so defaced the hedges, walks and gardens that a man who had known it before would think some enemies had passed that way and done their worst to disgrace it. Yet the owners[24] seem to please themselves with saying that by this course they have gained money to their purse, more light, better air, and larger prospect. . . .

I made a step to Oxford, which doth flourish as fast as other things decay. Sir Thomas Bodley's addition to the library is a fair and substantial building, suitable on the outside to the Divinity Schools. Master Wadham's new college would have been a fine, handsome fabric if it had been as well placed and contrived as it might easily have been. But the most pleasing thing I saw was the new quadrangle at Merton College, a graceful work, and that may stand for a sound foundation.

[149] September 11, 1612, from Ware Park: Sir Julius Caesar lay eight or ten days in this country at a house and piece of land he hath lately purchased of Sir Leonard Hyde, whither I went with Sir Henry Fanshawe and his Lady and was very kindly used by him both there and here at Ware Park, where he continued two half days in his way homeward. . . . He hath a special care of you, and of himself concurred in the conceit of drawing you nearer home upon the first occasion. He told me that, though your cousin Sir W. Cope arrogated much to himself in your advancement, yet he was but a secondary cause, and never showed himself till he [Sir Julius] as *primus motor* had set

---

[24] Sir Michael and Lady Dormer.

it on foot, and that diverse ways and diverse times, adding many particulars; not sparing to glance at the little great man[25] that is gone as occasion fell out, whom his Lady likewise makes no conscience to forbear as he comes in her way, for his coarse usage towards her husband.

Among other things he told me what a shift he was put to at his coming out of town, that the Prince having entreated him to provide him a thousand pound in so many Jacobus pieces against a certain day, and he having the promise of a prime man in London, when it came to the jump he failed him, so that his journey had been dashed if his daughter Vere at this pinch had not furnished him upon two hours' warning out of her own store.

[151] November 3, 1612, to Sir Ralph Winwood: Sir H. Wotton is thought to be down the wind and his business begins to quail. The King confronted him lately with a railing book of one Scioppius (as I take it) wherein he cites him as a dissembler and sent for the purpose, for having at his coming out of Italy written in a German book or *albo amicorum, "H. W. Legatus, vir bonus, missus ad mentiendum rei publicae causa."* [26] And though he would have avoided it as a merriment, yet the King told him it was no jesting matter, and that he should answer for himself, for he would have it cleared.

[155] November 26, 1612: The news I wrote you the last week touching Sir Walter Cope[27] is not so strange as true, for on Monday he took his place in the Court of Wards, and made a handsome and short speech at his entry. . . . I was to congratulate with him on Sunday and found him very jocund and cheerful, and attributes this his great

---

[25] Salisbury.

[26] "H. W. Ambassador, sent to lie for the good of his country." Wotton had written this or something very like it in the commonplace book of Christopher Flecamore in Augsburg, on his way to Venice in 1604. Gasper Scioppius was the most scurrilous, and most wounding to James's vanity, of the continental controversialists who replied to his *Apology* for the English oath of allegiance and its *Monitory Preface* against the Pope's claims to temporal power. Scioppius used Wotton's lighthearted autograph to cast aspersions on the honor of the English king.

[27] He had been appointed Master of the Court of Wards.

fortune to the King's own choice, protesting that he had no meaning
to stand for it till the day before he attained it, and professeth that he
will execute it sincerely, or (as he terms it) with clean hands. I cannot
cast up what benefit it may be to him, but the dignity is great, having
precedence of the Master of the Rolls, and of all the Chief Justices, or
any other officers that be not Councillors. . . .

He told me a long story at the beginning of this term, what entertainment he had given the Venetian Ambassador this summer, of hunting in Hyde Park, with a banquet and music at his house in Kensington, and all for your sake, and what large proffers and promises the
Ambassador made to requite this kindness towards you.

[157] December 31, 1612: The Lady Webb,[28] lying here sick of the
smallpox and past all danger to everybody's thinking, being exceedingly well tended and having her physician continually about her, on
Christmas Eve late at night began to change, and died the next morning between three and four o'clock; and according to her desire was
sent to Knebworth on Monday and there buried. She was grown a very
proper woman, but loved this town too well, which in short time would
have drawn her and her husband dry, as well in purse as in reputation.
For though I held her and assure myself that she was honest and
virtuous, yet some courses and company she kept began to breed
speech, so that, all things considered, her friends have the less cause
to lament her loss, specially seeing she made a very good and godly
end, and did so far foresee the misery that long life might have
brought her to, that she went away willingly.

[161] January 28, 1613: The Master of the Wards . . . told me he
was very willing to be rid of those papers you write of, and that he
had diverse times bethought himself how he might safely convey them
to you. I told him the readier and safer way were to burn them, which
course he allowed of, and said I should presently see him make a
sacrifice of them. And so he went to seek them, but returning after a
reasonable time, told me he could not find the key of his cabinet where
he had laid them up. Marry, he willed me tell you that they were in safe

---

[28] Anne, daughter of Sir Rowland Lytton, wife of Sir William Webb.

custody and that he would be as careful of them as of anything that concerned himself. . . .

The King is still at Newmarket, somewhat troubled with an humor in his great toe that must not yet be christened or called the gout. Presently upon his going hence, the Council took their several ways and gave themselves some liberty of recreation for a whole week, but are now as close at it again as ever, and indeed complain that matters find not that ready dispatch that were to be wished, for want of assistance in some secret business; so that no doubt they will importune the King at his return to resolve upon somebody. For though his Majesty at first took delight to show his readiness and ability in those causes, yet that vigor begins to relent, and he must daily more and more intend his own health and quiet.

[163] February 4, 1613, to Alice Carleton in Venice: Sir Rafe Winwood . . . hath no great fortune from Sir Thomas Bodley, where there was more reason to expect it, for . . . he hath left him little or nothing but his old armory that he could not tell well what else to do withal, and is in no way worth twenty mark. He died on Thursday last between four and five in the afternoon, having lain speechless and without knowing anybody almost thirty hours. His executors are Sir John Bennet and Master Hackwell, a young lawyer; Sir Rafe Winwood and Sir Henry Savile his overseers; and supervisors over them the Archbishop of Canterbury and the Lord Coke, to each of these last bequeathing a cup of gold of the value of fifty pound, whereas to his brothers he hath left very little, and to his brother's sons, who are his heirs and must hold up his house and name, scant anything. To Master Gent and Tom Allen, like a couple of almsmen, he hath left his best and second gown and his best and second cloak. But to cast a color or shadow of somewhat upon Master Gent, he makes a clause that he forgives him all he ought him, which Master Gent protests to be never a penny, and hath much ado to withhold from blazing how much and many ways he was beholding to him in former times, and indeed indebted; but . . . [he] deserved a better recompense and reward.

But his servants murmur and grumble most, with whom he hath dealt very mechanically, some of them having served him and her very painfully above two and twenty years, others sixteen, others fourteen, and the best not reaping after so long expectation above twenty pounds, the rest ten, and those not past two or three neither. . . .

But let good nature go, if he had had regard of conscience toward his wife's children, by whom he had all his wealth; but in truth he hath dealt hardly with one of them who hath many children and is in need and distress, and by his means, the story whereof is too long for a letter. And all this for a vainglory and show of good deeds, for he hath given about seven thousand pound to his library at Oxford, and two hundred pound to Merton College, besides mourning to all the students of that house from the highest to the lowest. This and such-like makes me know and esteem the world as it is, nothing but vanity.

[170] March 11, 1613: On Saturday last I was with Sir Henry Savile and found his lady[29] had been very sick and not without danger, but, in the opinion of the physicians and everybody else save herself, she was on the mending hand; and truly by her voice and hearty manner of speaking I could not judge otherwise, but yet she told me still she should never see Eton more.

The day before, the Lord Lisle, not knowing of her sickness, invited himself thither to dinner, and bringing his son with him made a tender of him to Sir Harry for his daughter. But he told him he was so far engaged already with Sir William Sidley, and all things so thoroughly concluded, that he could not go back; by which match the Lord Lisle is doubly disappointed, for he had destinated that young gentleman to his daughter Philippa. Indeed, Sir Henry told me that (if he had been free) this offer might have shaken his obstinate resolution not to match with nobility, for Sir Robert Sidney is a very proper gentleman and exceedingly well given every way, and his father's means augmented within this twelvemonth about £2000 a year; but sure young Sidley is like to prove in all likelihood a very good match, being an only child and of good education, and now they are in hand to send him over to travel with Master Brent of Merton College, till some few years may make them both more ripe for marriage.

Sir Henry Savile would needs have one see two fine standing cups

---

[29] Carleton's mother-in-law.

with a basin and ewer, all gilt, to the value of better than £50 that the Palsgrave sent him in requital of his Chrysostom he presented him withal, besides five pound to his man that brought it.

[173] May 6, 1613, to Sir Ralph Winwood at The Hague: It hath pleased God to restore me from the greatest weakness that ever I was in . . . and for mine own part (I speak it unfeignedly), if it had so pleased God, I was even as ready and willing to go as to tarry, which I take as an earnest of His grace and favor, and beseech Him that when my appointed time comes I may be no worse minded. . . . I have not, nor was not able to, set pen to paper many a day, but only about a fortnight since for a farewell to Master Gent, who, good man, is gone to God I hope. He died on Friday the last of April at Oxford, and was buried the next day very privately and without noise, not so much as the ringing of a bell. I cannot yet learn that he hath made any will, which makes me suspect (as I have done long) that he died in debt. The Vice-Chancellor, to show double diligence, presently sealed up his chamber and his study, where when they come to visit and search I think they shall find nothing but dust and cobwebs. . . . I have lost a very kind friend of him, and so he continued till the last gasp, for weekly I had letters from him as long as he could write, and afterwards from others by his direction, with some medicine or other advice proper for my disease . . . which continued with me night and day for seven weeks together and would not be stayed by any outward nor inward medicines . . . so that I resolved to leave all and commit myself only to God and good government.

[177] June 23, 1613: You had heard of Master Gent's decease, which I make no doubt was hastened by Sir Thomas Bodley's unkindness. . . . But the truth is he was so drunk with the applause and vanity of his library that he made no conscience to rob Peter (as they say) to pay Paul, for the which he hath his reward in verses and orations which the University heaps upon him for the present, though I make no question but they will quickly vanish and in short time come to stop mustard pots.

[180] August 1, 1613: Your letter of the 9th of the last found me out here at Ware Park, where I am, as it were, planted for this vacation, and where we are busied about new works and bringing of waters into the gardens, which have succeeded so well that we have a fine fountain with a pond in the lower garden where the fort was (if you remember the place), and a running stream from the river in the upper garden between the knots and the ranks of trees in the broad walk or alley, wherein we hope to have plenty of trouts fed by hand. These works with industry and cost are brought almost to perfection, and when they are well and come to the highest I would there might be an end, for else there is no end of new inventions; for hither came yesterday Signor Fabritio and stays till tomorrow . . . and as he is ignorant in nothing, so he takes upon him to propound many new devices, and would fain be a director where there is no need of his help. . . .

At the Assizes at Hertford about a fortnight since, Sir Rowland Lytton with his son William, his son Smith, and your nephew John Carleton lay here. Your nephew promised me . . . that you should have large relations from him. I cannot write you much of his courses because I have not much of his company, but I see him very fine and neat, or rather, curious, specially in cutwork bands, wherein our youths are become so vain that an ordinary band with double cuffs costs six or seven pound, and some much more. And upon speech of this and the like, his father told me he had a 100 pounds' worth of such ware. I doubt he is too idle to enjoy the place he holds in Court,[30] which requires daily attendance and diligence if a man mean to thrive by it. . . . I am of opinion that his father doth not perform his part, and I have heard it noted more than once that he seems to show more respect and observance to his son than his son to him. Indeed I can say it by more than him, that this is the age of *il mondo riverso*,[31] wherein parents observe their children more than children the parents. . . .

Sir Rowland Lytton and his son both told me how much good they heard diverse ways of your kind usage and bountiful entertainment of all English gentlemen that come in your way. . . . But you had not need meet with many such moths as Master Pory who must have both meat and money, for drink he will find out for himself if it be above ground or no deeper than the cellar; and this I had from his best

---

[30] He was Equerry to King James.
[31] The world upside down.

friends, as he terms them. And now that we are upon this point of kindness and courtesy, I will not conceal that your sister there with you, in every letter almost (specially of late) makes mention how much she is beholden and bound to you for extraordinary favors and kind usage.

[181] September 9, 1613: Our wants grow worse and worse, and all the engineers and projectors are put to their shifts how to supply the present need without sale of land. . . . The complaints are general for want of payment, and Sir Rafe is in arrearage for nine months, and Sir Tho. Edmondes for as much or more. I hope you be in better case. . . .

The Duke of Savoy's Ambassador, the Cavalier Gabaleone, liked his entertainment so well the last year at Ware Park that he hath brought and sent thither a present from his wife of salaccioni, cervellate, mortadelle, certain little cheeses (all these of her own handiwork, and yet not worth the carrying so far), besides a pair of gloves and a paper fan well perfumed for the Lady Fanshawe, and plenty of silk and copper ribbons of several colors for all the children.

[182] October 14, 1613: The choice of a new Lord Chief Justice hath bred great variety and much canvassing, but in conclusion it was once resolved and so stands still, for aught I hear, that the Lord Coke should be Chief Justice, Master Attorney Chief Justice of the Common Pleas, and all to make way for Sir Francis Bacon to be Attorney, whom the King hath promised to advance. These removes were looked for the first day of the term, but all things stand yet *in statu quo prius;* for the Lord Coke doth so stickle and fence, by all the means and friends he can make, not to remove, as being loath, he says, to be brought out of a court of law which is his element, and out of his profit, in regard whereof he values not the dignity, that he hath written very earnestly to his Majesty about it. And the King is so gracious that he will not force him against his will, but saith if he will accept it, he shall do it with as much honor as ever any went to that place, which is a kind of promise of a barony or a councillorship at the least.

[183] October 27, 1613: I imparted to Sir Rafe Winwood as much of your letter of the last of September as concerned him, specially touching the wine and oil that you mean to him, which he thought had been presently come, and gave you many thanks, saying he would write them himself when he should be assured of his going or stay: which will be now shortly, at the King's coming to town, for he means to move him for his dispatch, being willing to remove all jealousy that he lingers here after somewhat, and to cut off access of some persons nothing gracious, whom he cannot otherwise avoid. These reasons, together with the charge he is at, make him hasten away[32] sooner than he would, being grown so *intentus ad rem*[33] that he makes profession that before he retire he will spend three or four years more in those parts, and so finish his fortune where it began. Sure, as matters now stand, I cannot disallow this course, and I would his good friend Sir H. N. [Henry Neville] had taken no worse way, and not hung so long by a twine-thread till all is fallen to the ground; where, though he be no lower than he was before, yet it is with some loss, and imputation that he could not discern in time, but suffer himself to be sucked and drawn dry and then left, as it were, empty. . . .

On Monday, the Lord Coke (though ne'er so loath) was called up into the King's Bench and there sworn Chief Justice. He parted dolefully from the Common Place, not only weeping himself but followed with the tears of all that Bench and most of the officers of that Court. The next day Sir H. Hobart was made Chief Justice of the Common Pleas, Sir Fra. Bacon Attorney, and Yelverton Solicitor. There is a strong apprehension that little good is to be expected by this change, and that Bacon may prove a dangerous instrument.

[184] November 11, 1613: Upon Thursday last . . . the Lord Coke (with many good and gracious words) was sworn a Privy Councillor, which honor no man envies him, if he keep on his right course and turn not to be attorney again.

[187] December 23, 1613: We are here in state as when I wrote you last without any alteration, though here be much buzzing and whisper-

[32] Back to The Hague, without the coveted Secretaryship.
[33] Determined.

ing of some change every day. . . . Our good friend of St. Bartholomews[34] . . . is told by him whom he may believe that, but for Sir Thomas Overbury, he had been in the place long since, when he was sent for summer was twelvemonth. So that in reason there should be no let now, but that he speaks not to bye-saints, or that he is reputed somewhat harsh and too plain a speaker for the tender ears of this age. Indeed he is somewhat too quick and nimble to keep tune with the slowness and *fainéantise*[35] of this time.

The Treasurership is as much disputed and finds the like dispatch. . . .

Sir Fra. Bacon prepares a masque to honor this marriage[36] which will stand him in above £2000, and though he have been offered some help by the house, and specially by Master Solicitor Sir Hen. Yelverton, who would have sent him £500, yet he would not accept it, but offers them the whole charge with the honor. Marry, his obligations are such as well to his Majesty as to the great Lord, and to the whole house of Howards, as he can admit no partners. . . . He feasts the whole University of Cambridge this Christmas, and hath sent warrants to his friends and acquaintance far and near to furnish him with venison to bestow on the Colleges. He carries a great port, as well in his train as in his apparel and other ways, and lives at a great charge, and yet he pretends he will take no fees nor intermeddle in mercenary causes, but wholly apply himself to the King's affairs.

[**188**] December 30, 1613, to Alice Carleton: The Archbishop of Canterbury was at the marriage, but not the Bishop of London. Sir Rafe Winwood was there likewise, and had a very fair pair of gloves of three pound price; which he well deserved, for he made a suit of apparel against this wedding of only doublet, hose, and cloak, all black and without any kind of gold, silver, or embroidery, that cost him above fourscore pound—which I write that you may see how unreasonably things are risen here, and what a chargeable world we live in. He presented a very fair basin and ewer of 225 ounces that was given him by the States, and of so excellent workmanship that the goldsmiths have offered 20d. an ounce for it.

---

[34] Sir Ralph Winwood.
[35] Inertia.
[36] The marriage of Robert Carr, Earl of Somerset, and Frances Howard.

[189] January 5, 1614: I wrote somewhat the last week to your sister of this great marriage, which continues still in gallantry and triumphs. . . . The bride had a goodly rich coach which could not be furnished with four horses to their mind, so that Sir Rafe Winwood was moved on Sunday night to lend his (those that you may remember he had here four or five years ago and are now as fair or fairer than ever they were). He made answer that it was not for such a Lady to use anything borrowed, and therefore the next morning presented them to the great Lord, who made some difficulty at first to receive them of gift, but only as lent for this solemnity of going through the City,[37] but in the end took them in very good part. . . .

I fear our good friend will be led along as others have been, but what can he do? *Lupum auribus tenet.*[38] He knows not how to hold, nor how to let go, neither does he *constare sibi*[39] at all times, but suffers himself to be carried away from his own positions and judgment by some whose wisdom (though much esteemed) I never admired. . . . I think verily their company and conversation hath done him more harm and hindered him more than all the enemies he hath. He hath now changed his mind of demanding his dispatch, for he is told that he stands upright, and this might mar all.

The great man[40] had some conference with him lately touching your succeeding him, which he seconded by all the means he could; so that if matters fall out well, we hope to have you nearer, but yet refuse not any means or help you may have to further it.

[196] March 3, 1614: Touching our good friend,[41] I know he must follow the stream, and, now that he is embarked, be governed by the pilot[42] to whom he hath committed himself. . . But now we are almost out of the maze we have trodden all this while and are come to dance in another circle, I mean the Parliament, before the beginning whereof if nothing be done, *spes et fortuna valete.*[43] . . .

---

[37] The King had commanded the Lord Mayor to entertain the couple. (For other details of this marriage see Section VI.)

[38] He holds the wolf by the ears.

[39] Stand firm.

[40] Robert Carr, Earl of Somerset.

[41] Winwood.

[42] Somerset.

[43] Hope and fortune, farewell.

Yesterday I went a journey with Sir Ralph Winwood and his Lady to see a house they have taken at Thistleworth, for which they pay £56 a year, having nothing but a little reasonable convenient house, with a handsome garden and orchard. For my part I should have thought half the money a more indifferent rent, but they are willing to have a retiring place, and give the more for Doctor Burgess' neighborhood.

[198] March 31, 1614: Upon Tuesday the 29th of this month Sir Rafe Winwood, after so many traverses, was sworn principal Secretary; for by that title he was sworn, and Sir Thomas Lake of the Privy Council without any place or other title. . . . I am sorry at my heart for Sir Thomas Edmondes, that he would be present and see it done and troubled himself so much, solicited so openly, and labored so long in vain; but sure his coming over did him no good. . . . But the woman's violence (I doubt) prevailed with him more than his own judgment; and indeed in all this business women have had a great part, specially the Lady Lake.

[199] April 7, 1614: Though it be but yet young days both with the Parliament and our good friend's late advancement, yet having nothing else of moment, I will write that little that passeth in both. . . .

On Tuesday the fifth of this present, the King, Prince and Lords rode in their robes to the Parliament. There were many rich foot-clothes, specially that of the King and Prince, but the day proving very foul, it marred much of the show. . . .

The King made a long and an excellent speech, consisting of three principal parts wherein all his care lay: to continue to his subjects *bona animi, bona corporis,* and *bona fortunae,*[44] by maintaining religion, preserving of peace, and seeking their prosperity by increasing of trades and traffic. He made many fair promises, and that he would not press them beyond their own good will. In conclusion he wished they might not be strangers, but that they would have recourse to him in all their business, at whose hands they should always find easy

---

[44] Good for their souls, good for their bodies, good for their prosperity.

audience and gracious usage, and so dismissed them to choose their Speaker. . . .

Randall Crew was chosen Speaker without any contradiction, being nominated and recommended by Master Secretary, who made a fit speech for that purpose, which I have heard generally well allowed, and his assurance commended; only the manner of delivery was somewhat strange, being in a kind of an academical tune. But he is to be excused, having such a disadvantage that the first that ever he heard speak in that place was himself.

[200] April 14, 1614: Our Parliament goes on after the wonted manner, with many controversies and altercations. The Speaker was presented on Thursday and made a very orderly and convenient speech. The next two days were spent about the admitting or rejecting of Sir Fra. Bacon, who . . . was by reason of his place of Attorney thought not eligible. But in the end, seeing the matter like to grow to long and eager dispute, it was agreed to admit him *pro hac vice,*[45] without prejudice to their privileges. . . .

It is resolved the whole House shall receive the Communion together on Sunday next. The place was once agreed to be Westminster Church, but for fear of copes and wafer cakes and such other important reasons, it is now altered to St. Margaret's. . . .

The King made a speech to the whole assembly . . . wherein he laid out his wants and descended as it were to entreaty to be relieved, and that they would show their good affections toward him in such sort that this Parliament might be called the Parliament of Love, in which kind to begin and trace them the way, he offered them certain graces and favors—not in the way of exchange or merchandising (which course he will not allow nor cannot abide to hear of) but of mere good will and *motu proprio.*[46] . . .

Upon Tuesday Master Secretary brake the ice and entered into the matter of subsidies . . . and this speech, though not so pleasing for the matter, yet better allowed of for the manner than his former; but the conclusion was, after some speeches to and fro, to defer this cause to be more amply debated the Monday sevennight after Easter.

He is now going to Court, having Sir John Herbert's lodgings

---

[45] For this occasion only.
[46] By one's own motion or impulse.

appointed him, but for his diet I know not yet what course will be taken, whether to have the King's allowance or to have it in money and make his own provision. He hath his privy seal for £1400 for intelligence, as much as was ever granted to any.

[**201**] May 12, 1614: Master Secretary . . . doth promise that from henceforth every fortnight you shall be advertised how the world goes here, as likewise that he will have care of procuring your entertainment from time to time, and bade me wish Master Williams to repair to him when there is cause. The offer is fair, howsoever it can be performed, for I assure you the fountain of our means is drawn so dry that whosoever hath occasion to drink there is like to tarry till he be athirst.

Whensoever the King is abroad, he makes a step home, so that we have enjoyed him these two nights together. . . . The first night there was much company, but he bespake me for the next, and by good hap we were hand to hand, and then he received your letters of the 11th of April. . . . He says he hath saved me the labor of writing you Sir Thomas Parry's misfortune,[47] whereof no man could inform you better than himself, as being made the mouth to lay more load of disgrace upon him by pronouncing suspension of his place. . . . But he is grown so dull and stupid that unless this awake him, he is thought scant sensible of anything befalls or concerns him.

But he goes not away with this affront alone, for Sir Walter Cope, Sir Henry Wallop, and my nephew St. John have their part, being discharged the House and a new writ gone down for another election. . . .

The House is full of business and many irons are in the fire, but yet we see no great matter dispatched, for hitherto they have been much troubled with disputes about elections and privileges, about impositions (which, though it be a string should be tenderly touched, yet they make it speak loud), but specially about undertakers, wherein Sir Walter Chute did a very charitable deed by undertaking and offer-

---

[47] Parry, under whom Carleton had served unhappily in Paris in 1602, was dismissed from the Council and the Chancellorship of the Duchy of Lancaster for interfering in the Stockbridge election in behalf of Cope and Wallop. This was the only action the Commons found to take in spite of larger fears that the Crown had tampered with the elections.

ing to undergo the envy of all, and so accusing himself offered this enclosed writing to their consideration, whenas, poor man, nobody thought him worth the suspecting.

Master Secretary has gotten good reputation by speaking against recusants and idle churchmen, but what he hath gotten one way is lost another, for the bishops have him in conceit of a puritan.

Some beagles have Sir Lionel Cranfield in chase, and Spiller, and many hares more are on foot; but it falls out many times that too much game mars the sport.

In the meantime, the King hath a great deal of patience, and made his third speech to them . . . requiring they should fall in hand with the main business of his wants. And indeed I could wish they would not stand too stiff but take some moderate course to supply him by ordinary means, lest he be driven to ways of worse consequence, wherein he shall not want color both from law and pulpit.

[202] May 19, 1614: Master Secretary . . . hath now his head and his hands full of business, what with the Parliament where he is all the morning, and at committees in the afternoon, and with other affairs pertaining to his place wherein he is yet scant warm and not thoroughly settled. But the worst of all is that he hath brought the whole Clergy on his back from the highest to the lowest by the speech I mentioned in my last.

[203] May 26, 1614: I wrote you the last week how busy our Parliament was about impositions, wherein there hath been since much said *pro et contra*. Among the rest, Sir Henry Wotton made a very mannerly and demure speech for the maintenance of them, alleging Spain, France and Italy for example, in which argument he was seconded by Master Secretary and Sir Tho. Lake, with confirmation of his particular instance how many millions the impost of salt amounted to.

But it was replied that we were to be governed by our own laws, not by foreign examples, and that those exactions were rather *de facto* than *de jure,* as might easily be gathered by their histories; and that since they came to their height they have seldom or never had any

parliaments or assemblies; and for Italy there was no other consideration to be had of them than as of petty tyrannies rather than just
principalities.

Sir Edwin Sandy's went further and was more bitter, concluding
his speech with these words, pronounced at length: *"Ad Generum
Cereris sine caeda et sanguine pauci Descendunt Reges et sicca morte
Tyranni."*[48] But the boldest Bayard of all was Wentworth, who said
that the just reward of the Spaniards' impositions was the loss of
the Low Countries, and for France that their late most exacting kings
died like calves upon the butcher's knife.

[**205**] June 9, 1614: While the Parliament . . . grew every day more
fiery and violent in their speeches, the King sent them a letter the
third of this month whereby he signified unto them that for diverse
reasons and respects he meant to disolve the Parliament as this day
unless in the meantime they fell roundly in hand to consider and
provide how to relieve his wants. . . .

This peremptory message wrought diversly with them, and made
some of them put water in their wine, seeing the time of their reign
so near an end. But the greater sort grew more averse, and would not
descend to so sudden resolution. Many bold and petulant speeches
passed that day, for they sat long; but above all Christopher Neville,
younger son to the Lord Abergavenny, was most noted for a curious,
premeditate declamation, made for some other time (but should
have been lost if not spoken now) wherein among many other sen-
tences he said that *Nunc Principes ita grassantur ut potius sit mori
quam vivere;*[49] and spared not great personages about the Court, calling them *arrisores et arrosores,* which he Englished, "spaniels to the
King and wolves to the people." . . .

The truth is, it should seem by their carriage . . . that there was
never known a more disorderly House, and that it was many times
more like a cockpit than a grave council. . . .

Upon Tuesday . . . the commission directed to the two Archbishops, the Lord Chancellor, and all the Privy Council of [the

---

[48] Few kings descend to Pluto without slaughter and bloodshed; few tyrants
die a bloodless death.

[49] The Nobles now take such measures that they are more useful dead than
alive.

House of Lords] was read, whereby they had authority to dissolve the Parliament, and so they did. Whereby this meeting or assembly is to be held a blank parliament, or rather a parley only, not having so much as the name of a session but, as the words went, *parlamentum inchoatum*.[50]

Presently upon the dissolution, pursuivants were ready to warn diverse to be the next day at the Council table, from whence Christopher Neville, Sir Walter Chute, Hoskins and Wentworth were yesterday sent to the Tower. . . . Sir Samuel and Edwin Sandys, Sir Dudley Digges . . . and some others I remember not that had parts appointed them by the House in the matter of impositions, were enjoined to bring in their notes and papers to be burnt.

Sic transit Gloria mundi. The Lord Privy Seal,[51] that hath languished a long time and lain at Greenwich above this month, came home yesterday all along town with more than forty horse, which was much noted for the manner and the time.

[206] June 30, 1614: Sir Edwin Sandys so demeaned himself that he was dismissed without taint or touch, though upon examination it fell out there was a plot discovered to overthrow all orderly proceedings in this Parliament and to make it utterly void, by insisting upon dangerous points, as taking away impositions, restoring of silenced ministers, and removing the Scots, with other matters likely to make the King lose all patience. And for this purpose Hoskins was embouched, abetted, and indeed plainly hired with money to do that he did. . . .

You must understand there was much ado and great dispute before a Parliament could be procured, and the contrary part, to make good their opinion, sought by all means to embroil and bring it to nothing.

Christopher Neville upon submission found some favor and is removed to the Fleet. And Wentworth, because his offense is found to be rather of simplicity than malice, had leave this Whitsuntide to go home to his wife for five or six days, but is now returned to the Tower, where he hath the liberty of the place, and stays more to satisfy the French Ambassador than anything else. . . .

---

[50] Addled Parliament.

[51] Henry Howard, Earl of Northampton, enemy of Parliaments; he died a week later.

It is more than time we had a Treasurer, if that would any way mend the matter, for we are at a very low ebb for money. At the breaking up of the Parliament, the bishops agreed among themselves to give their best piece of plate or the value of it in present money as a speedy benevolence to supply the King's want. The Archbishop of Canterbury began with a basin and ewer, and redeemed it with £140, the Bishop of Winchester as much, Ely 120, *et sic de caeteris*.[52] The noblemen followed the example. . . . Master Secretary gave £100 and all officers toward the Law or Receipt according to their mind; Sir Henry Fanshawe £50, Sir Christopher Hatton as much, the Lord Coke £200; but the rest of the Judges came but slowly after, for I know where some presented but £20, which was refused. . . .

Letters shall be sent into all shires to see how they will follow the example. . . .

The King removed yesterday to Richmond, whither Sir Thomas Edmondes is gone to take his leave of him this morning. He can get but £400 with him of £1300 or £1400 that is owing him for entertainment, but he is promised he shall have the rest at a month.

---

[52] And likewise for the rest.

VI. The Howards and Robert Carr, Earl of Somerset

ONE of James's earliest schemes for achieving peace at Court was to unite opposing factions in happy marriages. Accordingly, he blessed the wedding of Catherine Howard to William Cecil, the stupid, agreeable son of Robert Cecil, Earl of Salisbury. On Robert Devereux, orphaned son of the second Earl of Essex, he bestowed Catherine's sister Frances. Unfortunately for the bridegroom, Lady Frances Howard embodied many of the characteristics that gave the second decade of James's reign a special reputation for scandal.

Young Essex, fifteen years old at the time of his marriage, spent the next three years travelling and returned in 1609 to find his bride's affections elsewhere engaged and her character vile beyond belief. During three more years of resolutely unconsummated marriage, her artistry in villainy matured. Then she took her equally vile great-uncle Henry into her confidence, persuaded her father, and sued for divorce on the grounds of her husband's impotence.

Lord Henry Howard was only too pleased to think that the King's favorite, Robert Carr, Viscount Rochester, upon whom Frances had fastened her affections, would thereby be drawn into the orbit of the Howard family and the pro-Catholic party. Carr had hitherto inclined alarmingly to the Puritan circle of Lord Chancellor Ellesmere and Archbishop Abbot, drawn by the sympathies of his good friend Sir Thomas Overbury. Overbury had all the distinction of mind that the amiable Carr would have liked to possess. More important, he foresaw clearly that Lady Frances would be the ruin of Carr, and said so.

While Lady Frances worked to win the sympathy of King James, she and great-uncle Henry organized the removal of Overbury with breathtaking decisiveness. Chamberlain did not suspect the full sordidness of the tale; he was sufficiently amazed and indignant at events that became public knowledge. King James's attitude to the divorce seems to have saddened but not surprised him. Overbury's death in the Tower seems to have disturbed him no more than it did anyone else at the time.

Carr, now Earl of Somerset, had two years of glory with his bride. Then an apothecary's boy, dying in exile in Brussels, poured out to a member of the English Agent's staff the story of his part, and Lady Frances', in poisoning Overbury. William Trumbull brought this delicate news in person to Secretary Winwood, who confirmed it in a poignant interview with Lieutenant of the Tower Helwys, Chamberlain's mild and gentle acquaintance.

Carleton left Venice in September, 1615, just as Chief Justice Coke began to examine the case, and remained on leave for the next five months; thus there are no letters to him from Chamberlain covering the trials of the unfortunate Helwys and Lady Frances' unsavory accomplices in poison. By the time Lady Frances herself appeared, a graceful confession was her only course. Somerset's stubborn insistence on his innocence is just barely credible.

Convicted, but reprieved, the Somersets were ordered to live in the Tower. Lady Frances obviously found it confining, but managed to amuse herself by scheming against fellow prisoner Northumberland and by being unfaithful to her infuriated husband.

[172] April 29, 1613: I doubt not but you have heard of Sir Thomas Overbury's committing to the Tower the last week. The King hath long had a desire to remove him from about the Lord of Rochester, as thinking it a dishonor to him that the world should have an opinion that Rochester ruled him and Overbury ruled Rochester; whereas he would make it appear that neither Overbury nor Rochester had such a stroke with him, but that he would do what he thought fit and what he intended without acquainting either of them with his purposes. And so caused the Lord Chancellor[1] and the Earl of Pembroke to deal with Overbury and to tell him the King's good meaning towards him, whereby he had an intent to make use of his good parts and to train him for his further service; and therefore they offered him his choice to be employed either by the Archduke, or into France, or into Muscovy (upon which place we have now new projects).

He excused himself as incapable of such places for diverse wants, and specially of language. They answered that he was young enough and with little labor might attain that in short time, or otherwise he

---

[1] Thomas Egerton, Lord Ellesmere.

might be assisted and supplied by sufficient secretaries and other fit persons about him. Then he alleged indisposition of body and want of health, as being much subject to the spleen; whereto they replied that change of air might be a special remedy for such infirmities. But he stood stiffly upon it that he was not willing to forsake his country, and at last gave them a peremptory answer that he could not yield to go, and that he hoped that the King, neither in law nor justice, could compel him to leave his country; with which answer the King was so incensed that he willed the Council to consider what it deserved, who upon this contempt caused him to be sent to the Tower.

Some take this as a diminution of my Lord of Rochester's credit and favor. But the King told the Council the next day that he would not have it so construed, for that he had and still did take more delight in his company and conversation than in any man's living. . . .

About Easter the Lord of Rochester showed a noble part and example, for seeing the world at a dead lift and at their wits' end for money, he sent for some of the Officers of the Receipt, and giving them a key of a chest bid them take what they found there for the King's use, which was £22,000 in gold. . . .

There was a divorce to be sued this term twixt the Earl of Essex and his Lady, and he was content (whether true or feigned) to confess insufficiency in himself. But there happened an accident of late that hath altered the case. His Lady sought out and had many conferences with a wise woman who, according to the course of such creatures, drew much money from her and at last cozened her of a jewel of great value; for which being prosecuted and clapped in prison, she accuses the Lady of diverse strange questions and propositions, and in conclusion that she dealt with her to make away her Lord (as aiming at another mark), upon which scandal and slander the Lord Chamberlain[2] and other her friends think it not fit to proceed in the divorce.

[174] May 13, 1613: On Thursday at night Sir Will. Waad was discharged of his Lieutenancy of the Tower, the particular reasons whereof I cannot tell you, more than that there were continual complaints of him, and some speak of certain jewels of great value and certain gold embezzled from the Lady Arabella, whereof either he or his Lady or his daughter cannot so clearly acquit themselves but that

---

[2] Lady Frances's father, Thomas Howard, Earl of Suffolk.

there is suspicion. One Sir Gervase Helwys of Lincolnshire, somewhat an unknown man, is put into the place by the favor of the Lord Chamberlain or his Lady. The gentleman is of too mild and gentle a disposition for such an office. He is my old friend and acquaintance in France, and lately renewed here in town, where he hath not lived past a year, nor followed the Court many a day.

[175] June 10, 1613: The divorcement twixt the Earl of Essex and his Lady is on foot, and I think will come shortly to a conclusion. It hath been heard at Lambeth before certain commissioners twice or thrice, but *à huis clos*.[3] All the difficulty is that, though he be willing to confess his insufficiency towards her, yet he will be left at liberty to marry any other, and stands upon it that he is *maleficiatus* only *ad illam*.[4] Now some lawyers are of opinion that if she will swear that he is impotent towards her there is sufficient cause of divorce, which is thought she will make no bones of, being as she presumes provided of a second—which I should never have suspected, but that great folks will have their ends without respect of friends or followers.

[177] June 23, 1613: The divorce now in question twixt the Earl of Essex and his Lady is thought shall be decided one way or other the first day of July. The opinions are diverse of the success, and the case is of so dangerous consequence that no doubt the commissioners will proceed with great wariness and maturity. For if such a gap be once let open, it will not be so easily stopped but that infinite inconveniences will follow.

In the meantime, the Lady hath been visited and searched by some ancient ladies and midwives expert in those matters, who both by inspection and otherwise find her upon their oath a pure virgin; which some doctors think a strange asseveration, and make it more difficult than to be discerned.

The world speaks liberally that my Lord of Rochester and she be in love one with another, which breeds a double question whether that consideration be like to hinder or set it forward.

---

[3] Behind locked doors.
[4] Impotent only toward her.

[180] August 1, 1613: Before the King's parting from Windsor, he sent for the commissioners employed in the divorce of the Earl of Essex and his Lady, and being desirous to see it at an end and to know their opinions, he found that the Bishops of Ely, Coventry and Lichfield, the two Chancellors of the Duchy and Exchequer, with Sir Daniel Donne, were directly for it and to pronounce it a nullity, but the Archbishop of Canterbury, the Bishop of London, Sir John Bennet, and Doctor Edwardes, Chancellor of London, were as directly against it; whereupon the King hath added two bishops more, Winchester and Rochester, and two deans, Westminster and Paul's, who together with the rest must labor in it twixt this and Michaelmas and then give their resolution—which, *computatis computandis*[5] and considering the King's inclination, is like to be for the dissolution.

At my last being with the Bishop of Ely not long before my coming out of town, I found which way he bent, for he made no dainty to tell me his opinion, which I could wish were otherwise if there be no more reason in it than I see or conceive.

[181] September 9, 1613: The main blow for the divorce will be given the 18th of this month when the commissioners are to give up their opinions. It is very likely to go forward, which in some sort were pity as well for the example and consequence as for that I have heard from some that may know, that all this business rises from willfulness and vain idle vows on both sides, when, upon her forwardness and untowardness at their first meetings or coming together, he grew to that impatience that he prayed God to damn him if ever he offered her any such kindness till she called for it, and she in the like heat wished to be damned if ever she did.

[182] October 14, 1613: Sir Thomas Overbury died and is buried in the Tower. The manner of his death is not known, for that there was nobody with him, not so much as his keeper; but the foulness of his corpse gave suspicion and leaves aspersion that he should die of the

---

[5] All things considered.

pox or somewhat worse. He was a very unfortunate man, for nobody almost pities him, and his very friends speak but indifferently of him. . . .

The marriage twixt the Earl of Essex and the Lady Frances Howard is dissolved and pronounced a nullity by the Bishop of Winchester, who with the Bishop of Rochester were only supernumerary to the first commissioners, and so cast the balance by weight of number, being seven to five. The morning that the matter was to be decided, the King sent express commandment that in opining they should not argue nor use any reasons, but only give their assent or dissent. And in the sentence there is no cause expressed but in these terms: *propter latens et incurabile impedimentum.*[6]

[184] November 11, 1613: Upon Thursday last, the Viscount Rochester was created Baron of Branspeth in Westmorland, and Earl of Somerset. . . . But it is thought he shall not stay here but ascend one step higher, and shortly be made Marquis of Orkney, that his mistress may be a better woman (if it may be) than she was before.

[188] December 30, 1613, to Alice Carleton in Venice: I thought I should have had a world of news to advertise this week, but it falls out in this as it doth commonly in other things, that the speech and expectation goes far beyond the matter. The marriage was upon Sunday, without any such bravery as was looked for. . . . She was married in her hair[7] and led to chapel by her bridemen, a Duke of Saxony that is here and the Earl of Northampton, her great-uncle. The Dean of Westminster preached and bestowed a great deal of commendation on the young couple, on the Countess of Salisbury, and the mother-vine (as he termed her), the Countess of Suffolk.[8] The Dean of the Chapel coupled them, which fell out somewhat strangely, that the same man should marry the same person, in the same place,

---

[6] Because of hidden and incurable impediment.

[7] In token of her virginity.

[8] Sister and mother of the bride respectively.

upon the selfsame day (after six or seven years, I know not whether), the former party yet living. All the difference was that the King gave her the last time, and now her father. . . .

I hear little or no commendation of the masque made by the Lords that night,[9] either for device or dancing, only it was rich and costly. . . . The presents indeed were more in number and value than ever, I think, were given to any subject in this land.

[189] January 5, 1614: I wrote somewhat the last week to your sister of this great marriage, which continues still in gallantry and triumphs, and the presents of plate and jewels increase daily. . . . The Queen gave certain silver dishes curiously enamelled, the Spanish Ambassador a jewel (they say) of £500—if it hold good, for the Lord Admiral's basin and ewer of gold, given him in Spain, is said not to prove pure metal now it comes to the touch. Sir Arthur Ingram gave a whole furniture or implements of a kitchen of silver, besides two pearls to the bride that cost him three hundred pound. It were to little purpose to go on further in this course, and therefore I will conclude with a curious bride-cake that cost five pound given by the Bishop of Bristol's wife.

The lofty masquers were so well liked at Court the last week that they were appointed to perform it again on Monday, yet their device, which was a mimical imitation of the Irish, was not pleasing to many, who think it no time (as the case stands) to exasperate that nation by making it ridiculous. . . .

The Lord Mayor was sent to by the King to entertain this newmarried couple with their friends and followers; but he making an excuse that his house was too little to receive them, it was not accepted, but word sent back that he might command the biggest hall in the town. Whereupon calling a council, it was resolved to do it at the charge of the City in the Merchant Taylors' Hall upon four days' warning, and thither they went yesternight about six o'clock, through Cheapside all by torchlight, accompanied by the father and mother of the bride and all the Lords and Ladies about the Court.

---

[9] Thomas Campion's *Masque presented at the Marriage of the Earl of Somerset.*

[206] June 30, 1614: On Wednesday in Whitsun week, the Lord
Privy Seal [10] departed this life, the same day sevennight that he came
through London as it were in triumph with only Sir Charles Cornwallis in his coach. He had a swelling in his thigh which increasing
daily it was thought good, after the applying of mollifying medicines,
to cut it, whereupon it grew so angry that it gangrened and made an
end of him. It should seem the matter was very venomous, when it so
poisoned Felton, the surgeon that lanced it, that he hath ever since
lain at death's door and the bell hath tolled for him twice or thrice.
. . . He was so heart-whole and so little expected death that he had
not made his will till the day before he died, and Sir Robert Cotton,
his old friend, was the man that put him in mind of it, telling him
there was no other way with him; but for his good news, among all
his friends and legacies, he gave him never a penny. . . . He gave
order his body should be buried at Dover, in a chapel within the
castle, whither it was carried the last week, whereupon there is much
descanting, and the more for that it is constantly reported that he had
extreme unction, and his body lay covered while it was here with a
velvet pall that had a white cross clean through it, with two burning
tapers upon his coffin day and night, where six of his gentlemen
watched continually by turns with torches borne by other servants,
and in that order he was carried all along through Kent in all the inns
where he rested.

[238] April 6, 1616: All the alteration we have since I wrote last is
that the very same day [March 27] the Lady of Somerset was committed to the Tower upon so short warning that she had scant leisure
to shed a few tears over her little daughter at the parting. Otherwise
she carried herself every way constantly enough, saving that she did
passionately deprecate and entreat the Lieutenant that she might not
be lodged in Sir Thomas Overbury's lodging, so that he was fain to
remove himself out of his own chamber for two or three nights till
Sir Walter Raleigh's lodging might be furnished and made fit for
her.[11]

---

[10] Henry Howard, first Earl of Northampton, who died a Catholic. His death
is significant here because several incriminating letters of his to the Lieutenant
of the Tower at the time of Overbury's death suggest that he escaped what
would have been a very ticklish situation had he lived till April, 1616.

[11] He had been released the week before, after fourteen years.

[240] April 30, 1616: The King went away the next day after St. George's feast towards Newmarket and Thetford, the Earl of Rutland and Sir George Villiers being that morning elected into the Order of the Garter, which seemed at first a strange choice, in regard that the wife of the former is an open and known recusant and he is said to have many dangerous people about him, and that the latter is so lately come into the light of the world; and withal it was doubted that he had not sufficient likelihood to maintain the dignity of the place according to the express articles of the Order. But to take away that scruple, the King hath bestowed on him the Lord Grey's[12] lands, and means (they say) to mend his grant with much more not far distant in the present possession of the Earl of Somerset, if he do *cadere causa*[13] and sink in the business now in hand.

[241] May 18, 1616: I thought I should this day have given you an account of our intended arraignments, but the matter is once more deferred till Thursday and Friday next. The stage in the midst of Westminster Hall, with numbers of scaffolds round about, was finished, the Lords assembled, and all things ready against Wednesday, when about Tuesday noon came order to put all off, whereby a great many that tarried of purpose after the term were disappointed and have since got themselves out of town with loss of their earnest for places. . . . I know a lawyer that had agreed to give ten pound for himself and his wife for the two days, and fifty pound was given for a corner that could hardly contain a dozen.

The cause of the stay is not certainly known, but this is certain, that warning being given the Lady on Saturday to prepare for her trial against Wednesday, she fell that night to casting and scouring and so continued till the next day very sick, whether it were that the apprehension wrought so violently with her, or that she had taken a dram. Some make this the reason; others say that her Lord begins to relent and makes show to reveal secrets of great importance.

[242] May 25, 1616: I come tired from hearing a piece of the Earl of Somerset's arraignment, who I think is but now in the midst of his

---

[12] Raleigh's companion in captivity, who had died in the Tower in 1614.
[13] Lose the cause.

answer, the proceeding against him having continued ever since ten o'clock in the morning till five that he began to answer for himself. . . .

He denies all, even his own letters, saying they be counterfeited, and will not be brought to write whereby to show the conformity of the character, but says it is against the law that he should be put to it. He had pen and ink allowed him to take notes, which is more than ever I knew any to have heretofore.

I was there at six o'clock in the morning, and for ten shillings had a reasonable place; but the weather is so hot and I grew so faint with fasting that I could hold out no longer—especially when I heard they had sent to provide torches. . . . The Lady Winwood is there, and more Ladies and other great personages than ever I think were seen at any trial. . . .

His Lady was arraigned yesterday and made shorter work by confessing the indictment, so that all was done and we at home before noon. She won pity by her sober demeanor, which in my opinion was more curious and confident than was fit for a lady in such distress; yet she shed, or made show of, some few tears diverse times. She was used with more respect than is usual, nothing being aggravated against her by any circumstance, nor any invective used, but only touching the main offense of murder. As likewise it was said today to be the King's pleasure that no odious or uncivil speeches should be given.

The general opinion is that she shall not die, and many good words were given to put her in hope of the King's mercy. . . . The Earl of Essex was at her arraignment, but somewhat more privately than this day, when he stood full in his face.

[243] June 8, 1616: When I wrote last, I left the Earl of Somerset pleading for his life, but that he said for himself was so little that he was found guilty by all his peers; which did so little appall him that when he was asked what he could say why sentence should not be pronounced, he stood still upon his innocence and could hardly be brought to refer himself to the King's mercy. . . .

Whether this or any other reason be the cause of stay of execution I know not, but they live yet and for aught I can learn so are like to do many a day.

[246] July 20, 1616: The new Knights of the Garter, the Earl of Rutland, Sir George Villiers, and the Lord Lisle, were installed at Windsor the seventh of this present, and there was a chapter held about taking down or continuing of the Earl of Somerset's hatchments or arms. But after long dispute, by warrant under the King's own hand, they were removed higher, as the manner is when new come in.[14] . . .

Yesterday he had the liberty of the Tower granted him; and Henrickson and his wife had the fortune to see him with his Garter and George about his neck, walking and talking with the Earl of Northumberland, and he and his Lady saluting at the window. It is much spoken of how foreign princes of that Order (to let our own pass) can digest to be coupled in society with a man lawfully and publically convicted of so foul a fact . . . but this age affords things as strange and incompatible.

The Lady's pardon was signed the other week. . . . The special reasons and inducements for it were four: the great and long service of her father, family and friends; her own penitence and voluntary confession . . . ; the promise of the Lord Steward and Peers to intercede for her; and lastly that she was not principal but accessory before the fact, and drawn to it by the instigation of base persons.

But it seems the common people take not this for good payment, for on Saturday last the Queen, with the Countess of Derby, the Lady Ruthin, and the Lord Carew, coming privately in coach to see somewhat here in town, there grew a whispering that it was the Lady Somerset and her mother; whereupon people flocked together and followed the coach in great numbers, railing and reviling, and abusing the footmen, and putting them all in fear. Neither would they be otherwise persuaded till they saw them enter into Whitehall.

[247] August 24, 1616: They say Sir George Villiers shall be created Viscount Beaumont tomorrow, once the coronet and robes are sent down [to Woodstock] for the purpose. In the meantime the Earl of Somerset and his Lady have the full liberty of the Tower and converse freely together both by day and night, and the Earl of Northumberland is much in their company, framing himself altogether to be friendly and sociable.

---

[14] I.e., he retained his place and precedence.

[**260**] March 8, 1617: The young Lady Sidney with her sister the Lady Lucy Percy, going . . . to visit their father in the Tower, after some few caresses he dismissed his daughter Sidney to go home to her husband and to send her sister's maids to attend her, for that he meant not to part with her but that she should keep him company, adding withal that he was a Percy and could not endure that his daughter should dance any Scottish jigs[15]; and there she continues, for aught I hear.

[**266**] May 24, 1617: The Earl of Northumberland could not divert his daughter, the Lady Lucy, from the Lord Hay; for while he had her in the Tower, giving her leave daily to visit the Lady of Somerset (thereby to have the better access himself), the matter was so plotted that where he thought he had her safest, there he lost her, and so was fain to send her away, seeing he could prevail no more with her. Her mother would not receive her neither, so that she retired to her sister at Baynard's Castle, and since the Lord Hay's going into Scotland, continues at the Wardrobe, he having left her £2000 for her maintenance till his return.

[**267**] June 4, 1617: There is a great falling out of late twixt the Earl of Somerset and his Lady in the Tower, but it is not yet so public that I can learn the original or particulars; but certainly there is a great jar, howsoever it will piece again or be smothered.

[**300**] October 14, 1618: I heard in the country of a great falling out twixt the Lord of Somerset and his Lady, for that he had taken her tripping, and that they were upon parting; but I have had no time to learn any certainty.

---

[15] Northumberland felt his daughter was throwing herself away on Lord Hay, Master of the Wardrobe, a Scotsman. He thought to dissuade her of her feelings by keeping her with him in the Tower, but Lady Frances, whose help he sought, undid him (see below, Letter 266).

[**401**] January 19, 1622: The Marquis Buckingham hath contracted with the Lord and Lady Wallingford [16] for their house near Whitehall, for some money and the making of Sir Thomas Howard [17] Baron of Charleton and Viscount Andover, and some think the delivery of the Lord of Somerset and his Lady out of the Tower was part of the bargain.[18] I hear they came out severally on Thursday in the evening and lay that night at Northampton House.

[16] Frances Howard's sister, Elizabeth.
[17] Her brother.
[18] Somerset was finally pardoned in October, 1624. Lady Frances had been pardoned in 1616 (Letter 246), a month after her conviction.

VII. Gazette, 1612-1619

[132] January 29, 1612: One Copley, a priest and domestical chaplain to the Lord Montague, falling in love with an ancient Catholic maid there that attended the children, they have both left their profession and fallen to marriage. . . .

Many of our pirates are come home upon their pardon for life and goods, but the greater part stand still aloof in Ireland, because they are not offered the same conditions, but only life; howsoever this course may serve the present turn, yet it is feared it may prove of ill consequence hereafter.

[133] February 12, 1612: This last Sunday Moll Cut-purse, a notorious baggage (that used to go in man's apparel and challenged the field of diverse gallants) was brought to [Paul's Cross], where she wept bitterly and seemed very penitent, but it is since doubted she was maudlin drunk, being discovered to have tippled off three quarts of sack before she came to her penance. She had the daintiest preacher or ghostly father that ever I saw in pulpit, one Ratcliffe of Brazenose in Oxford, a likelier man to have led the revels in some Inn of Court than to be where he was; but the best is he did extremely badly, and so wearied the audience that the best part went away, and the rest tarried rather to hear Moll Cut-purse than him. . . . A son of the Bishop of Bristol, his eldest, of 19 or 20 years old, killed himself with a knife to avoid the disgrace of breeching, which his mother or mother-in-law (I know not whether) would needs have put him to for losing his money at tennis.

[140] June 11, 1612: On Whitsun Eve there were four priests hanged at Tyburn who died very confidently and were suffered to talk their full; but whose fault it was I know not, but sure it was not well. They had been banished twice at least and would take no warning. The

124]

Earl of Arundel with his young son were present at the execution, and the Viscount Montague, with diverse ladies and gentlemen in coaches; and yet they were hanged early, between six and seven in the morning.

[148] August 11, 1612: Here is speech of a certain affront lately done the extraordinary Spanish Ambassador by a companion, that riding near his coach and saluting him, the Spaniard putting off his hat in requital, had it snatched from him and lost it with a rich hat-band and jewel.

[149] September 11, 1612: Sir Michael Hicks died not long since at his house in Essex of a burning ague, which came as is thought of his often going into the water this hot summer, which though it might seem to refresh him for the time, yet was thought unseasonable for a man of his years. . . .

There hath been great hurt done by fire of late, both at Ely, Birmingham, and other places, but especially at Tiverton, a great clothing town in Devonshire, where the 5th of August the whole town was burned saving the church, the parsonage, and an almshouse; and it is the more lamentable because it had the like mischance some eight or nine years agone (as I take it) and was now newly built and finished.

[155] November 26, 1612: The last week Norton the Stationer died of this new disease,[1] leaving a great estate they say in land as goods. It is observed that without any blazing star or other extraordinary sign this hath been a dismal year to great personages, and that within the compass of little more than twelve months, we have lost an Emperor, a King of Sweden, a Queen and a daughter of Spain, a Queen of Denmark, a Prince of Britain, a Duke of Orleans, a Duke of Venice, two Electors, besides our little great Lord Treasurer,[2] the Count Soissons, Count Hanau, and others.

---

[1] This "ordinary ague that hath reigned and raged almost all over England since the latter end of summer" (Letter 153), and which killed Prince Henry, was presumably typhoid.
[2] Robert Cecil, Lord Salisbury.

[161] January 28, 1613: Here is a proclamation come forth against pocket dagges,[3] and order is gone into most shires to disarm the papists. What secret cause there may be I know not, but the world here grows suspicious and apprehends great danger from them, and many rumors are raised, as namely the last week that the Earl of Huntingdon was slain by them in his own house; whereupon at Coventry and Warwick they shut their gates and mustered their soldiers, and at Banbury and those parts the people made barricades and all other manner of provision, as if they looked presently to be assaulted.

[169] March 10, 1613, to Sir Ralph Winwood: The King escaped a great danger at Newmarket, by reason the foundation of the house where he lay began to sink on the one side, with great cracks, so that the doors and windows flew open and they were fain to fetch him out of his bed with all possible expedition. About the same time the Lord of Rochester's chamber at Whitehall was robbed, but what he lost is not known, for they left his gay clothes and whole pieces of cloth of gold and rich stuffs.

Here be great store of coiners apprehended in diverse parts, which no doubt will multiply daily, now that the Lord Harington, in recompense of £30,000 (he saith) he hath spent in attending the Lady Elizabeth,[4] hath his suit granted of coining brass farthings: which is doubted to be but a shoeing-horn to draw on more of that metal to our mint. And you must think we are brought to a low ebb when the last week the Archduke's Ambassador was carried to see the ancient goodly plate of the House of Burgundy (pawned to Queen Elizabeth by the General States in anno '78, as I remember), and to know whether his Princes would redeem it, for otherwise it was to be melted. . . .

I know not whether I wrote you . . . of an odd fray that happened much about that time near the Temple twixt one Hutchinson of Gray's Inn and Sir Jermyn Poole, who assaulting the other upon advantage, and cutting off two of his fingers, besides a wound or two more before he could draw, the gentleman, finding himself disabled to revenge himself by the sword, flew in upon him and getting him

---

[3] Pistols.
[4] Princess Elizabeth had been brought up at his home in Warwickshire.

down tore away all his eyebrow with his teeth, and then seizing on his nose bit off a good part of it and carried it away in his pocket.

[171] March 25, 1613: I have kept my chamber now almost three weeks, and daily grow worse and weaker. I have been purged four or five times within this fortnight, and whereas when I entered into physic I complained only of want of appetite and a kind of heaviness all over, my head sound, my sleep good, I am now come to that pass that my stomach is quite gone and can receive nothing but broths, posset ale, or drink, my head extremely distempered, and my sleep utterly lost. Ever since Saturday that I took a vile purge, I have sunk very fast, and yesterday I took another to correct that, so that now I am come to mine old opinion that physic is a very casual thing and doth ordinarily more harm than good. And yet I have the advice of a man well reputed of and one that studied five years at Padua; but sure he hath mistaken his mark and missed the cushion[5] in my cure, so that now I am resolved to commit myself to good order and government and let physic alone, and if I had done so from the beginning I make no doubt but I had been a sound man by this time.

[174] May 13, 1613: Upon Friday one Bostock, an Under-Customer of Rochester, and one Waller were fined in the Star Chamber at 5000 marks apiece and censured further to stand on the pillory, lose their ears, and be whipped from thence through the streets, the one for reporting that presently after the Prince's death, four or five of the Council (whereof the Lord Privy Seal was principal) had kneeled to the King and besought him for toleration of religion; the other for writing this news to a Customer of Dover, who being dead before the letter came, his wife let it run from hand to hand. They have been in prison ever since Christmas or before. Sure if I were worthy to advise his Lordship I would rather wish him to contemn these barking whelps and all their bawlings than to trouble himself with them and bring these things to scanning; for it breeds but more speech, and to see silly men so severely censured begets commiseration, for it is thought

---

[5] Target.

somewhat a strange medley that 5000 marks and whipping should meet in one sentence. . . .

Here is the Marquis de Villa come Ambassador from the Duke of Savoy. They say he is a gallant gentleman and is well received. He hath had audience twice, but he makes no haste away, meaning to stay the Queen's coming, for whom it is given out he hath rich presents. He makes no great dainty of himself but goes with his troupe to the ordinary plays, to the Exchange, to the Pawn, and chaffers and bargains at every shop.

[179] July 8, 1613, to Sir Ralph Winwood: It may be you have not heard of the Earl of Northumberland's swaggering not long since in the Tower and beating Ruthven, the Earl Gowrie's brother, for crossing him in his walk in the garden. But the burning of the Globe or playhouse on the Bankside on St. Peter's day cannot escape you, which fell out by a peal of chambers that, I know not upon what occasion, were to be used in the play, the tampion[6] or stopple of one of them lighting in the thatch that covered the house, burned it down to the ground in less than two hours with a dwelling house adjoining. And it was a great marvel and fair grace of God that the people had so little harm, having but two narrow doors to get out.

[180] August 1, 1613: The Earl of Bedford, hunting in a park of his own, by the fall of his horse was thrown against a tree and so bruised that the report went he was dead, and it is doubted yet that he is in danger, for that his skull is said to be cracked. His Lady, who should have gone to the Spa but for lack of money, shows herself again in Court, though in her sickness she had in a manner vowed never to come there; but she verifies the proverb *nemo ex morbo melior*.[7] Marry, she is somewhat reformed in her attire, and forbears painting, which they say makes her look somewhat strangely among so many visards, which together with their frizzled, powdered hair makes them look all alike, so that you can scant know one from

---

[6] Wooden stopper for the muzzle of a gun; the "chambers" were short cannon used for celebrations and in the theatre.

[7] No one (learns) better from an illness.

another at the first view. Doctor Burgess, who is turned physician, was much about her in her sickness, and did her more good with his spiritual counsel than with natural physic; and his manner of praying was so well liked by Monsieur Mayerne or Turquet[8] that, thinking to do him a pleasure, he commended him to the King, who was so moved that he should dogmatize, as he called it, in his Court, that he commanded the Archbishop to look to it, who sending for him used him somewhat roughly, and enjoined him not to practice within ten miles of London.

[183] October 27, 1613: Dr. Carier, one of the King's chaplains, is turned papist and gone to Cologne, and there is cause to suspect that more will follow, seeing so many priests and Jesuits to the number of forty are said to be lately arrived here, and their companions pass as it were impune.

[184] November 11, 1613: On All Hallow day at night a vehement northwest wind that had lasted two or three days, meeting with the spring tides, brought in the greatest tide that hath been seen here by any man living (as they say) whereby there is much harm done, in Kent, Essex, Norfolk, and other places, as well by overflowing their marshes, bearing down their walls, and making many breaches, as by carrying away stacks of hay, many houses, and drowning great numbers of sheep and other cattle, insomuch that one man hath lost above 1500 sheep, besides other losses. And they make account that Kent alone is damnified to the value of £200,000; for not only all along the Thames side, but about Sandwich and that way there is great harm done, and six houses were carried away at Margate. And we hear that at Calais and all along that coast they have sustained great loss, which makes us fear that we shall have the same news or worse out of Zeeland.

On Thursday last two gentlemen, Skevington and Bray, having a suit one against the other in Chancery, met by mischance in Gray's Inn court, and upon the first encounter were both slain, and died at

---

[8] Theodore Turquet de Mayerne, Court physician of long standing.

one instant upon the place. Skevington was young, not above three or four and twenty, the last of his family, a man of £1500 land, which by his death is fallen to his sisters, whereof three are bestowed and one yet to marry.

[**193**] February 17, 1614: This week here came forth a long proclamation with a book annexed of reasonable bulk, against challenges and duels, which seems a curious piece of work, and though at first it was commonly attributed to Sir Fra. Bacon, yet by that little I have read of both, I did quickly acquit him, and did easily discern that it came from some higher hand.[9]

[**197**] March 17, 1614: I have not heard of so much contestation for places in Parliament as falls out this time. . . . Sir Henry Rich, going confidently into Norfolk with my Lord Chamberlain's warrant and letters, missed the mark by reason the Sheriff, upon less than half a day's warning, adjourned the County Court from Norwich (where it is usually held and where Sir Harry had more than 4000 freeholders ready) to a place twenty miles off and more, where Sir Henry Beningfield and Sir Hammond Lestrange carried away the goal. And though this were but trick of the Sheriff, yet they say he may do it by law and the other is without remedy.

[**214**] December 1, 1614: The Bishop of St. Davids, Doctor Rudd, is lately dead, and much posting and suing there is for his place, so sharp set men are nowadays for every little profit or preferment; and yet for all this penurious world, we speak of a masque this Christmas towards which the King gives £1500, the principal motive whereof is thought to be the gracing of young Villiers and to bring him on the stage.

---

[9] The higher hand was probably that of King James.

[**215**] December 15, 1614: The Bishop of St. Davids is not dead as I wrote you, but only in danger; but we are here so hungry and sharp set that there is nothing got by tarrying or showing modesty.

[**217**] January 5, 1615: There was lately speech of making fifty new barons at £6000 apiece, but it greatly quailed, for though the world be as vain and ambitious as ever, yet money goes low, and I think they should scant have found five at that rate. Now Master Hakewill hath a project in special request and this day the Council sit upon it, having appointed the judges and officers of the Exchequer to meet about it. The matter is a kind of general pardon of all offenses, debts and duties owing to the Crown, which should cost every man that takes it five pound. They make account the benefit would rise to better than £400,000, but I doubt they will find themselves mistaken in the reckoning if it go forward, and that it will scant amount to a quarter of the money.

[**219**] January 26, 1615: About ten days since there was a pink or small ship that came from Flushing robbed here in the river of Thames and great store of wealth taken away, but some of the thieves are taken and the rest sought after, being more than four or five and thirty.

[**222**] February 16, 1615, to Alice Carleton: The Lady Cheke, Master Osborne's sister of the Exchequer, would needs be let blood the last week for a little heat or itching in her arm, but by mishap the Queen's surgeon pricked her too deep and cut an artery, which fell to rankle, and in a few days grew to a gangrene whereof she died on Saturday, and was buried by night with above thirty coaches and much torchlight attending her, which is of late come much into fashion, as it should seem to avoid trouble and charge, but I rather think it was brought up by papists, which serve their turn by it many ways.

[224] March 2, 1615: There is now another project in speech, that whereas in the tenth year of the late Queen there was a decree made by the Earl Marshal and that Court, that no Arms should be given thenceforward without their allowance and consent, contrary where-unto the Heralds since that time are said to have dispensed above 7000 Coats, it is propounded that all these should be disarmed or ungentilized unless they will give twenty or thirty pound for confirmation of their gentry. But in the meantime, while this grass grows the horse starves and here is pitiful complaint on all sides for want of payment, specially those that deal for ambassadors who are wearied out with waiting.

[229] May 20, 1615: On Monday our new Knights of the Garter, Lord Fenton and Lord Knollys, ride to Windsor with great preparation to revie one upon another who shall make the best show, and though I am of the opinion that the latter will carry it by many degrees, by reason of his alliance with the house of the Howards, Somerset, Salisbury, Dorset, with many other great families that will bring him their friends and most part of the pensioners, yet most are persuaded that the other will bear away the bell as having the best part of the Court, all the Bedchamber, all the Prince's servants and followers, with an hundred of the Guard that have rich new coats made of purpose, besides Sir George Villiers, the new favorite, and Master Secretary,[10] whose presence had been better forborne, in my judgment, for many respects but that every man abounds in his own sense. . . .

On Saturday last the King went again to Cambridge to see the play *Ignoramus,* which hath so nettled the lawyers that they are almost out of all patience, and the Lord Chief Justice,[11] both openly at the King's Bench and diverse other places, hath galled and glanced at scholars with much bitterness, and there be diverse Inn of Court men have made rhymes and ballads against them, which they have answered sharply enough; and to say truth it was a scandal taken rather than given, for what profession is there wherein some particular persons may not be justly taxed without imputation to the whole? But it is an

[10] Sir Ralph Winwood.
[11] Sir Edward Coke.

old saying, *conscius ipse sibi*,[12] and they are too partial to think themselves so *sacrosancti* that they may not be touched. The King had a Latin sermon on Sunday, and disputations on Monday before his coming away.

[230] May 25, 1615: On Monday our new Knights of the Garter rode to Windsor very well attended both, and upon so even and indifferent terms that it were hard to judge whether had the advantage, save only that the Lord Knollys' troop was the better marshalled and ordered. Their number was in a manner equal as well of nobility and gentry as of other attendants not much above 300 apiece, but the Lord Fenton's people were generally better apparelled with many more chains of gold and better horses by means of the King's and Prince's stable. The Bishop of Ely sent eight men very well furnished and mounted which led the Lord Fenton's troop, which were seconded by a dozen of the Archbishop of Canterbury's. Daccombe, Master of Requests, went himself with the Lord Knollys, and sent four men to the Lord Fenton, who was likewise attended by two Councillors, Master Secretary and Sir Thomas Lake (though they did not ride together), and did him the honor to wear his feathers which were black and white, as the others were ash color and yellow. The King stood at Somerset House to see the show and would not suffer Sir George Villiers to ride. The Lord Knollys took horse at Salisbury Court in Fleet Street, and the Lord Fenton came from Arundel House. These particularities were not worth the repeating, but that the matter is come to that pass that every little thing is observed, now that they are grown as it were to siding and to open opposition.

[231] June 15, 1615. The project of pardons was on foot again, but finally defeated the last week, as likewise Sylvanus Scory's device for enlarging the privileges of baronets to be no Wards, to be Justices of Peace at 21 years of age, Deputy Lieutenants at 25, that their bodies should be free from arrests, with diverse other immunities, for which their rate should rise to £3000 a man, whereby the King's wants

---

[12] One knows oneself.

might be much relieved out of the vanity and ambition of the gentry. He had often access to his Majesty and pleased himself much with the invention and hope that he and his heirs (for this service) should be perpetual chancellors of that order. But after much discussing, the business was overthrown and he dismissed with a flout that *argentum eius versum est in scoriam, et aurum in orichalcum,* which that it might be the better understood was thus Englished, that his silver was turned to dross and his gold to alchemy.

But the inquiry after new-erected buildings within seven miles of this town since the King's coming in goes on amain, and the last week the whole Council from the highest to the lowest brought down a commission and sat at Guild Hall about it. If they should proceed with rigor and extremity, they might raise a great mass of money as is thought, but it would cause much murmur and complaint.

Here is much speech of new barons to be made for money, which were the less to be misliked if it came to the King's coffers, but the Lord Sheffield (I know not for what service) hath the grant of one, and hath already agreed with Sir Robert Dormer for £10,000, so that it is passed the seals and he is to be created some time this week unless some little controversy prolong it; for that the King will make none but such as must first pass through the order of baronets, and the question is whether must bear that charge, the buyer or the seller. Sir George Villiers hath likewise the grant of one, which is thought shall be Sir Nicholas Bacon upon the same rate or rather more; and withal he hath a pension of £1000 a year out of the Court of Wards.

[233] July 13, 1615: Sir Henry Neville died on Monday of the scorbut,[13] a disease easy to be cured if it be espied and taken in time, otherwise it draws on a number of other diseases and grows incurable.

[234] July 20, 1615: The King came to town yesternight, and goes this day towards Windsor, and so on Monday forward in the progress. The Queen is likewise going to the Bath, which comes ill to pass for

---

[13] Scurvy.

those countries they are to go through, who made petition to be spared this year in respect of the hard winter and hitherto extreme hot and dry summer, whereby cattle are exceeding poor and like to perish everywhere.

[236] September 15, 1615: We have had a long, hot and dry summer, and the best and fairest melons and grapes that ever I knew in England. Now of late the weather is turned moist and temperate, whereby we have the finest latter spring that hath been seen.

[239] April 20, 1616: Sir George Villiers hath been crasie of late, not without suspicion of the smallpox . . . but it proves otherwise; and we say there is much casting about how to make him a great man, and that he shall be now made of the Garter, but *non credo*. His great friend and favorite Sir John Grimes, a known courtier, died about a fortnight since, and was solemnly buried in the night at Westminster with better than 200 torches, the Duke of Lennox, the Lord Fenton, the Lord of Roxborough and all the grand Scottish men accompanying him. In apish imitation whereof (as it was suggested) certain rude knaves thereabout buried a dog with great solemnity in Tothill Field by night with good store of links, which was so heinously taken that diverse of them have been whipped by order from the Council; though upon examination the matter proved not so much in derogation of the Scots, seeing some of them were found to be ringleaders in that foolery.

[241] May 18, 1616: Yesterday was a woman condemned at the Sessions House for a lamentable murder of two of her own children. She dwelt at Acton and was a woman of good fashion both for means, shape and behavior, but being a violent recusant and urged by her husband to conform herself and to have her children otherwise educated, she took this course to rid them out of the world rather than to have them brought up in our religion.

[245] July 6, 1616: There was a seminary priest hanged at Tyburn on Monday that was banished before, and being taken again offered to break prison. That morning early there was a joiner's wife burnt in Smithfield for killing her husband. If the case were no otherwise than I can learn yet, she had *summum jus*,[14] for her husband having brawled and beaten her, she took up a chisel or such other instrument and flung it at him, which cut him into the belly, whereof he died. Another desperate woman coming from her execution, cut her own child's throat, alleging no other reason for it but that she doubted she should not have means to keep it. The same day likewise, another woman poisoned her husband about Aldgate; and diverse suchlike foul facts are committed daily, which are ill signs of a very depraved age and that judgments hang over us.

[247] August 24, 1616: We have a new ague or sickness that begins to spread itself in many places, and during the short time of my absence hath taken away diverse of good note, and upon short warning. . . . And it is the more strange for that we have had the finest and most seasonable weather now this whole twelvemonth that ever I knew, and as plentiful of corn, grass and all other fruits (saving apples) that hath lightly been seen, with as timely and goodly a harvest, insomuch that all manner of grain for forty or fifty miles about London hath been carried and laid up above a fortnight since. . . . They brag what rare plums they had there,[15] specially apricots, whereof some by their report were the fairest and weightiest that I have heard of, for they say they had three upon one tree the least whereof weighed four ounces or above, by trial. Indeed this hath been the greatest year of apricots that any man living hath seen in England, and I do not think that ever there were a quarter so many, so that they were usually sold in London before my going down six or seven for a penny.

[249] October 12, 1616: I came not to town till the very day before the term, the weather being so exceeding pleasant that we could

---

[14] The highest law.
[15] Chamberlain had been visiting Carleton's sister Elizabeth Williams at Gilston, Hertfordshire.

hardly be drawn to leave the sweet air and pleasures of the country for this misty and unsavory town. . . . Though the season now for these fourteen months hath been such and so good as I never saw so long together, yet the sicknesses are many and dangerous and dispersed in all places, which surely must be imputed to some influence from above rather than to any natural reason within our reach, specially if it be as we hear that this malignant fever reigns as well all over France, Spain, and Italy. . . .

Justice Warburton was in some disfavor for hanging a Scottish falconer of the King's at Oxford, contrary, they say, to express commandment of the King's that he should be reprieved. It was generally said that he should be displaced, and have a writ of ease as they call it; but howsoever it comes to pass, he sits still in the Court of Common Pleas. Justice Winch, likewise, and Sergeant Crew are somewhat discountenanced for hanging certain witches in their Circuit at Leicester, whereas the King, coming that way, found out the juggling and imposture of the boy that counterfeited to be bewitched.

[251] November 9, 1616: The Earl of Salisbury's young son died this day fortnight. The King was his godfather in person, held him at the font all the while he was christening, gave him the reversion of all his father's places and offices, and yet all these favors could not prolong life.

[252] November 14, 1616: On Saturday the Knights of the Bath were entertained by the Lord Mayor at Drapers' Hall with a supper and a play, where some of them were so rude and unruly, and carried themselves so insolently diverse ways but specially in putting citizens' wives to the squeak, so far forth that one of the Sheriffs brake open a door upon Sir Edward Sackville, which gave such occasion of scandal that they went away without the banquet, though it were ready and prepared for them. Neither did they forbear these disorders among themselves, for there were diverse piques and quarrels at their several meetings, but specially at the Mitre in Fleet Street, insomuch that young Parker, son to the Lord Monteagle, and Will Howard, the

Lord Treasurer's youngest son, went into the field, but were there prevented and reconciled. . . .

On Tuesday one Bartram, an aged gentleman, killed Sir John Tyndall, a Master of the Chancery, with a pistol charged with three bullets in Lincoln's Inn, pretending he had wronged him in the report of a cause to his utter undoing (as indeed he was not held for integerrimus), and afterwards stabbed himself once or twice but not mortally; and being apprehended and examined, showed no sign of remorse, saying that howsoever he had cast away himself, yet he had done the Commonwealth good. The cause breeds much discourse, the man being near fourscore years old that did it, and a comely grave man as is to be seen, but the strangeness and desperateness of the fact cuts off all commiseration. Mine author, Ned Wymark, cites Sir William Walter for saying that the fellow mistook his mark and should rather have shot hailshot at the whole Court, which indeed grows great and engrosses all manner of cases, and breeds generally complaint for a decree passed there this term (subscribed by all the King's learned Council) whereby that Court may review and call in question what judgments soever pass at the Common Law; whereby the jurisdiction of that Court is enlarged out of measure, and so suits become as it were immortal. This success is come of my Lord Coke's and some of the Judges' oppugning the Chancery so weakly and unseasonably, that, instead of overthrowing the exorbitant authority thereof, they have more established and confirmed it.

[253] November 23, 1616: On Sunday poor old Bartram that killed Sir John Tyndall, though he had a keeper and were narrowly watched, yet found means to hang himself in the King's Bench upon a nail. The King meant to have him respited until his coming that he might examine the depth and truth of his grievance, but it seems he was threatened or apprehended torture and the cutting off his hand for violence offered to a judge. He was above 75 years old and had a wife that was sister or half sister to Sir Robert Chamberlain's father.

[256] January 4, 1617: Yesterday there fell a great mischance to the Earl of Arundel by the burning of his house (built and left him by

the Earl of Northampton) at Greenwich, where he likewise lost a great deal of household stuff and rich furniture, the fury of the fire being such that nothing could be saved. No doubt the Papists will ascribe and publish it as a punishment for his dissembling or falling from them.

[258] February 8, 1617: I marvel how your letters of the 8th and 14th of the last month could find passage through these south and westerly winds that have continued so stiff and tempestuous now these three months, whereby we have yet felt no winter, unless perpetual weeping weather, extreme foul ways, and great floods may go under that name; for otherwise we have all the signs and shows of a warm spring, as well in all manner of herbs and sweet flowers as in buds of roses and blossoms of apricots and peach trees, which have been usually worn any time these three weeks. But among the many wonders that are spoken of in this kind, the greatest in my judgment is that my Lord of Canterbury had a nest of young blackbirds in his garden at Lambeth above twelve days since, and another sent him from Croydon about four days after. . . .

The King's *Works* (all save his poetry) are abroad in one volume, collected and set forth by the Bishop of Winchester with a large preface.

The Baron de la Tour[16] arrived here on Sunday last having had a hard and dangerous passage, and driven to land at Deal Castle in the Downs, where there lie at this present above 300 sail, more than ever were heard of to lie there so long.

[260] March 8, 1617: On the 4th of this present, being our Shrove Tuesday, the prentices or rather the unruly people of the suburbs played their parts in diverse places, as Finsbury fields, about Wapping by St. Katherine's, and in Lincoln's Inn fields, in which places being assembled in great numbers they fell to great disorders in pulling down of houses and beating the guards that were set to keep rule,

---

[16] The French Ambassador.

specially at a new playhouse (sometime a cockpit) in Drury Lane where the Queen's players used to play. Though the fellows defended themselves as well as they could and slew three of them with shot and hurt diverse, yet they entered the house and defaced it, cutting the players' apparel all in pieces, and all other their furniture, and burned their playbooks and did what other mischief they could. In Finsbury they brake the prison and let out all the prisoners, spoiled the house by untiling and breaking down the roof and all the windows, and at Wapping they pulled down seven or eight houses and defaced five times as many, besides many other outrages, as beating the Sheriff from his horse with stones and doing much other hurt too long to write. There be diverse of them taken since and clapt up, and I make no question but we shall see some of them hanged this next week, as it is more than time they were.

[261] March 15, 1617: On Sunday the Lord Mayor went to the Court to be knighted, where among many other good words the King gave them thanks for their forwardness in this loan of £100,000 which he borroweth of the City, though it be not yet raised; but it must be done *volens nolens*,[17] and they call in very mean men to help to bear the burthen. . . .

Two days since, the King gave the Lady Walsingham[18] £2000, for what service I known not.

This day was appointed to set forward for Scotland, but because it falls out this year forsooth to be a dismal day, the King, Queen, and Prince removed yesterday to Theobalds. On Monday the Queen accompanies him to Ware and then returns. . . . The King tarries nine nights at Lincoln, four at York, and twelve at Newcastle, besides other places. Half the pensioners are gone with him, and 24 of the chapel are to follow by sea. It is like to prove a very costly voyage every way. The Bishop of Winchester carries with him (besides all other provisions) 2000 Jacobus pieces in specie, and you may think the rest do what they can in that kind. I never knew a journey so generally misliked both here and there.

---

[17] Willy-nilly.
[18] Wife of Sir Thomas Walsingham, and a favorite of Queen Anne.

[262] March 29, 1617: On Monday the 24th of this month, being the King's day, the Archbishop of Canterbury, the Lord Keeper, Lord Privy Seal, the Earl of Arundel, the Earl of Southampton, the Lord Hay, the Controller, Secretary Winwood, the Master of the Rolls, with diverse other great men were at Paul's Cross and heard Dr. Donne,[19] who made there a dainty sermon upon the eleventh verse of the 22nd of Proverbs, and was exceedingly well liked generally, the rather for that he did Queen Elizabeth great right, and held himself close to the text without flattering the time too much.

[264] April 19, 1617: The King . . . is very much fallen in love with the country about Lincoln, so that he means henceforward to spend the best part of the winter there. At Worksop in Nottinghamshire he dated a proclamation that came forth this week that all gentlemen of quality should leave this town and repair to their own habitations. The greatest part of the prime Scots are here still and make no great haste homeward, which perhaps may be for want of moyens (as they term it) to carry them along and show themselves in equipage among their countryfolks. Indeed, for all these sums of money that have been borrowed, we are still in great straits . . . but new gifts and daily warrants under the privy signet do alter the course of orderly payments and disorder all. . . .

One Drope of Magdalen College in Oxford is called in question for a sermon at Paul's Cross on Sunday was fortnight, wherein out of the Proverbs, among other things, he would prove that kings might steal as well as meaner men, both by borrowing and not paying and by laying unreasonable and undue impositions upon their subjects.

[266] May 24, 1617: We have little out of Scotland since the King's being there, only here is an idle report that the King of Denmark should be come thither. Some speech there is likewise how the Burghers of Edinburgh received him in scarlet gowns, and more than 100 in velvet coats and chains of gold, and 300 musketeers in white satin doublets and velvet hose, and that they presented him with

---

[19] John Donne, Dean of St. Paul's.

10,000 marks in gold. But these things it is like you shall have there[20] sooner than we, for the King hath given order for cherries and other fruit to come over to him from those parts as being the shorter cut.

[268] June 21, 1617: We met with the news of a mischance fallen upon one belonging to my Lady Fanshawe, a man that had served Sir Harry from his youth and had now a place under him worth better than a hundred pound a year, who was found dead that morning in a ditch by Hoddesdon with almost £30 in gold about him and some silver. It should seem he was in some distemper, and putting his horse to leap the ditch miscarried, for he was found under him. His name was Ferdinando Lea, a very honest and sufficient man for any business, only he had the fault of good fellowship (as they call it) which brought him to this end. . . .

In Whitsun week the Countess of Arundel made a great feast at Highgate to the Lord Keeper, the two Lords Chief Justices, the Master of the Rolls, and I know not who else. It was after the Italian manner, with four courses and four tablecloths one under another; and when the first course and tablecloth were taken away, the Master of the Rolls,[21] thinking all had been done, said grace as his manner is when no Divines are present, and was afterwards well laughed at for his labor.

[273] October 11, 1617: It were to no purpose to write of the King's return out of Scotland, and what infinite numbers of people went out of this town to meet him when he came hither, and how well they were washed with a sound shower of rain for their labor.

[278] November 15, 1617: The King . . . stayed Sunday to entertain the Muscovy Ambassador, who had solemn audience, though with great confusion by reason of the throng; and Sir Ed. Coke, by

[20] At The Hague.
[21] Sir Julius Caesar.

what mischance I know not, stumbled and fell there before all the company. . . . Their presents were carried publicly by their own people and were the greatest that ever came thence, the very furs being estimated by those that are skillful at better than £6000, though some talk of much more. There were diverse hawks with coats or coverings of crimson satin and other colors embroidered with pearl, a rich Persian dagger and knife, bows and arrows, Persian cloth of gold with diverse other things I remember not. . . . The King was very much pleased, and the more when he understood Queen Elizabeth never had such a present thence.

[286] February 14, 1618: I told you of one Simpson of Cambridge that preached some Arminian points before the King, which being appointed to retract in the same place, when he came he made a very excellent sermon otherwise, but spake not a word of what was looked for and enjoined him, whereat the King was much displeased and hath since taken order that in another sermon he shall clearly deliver his mind in such and such points.

Here is one Trash or Thrash who was first a Puritan, then a Separatist, and now is become a Jewish Christian, observing the Sabbath on Saturday, abstaining from swine's flesh and all things commanded in the law. You will not think what a number of foolish followers he hath in this town and some other parts, and yet he hath not been long of this opinion. He and diverse of them are in prison, but continue obstinate, whereby a man may see there can arise no such absurd opinion but shall find followers and disciples. . . .

Here runs a rumor that we shall shortly have four or five Dukes made, that Sir John Villiers is to be created a Lord or Viscount, and his mother, the Lady Compton, a Countess or Marchioness (though her husband be not to rise but to continue where he is). I should not write these unlikely things, but that nowadays what seems most unprobable mostly comes soonest to pass.

[287] February 21, 1618: There was so good order taken and so strong watches and guards set in diverse places that our prentices did little harm on Shrove Tuesday; yet they had a cast at new Bridewell

beyond St. John's Street, and pulled down two or three houses in other places. They are grown of late to that number and insolency that they will hardly be suppressed without doing or receiving some great mischief.

[**293**] April 10, 1618: We were never at so low ebb for matter of news, specially public, so that we are even fain to set ourselves awork with the poorest entertainments that you have lightly seen or heard of, as on Wednesday with a race of two footmen from St. Albans to Clerkenwell, the one an Englishman belonging lately to the Countess of Bedford but now to the King, the other an Irish youth, who lost the day and I know not how much money laid on his head. The sums no doubt were very great, when the Lord of Buckingham for his part went away with £3000, and it is said for certain there was more than twice as much won and lost that day. The Irish youth serves Sir . . . Howard, a younger son of the Lord Treasurer, and the general opinion is that if the race had been shorter and the weather and ways not so extreme foul, our man had been put to the worse, though he had made good proof of himself heretofore and is a very lusty, able fellow, but carried it now by main strength, so that the other gives over twixt this and Highgate when he was not twice his length behind him. This story were not worth the telling but that you may see we have little to do when we are so far affected with these trifles that all the Court in a manner, Lords and Ladies (some further off, some nearer), went to see this race, and the King himself almost as far as Barnet, and though the weather were so sour and foul, yet he was scant *fils de bonne mère* that went not out so see, insomuch that it is verily thought there was as many people as at the King's first coming to London. And for the courtiers on horseback, they were so pitifully berayed and bedaubed all over that they could scant be known one from another. Besides, diverse of them came to have falls and other mishaps by reason of the multitude of horses. . . .

The Queen was yesterday at the Exchange, and though she meant to go privately, yet being discovered, she was no sooner in the Pawn[22] above but the press grew so great that they were fain to shut the doors.

---

[22] The arcade full of shops on the floor above street level.

[294] April 20, 1618: Yesterday Dr. Fotherby was consecrated Bishop of Salisbury at Lambeth, where (besides his oath) he made a loud protestation that neither directly nor indirectly (*per se aut per alium*[23]) he had given anything for the place, nor ever meant to do, and if any other in his name had condescended to any simoniacal conditions he utterly renounced them and vowed not to perform. Only he gave rich gloves to his friends that were present, as to the Archbishop, Earls and Bishops with five laces, to Barons with four, to Knights with three, *et sic de caeteris.*[24]

This morning two coiners (of three that were condemned) were hanged, drawn and quartered at Tyburn. They were in a good way (if they might have been let alone) of making Jacobuses not worth above four shillings apiece.

[297] August 8, 1618: This next week we are to have a great commission sitting at Guildhall about the tumult and riot committed upon the Spanish Ambassador's people and his house,[25] the King being much exasperated against the Lord Mayor and City for letting it pass so quietly, and therefore will have it re-examined and sifted to the full, to which end he hath appointed the Lord Coke for a principal commissioner.

Mistress Vavasour (old Sir Henry Lee's woman) is like to be called in question for having two husbands now alive. Young Sir Henry Lee (the wild oats of Ireland) hath obtained the confiscation of her, if he can prove it, without touching her life.

[298] August 13, 1618: The Commission I wrote of held on Wednesday at the Guildhall, where there were none but poor-snakes indicted for the riot committed at the Spanish Ambassador's. Seven were found guilty and adjudged to six months' imprisonment and to pay £500 apiece. The other two were acquitted. There were likewise

---

[23] By his own means or through another's.

[24] And so forth.

[25] One of Gondomar's men had ridden over a child in Chancery Lane and taken refuge in the Spanish Embassy. Several thousand angry Londoners had broken down doors and windows before Chief Justice Montagu and Lord Mayor Sir George Bowles arrived to quiet them.

certain Brownists fined and imprisoned for following of conventicles. Captain Bubbe (a man not unknown to you) was sentenced the last week at the Sessions to stand on the pillory for cozenage and telling of fortunes and other knaveries. . . . Bubbe was on the pillory all this morning in Cheapside, in as sound a shower of rain as we had any this year.

[299] August 20, 1618: Here is much ado about buildings, both in suppressing great numbers that have been built heretofore and in exacting such as are now in hand to be done, according to a proclamation come forth since your going, which makes diverse stand at a stay now they are more than halfway up.

Diverse patents or licenses have been lately granted that breed much speech, as a groat upon every cauldron of sea-coal, a certain rate (I know not what) for every ton of shipping that passes toward the northern coast, for maintenance of lights, as is pretended.

[300] October 14, 1618: This last night there was a great fire in Cornhill a little above the Exchange, where a house or two were burned and as many pulled down, and not without need, for the house where the fire began belonged to one that sold oil, which gave fuel to the flame.

[304] November 14, 1618: On Tuesday . . . one Robinson, that had sometime been a clerk in an office, was arraigned at the King's Bench and condemned for counterfeiting the Great Seal and, under color of letters patents, exacting sums of money of alehouse keepers and of fellows that let out money at use in the country. For which and such other abuses he was yesterday hanged, drawn and quartered about Charing Cross. Another course of his, they say, was by virtue of this commission to take up rich yeomens' daughters (or drive them to compound) to serve his Majesty for breeders in Virginia. . . .

Mistress West, the Lord Delaware's daughter, one of our prime and principal beauties, is seized on by the smallpox, which if they deal not mercifully with her she is quite undone, seeing her good face is the best part of her fortune.

[305] November 21, 1618: On Wednesday . . . was the first day we took notice here of the great blazing star, though it was observed at Oxford a full week before. It is now the only subject almost of our discourse, and not so much as little children but as they go to school talk in the streets that it foreshows the death of a king or queen or some great war towards. Upon which occasion (I think) it was given out all this town over that the Queen was dead on Thursday; but yesterday I heard for certain that she is in a fair way of amendment, and looked out of her window to see the hunting of a fox.

[306] November 28, 1618: We hear little or nothing from Newmarket but that they devise all the means they can to make themselves merry, as of late there was a feast appointed at a farmhouse not far off, whither every man should bring his dish. The King brought a great chine of beef, the Marquis Hamilton four pigs encircled with sausages, the Earl of Southampton two turkeys, another six partridges, and one a whole tray full of buttered eggs, and so all passed very pleasantly.

[307] December 3, 1618: There was no Star Chamber kept on Monday as there used to be the day after the term, not that the Lord Chancellor[26] is sick (as far as I can learn) but only out of tenderness that he cannot endure the cold, which is since somewhat abated; for if it had lasted with that extremity, no doubt the Thames had by this been quite frozen over, as already it was become impassable for boats. It came well to pass, I hope, to stay the violence of the smallpox, which are so generally spread that it is verily thought every third house in this town hath been infected with them.

---

[26] Francis Bacon, Lord Verulam.

[310] December 19, 1618. It is grown altogether in fashion to bury now by night, as on Sunday last the Lady Haddington had a solemn convoy of almost an hundred coaches, and torches in abundance, that accompanied her from Westminster to Whitechapel on her way to Newhall in Essex where she is to be buried.

[311] January 2, 1619: On Christmas eve a desperate fellow in Thames Street had gotten a barrel of powder, pitch, tar, and suchlike stuff of purpose to have blown up and burned his house, but, being discovered and interrupted by his servant and some others, he made away to the Thames and there drowned himself, diverse others looking on and some boats offering him all the help they could, which he obstinately refused. The cause is not certainly known. Some say he was grown in decay, others that it was to be revenged of some bad neighbors. The day before, a woman in Whitefriars held her maid's head so long in a tub of water that she drowned her. And a player about the town, upon some displeasure to the Lord of Doncaster's barber (that was very dear to him) ran him through and killed him unawares.

[313] January 16, 1619: Since my last we have had here a great mischance by fire at Whitehall, which beginning in the banqueting house hath quite consumed it, and put the rest in great danger, but that there was so much help at hand besides that which was sent out of London on all sides, and so good order taken by the presence of the Lord Chamberlain,[27] the Duke,[28] and the Earl of Arundel, that all passed with as much quiet as was possible in such a confusion; and the fire, though it was exceeding furious, kept from spreading further than the limits of that building, saving only that the vehemency of the heat burned down one of the rotten terraces or galleries adjoining and took hold of the pulpit-place, which was soon quenched. One of the greatest losses spoken of is the burning of all or most of the writings and papers belonging to the Offices of the Signet, Privy

---

[27] William Herbert, 3rd Earl of Pembroke.
[28] Ludovick Stuart, 2nd Duke of Lennox.

Seal, and Council Chamber, which were under it. And in such a mishap it fell out happily to be in the daytime, about eleven o'clock on Tuesday the 12th of this month, for if it had happened in the night, the whole house and all in it had been in great danger, for though it were at high noon yet there was much embezzling and much spoil, though there was as much provision made against it as the shortness of time could permit, and diverse taken with the manner and committed. There is speech of diverse miscarried, but we hear yet no certainty, only some are hurt and maimed, and the fire is not yet so thoroughly quenched that they can search every corner. You may guess at the fury of it when it lasted not in any strength above an hour. Diverse reports run how it came, but the most current is that a mean fellow searching in the masking or tiring house with a candle for certain things he had hid there, fired some oiled painted cloths and pasteboards, with such other stuff, and seeing he could not quench it alone, went out and locked the door after him, thinking so to conceal himself. There is doubt that this will hinder the King's coming to town this Candlemas.

[314] January 23, 1619: There is speech of setting up the banqueting house again very speedily, and some will undertake for seven or nine thousand pound (I know not whether) to make it more fair and beautiful than before.[29] . . .

This week there went a great many to Tyburn, among the rest one Nicholls, a notorious thief, who, being condemned last Easter term at the King's Bench for a robbery, had his pardon and was this Christmas taken with the manner again, and in a sullen humor would needs die a Catholic forsooth, saying in direct terms that he trusted to be saved by the merits of Jesus Christ and his own. There was a broker likewise hanged at his own door in Houndsditch for receiving goods stolen at the fire at Whitehall. We hear of a certain Lady Sandys that hath done a robbery in her own person. Her husband was hanged for the like about a year since. About the beginning of this month a Lady Ogle, wife to Sir Richard . . . attempted to cut her own throat and missed it very narrowly, but the hurt is well cured again and she seems to be now of another mind; she hath

---

[29] Inigo Jones's famous Banqueting Hall, which is the most notable survival of James's Palace at Whitehall, was the result.

been held a very handsome woman and modest, and no cause known that should move her but that her husband lies in the Fleet for debt. . . .

Mistress Prescott, . . . having a daughter ready to be married that fell sick of the smallpox, with good tending saved her but lost herself and is dead of them, which I write the rather because I think my Lady knew her. The Lord Mordant and the Lady Lisle (the Earl of Northumberland's daughter) lie likewise very sick of them. And if this cold weather do not cool and abate their fury, God knows how we shall do in summer.

[321] March 19, 1619: We have every week almost a new proclamation for somewhat or other, as for buildings (forward and backward), for weights and measures, for inns and alehouses, for horse meat, and I know not what else, all for the good of the subject, and yet they either believe it not or will not acknowledge the good pretended.

The Queen's funeral[30] is put off till the 29th of the next month, to the great hindrance of our players, which are forbidden to play so long as her body is above ground. One special man among them, Burbage,[31] is lately dead, and hath left they say better than £300 land. One Frith, a scrivener, that had scraped together four or five hundred pound land a year and yet lay in prison for debt, dispatched himself with a pistol the last week in the King's Bench.

[322] March 27, 1619: The Queen's funeral is put off till the 29th of April and perhaps longer, unless they can find out money faster, for the Master of the Wardrobe[32] is loath to wear his own credit threadbare, or to be so ill an husband as to use the King's credit and so pay double the price, which is now become ordinary because they stay so long for their money. In the meantime the Ladies grow weary of watching at Denmark House, though all day long there is more concourse than when she was living. . . .

---

[30] She had died at the beginning of the month.

[31] Richard Burbage, the leading actor of his day, who first played many of Shakespeare's greatest roles.

[32] Sir Lionel Cranfield.

Now for yearly incomes the King shall have £60,000 that her household, her servants and stable stood him in, besides £24,000 that was her jointure and allowed for her own person, and £13,000 she had for certain years out of the sugars and a late grant of clothes, which they say the King hath bestowed on the Prince. . . .

Most of the Court Lords, as the Duke, Earls of Arundel, Pembroke, Montgomery, the Viscount Doncaster, and others, were gone post to the King upon notice of a violent fit of the stone, whereupon the Prince was sent for on Monday and met the King twixt Newmarket and Royston, whither he came weak and faint, but with better hope the next day for that he voided three stones, whereby it is hoped the passage hereafter will be more easy. . . . I am glad to see the world so tenderly affected toward him, for I assure you all men apprehend what a loss we should have if God should take him from us, and do earnestly inquire, and in general heartily wish and pray for his welfare.

We had a great alarm the last week by the firing of almost all the beacons in Sussex and Kent, upon a mistaking by reason of the burning of certain furzes or fern near a beacon in Sussex. But it fell out not altogether amiss, for the people showed themselves forward enough to arm and make head.

[324] April 17, 1619: The Bishop of London preached on Sunday at Paul's Cross to give thanks for the King's recovery, and made a very pleasing piece of work upon the 17 verse of the 38th chapter of Isaiah. I did not conceive before I heard him that the extremity of the danger had been such as he delivered it, that there was little or no hope left, and that the physicians themselves were of that opinion. The audience was the greatest that I remember to have seen there, for besides the Lord Mayor and Aldermen, with all the rest of the City Companies in their best array, there were almost all the Council and great men about this town, as the Archbishops of Canterbury and Spalato, with diverse other bishops, the Lord Privy Seal, the Duke of Lennox, the Lord Chamberlain, the Earls of Arundel, Leicester, Devonshire, with many others that come not now to mind; but I must not forget four of the Earl of Suffolk's sons, who were the more noted because they came somewhat late and by themselves, but specially because it had been given out (and perhaps believed) that during the King's sickness they carried their heads high

with all manner of feasting and jollity, more than needed. All the Council and noblemen that were present dined with the Bishop, who they say made a great feast.

[**325**] April 24, 1619: The day of the Queen's funeral is not yet set down. . . . The number of mourners and the whole charge spoken of is beyond proportion, above three times more than was bestowed upon Queen Elizabeth, which proceeds not of plenty, for they are driven to shifts for money, and talk of melting the Queen's golden plate and putting it into coin, besides that the commissioners for her jewels and other movables make offer to sell or pawn diverse of them to good value. . . .

Another piece of difficulty there is, that some Catholic ladies nominated for mourners give out that they will not stain their profession with going to our church or service upon any show of solemnity, a strange boldness, and such as would not have been so easily digested in some times.

[**327**] May 14, 1619: The funeral[33] . . . was but a drawling, tedious sight, more remarkable for number than for any other singularity, there being 280 poor women, besides an army of mean fellows that were servants to the Lords and others of the train; and though the numbers of Lords and Ladies were very great, yet methought altogether they made but a poor show, which perhaps was because they were apparelled all alike, or that they came laggering all along, even tired with the length of the way and weight of their clothes, every Lady having twelve yards of broadcloth about her and the Countesses sixteen. . . .

It was full six o'clock at night before all the solemnity was done at church, where the hearse is to continue till the next term, the fairest and stateliest that I think was ever seen here. The business passes not without some disaster (as is commonly seen in such assemblies), a young man being killed outright by the falling of a stone from Northampton House, which was one of the letters S that serve for

---

[33] Held, at last, on May 13.

the battlements and thrust out by mischance and carelessness of those above.

[**328**] May 31, 1619: On Trinity Sunday . . . Paul's Cross mourned, being hanged with black cloth and scutcheons of the Queen's arms, and all our aldermen and officers of this town came together in black, as it were *postliminio*.[34] Because they were forgotten or neglected at the funeral, the King to please them would needs have it done now.

Only the Lord Mayor was not there, being very sick and surfeited upon messages sent him by the King about his only daughter, whom the Countess of Buckingham will needs have for her son Christopher, and the Mayor, being a willful and dogged man, will not yield by any means, fair nor foul, as yet, and wishes himself and his daughter both dead rather than to be compelled. The truth is she is not past fourteen and very little of growth, so that he protests he will not marry her these four or five years by his will. But yet he hath taken the King's messages so to heart that he hath been at death's door.

[**329**] June 5, 1619: The King came from Theobalds on Tuesday to Whitehall all along the Fields, and on the back side of Gray's Inn was met by a fair troop of our citizens on horseback, with their chains of gold or pearl or diamonds, and the Aldermen in scarlet. . . . The King was attended by the Prince and all the nobility in very good equipage, himself very fresh in a suit of watchet[35] satin laid with silver lace, with a blue and white feather, as also his horse was furnished with the like both before and behind; insomuch that all the company was glad to see him so gallant, and more like a wooer than a mourner. But what decorum it will be when ambassadors come to condole (as here is one now from the Duke of Lorraine with three or four and twenty followers all in black), let them consider whom it more concerns. . . . The King was gone early the next morning on hunting, and that night to Greenwich, so that it seems his only coming hither was to receive these applauses and gratulations.

---

[34] Restored to rights and privileges.
[35] Pale blue.

[330] June 19, 1619: The smallpox had seized on the Lady of Bedford and so seasoned her all over that they say she is more full and foul than could be expected in so thin and lean a body. . . . The Lady Delaware likewise lies now sick of the smallpox, which is somewhat strange that this disease should nowadays take hold of persons that for years and other respects thought themselves privileged long since from the boiling and fury of maladies that follow young blood.

[338] October 16, 1619: About a fortnight since, Sir John Whitbrooke was stabbed and killed in the Fleet by Boughton, one of his fellow prisoners. The case is the harder for that he had made means diverse times before to the Warden or Keeper to be separated from such an unruly chamber fellow and could not obtain it.

There be likewise two or three deer-stealers in the King's Bench for hunting in Hyde Park and killing a keeper. . . .

[339] October 30, 1619: Three of the deer-stealers I wrote you of were arraigned the last week at the King's Bench and executed at Hyde Park Gate the day following. One of their names was Wornall, a very proper gentleman (they say) and spake very well for himself; but a poor laboring man was most pitied, that was hired for sixpence to hold their dogs and bear them company to the gallows.

All the clergy in this town were called of late before the Bishop of London upon a letter sent from the King, complaining that they used to neglect or curtail his titles of Defender of the Faith and Supreme Head or governor in all causes and over all persons as well ecclesiastical as civil; as likewise that they did not particularly mention and pray for the Archbishops and Bishops, all which they are enjoined to do from henceforth, not perfunctory but severally and at large. . . .

They complain of drought almost everywhere, and that the ground is so hard that they can neither till, sow, hunt nor hawk, but sure otherwise it hath been a very sweet season, and pity it is that such fair weather should do harm.

VIII. Private Lives and Public Service, 1614-1617

MR. SECRETARY WINWOOD

THE *period of Winwood's Secretaryship must in many ways have been the happiest of Chamberlain's life; it was then that his special talent for friendship brought him closest to the events he enjoyed recording for Carleton. But these were also the years in which he was beginning to outlive the friends of his own generation. He was kept busy helping their wives with the vexed problems of wardship, and worrying about their orphans.*

Wardship was the feudal anachronism whereby the King could treat the minor children of his deceased landholders as his wards, and their revenues as his own, until they came of age. Fathers had to arrange in their wills for the purchase of the wardship of their children from the King by their widows or a trusted friend. Courtiers competed for the wardship of profitable orphans. Commons had tried to end the practice in 1604, offering instead a fixed revenue for the Crown, but were rebuked. The same bargain formed part of Cecil's Great Contract in 1610; but royal prerogative and Parliamentary grievances conspired to defeat it, and the practice continued, universally condemned.

The not-altogether-edifying adventures of Cecil's niece Elizabeth, Lady Hatton, and his grand-nephew William, Lord Roos, occupy Chamberlain in passing. Francis Bacon's star rises at last in Council; Edward Coke's as rapidly sinks in Westminster Hall. We are familiar with Chamberlain's incidental characterization of them both.

Carleton's brother-in-law and later his brother both stand in mortal terror of being "pricked for Sheriff," formerly a position of considerable honor, but now one where the honor does not compensate for the cost. His great friend Tobie Matthew returns from the long exile to which his conversion to Catholicism had condemned him. There do not seem to have been any personal or theological scruples about friendship with Catholics, but the equivocal public status of recusants —those who refused to take the Oath of Supremacy—and of foreign Catholics in English society continued to be a matter of comment and worry.

Bacon called Winwood "the boisterous Secretary," a nice example of his talent for the subtly derogatory epithet. Councillor Winwood obviously accepted as little advice from Councillor Bacon as he did from his close friends. It is fascinating and fruitless to speculate about what would have become of Winwood had he not died so suddenly. Would James have sacrificed him, with Raleigh, to Gondomar? Could Winwood have achieved everlasting popularity by persuading James to become an active Protestant champion in 1619? Might Parliament have found grounds for making him a scapegoat in 1621? No matter; he was dead in 1617, and the field was clear for the rise to influence of George Villiers, first Duke of Buckingham.

[204] June 1, 1614: Our good friend[1] . . . is neither idle nor always well occupied, neither greatly giving nor receiving satisfaction, but held *opiniastre*[2] and peremptory to the proof, which kind of carriage is nothing pleasing, which makes him subject to much censure; neither do they forbear him a whit. I am of opinion that this Parliament will mend him or quite mar him. Yet hitherto it fadges but ill-favoredly; and though he be an old scholar, yet he never was in such a school before.

[206] June 30, 1614: Our old friend rubs on, and for aught I see stands alone, without much dependence upon any, which as the world goes I think is no ill. I have been with him here at his house twice or thrice within this sevennight and find him still the old man.

He wishes you would think of succeeding Sir Thomas Edmondes when the time comes.

---

[1] Sir Ralph Winwood.
[2] Stubborn.

[207] June 30, 1614, to Alice Carleton in Venice: At my coming to town on Friday last, I received your letter of the 13th of this present and found here with my brother Richard the box of seeds and plumstones which you wrote I should receive of Master Blunt in Paul's Churchyard. It was brought in my absence by a sailor, who would not deliver it without a note of my brother's hand for the receipt; and he would not be persuaded but there was matter of great value in it, as pearls or diamonds at least.

I thank you for it, though there be little or nothing in it that will be now of any use; yet we will set the plumstones at all adventures, though we have no great hope of them that they will grow. Neither if they should have I any opinion of the goodness of Italian plums; they may brag of their melons and grapes, for the rest of their fruit is not worth the talking of.

We have set the vine plants that came from Master Wake[3] as carefully as we could, and I am not out of hope but they may prove, though they be very dry and promise little by their looks. . . . I have promised my Lady Winwood some of them if they live and do well, for she takes great delight in flowers and plants, and is as busy herself in setting and tending of melons as any gardener of them all. She is not greatly sorry that this year is like to prove no better for fruit, for she says she should surely have killed herself. We have had some plants of muscadine grapes from her that were sent her out of the Low Countries for excellent good, and we truck and live much by exchange that way, for we furnished her with melon seed in the spring and sent her some grown plants from Ware Park before Whitsuntide. . . .

I have not seen your sister Williams since I came to town, though I have been there twice. The first time she was at a neighbor's house at cards, and the next she was gone to the new Globe to a play. Indeed I hear much speech of this new playhouse, which is said to be the fairest that ever was in England, so that if I live but seven years longer I may chance make a journey to see it. . . .

On Sunday morning your cousin Smith[4] was brought abed . . . of a son, which, though he came almost six weeks before he was looked for, yet is very lively and like to hold out, though but a little one. Sir Rowland is much joyed at it, for I must tell you she is his darling.

---

[3] Carleton's First Secretary in Venice.
[4] Judith, wife of George Smith and daughter of Sir Rowland Lytton.

[208] July 7, 1614: Good Sir Rowland Lytton grows fast into decay as well of mind as body, though his looks made no such show. As well as I love him, I should less grieve to lose him than to see him outlive himself.

[209] July 14, 1614: In answer to yours of the 17th of June, I will begin with the point that most presseth. I mean your remove nearer home. . . . Sir Henry Wotton is presently to go [to The Hague] Ambassador Extraordinary, for ordinary lieger there is not yet appointed. . . . Our uncertainties are such, and slackness together, that nothing is done that doth not in a manner do itself. . . . In the meantime you may think there want no wooers for your place and such as make fair offers, when a knight whom you know well, and whose name begins with R. Dru., would part with £2000 for the purchase; but it were pity things should pass that way, for then we might well say *omnia Romae vaenalia.*[5] And I see not how there could be much gotten by such a bargain, when there is already £12,000 owing to Ambassadors.

[210] July 21, 1614: Sir Henry Wotton goes away out of hand to see if he can compound this business of Cleves without blows . . . ; his allowance is four pound a day with forty days' advancement, but he complains of hard measure in both. . . .

In the meantime you are not to think of removing till the spring, and many alterations may fall in that time. One thing I cannot keep from you, that [Sir Ralph Winwood] thinks you neglect him more than needs; but howsoever there may be mysteries and cabals twixt you and the great man,[6] yet he is not to be altogether forgotten. As likewise there is another point which, though I am loath to touch or to intermeddle with matters above my compass, yet seeing I have heard it two several ways from good hands, I cannot conceal: that your sedulity and length are not always so welcome as perhaps you imagine, for even the best things may breed satiety. But, as I said, though this

[5] Everything in Rome is for sale.
[6] The Earl of Somerset.

be beyond my reach, yet I hope you will think it no presumption seeing it proceeds of mere zeal and good meaning.

[211] August 4, 1614: I doubt not but before this come to your hands you have received the letters I sent you last week from Master Secretary whereby he gave you to understand that you were to leave Venice and make towards the Low Countries, which I would wish you do with the best speed you may to avoid the foul weather, which commonly begins early in those parts. And though he advised you to come by Milan and so to Basel, yet I take it to be the longer and the worse way, and therefore you shall do well to inform yourself and take the course that you shall find most convenient. Your letters of revocation, and to authorize Master Wake to tarry there as Agent till your successor come, shall be sent with the first opportunity. . . .

We have lost Sir Walter Cope upon a very short warning, for whiles he was preparing to go to his brother's funeral, he was buried the same day himself at Kensington. He fell sick on Tuesday in the afternoon and died on Sunday morning. It is thought the loss of his brother and the speech of losing his place[7] brake his heart.

[212] October 12, 1614, to Isaac Wake in Venice: Coming to town the last week I met with the unexpected news of my Lord Ambassador's removing from Venice countermanded, which I could not at first believe till Master Secretary himself confirmed it unto me and that there was order gone three or four several ways to stay and cause him to return, though he were well advanced in his journey (as I make no question but he was). . . . I doubt he will return but slenderly accompanied if he meet with these directions on this side of the mountains. . . . But howsoever it be, seeing *sic visum est superis*,[8] they must break through all difficulties and digest all as well as they may, being as I presume but for a small time, or till the spring at farthest. I shall long very much to hear the success of this business and to have them handsomely settled there again; till

---

[7] As Master of the Court of Wards.
[8] It is thus understood by the powers that be.

when I shall not know how nor to whom to write but to yourself as occasion shall be presented, wishing that if I write anything worth their knowledge you would acquaint them with it.

[214] December 1, 1614, to Carleton, back in Venice: There is now order taken (they say) to satisfy Sir Walter Cope's debts and to clear his estate. The rest of the executors declining the business, Sir Henry Rich and Sir William Cope have undertaken it. Sir Harry is to have the house at Kensington with the land about it and all the appurtenances for his part; Sir William certain parsonages and chantries, the key at the Custom House, and some other things to discharge debts for six or seven and twenty thousand pounds, which sum added to his own debts of eleven or twelve thousand pound at least may chance prove a heavy burthen. The Lady Cope hath compounded for her jointure[9] of £550 and is to receive £3500 ready money, which if she dispose not the sooner and to good purpose may prove to her but an indifferent bargain. . . .

Because you seem to long to know mine opinion of your abode there, though I am able to say little nor so much as make any probable conjecture, yet I will deal with the same freedom and plainness that I have always used to my best friends. It seems you are embarked in diverse intricate business,[10] wherein you have made yourself so necessary that you cannot be spared. . . . And though I make no question but you do all or most by commandment, yet . . . if matters should not succeed *à souhait*[11] you may well think where the blame would lie, specially if there be not sufficient warrant for every particular. But the pleasure of dealing in great and high matters carries men sometimes further than they meant at first; and some, that only to avoid idleness have entered into business, have been drawn along to cut out more work than they were afterwards well able to overcome, in which regard I should be sorry, instead of recompense for your care and travail, to see you put to apologies. I doubt not but you have many and sound reasons for that you do, and in an active age there were great and good use of such diligence; but

---

[9] Income per year.
[10] Carleton was helping to negotiate peace in a dispute between Savoy and Mantua that also involved Venice and Spain.
[11] As is wished.

as the times stand, wherein we have neither will nor means to undertake great matters, *Tuta consilia speciosis praeferenda.*[12] I presume
you will pardon this boldness, and make the best construction of my
good meaning . . . for it is but mine own bolt, and though perhaps
it be shot wide, yet my care and affection are not to be rejected.

[216] December 22, 1614: I know not what to write touching your
remove, which I see you linger so much after. . . . I put our good
friend in mind of you as often as I come in his way, but his silence
or cold answers give me no great comfort. I find him as friendly and
familiar towards me as ever heretofore, and he never comes home but
I am summoned and sent for. . . . Indeed I perceive I should not
need to ask anything concerning you when he hath aught that is
pleasing, for he poureth it out as soon as he sees me; and therefore
be assured you cannot want what lies in him to do. . . . But the
worst I gather is that Sir Harry Wotton would build his tabernacle
where he is[13] and labors to put off his extraordinaryship for the
ordinary place.

[219] January 26, 1615: Your brother Williams is half out of heart
that with all his pains and travail he cannot yet procure your money,
and it would discourage any man to do as he doth, *omnem movere
lapidem* and yet not *promovere;*[14] for sometime he flies to the Chancellor, sometime to the Lord Treasurer, and sometime to Master Secretary—whom he need not solicit if it lay in his power, for, more than
a fortnight since, he moved both the Lord Treasurer and Master
Chancellor severally and together, as well for you as for Sir Thomas
Edmondes, who presseth hard and protesteth he can stay no longer
where he is if he be not presently supplied, being brought so bare that
he is altogether both out of money and credit. . . . Poor Quester, the
postmaster, runs up and down from one to another, and though they
have continual and daily use of him, yet can he not get a penny of

---

[12] All plans should be revealed to the brilliant pretenders.
[13] I.e., at The Hague.
[14] To leave no stone unturned and yet not succeed.

£600 they owe him for postage, whereby you may see how the world goes here.

[**220**] February 1, 1615, to Alice Carleton in Venice: Yesterday by your brother Williams I received your letter of the 16th of January, but I cannot follow your advice therein to sell the glasses[15] you sent me, for I have not one left within three days after they came to my hands, having disposed of them all so soon as might be. . . .

I brought the Lady Winwood and the Lady Fanshawe to see in one room and in one view above eight hundred dozen of glasses that came all in the same ship with mine, whereby you may see that this town is thoroughly furnished of that commodity, and no great estimation to be made of them unless they be somewhat extraordinary and rare. . . .

One thing I will entreat more, if it may be had: that you would procure half a dozen such looking glasses as you sent me, which are so well liked of that my Lady Winwood hath been in hand with me twice or thrice, and no longer ago than yesternight, to get her so many to furnish both her houses.

[**221**] February 9, 1615: I was drawn the last week for a day of two to Knebworth, where I took small comfort to see so good a friend and such a spirit in the case that he is become *bis puer*.[16] In truth it was a pitiful and mortifying spectacle and did affect me extremely, but God's will must be done. . . .

Master Secretary came home yesternight from Newmarket in a day, which was a sore journey as the ways are, being at least 54 miles, but he had coaches laid for him in three places. He told me that he could not write to you this week, for that he was going this morning to the Spanish Ambassador[17] to salve somewhat.

[**223**] February 23, 1615: Master Secretary keeps altogether at Court and comes not home whiles the King is here, wherewith his lady is

---

[15] Venetian drinking glasses.
[16] A boy again.
[17] Sarmiento, later created Count Gondomar.

nothing pleased, but murmurs and mutinies that they should live both in a town and meet so seldom.

[225] March 16, 1615: I am newly returned from Cambridge, whither I went some two days after I wrote you my last. The King made his entry there the 7th of this present with as much solemnity and concourse of gallants and great men as the hard weather and extreme foul ways would permit. The Prince came along with him, but not the Queen, by reason (as it is said) that she was not invited, which error is rather imputed to their Chancellor[18] than to the scholars that understand not those courses. Another defect was that there were no ambassadors, which no doubt was upon the same reason. But the absence of women may be the better excused for default of language, there being few or none present but of the Howards or that alliance, as the Countess of Arundel with her sister the Lady Elizabeth Grey, the Countess of Suffolk with her daughters of Salisbury and Somerset, the Lady Walden, and Henry Howard's wife, which are all that I remember.

The Lord Treasurer kept there a very great port and magnificent table, with the expense of a thousand pound a day as is said, but that seems too large an allowance; but sure his provisions were very great, besides plenty of presents, and may be in some part estimated by his proportion of wine, whereof he spent 26 tun in five days. He lodged and kept his table at St. John's College, but his Lady and her retinue at Magdalen College, whereof his grandfather Audley was founder. The King and Prince lay at Trinity College where the plays were represented, and the hall so well ordered for room that above 2000 persons were conveniently placed.

The first night's entertainment was a comedy, made and acted by St. John's men, the chief part consisting of a counterfeit Sir Edward Ratcliffe, a foolish doctor of physic, which proved but a lean argument, and though it were larded with pretty shows at the beginning and end, and with somewhat too broad speech for such a presence, yet it was still dry.

The second night was a comedy of Clare Hall with the help of two or three good actors from other houses, wherein David Drummond in a hobby-horse and Brackyn, the Recorder of the town, under the

---

[18] Thomas Howard, first Earl of Suffolk, Lord Treasurer.

name of Ignoramus, a common lawyer, bare great parts. The thing was full of mirth and variety, with many excellent actors (among whom the Lord Compton's son, though least, yet was not worst), but more than half marred with extreme length.

The third night was an English comedy called *Albumazar* of Trinity College's action and invention, but there was no great matter in it more than one good clown's part.

The last night was a Latin pastoral of the same houses, excellently written and as well acted, which gave great contentment as well to the King as to all the rest.

Now this being the state of their plays, their acts and disputations fell out much after the same manner, for the Divinity act was performed reasonably well but not answerable to expectation, the Law and Physic acts stark naught, but the Philosophy act made amends and indeed was very excellent, insomuch that the same day the Bishop of Ely sent the moderator, the answerer, the varier or prevaricator, and one of the repliers that were all of his house, twenty angels apiece. . . . The King was exceeding pleased many times, both at the plays and disputations, for I had the hap to be for the most time within hearing, and often at his heels, he would express as much. . . . Though I endured a great deal of penance by the way for this little pleasure, I would not have missed it, for that I see thereby the partiality of both sides, the Cambridge men pleasing and applauding themselves in all, and the Oxford men as fast condemning and detracting all that was done; wherein yet I commend Corbet's[19] modesty whiles he was there, who being seriously dealt withal by some friends to say what he thought, answered that he had left his malice and judgment at home, and came thither only to commend. . . .

Almost all the courtiers went forth Masters of Art at the King's being there, but few or no Doctors saving Young, which was done by a mandate, being son to Sir Peter, the King's schoolmaster. The Vice-Chancellor and University were exceeding strict in that point and refused many importunities of great men . . . ; neither the King's entreaty for John Donne[20] would prevail, yet they are threatened with a mandate which if it come it is like they will obey, but they are resolved to give him such a blow withal that he were better be

---

[19] Richard Corbet, proctor of Christ Church, Oxford.
[20] John Donne had been ordained January 23, 1615.

without it. Indeed the Bishop of Chichester, Vice-Chancellor, hath been very stiff and carried himself very peremptory that way, wherein he is not much to be blamed, being a matter of more consequence than at first was imagined. He did his part every way, as well in moderating the Divinity act as in taking the great pains in all other things and keeping exceeding great cheer.

[226] March 30, 1615: John Donne and one Cheke went out Doctors at Cambridge with much ado after our coming away, by the King's express mandate, though the Vice-Chancellor and some other of the heads called them openly *filios noctis et tenebriones*,[21] that sought thus to come in at the window when there was a fair gate open. But the worst is that Donne had gotten a reversion of the Deanery of Canterbury, if such grants could be lawful, whereby he hath purchased himself a great deal of envy, that a man of his sort should seek *per saltem*[22] to intercept such a place from so many more worthy and ancient divines.

[227] April 4, 1615: Truly I doubt you have leaned too long upon a broken staff [23] that cannot, or will not, or (I am sure) hitherto hath not given support to any that relied upon it; and in respect thereof neglected those that in all occasions would have stood more firmly to you. Yet I make no question but all things shall succeed *à souhait*[24] for the main matter, though peradventure the manner may not be altogether as you wish.

[228] April 6, 1615, to Alice Carleton in Venice: I went last day to visit the Lady Cope and found her busy in removing household, for she hath sold her house in the Strand to one Walter, a lawyer (the Prince's attorney), and hath taken a smaller house in Drury Lane of

---

[21] Shadows and sons of night.
[22] At a leap.
[23] I.e., on Somerset.
[24] As is wished.

£30 a year. I cannot but pity her now a little, that after the loss of her husband must leave her daughter and her children, that never parted yet since they came together, leave her fair houses and her port, and betake herself to a poor cottage. But they that love to carry a greater show than their substance will bear must either pull down their sails or sink if foul weather come; wherein I commend her course and good mind that can so soon settle herself to it without grudging or repining.

[231] June 15, 1615: Master Camden hath set out *Annales*[25] from the beginning of Queen Elizabeth's reign till the end of 'eighty-eight. He sent me one of them yesterday, which I would you had with a wish, for I presume they are as well and indifferently[26] written as time will afford, and that they will be well received abroad.

[232] June 29, 1615: We have . . . lost Sir Rowland Lytton, who left this world on Friday last; but the greatest part of that grief was passed over long since.

[233] July 13, 1615: Touching the order given for the address of your packets, it was but from Master Packer,[27] for from the Lord himself you never had any matter of moment. And you might perceive by the dispatches and instructions who had the managing of business, and consequently, both in reason and right of his place, was to receive the answers, unless it were in some privy particulars or reserved cases. . . . And I am assured that Sir H. Wotton and Sir Thomas Edmondes make their addresses to him, for Sir Thomas Edmondes told me himself, before his going hence, that he was so

---

[25] William Camden's *Annales rerum Anglicarum et Hibernicarum regnante Elizabetha*, 1615.

[26] Impartially.

[27] Secretary to the Earl of Somerset; Carleton had been sending his dispatches to Somerset instead of to Winwood.

careful in that point that he asked his Majesty to whom he should send his dispatches, who answered, "To whom but the Secretary?" . . . The truth is he takes it worse from you than from another, for the least unkindness from a friend is commonly taken more to heart than the malice or injury of an enemy . . . ; but howsoever this may be a flaw for the time, yet it will be no such crack but that it will solder together again without any scar.

[234] July 20, 1615: I acquainted Master Secretary with your desire of taking the Spa in your way hitherward, but as far as I can gather by him there is no hope of it this year, seeing Sir Henry Wotton[28] must first come to you before you can come away. . . . I fear it will be toward Michaelmas before you remove. . . .

He wins upon the world daily as well in Court as abroad by his upright and sincere carriage (whereof he makes profession), and is very like to wear out all disadvantages that he came in withal, and to overcome the malice and malignity of his emulators.

[235] August 24, 1615: I come now from reading your letter of the 4th of this present, whereby I understand your safe return to Venice, having since Sunday last heard of your departure from Turin by a letter of Master Secretary's to his Lady at Ditton, whither I was invited by three or four messages (besides that I was engaged by promise), and stayed there a whole week, which, though I were never so welcome, was a penance to me, being grown so in love with home (or that which I make account of as home) that I love no straggling journeys abroad, because travelling by horse (for want of use) is become wearisome to me; so that for these three whole years I have not been at any of my western friends' nor old haunts as Ascott, Bockmer, Swallowfield, and the rest. Now so soon as I have closed this letter, I am for Ware Park, whence I have been absent these ten days, and there to take up my lodging (for aught I know) till the term.

---

[28] Who replaced Carleton, for his second tour as Ambassador to Venice.

[236] September 15, 1615: Sir Henry Fanshawe hath been busied all this week and the last in taking of musters. Yesterday your cousin Lytton trained his company at Hitchin. I had much ado to dissuade him from putting off his captainship, which would have been taken for a scorn, there being a dryness already twixt him and the Earl of Salisbury, their Lord Lieutenant.

[237] March 27, 1616, to Carleton (installed at last as Ambassador in The Hague): Since you went we have lost Sir Henry Fanshawe, who, being at dinner the 9th of this present at the Assizes at Hertford, was suddenly stricken with a dead palsy that took him away in 40 hours. He is much lamented and so generally well spoken of as I have not known any man, which is no small comfort to them that loved him, as it was likewise a great happiness to himself that his memory continued till the very end, and his speech did not quite fail till some three or four hours before his departure. He hath left all in good order and had made his will above two years agone.

But the reversion of his office[29] was in great hazard, by reason his son, lacking almost two years of 21, was said to be unfit, or rather uncapable, to execute it. But by Master Secretary's good means, it is now settled in Sir Christopher Hatton and Sir Arthur Harris for his use till he come of age . . . which will be a great stay and settling to the whole state and relief of those children whose portions depended principally upon it. . . . Master Secretary went so frankly and roundly through it that, though he get little or nothing else (or at most but a trifle), yet he hath gotten a general applause and approbation of a good work and of a sound and sure friend. . . .

I have had likewise another near loss, God having taken away my brother George this last week who, lingering ever since Christmas of a consumption, *placide obdormivit in Domino*.[30] Among other discommodities of old age and long life this is not the least, to lose our best friends. . . .

And some three or four days since died Sir Rafe Coningsby, upon whom and Sir Henry Fanshawe rested the greatest part of the business of Hertfordshire, which country in less than three quarters of a year

---

[29] He had been Remembrancer of the Exchequer, following his father.
[30] Fell asleep peacefully in God.

is left naked of three good patriots and deputy-lieutenants, Sir Rowland Lytton and these two last named.

[239] April 20, 1616: [Lady Fanshawe's] younger daughter Mary was married the 9th of this present to one Master Newce of Haddam in Hertfordshire, the only child of his parents, and on Monday last I was entreated (for want of better company) to convoy the bride home and reconduct Mistress Alice Fanshawe and Bessie Hatton that went to accompany her. We found all things answerable to promise and beyond expectation, so that there is no doubt but she is well bestowed and like to prove a happy match.

Whiles I was there I made a step over to Gilston[31] (being but three miles distant) where I found all well and glad to hear you were all so safely arrived and well settled. . . .

Your brother Williams went home this day, though it be term, to solemnize his annual wedding feast of I cannot tell how many years. God send them to hold many more together.

[240] April 30, 1616: The Lord Roos[32] is appointed to go Extraordinary Ambassador into Spain, which honor he and his new father-in-law take so to heart that they make profession to perform it very honorably and to spare no expense; and though they should stretch themselves very far, yet it is thought they will come much short of the Lord Hay who provides for France.

[241] May 18, 1616: Touching the letters you left behind, I heard nothing of it till five or six days after [Winwood] came to town; and then he brake with me and said you had a strange conceit of him, and that if he were such a man as you described him, he were not worthy to be esteemed by any man, much less of his friends, of whom

---

[31] To the new home of Alexander Williams and his wife, Carleton's sister Elizabeth.

[32] William Cecil, Lord Roos, grandson of the second Lord Burghley, had just married Anne Lake, daughter of the ambitious Sir Thomas.

he had always studied to deserve well. I told him it must needs be that passion transported him, for otherwise I knew you so well, and to be of so sound affection and judgment, that you could not commit such an error. Perhaps you might represent unto him the speeches of other men, or the opinion of some malignant persons, which was a friendly part in you to perform, and proceeded of much care and confidence. He alleged diverse passages after the worst construction that could be made, but would not show me the letter, which I did somewhat mannerly crave.

In the end he asked me if you had not made me privy to it. I told him, only thus far: that at parting you said you had written somewhat to him which you wished might be as well taken as it was meant. But one thing I perceived wrought much upon him, that he doubted that you had communicated it to others and given copies of it, which I did so stiffly withstand, and withal gave him so many reasons and arguments to the contrary, besides taking it on my conscience (as I assured him I might), that I wiped away that suspicion clean. . . . And I do verily and assuredly believe he is come home to himself again and never thinks more of it. But by this I perceive it is a tickle point for one to deal by way of advice with a man well conceited of himself and of his own sufficiency, be it in what manner it will.

[243] June 8 ,1616: The Lord Coke of late is fallen (I know not how) into disfavor, so far forth that the King hath been very bitter to him, both in private and public; as upon Thursday last, when all the Judges were called before the King at Whitehall to give a reason of their proceeding in the Exchequer Chamber to argue a case of commendams contrary to his commandment by express message,[33] and sending a letter subscribed by them all, not so respectively and reverently written as might become them, they all stood upon the very words and terms of law and statutes and upon the strictness of their oath, but the heaviest burden lighted on him. Wherein he behaved and

---

[33] King James had given Bishop Neile a benefice to hold *in commendam,* Neile receiving the revenues while appointing a deputy to perform the duties. Two subjects had claimed that this benefice was theirs to grant, and the Court was daringly arguing the King's right, while refusing to allow the King to interfere.

carried himself so well and confidently that the matter goes on, and they argue it again this day, contrary to the expectation and hope of all the Bishops.

But the worst is that the Lord Chancellor, the Attorney, and Solicitor[34] prosecute him implacably . . . and withal the whole course of his life is like to be ripped up and looked into, which if it be severely followed, many men fear it may be his utter overthrow.

[244] June 22, 1616: Sir Francis Bacon was sworn of the Council,[35] and in election, by every man's account, to be presently Lord Keeper; but that rumor is since reasonably cooled, and it is said he must tarry the time till he may be Lord Chancellor, for (as a Lady told the King) it is to be doubted he will never be a good keeper. . . .

The Lord Coke hath had much ado to bear of the storm. . . . His Lady hath stood him in great stead both in soliciting for him in private and pleading for him at the Council table, wherein she hath done herself a great deal of honor, but specially in refusing to sever her state or cause from his (as she was moved to do), but resolving and publishing that she would run the same fortune with him.

Our good friend stood to him as long as there was any hope, but when the King was so incensed that there was no more good to be done, was fain to retire and leave him to himself sink or swim. This is thought not to be the least motive of his safety, that it was told the King that he could not do him a greater honor than to take him down now; for whereas he was nothing well-beloved before, if he should suffer in this cause, he would be accounted the martyr of the Commonwealth.

[245] July 6, 1616: The Lord Hay is upon parting, having lingered thus long in hope to be made of the Garter,[36] the success whereof

---

[34] Lord Ellesmere, Sir Francis Bacon, and Sir Henry Yelverton respectively.

[35] He was fifty-six, had hoped for a Councillorship since the 1580's.

[36] The extravagant Master of the Wardrobe, on his way to Paris as Ambassador Extraordinary, hoped in vain for Somerset's place among the Knights of the Garter.

cannot be held now in suspense beyond this day. He goes with great pomp, but they say is like to be shrewdly disappointed; for, having made twenty special suits of apparel for so many days' abode (besides his travelling robes), news is very lately come that the French have newly changed or altered their fashion, whereby he must needs be out of countenance if he be not set out after the last edition. . . .

On Sunday last the Lord Coke (by the King's express order, delivered by Secretary Winwood) was sequestered from the Council table, from riding his circuit, which is supplied by Sir Randall Crew, and willed to review and correct his Reports, as many ways faulty and full of novelties in points of law. This was the sum of the censure for his corrupt dealing with Sir Robert Rich and Sir Christopher Hatton in the extent of their lands and installment of the debt due to the King, and for words spoken touching the premunire[37] the last day of Easter term, and for his insolent behavior when he and the judges were before the King at Whitehall.

Some that wish him well fear the matter will not end here, for he is willful and will take no counsel, but seeking to make good his first errors (which in truth were foul) runs into worse, and entangles himself every day more and more, and gives his enemies such advantage to work upon the King's indignation towards him that he is in great danger.

The world discourses diversely how he should run so far into the King's displeasure, and will not take these alleged causes for sound payment, but stick not to say that he was too too busy in the late business[38] and dived farther into secrets than there was need and so perhaps might see *nudam sine veste Dianam*.[39] Howsoever it be, he is not well advised that he doth not *cedere tempori*[40] and carry himself more dutifully and submissly to his Majesty. . . . His Lady hath likewise carried herself very indiscreetly of late towards the Queen, whereby she hath lost her favor and is forbidden her Court, as also the King's. The story were too long to tell, but it was about braving and uncivil words to the Lady Compton, Sir George Villiers' mother.

---

[37] Premunire: to forbid the right of appeal from one court to a higher one; in this case from King's Bench to Chancery, but originally to prevent appeal from English courts to Rome.

[38] The trial of the Somersets for the murder of Sir Thomas Overbury.

[39] Diana undressed, i.e. Frances, Countess of Somerset, exposed.

[40] Yield for the time.

[246] July 20, 1616: The King came hither . . . the 9th of this month, and within an hour after his arrival Sir John Holles was created Baron of Houghton and Sir John Roper Baron of Teynham —or Ten M's,[41] as Ned Wymark terms it, being the sum they were rated at. This money was presently delivered to the Lord Hay, for that he could not move till this weight set his wheels going. / . . . Our good friend was promised and made full account to have had Sir John Holles for his prize, but the present necessity would not permit it.

[249] October 12, 1616: I saw not Master Secretary since the beginning of the progress till yesternight that he came from Royston. . . . In truth, I have not found him in so good mood and so kind a mind toward you many a day, which I was very glad of and do verily think you may safely build upon the foundation of your old friendship, howsoever he be sometime harsh in words and fashion to those he loves best. But he continues still the same man, and loseth nothing of the good opinion of those that know him.

[250] October 26, 1616: We are now at as low an ebb for matter of news as we were this time twelvemonth in our full tides, he being now become the patient, and as it were the only subject of discourse, that was then the principal agent and *primus motor* in all those business:[42] I mean the Lord Coke, who hath been called twice or thrice this term before the Lord Chancellor and the King's learned Council to give a reason of diverse things delivered in his reports. The objections at first were eight and twenty, which either were so weak in themselves or so well answered that they are now reduced to five, wherein they are not so sufficiently satisfied, but have referred his answers over to the King.

It is not the least part of his humiliation to be convented in these points before such judges as Sergeant Crew, Sergeant Montagu, and Sergeant Finch, the Attorney, and Solicitor, whereof the greater part

---

[41] £ 10,000 was the price paid for these titles.

[42] Sir Edward Coke, as Lord Chief Justice, had assembled the case against the Somersets, and had conducted the six trials that preceded theirs.

(excepting the Solicitor) are held no great men of law; and withal to find so coarse usage as not to be once offered to sit down. . . . The Attorney is thought to be come about, as well for that he ever used him with more respect than the rest, as for diverse speeches he gives out in his favor, as that a man of his learning and parts is not every day to be found, nor so soon made as marred. . . .

If you can spare your Gazettes when you have done with them they should be welcome, for I am disappointed of those I was wont to have by the means of Ned Blount[43] from Fishborn and Browne. If you would have them back at any time, they should come readily; otherwise I would lay them up safe for you by themselves.

[251] November 9, 1616: Your brother Carleton . . . hath been here now a whole week and thinks every day ten till he may get out of town. The cause of his stay is to attend for his son,[44] who like a good husband got himself out of the way and plays least in sight whiles our gallants flaunt it out in their greatest bravery at the Prince's creation, which was performed on Monday at Whitehall with all solemnity, within doors, for ˙ the sharpness of the weather and the Prince's crasiness did not permit any public show. I have not the list of the 24 Knights of the Bath that were made at this time, but it may suffice that they were all of noble houses, and the Lords Maltravers, Percy, and Wriothesley were the ringleaders, and young Seymour that married Arabella did *cladere agmen*[45] and was the last. Tom Carew[46] and Phil Lytton, as I hear, were squires of high degree for cost and bravery, the one to the Lord Beauchamp, the other to his cousin Rowland St. John. There is little else to be said touching this troop but that it was generally observed that the least became themselves best.

[252] November 14, 1616: The Lord Coke is now quite off the hooks, and order given to send him a supersedeas from executing his

---

[43] The Stationer by St. Paul's Churchyard.

[44] I.e., to attend the creation of Prince Charles as Prince of Wales, in place of John Carleton, Equerry to King James.

[45] Lose the crowd.

[46] The poet Thomas Carew, who had been at The Hague with Carleton.

place. The common speech is that four P's have overthrown and put him down, that is Pride, Prohibitions, Premunire and Prerogative. . . .

The Sheriffs were pricked on Sunday. Those that I remember are Master Paulet for Somersetshire, Sir Thomas Temple for Buckingham, Sir Thomas Spenser for Oxford, one Beswick for Kent, Thomas Lucas for Essex, Master Newce (whose son married Moll Fanshawe) for Hertford, and one Standen, a widower (a near neighbor of Sam Backhouse and shall marry his youngest daughter) for Berkshire. It is become a matter of great canvass and suit to avoid the place, and your brother Harrison was in bodily fear it would light upon him.

[253] November 23, 1616: The Lord Coke, after so long suspense, is at last displaced, and Sir Henry Montagu sworn in his place upon Monday, who went the next day with great pomp to the Hall, accompanied with some Earls, Lords, and others of great quality to the number of fifty horse, besides the whole fry of the Middle Temple and swarms of other lawyers and officers.

The Lord Chancellor, though he were crasie and had not come at Westminster five or six days before nor since, yet made shift to give him his oath, and withal many admonitions how to carry himself in the place, wherein he glanced (not as they say obscurely but in plain terms) at his predecessor for many errors and vanities, but specially for his ambitious popularity. . . .

If Sir Edward Coke could bear this misfortune constantly, it were no great disgrace to him, for he goes away with a general applause and good opinion; and the King himself, when he told his resolution at the Council table to remove him, yet gave him this testimony, that he thought him no way corrupt but a good justicer, with so many other good words as if he meant to hang him with a silken halter. Hitherto he bears himself well, but specially towards his Lady, without any complaint of her demeanor towards him, though her own friends are grieved at it. And her father sent to him to know all the truth and to show how much he disallowed her courses, having divided herself from him and disfurnished his house in Holborn and at Stoke of whatsoever was in them, and carried all the movables and plate she could come by God knows whither, and retiring herself into obscure places both in town and country.

He gave a good answer likewise to the new Chief Justice who sending to him to buy his collar of SS, he said he would not part with it but leave it to his posterity, that they might one day know they had a Chief Justice to their ancestor.

[254] December 7, 1616: The King's and Queen's absence, together with the ending of the term, hath made this town as barren of news as it is of good company. Most of the Council are likewise dispersed, the Lord Treasurer gone to Audley End, as much to avoid the importunate clamors for money as for recreation.

The Lord Coke continues at his daughter Sadler's and hath been twice within these two weeks at Newmarket. The first time he had good access and kissed the King's hand. What success he had this second time I cannot yet learn, for the news is as new as most certain and true.

The motive of his first journey was the report of some of his friends to the King how much he was dismayed and dejected; whereupon the King answered that if he came to him, he should find that he ought him no further displeasure, and indeed had given order before to dash certain suits commenced in the Star Chamber against him. And Master Attorney committed two of his own men to the Fleet for presuming to give order for process against him in his name or as by his direction.

His friends are in hope that he shall very shortly be restored to the Council table. His Lady hath somewhat changed her copy, and, finding how harshly her former carriage sounded as well with friends as foes, hath reclaimed herself and a little mollified the matter, as if she had no such meaning as was conceived; though her trunks by mischance were stayed, and so her course interrupted. But yet she affords him no manner of comfort either by her counsel or company.

[255] December 21, 1616: The Lord Coke . . . is as jocund and jovial as ever he was. It is generally said he shall shortly be made a Baron, but some interpret this kindness to be but for the compassing

of a match for the Lord Villiers' brother with one of his daughters. . . .

Sir Thomas Edmondes came to town on Thursday, but hath not taken his solemn or last leave at Paris, thinking it better to pause a while and see what contentment he shall find here, and withal to let his entertainment[47] run on till he see cause to leave it.

[256] January 4, 1617: I moved Master Secretary about your money, and he remembered well what you had written to him touching that point, but says there can no more be done than hath been, to put both the Lord Treasurer and the King in mind of it; but all is one, for it is *surdo canere*[48] to either, and as the case stands it is *commune malum*[49] which God knows how or when to remove, being past the wit of man. The best is you have had some small refreshing of £400 of late, which must keep life and soul together till the world mend.

Sir Thomas Edmondes was made Comptroller, and had the white staff delivered him the first hour he saw the King, and doth execute the place with courage and authority enough, but they say he doth somewhat too much flourish and fence with his staves, whereof he hath broken two already—not at tilt, but stickling at the plays this Christmas. I wish him all honor and good success, and specially a fair, young, rich widow lately fallen, Sir Francis Anderson's Lady, if he have a mind to her, and which is more, *rebus sic stantibus*,[50] niece to the Lord Villiers by his sister, Sir John Butler's Lady.

[257] January 18, 1617: I forgot in my last to give you notice that there was a meaning before the end of Christmas to make the Lord Villiers an Earl . . . which fell out the next day to be performed with all usual solemnity, and he bears the name of Buckingham. On Twelfth Night was a masque wherein the new-made Earl and the Earl of Montgomery danced with the Queen.

---

[47] I.e., his allowance.
[48] To preach to the deaf.
[49] A universal evil.
[50] Things standing as they do.

[258] February 8, 1617: The Earl of Buckingham was [on Sunday last] sworn of the Council, being they say the youngest that hath been seen sit at that board. He is become somewhat crasie of late and takes much physic. His brother Christopher is come to be of the Bedchamber, but whether in quality of a gentleman or groom I cannot yet learn. I cannot but commend that Lord's good disposition in doing good to his kindred and friends, though some rhyming companions do not forbear to tax him for it, as one by way of a prognostication says,

> Above in the skies shall Gemini rise,
> And Twins the Court shall pester:
> George shall call up his brother Jack
> And Jack his brother Kester. . . .

I am sorry to hear you have such animosity in those parts about such nice questions.[51] . . . I understood much of that business by a book or oration of Grotius that Master Secretary gave me before Christmas. I congratulate the warming of your house by so great and worthy guests, but I was afraid when I read it that their healths would put you to the trial and hazard of your own; and I am of the opinion of the Scottish man that preached before the King the same week I received your letter, that it is *una salus sanis nullam potare salutem.*[52]

[259] February 22, 1617: The French Ambassador and his company were feasted at Whitehall on Sunday, and yesterday at Theobalds, and last night had a great supper at the Lord Mayor's. . . . The Duke of Lennox feasted him before the King, and this night he is solemnly invited by the Lord Hay to the Wardrobe to a supper and a masque, where the Countess of Bedford is to be Lady and Mistress of the feast, as she is of the managing of his love to the Earl of Northumberland's younger daughter, with whom he is far engaged in affection. . . . But (*pour retourner à nos moutons*[53]) this feasting begins to

---

[51] Carleton had to support the Calvinist Prince of Orange against the Arminian Prime Minister without losing face for the (Arminian) position of King James that the church should be under state patronage. At the same time, James ferociously defended the Calvinist theology of predestination against Arminian teachings about free will.

[52] One safeguard to the healthy is to drink no health.

[53] To get back to our sheep.

grow to an excessive rate, the very provision of cates[54] for this supper arising to more than £600, wherein we are too apish to imitate the French monkeys in such monstrous waste.

[261] March 15, 1617: I went to Gilston on Monday, and the next day we christened your Godson Dudley Williams, and so returned on Wednesday. Sir John Bennet a good while made show to go himself,[55] then appointed his son; but, I know not what mischance coming in the way, Master Brent was delegated to the business, who (together with your sister Mistress Alice Carleton) was my assistant, and all was well and orderly performed. Sir John sent a gilt cup of some five pound value. I presented in your name a pair of silver candlesticks, having some inkling that they would be most welcome, that came to about nine pound fifteen shillings, and I received more of Sherburn[56] two angels for the midwife and nurse, and half an angel for the keeper. Master Brent's commission stretched but to five shillings apiece, and fain he would have been more bountiful, but durst not exceed. . . .

The Lord Coke is left in the suds,[57] but sure it is God's doing according to the old saying, *Perdere quos vult Jupiter prius dementat.*[58] For if he had had the grace to have taken hold of the match offered by Sir John Villiers, it is assuredly thought that before this day he had been Lord Chancellor; but standing upon terms to give but 10,000 marks[59] with his daughter, when £10,000 was demanded, and sticking at £1000 during his life (together with some idle words that he would not buy the King's favor too dear, being so uncertain and variable), he hath let slip the occasion and brought himself in danger (besides the disgrace) of paying double that sum, if he be convicted in the Star Chamber of somewhat that is thought will be proved against him.

---

[54] Sweets, delicacies.

[55] He was preparing to go to Brussels to demand punishment of Scoppius, the author of *Corona Regia,* an attack on King James.

[56] Edward Sherburn, temporarily employed by Carleton to deal with his affairs in England.

[57] In difficulties.

[58] Those whom Jupiter would destroy, he first makes mad.

[59] A mark equalled three-quarters of a pound.

[**263**] April 5, 1617: Sir John Bennet set forth yesterday toward Margate. . . . On Sunday Sir John Bennet invited the Lord Hay, Master Comptroller, and Master Secretary to a poor, pitiful supper, if all were as Sir Thomas Edmondes related it to me the last night at Master Secretary's, and as John West confirmed it, who poor man was extreme sorry to see him invite such friends to shame himself, and to make show what a hand his wife hath over him. The Lady Winwood was solemnly invited but had no stomach to go.

[**264**] April 19, 1617: Your brother Carleton . . . would fain tempt me to a journey to the Spa with him, being lately overtaken with an infirmity which he suspects to be the stone, but . . . I should be twice advised before I adventured on that cure at this age, for I do verily think it overthrew Sir Rowland Lytton, for he did even sensibly decay presently upon his return thence, both in body and mind. It may prove well with younger folks that have stronger stomachs and a firm constitution, but I have no belief in it for elder people. But it may be a good errand for him, as well for his health as to visit you in his return.

His son is not gone with the King[60] as he was borne in hand he should, which in mine opinion falls out never the worse for him, seeing that by staying he makes at least a saving bargain.

[**265**] May 10, 1617: We came to town after the old manner the day before term, and the rather to see the new Lord Keeper[61] ride in pomp to Westminster as he did the next day, accompanied by most of the Council and nobility about this town, with other gallants to the number of more than 200 horse, besides the Judges and Inns of Court. There was a great deal more bravery and better show of horse than was expected in the King's absence, but both Queen and Prince sent all their followers, and his other friends did their best to honor him. . . . The greatest part of his train dined with him that day, which cost him the setting on, if it be as is generally reported that the charge of that dinner came to £700; wherein he followed not his pattern he

---

[60] To Scotland.
[61] Sir Francis Bacon.

seemed so much to approve. For, dining the week before with the rest of the Council at Secretary Winwood's, besides all other good words and commendations of that entertainment, both he and the Earl of Worcester (whose turns came to feast next) sent to entreat to have the bill of cates, and to have the same cooks. But sure for aught I can learn since I came, the expense of that dinner was in no sort proportionable to that sum. . . .

Indeed I have not been much in my wonted walks, but by reason Master Secretary is at so good leisure I am most there. On Wednesday night he made a feast to Master Comptroller for his farewell,[62] which held us till after midnight and had no guests but those he named. I have not seen a finer supper for so little company, there being no more but the Lady of Arundel, the Lady Grey of Ruthin, the Lady Windsor, and Lady Wood, his little daughter, Sir Horace Vere, Sir Thomas Tracy, and myself. The next day we went to Highgate; and yesternight late we parted with him, being to take his leave this day of the Queen in his way. She threatened to make him a feast, but he goes in such haste that he cannot tarry for it.

[266] May 24, 1617: Most of the Council keep [at Greenwich] about [the Queen],[63] saving such as have necessary attendance at the term, and those come still on Saturday night and tarry Sunday. The rest are only absent on Star Chamber days, which have been few or none this term, or not past once at most, by reason of the Lord Keeper's indisposition, which hath greatly hindered both that Court and the Chancery, and if it should continue would much disturb the whole course of Westminster Hall and the Council table, where matters of greatest moment are still put off and reserved till he may be present.

His infirmity is given out to be the gout, and the greatest harm or sense he hath of it is in his heel. And sometimes he takes pleasure to flout and play with his disease, which he says hath changed the old covetous course and is become ambitious, for never beggar had the gout but he.

But in truth the general opinion is that he hath so tender con-

---

[62] Sir Thomas Edmondes was going back to Paris on a special mission to mediate between Marie de Médicis and her sons.

[63] The Queen aspired to be Regent while the King was on his progress to Scotland.

stitution both of body and mind that he will hardly be able to undergo the burden of so much business as his place requires, and that if he do not rouse and force himself beyond his natural inclination, both private subjects and the commonwealth will suffer much.

[**270**] July 19, 1617: Master Tobie Matthew is come,[64] and was last night with Master Secretary, who called me out of the garden into his gallery to salute him. He used him kindly, and dealt earnestly with him to take the oath of allegiance; but as far as I could perceive it was lost labor, though he told me that without doing it he is verily of opinion that the King will not endure him long here. But perhaps he presumes upon the Lord Keeper's favor, which indeed is very great now at first, if it continue, for he lodgeth him in York House and carries him the next week along with him to his house at Gorhambury near St. Albans. . . .

These eight or ten days here have been great stirs twixt the Lord Coke and his Lady about conveying away the younger daughter, which she will noways consent should match with Sir John Villiers as the Lord Coke had agreed, with £20,000 ready portion, 2000 marks yearly maintenance during his life, and £2000 land after his decease. If he had offered these conditions when time was and taken occasion by the forehead when she presented herself, they might have stood him in great stead, whereas now perhaps he doth but catch at the bald side.

The daughter was first carried to the Lady Withipole's, from thence privily to a house of the Lord of Argyll's by Hampton Court, whence her father with a warrant from Master Secretary fetched her, but indeed went further than his warrant and brake open diverse doors before he got her. His Lady was at his heels, and if her coach had not tired in the pursuit after him, there was like to be strange tragedies.

---

[64] Tobie Matthew, an Oxford contemporary and lifelong friend of Carleton, was the son of a Puritan bishop, later Archbishop of York. In trouble with his father as early as 1597 for his extravagance and dissipation, he finally became financially independent in 1604 on a grant from the Crown. Upon receiving the grant he retreated into Italy. Unfortunately, his conversion to Catholicism became public knowledge soon after the discovery of the Gunpowder Plot. Now, at last, he returned to England, to charm King James and be knighted by him.

He delivered his daughter to the Lady Compton, Sir John's mother, but the next day Edmunds, Clerk of the Council, was sent with a warrant to have the custody of her at his own house. The next day, being all convented before the Council, she was sequestered to Master Attorney; and yesterday upon a palliated agreement twixt Sir Ed. Coke and his Lady, she was sent home to Hatton House, with order that the Lady Compton and her son should have access to win her and wear her. It were a long story to tell all the passages of this business, which hath furnished Paul's and this town very plentifully for a whole week.

The Lord Coke was in great danger to be committed for disobeying the Council's order, for abusing his warrant, and for the violence used in breaking open the doors, to all which he gave reasonable answers, and for the violence will justify it by law, though order be given to prefer a bill against him in the Star Chamber. He and his friends complain of hard measure from some of the greatest at that board, and that he was too much trampled upon with ill language.

And our friend passed not scot-free for the warrant, which the greatest there said was subject to a premunire, and withal told the Lady Compton that they wished well to her and her sons, and would be ready to serve the Earl of Buckingham with all true affection, whereas others did it out of faction and ambition; which words glancing directly at our good friend, he was driven to make his apology and to show how it was put upon him from time to time by the Queen and the other parties, and for conclusion showed a letter of approbation of all his courses from the King, making the whole table judge what faction or ambition appeared in this carriage, *ad quod non fuit responsum.*[65] And indeed hitherto I do not see in all these oppositions but that he maintains his ground, and goes away with general applause. But *hinc illae lachrimae,*[66] that they doubt the Lord Coke's rising by this match and his coming again among them, and therefore would either hinder it or have the thank to contrive it.

But if it be as is said, both mother and daughter are far enough from it, and have another aim at a younger son of the Lord Treasurer.[67]

---

[65] To which there was no reply.

[66] But here is the reason for regrets.

[67] Perhaps Sir Robert Howard, whose child the unhappy Frances Coke bore in 1625; which the fond, inadequate John Villiers was willing to claim as his own.

[271] August 9, 1617: I came newly from Ditton, whither Master Secretary carried me and kept me ten or twelve days, though himself made no long stay there at any time but was still going and coming as occasions called him.

They have brought that place to a very good pass, wherein my Lady challengeth the chief part, as well in building a new dovehouse, in paving the court, in bringing a spring or conduit of excellent water, in making of fair and large ponds, in damming or filling up the moat, in planting a great orchard, in making a reasonably spacious garden with delicate arbors and fencing it with as fair a brick wall as I have lightly seen, as also in furnishing the house very sufficiently, though without any great cost or curiosity; and all this (besides other conveniences of offices within doors and of utter courts and out-housing abroad) in so short time that the speedy dispatch deserves as much commendation as the contriving or cost. . . .

Our good friend means not to make toward the Court till it come to Woodstock, wherein I know not whether he will do well or no, but he is so confident in all his courses that there is no advising or arguing to the contrary. . . .

Soon after my last to you there came new letters out of Scotland to approve all his dealings in the Lord Coke's business, which made the most forward on the other side to pull in their horns. And order was taken that his daughter should be delivered him, and disposed of as he should think fit, whereupon he sent her to Kingston to his son's, Sir Robert Coke, where she yet remains. And her mother having permission to resort unto her but not to lie in the house, she hired a lodging in the town and kept her such company all day that nobody else could have access, whereupon her coming is moderated, and diverse of her instruments in conveying her away are called in question and committed.

Whereupon finding herself forsaken of her friends, who dare not show themselves too far in the business, and seeing her struggles in vain, she begins to come about; and upon a letter to her from my Lord of Buckingham, hath returned answer, as I hear, that if this course had been taken with her at first, things might have proceeded better, and upon some conditions can be content to double the portion her husband hath offered, and so make up the match and give it her blessing.

The Lady Compton and her son have been at Kingston these two or three days, which makes the world think they grow to conclusion.

But it seems the Lady Hatton would have all the honor and thanks, and so defeat her husband's purposes, towards whom of late she has carried herself very strangely, and indeed neither like a wife nor a wise woman.

The Lord Keeper[68] hath been this fortnight at Gorhambury, and means to continue there a fortnight or three weeks longer. The world begins already to complain of some encroaching courses and say if things should thus proceed and hold on, that one should have as it were all men's estates *in scrinio pectoris*.[69] The distastes continue still twixt him and the "boistrous Secretary" [70] as he terms him, though some friends have mediated a reconciliation; but at the worst, the world is of opinion that if they should come to justle, both of them are made of as brittle metal the one as the other. . . .

The Lord Roos, pretending a journey into Yorkshire in good equipage with 16 or 20 men and being on his way as far as Huntington and Stilton, there left them till his return from London, whither he feigned to be called back upon some urgent occasion. But there hath been no news of him till Thursday last that an unknown French foot-post brought Master Secretary a letter from him without date of time or place, wherein he complains that the diabolical dealings of the Lady Lake[71] have driven him to absent himself, excusing himself towards him very much for not acquainting him with it, but within 25 days he should hear further from him the reasons of his departure. In the meantime he had sent him therewithal, in a box, security for £4000 he had borrowed of him, and should have been paid the first of this month, which was a grant and conveyance of certain woods, worth £8000 as he says. Howsoever it be, I make no doubt but Master Secretary will make shift to come by his money. The letter was very well and affectionately written, and with a great deal of acknowledgment towards him. This is all we hear of him yet, saving that the fellow said he left him at Calais, and had charge to deliver the letter and box to his own hands. If he chance to come by you, I pray you take no more notice of this than you shall find convenient. . . .

Touching Fabritio's precious advertisement,[72] I know no more than

---

[68] Sir Francis Bacon.

[69] In his private cupboard.

[70] Winwood.

[71] His mother-in-law.

[72] Wolton sent one Tommaso Cerronio, a Jesuit from Milan, to tell a story of conspiracy between France and Spain to murder King James and Prince Charles. The Council was unimpressed.

when I wrote you that I had seen the man, only finding our good friend methought more sparing than usually he is when I inquired of him. I urged a little the more, whereupon he gave me this answer: "I cannot precisely say what it may come to; but as far as I can gather, never trust my judgment if it prove any matter of worth." So that I doubt this *legatus pergre missus* will make good his *mentiendi causa*,[73] as well in that as he doth in his last letters (which I saw yesterday) that the Venetians had lost more than a million and a half in merchandise upon two galleys taken by the Neapolitan fleet. I would scant change states with him, nor with all I know of his name, if I had but as much as there was lacking of that sum!

The Lord Hay thinks long till the King's coming that he may consummate his marriage,[74] for the King hath promised to give the bride. He is wonderful observant and obsequious to her and her mother, and spends most part of his time there, having taken Sir Fra. Darcy's house by Sion, where he makes solemn feasts twice a week at least, with that cost and expense that the Lady of Northumberland dares not so much as once invite him, by reason of his curiosity,[75] though he be commonly in her house from morning till dinner, from after dinner till supper, from after supper till late in the night. It comes well to pass that he begins this course in a year when there is so great plenty of excellent venison, and such store of salmon that the like hath not been seen in the Thames these forty years. . . .

I have not seen Master Matthew since I wrote last but once in Paul's, when we dealt as confidently one with another as need to be, and so will I do whensoever he shall give me occasion. He hath been ever since, I think, at Gorhambury, being so exceedingly favored and respected by that Lord that it is thought *aliquid nimium*,[76] that a man of his place should give countenance to one so affected; and some stick not to say that former private familiarity should give place to public respects. It is likewise noted that he showed himself somewhat too soon upon the Exchange; but these are but peccadilloes and may pass well enough if he have the principal verb[77] so much his friend as he makes account of. . . .

And now I had done, if I could tell you how to thank my Lady for

---

[73] "The Ambassador sent abroad" will make good his "opportunity for lying."
[74] To Lucy Percy, younger daughter of the Earl of Northumberland.
[75] Fastidiousness.
[76] Somewhat too much.
[77] Buckingham.

her fine and bountiful present which hath made me finer than ever I was or ever meant to have been; but seeing it is her pleasure, I will make use of her favor, the rather for that they come in a time when I was even the next day going about the like provision, I mean of that kind though not of that worth. I beseech you let me entreat you to supply and excuse my weakness that way, for you know how awkwardly and untowardly compliments come from me; and if I had the means I should rather show my thankfulness with real deeds than formal words. And I assure you it is the greatest worldly want I find, not to be able in any proportion to requite such friendly kindness.

[273] October 11, 1617: I cannot relate all the passages of the Lady Hatton's business because I was absent, but sure she hath done herself a great deal of wrong in kicking against the prick and by indirect courses to hinder that which lay not in her power. Her daughter was married to Sir John Villiers at Hampton Court on Michaelmas day. The King himself gave the bride, and they were thrice publicly asked in the church. The pretended contract with the Earl of Oxford proved nothing, and since the marriage, letters are come whereby he disavows it. Yet to say my conscience, methinks there needed no such haste, but that they might have tarried for his answer, specially the bridegroom being in no such perfect state of health but that wedlock was rather like to hurt than heal him. But her mother's willfulness and animosity, together with the danger of her continual plottings, made the business go on the faster. . . .

But sure she is in a wrong way now, and so animated towards her husband that it is verily thought she would not care to ruin herself to overthrow him. He is admitted again to the Council table, but his friends cannot yet foresee any further advancement. . . .

The Jesuit that came from Milan[78] is sent away without seeing the King, who gave order that the Lord Archbishop and Master Secretary Winwood should hear what he could say. They dealt with him by all manner of good means, and drew from him as he protested the uttermost of his knowledge, which was not all worth the whistling, being certain strange chimeras and farfetched imaginations of plots and dangers not worth the knowing, much less the relating. Whereupon it

---

[78] Tommaso Cerronio. (See Letter 271, footnote 72.)

was thought good to dispatch him away, the rather for that he grew scandalously debauched with boys and otherwise. He had a hundred pound in gold delivered him, which the searchers at seaside took from him, a thing that should not have been done, but now there is no remedy, neither do they know how or whither to send it after him. And here is the end of that play, to the small honor of the author.[79] . . .

The Queen lately asked the Lord Keeper what occasion the Secretary had given him to oppose himself so violently against him, who answered prettily, "Madam, I can say no more but he is proud and I am proud." But the King, according to his pacifical disposition, hath made all friends, and in the admonition he gave some of them did him this honor, to say, "You may perhaps think that he hath informed these and these things against you, but I assure you in the word of a prince, that neither by word nor writing did he ever suggest aught to any particular man's prejudice, either to me or to Buckingham, as he is here ready to protest before you."

[274] October 18, 1617: Your brother Carleton is not in town, neither do I know when he will be; but if he come not the sooner, I will find means to write to him concerning his son,[80] who I think will be the fittest for you when all is done. And God knows how much such a breeding may be to his advancement and to the comfort of all his friends; for I have little hope of your nephew John, who is grown so negligent and idle that he is generally noted for it, and I hear from good place that when the King reproves any man for ill waiting, he tells him he will prove a Carleton. . . .

Master Sherburn[81] . . . is in great hope to do himself good, and no doubt industry and diligence will prevail much with any man, specially with one that is attended by a sort of loose companions. I inquired of him after Master Matthew, who continues still very intimate with that Lord. I hear he is grown very gay, or rather, gaudy, in his attire, which I should not have suspected of his years and

---

[79] Sir Henry Wotton.

[80] Dudley, who became Carleton's Secretary at The Hague in spite of the fellowship he held at King's College, Cambridge.

[81] Sherburn, formerly manager of Carleton's affairs in London, was now working for Bacon.

judgment; but peradventure it is more noted of him than needs. But that which is worse (and which I must tell you under the rose), he is noted for certain night walks to the Spanish Ambassador;[82] but if it be so, perhaps he presumes upon the forwardness of Sir John Digby's business,[83] who landing at St. Andros about the end of August (the fifth day after his parting from Plymouth), found there great provision for his entertainment. . . . I was present yesternight when letters came thence full fraught with large promises of success. But God knows what is best, and to Him must we leave it.

[275] October 25, 1617: Secretary Winwood came from Whitehall on Wednesday ill at ease, and sending for me I found that he had *lentam febrem*[84] upon him ever since Monday before by his own relation. He made then no reckoning of it, but since it hath increased so fast upon him that yesterday, about noon, he was let blood, which was very bad and foul, and withal it had brought him so low that he fainted diverse times for an hour or two after. My Lady came post from Ditton and found him in those faintings, which so dejected her that I did as much pity her as him. He continued very ill till ten o'clock at night when I came away after we had had prayers; and sending this morning to know how he had rested, word is brought that he had a very ill night and grows weaker. God comfort him and send us better news. . . . The worst I like in him is that he is very talkative, which is an ill sign in a man otherwise so silent, and he found it so himself the first night I was with him. The continual visits and messages of great folks are a great vexation to him, and can hardly be avoided.

[276] October 31, 1617: My fear was not in vain which I conceived of Master Secretary's disease, and I presaged too truly of the success; for after my last writing to you he daily decayed even visibly, so that by Monday in the afternoon he was plainly *deploratus,* though he lived till Tuesday morning toward seven o'clock. He had all the

---

[82] Count Gondomar.
[83] He had gone to Spain to arrange a marriage for Prince Charles.
[84] A slight fever.

help that our physicians could afford, but Mayerne never saw him after he had let him blood, for he went straight to the King. Of all men I have no fancy to him, at leastwise for luck sake, for by that I have observed he is commonly unfortunate in any dangerous disease. But I will not blame him too much for this, seeing it appears upon the opening of the body that he could not possibly last long, having his heart withered almost to nothing, his spleen utterly rotten, one of his kidneys clean gone, the other perished, his liver full of black spots, his lungs not sound, besides diverse other defects, so that it was a wonder how he held out so long and looked so well. But there appeared no signs of any ill measure as was first generally suspected.

Upon Sunday he received a gracious letter from the King to this effect, that he doubted the multiplicity and care of business had cast him down, wherefore he advised him to cast off all cogitations saving such as might best procure his recovery, wherein he should do him the best service that he ever had or could do him. At the same time he had one likewise from the Lord of Buckingham to the same purpose. And seeing it was God's pleasure to call him, he could never go in a better time than when he was in his highest favor with the King, Queen, Prince, and principal favorite, and was generally grown into so good opinion that his sickness, first, and then his death was as much lamented as ever I knew any of his rank, though I will not say but he had some ill-willers that are as glad he is gone as most are sorry.

We buried him privately yesternight at ten o'clock, with as little noise or show as might be. Only his household and some few friends and kinsmen had mourning.

He decayed so suddenly on Monday, after many good signs (by the physicians' account) and so unexpected by himself and us all about him, that there was no time to finish his will whiles he was in perfect memory, but the best is he had set his things in order this last summer (specially the conveyances of his lands) when he was to go into Scotland. . . . He hath left a very good estate.

The Archbishop of Canterbury professes very great affection towards the memory of him, and expresses very much care and kindness towards his Lady and her children. The King hath granted her the wardship of her son, but in what terms I do not yet know, for it is but new done. The Queen wrote earnestly in her behalf, and failed not every day to send to him after she heard he was let blood.

Now all the speech is who shall succeed him. . . . You are not the last nor the least spoken of, but I doubt your absence is your greatest hindrance, unless the Lady Hatton have the grace in this conjuncture to have you in remembrance; for if it be as I hear, it never was in her power to stand you in so much stead. For, the King coming to town yesterday, it was told me that the Earl of Buckingham meant to go himself and fetch her as it were in pomp from Sir William Craven's (where she hath been so long committed) and bring her to the King, who upon a letter of her submission is graciously affected towards her. But another cause is that, seeing her yielding and as it were won to give her allowance to the late marriage, he will give her all the contentment and countenance he can, in hope of the great portion she may bestow upon her, for there is little or nothing more to be looked for from Sir Ed. Coke, who hath redeemed the land he had allotted his daughter for £20,000, so that they have already £30,000 of him paid down.

I would I knew any means how to insinuate this business unto her. If your father Savile or his Lady were in town they might easily do it, and I am persuaded that considering all circumstances it were no hard matter for her to obtain it upon this reconciliation and new league of alliance. And it might concern herself very much, considering that she lays all the fault of her late troubles upon the deceased Secretary. . . .

You may think what a loss I have of so good a friend, now in my latter age when I have most need of comfort; and indeed it was a kind of new life to me to see his kindness increase daily towards me, and that we still grew nearer. But God knows what is best, and I hope by this means and the like would more and more wean me from the world.

IX. Sir Walter Raleigh

LUCK and an incomparable style had raised Sir Walter Raleigh's fortune far above his Devonshire beginnings during nearly twelve years of "warfare in love" with Queen Elizabeth. However, in 1591 he married, secretly, her lady-in-waiting, Elizabeth Throckmorton. Raleigh's luck deserted him then. To have married a lady-in-waiting without the Queen's consent was bad enough; for a favorite of the Queen to have done so was doubly bad. By August, 1592, Raleigh and his Lady were in the Tower.

He had spent the spring of 1592 fitting out an expedition to intercept the Spanish silver fleet and attack Panama, hoping himself to be in full command. In September his ships returned to the West Country ports with the Madre de Dios, richest prize of the privateering war. Raleigh was released to recover the treasure, which was vanishing into the pockets of every sailor who could lay hands on it. Sir Robert Cecil went too. The treasure was mostly recovered, thanks, Cecil says, to the smell of musk that stuck to everything. Raleigh received a tiny portion and complete silence from the Queen, and retired to his country estate.

After three years of rustication, broken only for service in Parliamentary affairs and duties as Warden of the Cornwall Tin Mines, Raleigh set off to Guiana, hoping to find gold up the Orinoco and win back royal favor. In 1596 Raleigh took brilliant part in the capture of Cadiz, and was much blamed for allowing the fleet to return home without waiting to intercept the Spanish treasure fleet. He led the only successful action of the anticlimactic Islands Voyage of the following year, for which Essex's jealous friends wanted to court-martial him. He was readmitted to the Captaincy of the Bodyguard, but never to a more coveted seat on the Council. From 1600, except for a few minor errands, he had to be satisfied to watch out the reign of Elizabeth as Governor of the Island of Jersey.

With the accession of King James, Raleigh's luck became melodramatically bad. Aubrey reports James's chilly salutation: "On my soul, mon, I have heard rawly of thee." Raleigh's equally typical *opening (he had neglected any preliminary flattery) was to present a* Discourse Concerning *a War with Spain, offering to raise 2000 men at his own expense—the exact opposite of James's intentions. Chamberlain gives us the briefest glimpse of Raleigh's circle at this time, and has left no letters covering Raleigh's trial for treason in November, 1603.*

Sentenced to death, but reprieved at the last minute by the King (though not pardoned), Raleigh lived his next thirteen years in two rooms on the second floor of the Bloody Tower. He was allowed the use of a shed for his chemical experiments, and his wife and child lived with him. Prince Henry began to come to him for advice about shipbuilding ("Who but my father would keep such a bird in a cage?"), and Raleigh planned his History of the World *for this teachable young man. The Prince even obtained his father's promise to release Raleigh for Christmas, 1612, but died before the promise could be made good.*

Sir Ralph Winwood was fundamentally as anti-Spanish as Raleigh himself; through his good offices—and a £1500 bribe to the new favorite Villiers's brother—Raleigh was released, unpardoned, in March, 1616. He promised the King he could find gold in Guiana without entrenching on Spanish possessions, and mounted an expedition. Raleigh must have known the impossibility of keeping his promise, and so must James, who promised Gondomar, the Spanish Ambassador, that Raleigh's life was forfeit if Spanish property suffered any damage.

While Raleigh lay off Trinidad weak with fever, his rash twenty-two-year-old son dashed in to attack San Tomé and was killed while the settlement burned. Captain Keymis, who had been faithful to Raleigh from the first voyage to Guiana, committed suicide when reproached for failing to find the gold mines that had to be there. Londoners expected Raleigh to turn pirate and stay abroad, but he played out the denouement of his tragedy in true Elizabethan style.

[9] October 20, 1598: Sir John Gilbert with six or seven sail one and other is going for Guiana, and I hear that Sir Walter Raleigh should be so deeply discontented because he thrives no better, that he is not far from making that way himself.

[**26**] March 5, 1600: Our peace goes but slowly on, and when all is done it is thought it will prove but a cessation, or truce, for seven or ten years at most. Neither do I think any great[1] person shall be employed in the treaty, when Sir Walter Raleigh is like to be second in the commission as himself says in secret. He attends the Ambassador[2] much, by the Queen's appointment, and carries him up and down to see sights and rarities hereabout. He hath had him at Paul's, at Westminster, at Whitehall, and where not? This day he is feasted at the Lord Treasurer's and tomorrow at the Lord Chamberlain's, where methinks it should be somewhat strange to see carouses to the King of Spain's health.

[**57**] December 23, 1602: There is no show of any great doings at Court this Christmas. Sir Walter Raleigh hath carried away the Lord Cobham, the Lord Compton and others to Sherborne, and Sir John Harington means to keep a royal Christmas in Rutlandshire, having the Earls of Rutland and Bedford, Sir John Grey and Sir Harry Cary with their Ladies, the Earl of Pembroke, Sir Robert Sidney, and many more gallants.

[**109**] January 10, 1609: Sir Walter Raleigh's estate is fallen into the King's hands, by reason of a flaw in the conveyance,[3] who hath bestowed it on Sir Robert Carr . . . and though the Lady Raleigh have been an importunate suitor all these holidays in her husband's behalf, yet it is past recall; so that he may say with Job, naked came I into the world and naked shall I go out. But above all, one thing is to be noted, that the error or oversight is said to be so gross that men do merely ascribe it to God's own hand that blinded him and his counsel.

---

[1] Royal.

[2] Ludovic Verreyken. The problem was the continuing one of peace with Spain, which the Dutch at this point opposed.

[3] In 1603 Raleigh had made a writ of trust conveying the land to his eldest son and heirs male with a life interest only for himself. The clerk miscopied the deed, making it illegal. Therefore the land was still Raleigh's own and forfeit for treason.

[116] December 30, 1609: Sir Walter Raleigh hath a ship come from Guiana richly laden they say with gold ore, and Sir Thomas Roe with a ship and pinnace is going that way to seek his fortune.

[147] August 10, 1612: The widow Countess of Rutland died lately and is privately buried in Paul's by her father Sir Philip Sidney and Secretary Walsingham. Sir Walter Raleigh is slandered to have given her cetrain pills that dispatched her.

[153] November 12, 1612: In [Prince Henry's] extremity they tried all manner of conclusions upon him, as letting him blood in the nose, and whatsoever else they could imagine, and at the last cast gave him a quintessence sent by Sir Walter Raleigh[4] (which he says they should have applied sooner) that brought him to some show of sense and opening of his eyes, and (some will needs say) speech, but all failed again presently. Amongst the rest he hath lost his greatest hope, and was grown into special confidence with him, insomuch that he had moved the King diverse times for him, and had lastly a grant that he should be delivered out of the Tower before Christmas.

[217] January 5, 1614: Sir Walter Raleigh's book[5] is called in by the King's commandment, for diverse exceptions, but specially for being too saucy in censuring princes. I hear he takes it much to heart, for he thought he had won his spurs and pleased the King extraordinarily.

[4] Raleigh's "Greal Cordial" was "a compound of pearl, musk, hart's horn (ammonia), bezoar stone (a concretion found in the intestines of ruminants), mint, borage, gentian, mace, aloes, sugar, sassafras, spirits of wine, etc." Queen Anne used it; John Evelyn reports that one of Charles II's first entertainments after his Restoration was to watch it being prepared; the dying William III was given it in 1702.

[5] *The History of the World*. The reception of this volume, which reaches 130 B.C., led Raleigh to destroy his notes for two further volumes. When it was banned by James, three issues of the first edition were snapped up, without Raleigh's name or portrait; two further editions, name restored, were issued in 1617.

[223] February 23, 1614: Sir Walter Raleigh hath been dangerously sick of an apoplexy or some like disease in the head, caused as is thought by his chemical experiments, but they say he is on the mending hand.

[237] March 27, 1616: Sir Walter Raleigh was freed out of the Tower the last week, and goes up and down seeing sights and places built or bettered since his imprisonment. He prepares for a journey to Guiana, whither he pretends to set forward sometime in August, and shall have many adventurers besides £16,000 he makes show to employ of his own. I hear of diverse of good account and experience that offer to go with him, as Sir William St. John that hath some command in the King's ships, Sir James Lancaster, Sir Edward Harwood that hath a company in the Low Countries, and others. The world says that our good friend[6] was a principal means of his delivery, as likewise of the Countess of Shrewsbury.

[252] November 14, 1616: Being last night at Master Secretary's, I understood that Dieston was to be dispatched this day towards you, who must not come empty though I wrote so lately. There supped divers of your good friends, Sir Walter Raleigh, Sir Henry Savile, Sir Maurice Berkeley, Sir . . . Seymour, Sir Harry Neville, Sir Robert Killigrew, with I know not how many Ladies and gentlewomen of that race and alliance. The absence of the Court gives Master Secretary leave and leisure to entertain his friends.

[261] March 15, 1616: The Spanish Ambassador had so practiced, and found so good seconds, that Sir Walter Raleigh's voyage was within these few days in question and in great hazard to be overthrown here at home, when he was now *in procinctu*[7] and in a manner ready to be gone.

---

[6] Secretary Winwood.
[7] Prepared for battle.

[262] March 29, 1617: Sir Walter Raleigh took his leave yesternight of Master Secretary and goes this morning toward Dover where he hopes to find his ship, though his followers are yet in the river and make no great haste after him. He makes away with all the speed he can for fear of a countermand, by reason of some message brought by the Lord Roos,[8] and of Master Vice-Chamberlain's going to Court now his friends be away, and it is observed that the Prince is no friend to the journey, but hindered the Queen from going to see his ship as she had appointed on Wednesday last. God knows there needs no such great working to overthrow the voyage. For aught I can understand, I fear he doth but go (as children are wont to tell their tales) to seek his fortune.

[269] July 5, 1617: Sir Walter Raleigh hath met with a tempest at sea that hath dispersed and scattered his ships, whereof one was driven almost to Bristol. Himself and some others are in several ports of Ireland. He hath seven ships and three pinnaces, the whole adventure of him and his followers being near £37,000, whereof £14,000 for his own account, as I saw under his own hand; God speed him and send him a better voyage than I can hope for.

[274] October 18, 1617: Here is one Captain Bayley, stolen away from Sir Walter Raleigh, who gives out that he is turned pirate but the world hopes he speaks of malice and that there is no such matter.

[283] January 17, 1618: On Sunday, Captain Bayley that came away from Sir Walter Raleigh was from the Council table committed close prisoner to the Gatehouse.

[285] February 7, 1618: Here is one Captain Alley come from Sir Walter Raleigh whom he left in November near the place he went

---

[8] William Cecil, Lord Roos, had just returned with messages from the King of Spain.

for in Guiana. He hath brought diverse letters but no matter of any moment, but that more than a hundred of his company are dead of a calenture,[9] among whom are many gentlemen as Hastings (a brother of the Earl of Huntingdon's), Captain Pigott,[10] Hammond, Whitney, and diverse others that I knew not. He himself [Raleigh] hath been sick and brought so low, that there is doubt how he can recover.

[**297**] August 8, 1618: Sir Walter Raleigh was at Salisbury[11] but had no audience either of King or Council, by reason that he is so sick and weak and withal so broken out all over that it is verily thought to be a kind of leprosy, or else that he hath taken a dram of somewhat to do himself harm. He came to town (they say) yesternight to his old habitation in the Tower, but not to his own lodging which was taken up a good while since by the Count and Countess of Somerset.

[**298**] August 13, 1618: Sir Walter Raleigh went to the Tower on Monday, having attempted the night before to make an escape and get oversea, but he was bewrayed, or in a sort betrayed by Sir Lewis Stukeley (who had the charge of him) and brought back by certain boats that waited for him about Woolwich. Sir Lewis did nourish him in the humor with promise to assist and accompany him, but it was a foul *pas de clerc*[12] for an old cozener to be so cozened and overtaken.

[**301**] October 24, 1618: It went current all this week that Sir Walter Raleigh had the liberty of the Tower, but it grew only upon the discharge of his guardian Sir Thomas Wilson, your old acquaintance. But for aught I hear he is not secure yet, though he have now good means to redeem his demerits if he can speak to the purpose in a

---

[9] Fever.
[10] Raleigh's second-in-command.
[11] He had been arrested upon his return in June from his disastrous expedition to the Orinoco.
[12] Blunder.

cause wherein he was lately examined, about the conveyance of jewels and suchlike matters at the King's first coming, and for which and other abuses in the sale of lands etc. there is a commission come forth, which is thought will shrewdly reflect upon the Earls of Suffolk, Salisbury, and others.

[**302**] October 31, 1618: I remember that in my last letter I said that Sir Walter Raleigh was not secure, but now he is past all peradventure, for upon Thursday morning he was beheaded in the old palace at Westminster twixt the Parliament House and the Church.

On Wednesday he was brought from the Tower to the King's Bench Bar (as they say the manner is when a man lives above a year and a day after he is condemned) and there demanded what he could say for himself why the sentence pronounced against him at Winchester[13] should not be put in execution. The sum of his answer was, that the King had employed him in his service and given him a commission wherein he styled him his loyal subject, and withal given him *potestatem vitae et necis*,[14] which did amount to a pardon, for in all reason he must be master of his own life that hath power over other men's. The judges replied that there is no pardon for treason by implication, wherefore he must find a better plea or undergo the sentence.

Then he spake of his trial at Winchester and avowed that all or the far greater part of those that were present did acquit him in their conscience, and that the King's gracious forbearing him so long (and but for this late accident longer would have done, even to an hundred years if nature could have drawn out his life so long) did show that his Majesty approved his innocence.

But in conclusion he was willed to prepare himself, and so was delivered to the Sheriffs of London and conveyed to the Gatehouse, where he spent the rest of that day in writing letters to the King and others and in prayer with the Dean of Westminster, who came the next morning at five o'clock and ministered to him the Communion, and when he had broken his fast about eight o'clock came to the scaffold, where he found the Earls of Arundel, Oxford, Northampton, the Lord of Doncaster and diverse others.

---

[13] In 1603.
[14] Power of life and death (over his followers).

He made a speech of more than half an hour, wherein he cleared himself of having any intelligence with France (which had been objected to him) more than to save his life and hide himself from the King's indignation: then that he never had any ill intent towards his Majesty not so much as in thought, that he had no other pretense nor end in his last voyage than the enriching of the King, the Realm, himself, and his followers: that he never had any undutiful speech concerning his Majesty with the runagate French physician, nor ever offered to Sir Lewis Stukeley £10,000 to go with him into France, nor told him that the Lord Carew had given him advice to be gone, and that he and the Lord of Doncaster would maintain him in France, of which points he had been accused by them, and though he protested not only to forgive them but to pray God to forgive them, yet he thought fit to give men warning of such persons.

To all this and much more he took God so often and so solemnly to witness, that he was believed of all that heard him. He spake somewhat of the death of the Earl of Essex and how sorry he was for him, for though he was of a contrary faction, yet he foresaw that those who esteemed him then in that respect, would cast him off as they did afterward. He confessed himself the greatest sinner that he knew, and no marvel, as having been a soldier, a seaman, and a courtier. He excused the disfiguring of himself by the example of David who feigned himself mad to avoid danger, and never heard it imputed to him for a sin. In conclusion he spake and behaved himself so, without any show of fear or affectation, that he moved much commiseration, and all that saw him confess that his end was *omnibus numeris absolutus*,[15] and as far as man can discern every way perfect.

It will not be amiss to set down some few passages of diverse that I have heard. The morning that he went to execution there was a cup of excellent sack brought him, and being asked how he liked it, "As the fellow," said he, "that drinking of St. Giles' bowl [16] as he went to Tyburn said, it was good drink if a man might tarry by it." As he went from Westminster Hall to the Gatehouse, he espied Sir Hugh Beeston in the throng and calling to him prayed he would see him die tomorrow. Sir Hugh to make sure work got a letter from Secretary Lake

---

[15] Complete in all respects.

[16] At St. Giles in the Fields "prisoners conveyed from the City of London to Tyburn, there to be executed for treason, felonies, or other trespasses, were presented with a bowl of ale, thereof to drink at their pleasure, as to be their last refreshing in this life." (Stow, *Survey of London*.)

to the Sheriff to see him placed conveniently, and meeting them as they came near to the scaffold delivered his letter; but the Sheriff by mishap had left his spectacles at home and put the letter in his pocket. In the meantime, Sir Hugh being thrust by, Sir Walter bade him farewell and said, "I know not what shift you will make, but I am sure to have a place."

When the hangman asked him forgiveness he desired to see the axe, and feeling the edge, he said that it was a fair sharp medicine to cure him of all his diseases and miseries. When he was laid down some found fault that his face was westward, and would have him turned, whereupon rising he said it was no greater matter which way a man's head stood so his heart lay right. He had given order to the executioner that after some short meditation when he stretched forth his hands he should dispatch him. After once or twice putting forth his hands, the fellow out of timorousness (or what other cause) forbearing, he was fain to bid him strike, and so at two blows he took off his head, though he stirred not a whit after the first.

The people were much affected at the sight, insomuch that one was heard to say that we had not such another head to cut off. Another wished the head and brains to be upon S. N. shoulders.[17] There was great means made for his life; and I hear the Queen wrote very earnestly to the King, as he tendered her health, to spare him for that she had received great good by his receipts. I hear not so much of her recovery of late as when I wrote last, but rather that she goes *peggiorando*,[18] insomuch that it is doubted whether the King come hither today from Theobalds or go directly to Hampton Court where she lies.

The Spanish Dominican lately come hither is said likewise to have labored for Sir Walter Raleigh, as finding his death would much

---

[17] "One Mr. Wymark, a wealthy man, great novellant, and constant Paul's-walker, hearing the news that day of the beheading of Sir Walter Raleigh, 'His head,' said he, 'would do very well on the shoulders of Sir Robert Naunton, Secretary of State.' These words were complained of, and Wymark summoned to the privy council, where he pleaded for himself, that he intended no disrespect to Mr. Secretary, whose known worth was above all detraction; only he spake in reference to an old proverb, 'Two heads are better than one.' And so for the present he was dismissed. Not long after, when rich men were called on for a contribution to St. Paul's, Wymark at the council table subscribed a hundred pounds: but Mr. Secretary told him two hundred were better than one; which, betwixt fear and charity, Wymark was fain to subscribe." (Fuller, *Worthies of England,* iii, 175-176.)

[18] Worse.

alienate the minds of our people as if he were sacrificed to the malice of the Spaniards; but it is verily thought some unseemly speeches fathered upon him, whether truly or falsely, by those two fellows were the principal motives of his ruin. It is said we should have some declaration set out touching the causes of his execution at this time, but whether his protestations and manner of dying may alter the case God knows; for he died very religiously, and every way like a Christian, insomuch that the Dean of Westminster (they say) commends him exceedingly and says he was as ready and as able to give as take instruction.

[303] November 7, 1618: This week I received yours of the 29th of October together with the printed papers, which I understand no more than children do that look upon the babies, because they be all Dutch, yet I had seen one of them before with a French coat or copy. For some part of amends I return you two papers in exchange, the one from Sir Walter Raleigh to the King before he came to Salisbury, and withal half a dozen verses he made the night before his death, to take farewell of Poetry wherein he had been a piddler even from his youth. The other is a remembrance left with his Lady, written likewise that night, to acquaint the world withal, if perhaps he should not have been suffered to speak at his death, as he was cut off from speaking somewhat he would have said at the King's Bench: and they had no thanks that suffered him to talk so long on the scaffold, but the fault was laid on the Sheriffs and there it rests.

His Lady had leave to visit him that night, and told him she had obtained the disposing of his body, to which he answered smiling, "It is well, Bess, that thou mayest dispose of it dead, that hadst not always the disposing of it when it was alive"; and so dismissed her anon after midnight, when he settled himself to sleep for three or four hours. His body and head were buried together in St. Margaret's Church at Westminster.

Sir Lewis Stukeley makes suit to the King that his reputation may be repaired, and offers to take the Sacrament solemnly in Paul's or any other public place, that all he related of him is true. But Sir Thomas Badger told him, in good company, that all that would not serve his turn unless he should be presently hanged and so seal it with his death.

[306] November 28, 1618: You will find little in Sir Lewis Stukeley's apology but that they strive to bewray one another; it is like we shall have no further declaration, if this may satisfy, which hitherto finds little credit. But now when I was come thus far my man brings me an authentical declaration of all that business. I have not read a word of it (more than the title) for it came forth but this morning, and as I hear it is the work of the Lord Chancellor,[19] Master Attorney,[20] or Secretary Naunton: or rather fathered upon all three so that in all probability it must be as true as well written.

[308] December 4, 1618: I forgot in my last that Sir Lewis Stukeley's pamphlet was penned by Dr. Sharpe. He is now most commonly known and called by the name of Sir Judas Stukeley.

---

[19] Francis Bacon, Lord Verulam (see *Letters & Life of Francis Bacon*, vi, 356).
[20] Sir Henry Yelverton.

X. Trade and Empire

THE *production of silver increased sixfold between the discovery of America and the defeat of the Armada; and gold poured into Europe from West Africa and Central America. Coinage thus more than kept pace with the increasing demand for money to pay rent and taxes, to hire soldiers, and to pay salaries. The continued arrival of treasure ships led to enormous inflation of prices in Spain and, gradually, in the countries with whom Spain dealt. The French or English merchant who sold his cargo in Spain profited enormously; the farmer who sold his grain for cash locally did well; the landlord who collected a fixed rent suffered, and sought to share the profits of inflation by helping to finance a voyage.*

Overall wealth was increasing. But bad harvests were still catastrophic, and the role of the new supply of money in the rapid cycles of plenty and want continued to mystify its users. Jean Bodin laid down the principles of mercantilism: export more goods than you import; keep your balance of trade favorable to your supply of hard cash; money is wealth.

War with Spain and a succession of bad harvests from 1595 to 1598 serve as a background to the early Chamberlain letters. After the peace with Spain in 1604, commerce began again fitfully with Spain, but English ships constantly complained of their usage in Spanish ports where they were held on suspicion of being pirates or of trading with infidels. French experiments in mercantilism were a bother. Colonization became a more attractive form of investment. Chamberlain himself invested in the Bermudas and Virginia.

Relations with the traditionally friendly Dutch deteriorated during the whole of James's reign. Rivalry over fisheries in "Greenland" (Spitsbergen) and the North Sea; rivalry over trade in the Far East, in which the Dutch had the advantage of five years' start; and the ultimate fiasco, the fight over the import of dyed cloth, all put cracks into what had been a natural alliance against the Catholic powers and a natural partnership in finance and industry.

The fate of the Merchant Adventurers raised the loudest cry of frustration. That prosperous company had been exporting unfinished

204]

woolen cloth to their factory in Middleburgh, where Dutch artisans finished and dyed it for sale all over the continent. In 1614, Alderman William Cockayne persuaded King James that this was bad both in theory and in practice, and that he should forbid export of unfinished cloth and form a new company to finish and dye cloth in England. The Dutch immediately retaliated by refusing to import the finished cloth, and the whole English woolen industry was thrown into chaos.

The treatment of the Strangers, the foreign merchants and financiers who played an important part in the financial life of the City, is an even more scandalous if less serious example of how little the role of money was understood. When suddenly gold and silver became scarce in London in 1620, James clapped the Merchants Strangers into prison and fined them heavily for their allegedly criminal export of precious metals.

King James was an enthusiastic and maddening patron of overseas enterprise. Twice he undermined the position of the East India Company by granting rival charters to adventurers who seriously hampered the activities of the original company. No sooner had the colony in Virginia begun to make its way by exporting tobacco than a series of pamphlets against the foul weed streamed from his Majesty's pen. The ambitious schemes for trade with Russia and Persia yielded little of substance, partly because of political disturbances there, partly because the Dutch got in first. And always the revenues from charters, loans and customs disappeared into the pockets of James's courtiers.

[27] May 10, 1600: Nine or ten good merchant ships are come out of the Levant, whereof the owners are not a little glad because they heard they were strongly laid for in the Straits and in the Sleeve twixt England and France. Not far from the North Cape they met two of the King of Spain's armadas or galleons, and after some fight sunk the one and were possessed of the other, but having taken out some few men, shot and powder, with some other things they wanted, they let her go because they knew not how to bestow her men, which were almost five hundred; and withal the Spaniards gave out that the peace was concluded twixt England and Spain, which made them the more merciful.

[38] May 27, 1601: The Spaniards have taken a rich ship worth £40,000 of our Turkey merchants coming out of the Levant.

[45] April 26, 1602: I hear much talk of three prizes taken by a ship of Sir John Gilbert's (with two or three more in consort) as they were coming out of the mouth of the river of Lisbon. Two of them were laden with corn, munition, and money for the pay and provision of a garrison town on the coast of Africa. The other was a ship of 500 ton, very rich of peppers, sugars, and other rich commodities, besides 300-weight of pearl. The Italians lay a colorable claim to the best part of this lading, which, if it prove prize, is assuredly thought will amount to almost an hundred thousand pound.

[46] May 8, 1602: This week two pretty ships went out of the river very well furnished and victualled by our merchants for almost two years, under the conduct of one Captain Waymouth, to seek the north-west passage to the Indies, which if it hit right will be a matter of great importance. He carrieth letters in diverse languages from the Queen to any princes of name he shall light on.

[49] June 27, 1602: We hear of 6,000 Italians ready in Spain[1] to come thither and stay for nothing but shipping, which I doubt they shall too easily compass now our fleet comes away to convoy home the carrack they have taken within the mouth of the river of Lisbon.

If our people had not played the men every way, she had escaped their fingers, by the reason she was got so far within the river among flats and shallows, and had received a supply of three or four hundred fresh men, besides a guard of ten galleys to tow her up and defend her; but our ships so plied the galleys that I think they will have no list to encounter them any more. . . . What her value may be we cannot yet guess, but sure she was a rich ship. Marry, there goes a report all the short ends were conveyed away before our men could come at her, but most men think that but a color for them

---

[1] Mercenary soldiers to be sent to Ireland to help the rebels.

that have and mean to make their market. Once here, is order taken that no goldsmiths or jewellers shall go into the West Country, and Fulke Greville is gone down post to Plymouth and so to the sea to meet her and keep her from coming into that pilfering town (as they term it), but to bring her along to Portsmouth.

[59] January 27, 1603: The Queen seeks to discharge herself of her great charge in Ireland, and hath lately cashiered 4000 men there. Here be likewise projects to ease her of the burthen of keeping the narrow seas; for, seeing her ships serve to so little purpose against the Dunkirkers,[2] it is propounded that the City should maintain two ships and a pinnace, the northern coast as many more, and the West Country in like proportion, and so to make trial what good may be done upon them. In the meantime, the Queen's ships shall serve for the coast of Spain, and Sir Richard Leveson is preparing thitherward with eight of her navy and some other assistants.

[70] February 16, 1605, to Ralph Winwood: The Spanish Ambassador complains that our people on the seacoast show more favor and familiarity upon all occasions to their old friends the Hollanders than to the Dunkirkers; and Caron[3] cries out as fast (and with more reason) that the King's ships in the narrow seas do all the contrary.

[90] February 6, 1607: Two men-of-war of Holland, that have watched a Dunkirker above these two years in Portsmouth, lighted upon him as he came forth on Sunday last and have carried him away.

[110] January 23, 1609: The Council have been very busy of late in plotting how to plant Ireland with English and Scots. The whole

---

[2] Ships from the Spanish Netherlands.
[3] Noel Caron, the Dutch Ambassador; peace with Spain had been signed in August, 1604.

project with the particulars is like to come forth shortly in print.

We were like enough to fall out with the Duke of Florence, if we knew how to hurt him. Our merchants are forbidden to trade any more to Leghorn, who are thereupon minded to translate that traffic to Genoa.

The least of our East Indian ships, called the Pinnesse, is arrived at Dartmouth with a 100 ton of cloves, without seeing or hearing anything of her consorts since they parted from the coast of England.

Here is likewise a ship newly come from Virginia with some pretty commodities and hope of more, as diverse sorts of wood for wainscot and other uses, soap ashes, some pitch and tar, certain unknown kinds of herbs for dyeing, not without suspicion (as they term it) of cochinilla.

[117] January 13, 1610: Our East Indian merchants have lately built a goodly ship of above 1200 ton, to the launching whereof the King and Prince were invited and had a bountiful banquet. The King graced Sir Thomas Smith, the Governor, with a chain in manner of a collar better than £200, with his picture hanging at it, and put it about his neck with his own hands, naming the great ship Trades Increase, and the Prince a pinnace of 250 ton (built to wait upon her) Peppercorn.

[128] December 4, 1611: Sir Harry Wotton's friends give out that he hath refused the employment to Brussels; and now Sir Dudley Digges is in consideration, if this new discovery of the north-west passage (wherein he is a great undertaker) will give him leave to think of anything else, for it possesseth him wholly, and they are preparing ships against the spring as if there were no doubt nor difficulty at all in the matter. And the Prince is become patron and protector of this new discovery.

[133] February 12, 1612: The last week four good ships went hence for the East Indies, but missed some of their mariners who, seizing

on a Low-Country vessel that lay in the river, have carried her away no man knows whither.

There is a lottery in hand for the furthering of the Virginia voyage, and an under-company erecting for the trade of the Bermudas, which have changed their name twice within this month, being first christened Virginiola as a member of that plantation, but now lately resolved to be called Summer Islands, as well in respect of the continual temperate air as in rememberance of Sir George Somers[4] that died there.

[144] July 9, 1612: The Spanish Ambassador Don Pedro de Zuñiga, Marquis de Villa Flores, had his first audience on Sunday last at Hampton Court. . . . It is generally looked for that he will expostulate about our plantation in Virginia, wherein there will need no great contestation, seeing it is to be feared that that action will fall to the ground of itself, by the extreme beastly idleness of our nation which, notwithstanding any cost or diligence used to support them, will rather die and starve than be brought to any labor or industry to maintain themselves. Two or three of the last ships that came thence bring nothing but discomfort, and that Sir Thomas Gates and Sir Thomas Dale are quite out of heart. And to mend the matter, not past five days since, here arrived a ship with ten men who, being sent forth to fish for their relief and having taken great store, have given them the slip and run away, and fill the town with ill reports which will hinder that business more than the Lottery or any other art they can use for the present will further it. And yet they have taken good order to have these runaways apprehended and punished or at least sent back again.

[172] April 29, 1613: The Council have been much busied of late about certain projects for Muscovy, for that, about two years since, some of the nobility offered to Master Merrick (my brother George's wife's uncle) to put themselves and their country under the King's protection. Master Merrick is a man that was from his youth brought

---

[4] Sir George Somers, discoverer of the Bermudas, died in 1610.

up amongst them, and of as great credit and reputation as ever was Englishman in that country, so that the King hath had much conference with him and will needs have him go again presently to negotiate this business.

But sure the world is much altered since that time, and the King had then another son, whereby they might hope he would send them his second to be their Emperor, for I can never believe they will be content with a deputy. But the King doth so apprehend the matter that he saith he never affected anything much and seriously but it came to a good pass, and he never affected anything more than this, so that he doth not doubt of success, and makes account of sending ten or twelve thousand men thither at the least if the business grow to any conclusion. And withal there be many farfetched projects and devices on foot, how to draw all the traffic of Persia and the inland parts of the East Indies up the river Hidaspes into the river Oxus that falls into the Caspian Sea, whence with certain small ships that shall be built, the commodities are to be brought up the Volga to a strait of land not above forty miles and so into the river Drina that comes to St. Nicholas or the town of the Archangel, the ordinary ports and stations of our shipping in those parts. These I doubt are but discourses in the air, and yet Sir Henry Neville hath been much employed in them.

[**180**] August 1, 1613: There is a ship come from Virginia with news of their well-doing, which puts some life into that action, that before was almost at the last cast. They have taken a daughter[5] of a king that was their greatest enemy, as she was going afeasting upon a river to visit certain friends, for whose ransom the father offers whatsoever is in his power, and to become their friend, and to bring them where they shall meet with gold mines. They propound unto him three conditions: to deliver all the English fugitives, to render all manner of arms or weapons of theirs that are come to his hands, and to give them 300 quarters of corn. The first two he performed readily, and promiseth the other at their harvest, if his daughter may be well used in the meantime.

But this ship brought no commodities from thence, but only these

---

[5] Pocahontas.

fair tales and hopes. Marry, touching at the Bermudas, she hath brought thence some quantity of pearl, and between 20 and 30 pound weight of ambergris, worth £ 900 at least; and by the next that is to come thence, they are promised to have a return of four times as much.

When the business of Virginia was at the highest, in that heat many gentlemen and others were drawn by persuasion and importunity of friends to underwrite their names for adventurers. But when it came to the payment (specially the second or third time), their hands were not so ready to go to their purses as they were to the paper, and in the end flatly refused; whereupon they are sued by the Company in the Chancery, where this action finds such favor that they have ready dispatch, and the underwriters are forced to make payment, which amounts to a round sum between three and four thousand pound. Among the rest, your cousin Will Lytton was drawn on by Sir Walter Cope, with persuasion that he should not need to adventure anything unless he list, but only to give his name for encouragement to others and for a countenance to the cause; but Sir Walter cannot protect him.

[183] October 27, 1613: Our Company of Muscovy have for these three or four years found out a new and rich trade of fishing for the whale, about Greenland or certain islands there along, which yields above *cento pro cento*,[6] with a short return and small charge. They enjoyed it quietly till this year that both Hollanders, Frenchmen and Spaniards would have come in for a share; but our men, having some inkling of it, went well appointed with seven good ships and so put them by and sent them away, whereat there is much murmuring and complaint, specially by the Hollanders, who have sent certain deputies hither about it. But our men pretend possession, and mean to maintain it, though peradventure it will come to blows. This year they killed almost fourscore whales, and almost ten times morses or sea horses, whose oil, fins and teeth are a great commodity.

From the Bermudas or Summer Islands there hath come great store of ambergris this year, which is the only commodity they have thence as yet, but they hope for more hereafter of many kinds, though

---

[6] One hundred percent.

nothing so rich; and begin to nestle and plant there very handsomely, wherewith the Spaniard is nothing pleased but threatens the next year to remove them, which advertisement they have by good means and many ways. But they seem nothing dismayed therewith, trusting rather to the difficulty of access than to any strength of their own. The greatest piece of amber in one lump that hath been heard of was found there this year, being as big as the body of a giant, and answerable or resembling almost in all points saving for the want of the head and one arm; but they handled the matter so foolishly that they brake it in pieces, and the biggest they brought home was not above 68 ounces, which sells better by twelve or fifteen shillings in an ounce than that which is smaller.

Since Michaelmas we have had four ships come from the East Indies well and richly laden, and though they have been long missing yet this return doth recompense their stay, the rather for that, of three Hollanders that came with them, one was blown up by mischance at St. Helena's, the second coming in at the Texel was cast away in the very port, and the third is not yet heard of, so that they account their loss to be no less than £500,000.

[205] June 9, 1614: Captain Best is newly come from the East Indies and brought home the Red Dragon richly laden. He brings news that Sir Henry Middleton is dead at Bantam, and the Trades Increase lost there by mischance as she was careening (as they call it), which is a great pity, being the goodliest ship of England and never made voyage before. The best is, there was nothing lost but the bulk, her ordnance and lading being laid safe on shore.

[212] October 12, 1614, to Isaac Wake: The Company of Merchant Adventures is dissolved and their charter cancelled, which may prove a matter of dangerous consequence many ways; but we are in the course of trying conclusions.

[213] November 24, 1614: Here is a Jew Pirate arrested that brought three prizes of Spaniards into Plymouth. He was set out by the King

of Morocco, and useth Hollanders' ships and, for the most part, their mariners. But it is like he shall pass it over well enough, for he pretendeth to have leave and license under the King's hand for his free egress and regress, which was not believed upon the first sight, till he made proof of it.

Sir Thomas Roe is in speech to be sent ambassador as from the King by the East Indian Company to the Great Mogul; and if his allowance be so large as is reported, it goes far beyond the best ambassadors the King hath abroad.

[223] February 23, 1615: The Merchant Adventurers have, two days since, voluntarily delivered up their charter to the King, and the new company have all at their will. Yet they are already puzzled, for that the clothiers begin to complain and make petitions, for want of utterance of their cloth; which, besides all other incommodities abroad, may turn to a matter of dangerous consequence at home if it be not prevented. They have made the best provision they can and called in strangers to their assistance, having liberty likewise to carry them out undyed and undressed till they can provide sufficient store of workmen and materials, which will be God knows when; which is thought hard, that the ancient possessors should be turned out to make place for newcomers and strangers upon the same conditions. And it is found strange that the wisdom of the state could be induced to remove such a cornerstone upon so weak assurance as the vain promises and projects of idle brains.

[230] May 25, 1615: The great project of dyeing and dressing of cloth is at a stand, and they know not well how to go forward nor backward; for the clothiers do generally complain that their cloth lies on their hand, and the cloth workers and dyers weary the King and Council with petitions wherein they complain that they are in worse case than before, having taken more servants and provided better means of housing and other necessaries, and have less work than before. And indeed upon search it is found that there hath not been a cloth dyed nor dressed since Christmas more than usual. . . .

Whereby the customs do fall and many other inconveniences follow both at home and abroad, whiles the new companions differ among themselves and draw diverse ways; so that the old Company have been dealt withal to resume the trade and to set all straight again if it may be, whereabout they are now in consultation, to see how the confusion may be prevented whereinto private ends and interests have cast us under pretense of public good.

[235] August 24, 1615: Our merchants have had great losses of late, by a rich ship cast away in the river of Hamburg. Another was seized at Rouen for exporting forbidden commodities, specially coin, having besides other gold above 7000 Jacobus pieces in specie. But the worst of all was a ship arrested and taken by force in Spain that had better than £30,000 in gold and silver.

[244] June 22, 1616: Sir Thomas Dale is arrived from Virginia and brought with him some ten or twelve old and young of that country, among whom the most remarkable person is Pocahontas, daughter of Powhatan, a king or cacique of that country, married to one Rolfe, an Englishman. I hear not of any other riches or matter of worth, but only some quantity of sassafras, tobacco, pitch and clapboard, things of no great value unless there were more plenty and nearer hand.

All I can learn of it is that the country is good to live in, if it were stored with people, and might in time become commodious, but there is no present profit to be expected. But you may understand more by yourself when he comes into those parts, which he pretends to do within a month or little more.

[245] July 6, 1616: Here is a rich ship called the New Year's Gift lately arrived from the East Indies, valued at better than £140,000.

[248] September 3, 1616: Our Greenland ships are come home and have made a good voyage, having made more oil than they could bring away and killed 130 whales.

[253] November 23, 1616: Our old Merchants have many consultations and disputes among themselves how to content the King, who doth not accept any of their offers, so that they are at their wits' end; for with the new Company they will in nowise join, who are now casting about to vent their cloths at Antwerp or Bruges. And many meetings they have with the Spanish Ambassador, who makes them large promises. . . .

I forgot heretofore to write of five men safely arrived from the Bermudas in a boat of hardly two ton, being thought half a miracle how so small a vessel should brook those seas seven whole weeks and not be swallowed up in the vast ocean.

[256] January 4, 1617: After so long and vehement debating, the old Company of Merchant Adventurers is to be set up again and this day their charter to be restored them, but with what conditions and limitations I have not yet learned.

We have hitherto the warmest winter that I think hath been seen, which proceeds from the settling of the wind continually at southwest, whereby there lie above 250 sail one and other in the Downs that are to go southward. And some of our East India ships have lain there for wind for almost ten weeks.

[257] January 18, 1617: The Virginian woman Pocahontas, with her father-counsellor, hath been with the King and graciously used, and both she and her assistant well placed at the masque. She is on her return, though sore against her will, if the wind would come about to send them away.

[258] February 8, 1617: Our East India Company are in a great bravery, having closed up their books for underwriters the last of January and find adventurers of £1,400,000 for these four years following, which in truth is a very great sum and a great deal more than was expected; but diverse have underwritten for ten, twelve, and fourteen thousand pound apiece.

[259] February 22, 1617: Here is a fine picture of no fair Lady.[7] And yet with her tricking up and high style and titles, you might think her and her worshipful husband to be somebody, if you do not know that the poor company of Virginia, out of their poverty, are fain to allow her four pound a week for her maintenance.

[262] March 29, 1617: The Virginian woman whose picture I sent you died this last week at Gravesend as she was returning homeward.

[277] November 8, 1617: This week Sir John Merrick is arrived from Muscovy, where he hath been these three years and a half and hath effected his business with good approbation. He was yesterday with the King who used him very well and graciously, and had long conference with him. There is come an ambassador with him thence, accompanied with 75 persons, to the great charge of that Company upon whose account they are like to tarry here seven or eight months. He would fain have had audience before the King's going, but his furniture and some of his company being not yet come to town the King would not stay his leisure, though he have brought some presents to his liking, as white hawks, live sables, and I know not what else.

[283] January 17, 1618: Our Merchant Adventurers have lately lent, or rather given by way of present, to the King £50,000 for

---

[7] Pocahontas.

their ancient privileges and immunities, and to be protected and secured from interlopers, wherein there will be some difficulty, seeing they claim and challenge free traffic by the laws of the realm and their birthright; and diverse of them are committed to the Marshalsea for refusing to enter into bond to desist. In the meantime, the Merchants, having paid in the most part of this money, hold their hand for the remainder till this point be better cleared, wherein the present necessity makes for their advantage, howsoever they speed hereafter.

[284] January 31, 1618: Our East Indian fleet is setting out and some of them gone down to Gravesend. They go stronger and more than ever heretofore, being nine good ships and of great burden, three or four of them new-built. Sir Thomas should go General, but if he come not back from you the sooner, he is like to be left behind and so lose his employment.

The King hath given a patent to one Sir James Cunningham, a Scottish knight, to raise an East Indian Company there, whereof he and his heirs are to be Governors and none to be admitted but by his and their approbation. They have liberty to trade into the East and West Indies, Turkey, Muscovy, Greenland, or to any other place already discovered or to be discovered. They may furnish themselves of shipping, mariners, victual, or anything else they need in any port of England, where all officers are to assist them, as likewise they may vent their commodities here, and—that which in the reading it seemed to me most strange—that not only Scots, but English or any other stranger may be admitted into this Society . . . with a number of other large privileges which do directly infringe former grants and cross the whole course of our traffic. . . .

The Lord Delaware is returning to Virginia and carries with him seven- or eightscore men. Sir Thomas Gates makes account to follow him some time this next summer.

[290] March 16, 1618: The King and Council have been much troubled since his last coming to town about the Scottish patent I

wrote you of, and many meetings, debatings and consultations there have been about it. But it is found so prejudicial to the East Indian, Muscovy, and Turkey Companies that if it should go on it would apparently ruin them all and bring confusion into all trade and intercourse, breeding, moreover, distraction and separation instead of union twixt us and them; wherefore it is thought it shall be recalled, cashiered and quite dissolved, though they had gotten many interlopers and partners here.

Our Merchant Adventurers are likewise forbidden to forsake and leave their residence at Middleburgh, which they were very forward to have done without this prohibition.

[292] April 1, 1618: Here is a great business agreed upon yesterday betwixt the East Indian and Muscovy Company for the furnishing of the Emperor of Russia with a hundred thousand marks by way of loan, whereby they hope to engross that trade so necessary for this state, both in respect of the quantity and goodness of all manner of cordage that comes thence, as of many other real commodities, besides the hope of a trade into Persia that way, which may prove a matter of great importance. The Muscovy Company was not able to undergo the burden without the assistance of the East Indian merchants, who for their assistance are to have an equal stock and adventure for eight years in all those northern voyages. And for their better encouragement, the King hath recalled and delivered into their hands the Scottish patent I wrote of.

[300] October 14, 1618: The Lord Delaware is dead in his voyage to Virginia. He touched in his way thither at the Terceras, where he was feasted and well used, to seeming, but the sickness and death of him and most of them that landed with him makes it suspected that they had ill measure.

The City is now shipping thither an hundred young boys and girls that lay starving in the streets, which is one of the best deeds that could be done with so little charge, not rising to above £500.

[306] November 28, 1618: Here be two or three ships ready for Virginia, and one Captain Yeardley, a mean fellow by way of provision, goes as Governor; and to grace him the more, the King knighted him this week at Newmarket, which hath set him up so high that he flaunts it up and down the streets in extraordinary bravery, with fourteen or fifteen fair liveries after him.

[307] December 3, 1618: The greatest news I have is that Master Pory is in the way of high preferment, for yesterday he was chosen Secretary of Virginia for three years, and is upon his departure thither the end of this week with the new Governor, Sir George Yeardley, who married his cousin-german as he tells me. No question but he will become there a sufficient sober man, seeing there is no wine in all that climate.[8]

[311] January 2, 1619: We hear of a ship upon the coast come from the East Indies called the Bull, but what her lading is we hear not yet, for the news came but yesterday. They say she brings word that the Lord Rich's two ships that were in those parts are cast away.

[332] July 15, 1619: Our Turkey merchants have made choice of a new ambassador for Constantinople, one Sir John Ayres. . . . This last week likewise the East Indian Company with some difficulty have chosen Sir Thomas Smith their Governor for this year.

[334] August 10, 1619: Our Merchants complain . . . of these new impositions upon cloth under the name of pretermitted cus-

---

[8] Chamberlain had met Master Pory, who had been on Carleton's staff in Venice, in October, "in such a pickle that I perceive the pot and he are so fast friends that they cannot easily be parted."

tom, and say they were taken at advantage when they had already shipped their goods, or else they would have been advised how they had bought; but sure it is like to turn the realm to great hindrance. And that which they take worst is to see it so bestowed, as they say: £3000 a year to the Marquis Hamilton, £1000 to Sir Edward Doncaster, £2000 to Sir George Goring, £2500 to the Lord of Zouche, and the rest to others.

Here is the proclamation for gold,[9] which I cannot conceive to what great end it is or *cui bono*,[10] but rather that all that have any store by them shall be great losers, without gain to any but to the Master of the Mint.

[**336**] September 11, 1619: Sir Thomas Roe is come home rich, they say, from the East Indies, and we hear that our men there have repaid themselves and repaired our honor upon the Hollanders.

[**337**] October 2, 1619: The King was here yesterday at Whitehall but is now gone to Theobalds. He came from Hampton Court, where Sir Thomas Roe presented him with two antelopes, a strange and beautiful kind of red deer, a rich tent, rare carpets, certain umbrellas, and suchlike trinkets from the Great Mogul. For aught I hear, he hath not provided so well for himself as was thought at first, but must rely upon the Company's liberality.

[**343**] January 1, 1620: The Merchant Strangers that are in the Fleet have made means and petitions to the King by Sir Noel Caron, by the Dutch and French churches, and by their wives, children and friends, but I hear not yet with what success. . . . But when all is done, they will have much ado to make up any great sum, for many of them are but poor men, not worth what they be fined at. . . . But the worst is diverse of them do with deep execrations forswear the fact for which they are censured, as van Lore, for one, who in

[9] By the King, *For reforming the Coynes.*
[10] For whose good.

good company at dinner of late said that, when he had ended this business, he would bid England farewell; and being told that it was no great loss to him, being otherwise so well feathered, having good store of land in England, to which he answered he had children here to leave it to, but for himself he would go to save his skin— for they that upon such witness could take away his goods might, when they pleased, take his life. To say the truth, the carriage of the whole business sounds not so well with us here at home, whatsoever it doth abroad. . . .

What the consequence for matter of trade, and for our merchants elsewhere may be hereafter, *viderit utilitas*;[11] but the Farmers of the Customs feel it and complain already, among whom Sir John Wolstenholme was by the King's commandment committed of late to his house for muttering against a patent and new-erected office in the Custom House, to the prejudice and undoing of their underclerks and writers.

[345] January 22, 1620: Most of the Strangers lie by it still in the Fleet, till they find means to satisfy their fines. In the meantime all our English that used to trade with them are sworn to reveal what sums of money they owe them, which debts are seized to the king's use; and Robert de l'Eau having ten or eleven thousand pound in the East Indian Company, it is sold by commission at twenty in the hundred loss and £9000 of the money paid in this day sevennight. I hear Burlamachi hath made his peace by lending £10,000 down.

[348] February 26, 1620: I hear of some cross language passed twixt [the Lord Digby] and the Lord North at a table in Court about a journey [Captain Roger] North is making to the River of Amazons in Guiana, which the Lord Digby argued against as being to the prejudice of the King of Spain, and that the Ambassador at his coming would hinder it; to which the Lord North replied that then he wished he might never come, and withal that he took the Lord Digby for the King of England's Ambassador in Spain, but it seemed he is rather the King of Spain's Ambassador in England.

---

[11] Use will discern.

[349] March 11, 1620: I hear upon inquiry that we shall have a ship ready in April to go for Virginia, so that if you please to write Master Pory you may send your letters against that time. We have had foul weather this week, and two lighters laden with merchandise sunk, besides a boat or two with passengers; but the worst is that our best and biggest ship going now for the East Indies is set on ground not far from Gravesend, in danger to be lost.

[353] May 20, 1620, to William Camden: Here is a sharp proclamation come forth against Captain North, who upon letters patents was employed by diverse noblemen in a discovery and plantation about the River of Amazons, but the Spanish Ambassador excepting against it, he was willed to attend further order, for infringing whereof he is run into a kind of contempt and rebellion, though no doubt he be long ere this out of hearing and so knows not his danger.

[354] May 27, 1620: The bad news of the taking of 4 or 5 of our ships by the Hollanders in the East Indies doth trouble us all, and sure the disgrace and dishonor is more than the loss, though it be great, and I know not how it can be repaired, specially so many of our best men being slain and taken. The King, I hear, is much incensed by reason of their insolencies used towards him, as is reported—which I give no great credit to, but think them made and given out of purpose to kindle him. Howsoever it be, this accident falls out in an ill time, to weigh down the balance that did but sway before toward the Spaniard. . . .

The Virginia Company being to choose a new Governor or Treasurer this last week in place of Sir Edwin Sandys, the King sent them a peremptory message by Master Kirkham to make choice of Sir Tho. Smith, or Sir Tho. Lowe, Alderman Johnson, or Maurice Abbotts, whereupon the Company entreated the Earl of Southampton, the Lord of Doncaster, the Lord Sheffield, the Lord Cavendish, with 2 knights, 2 lawyers, and some 4 more, to inform his Majesty of the unfitness of most of those parties, and to excuse their not making any choice at that time. The King was much displeased at the first, and took great exceptions to Sir Edwin Sandys as principal man that had withstood him in Parliament and traducted his government, with much more; but in conclusion told them the message was mistaken by him that brought it and that he did but only recommend those men, but still excepted against Sir Edwin Sandys that he should not be continued. Whereupon Sir Edwin looks by all means to make his peace and hath many good friends speak for him. I send you here a note of what he hath this last year: more, they say, than in 7 years before. . . .

The last week the Lord North's house was searched and the copy of a letter found to his brother, which . . . animated him to be gone, for which on Monday he was committed to the Fleet and lay there till Thursday, being all the while so exceedingly visited that he had sometimes 6 earls there at once.

[356] July 8, 1620: The last week the Virginia Company chose the Earl of Southampton for their Treasurer or Governor, who accepted it. And there is hope matters will go forward there better than heretofore. . . .

On Tuesday Sir Thomas Smith, without any contradiction, was re-established Governor of the East India Company, by reason of a letter from the King wishing them not to alter their officers and committees.

[363] October 28, 1620: Many new patents come forth and more daily expected, as first for tobacco, whereby the new plantations of Virginia and the Bermudas are like to be stifled as it were in the cradle; another for saltpeter, which (the Earl of Worcester being in a manner forced to surrender by reason of the continual complaints) is not like to be lighter or less burdenous in the Lord of Buckingham's hands; another for scouring and trimming of armor throughout England; another for sixpence a load of hay of all that comes to this town by land or by water; another for whatsoever is printed but on the one side, whether in paper or parchment, which besides many other things I know not how far it may concern ballads and play-bills.

[**368**] January 13, 1621: Captain Roger North was committed [to the Tower] this day sevennight upon his return from Guiana, and his ship and goods arrested, though he have many great partners in his adventure and pretends to have done nothing against the peace nor to have in any way offended the Spaniard. Yet it seems his great patrons and friends cannot protect him.

We hear of an East Indian ship of Holland cast away about Guernsey or Jersey.

[**390**] August 18, 1621: Here be two merchants, James and Greene, men of good estimation both for wit and wealth, lately broken for great sums, and it is doubted more will follow.

Ten, or rather twenty as others say, of our best merchants' ships are pressed here in the River for some service, which is thought to be either to keep the Hollanders *in cervello* about the East Indian trade, or to relieve Rochelle in case of need, or (as is most likely) to repress the insolency of the French fishermen who of late have usurped and encroached extremely upon the coast of Rhé and those parts without all limitation, and what with unlawful nets and other disorders have quite spoiled all the fishing of all that coast.

I perceive our East Indian merchants have here a strong apprehension that the Hollanders' General or Principal Factor in the Indies is not sound, which they collect by diverse arguments not only touching their own past differences and that concern the common alliance, but that he is false to his own masters, and, as they stick not to say, popishly affected and even Jesuited; whereby he doth still *bellum ex bello serere*[12] in those parts, and so by overlaying the business to overthrow all.

[**392**] October 20, 1621: Sir Thomas Roe is gone ambassador for Constantinople and carried his Lady along with him. God send them to escape the pirates who are strong and busy abroad, for two days since we had news that they have lately taken 57 sail of ours, whereof two were of London, 43 of the West Country, and 12 Scots;

---

[12] Engage in continual war.

and though most of their lading were but corn, fish, and such other slight merchandise, yet the loss of so many mariners and ships is no small matter, besides the impoverishing and discouraging of those poor towns, and the heartening and enabling of those thievish companions. It seems our fleet set out against them the last year did little good and went neither to Gravesend nor Ostend, nor to no end . . . but *irritare crabrones*.[13]

[406] April 27, 1622: Captain Walsingham (that had been a pirate) was sent to the Tower . . . for, being employed in the voyage to Algiers and ill satisfied for that service at his coming home, he began to prattle of returning to his old occupation, and for that purpose of surprising the Dreadnaught, one of the King's ships. Sir Robert Mansell and the rest of that crew are nothing well apaid neither, insomuch that Sir Richard Hawkins, the Vice-Admiral, finding his reckonings come short of that he expected, of mere grief and discontent sunk down before the Lords and died the next day.

[408] June 8, 1622: We have news this morning of two East India ships come into the Downs, which I hope will put some life into that company that did languish and was brought very low. They bring word likewise of three Hollanders come thence . . . for they left them at their last watering place.

[411] July 13, 1622: This week the Charles, a rich ship of 800 tons, is arrived here from Bantam and brings hope of one or two more coming after. Another likewise is come from Virginia with ill news that the savages have by surprise slain about 350 of our people there one and other. It was by their own supine negligence, that lived as careless and securely there as if they had been in England, in scattered and straggling houses far asunder, whereby they were so easily subject to the surprise of those naked people, who besides other spoil and booty have possessed themselves of arms and weapons;

---

[13] To stir up the hornets.

but the best is they have no skill to use them. Among them that are lost is one Captain Barclay and Captain Thorpe, whom I was well acquainted withal and had been a pensioner.

The disgrace and shame is as much as the loss, for no other nation would have been so grossly overtaken.

[428] April 19, 1623: There is a great faction fallen out in the Virginia Company. The heads of the one side are the Earl of Southampton, the Lord Cavendish, Sir Ed. Sackville, Sir John Ogle, Sir Ed. Sandys with diverse other of meaner quality. On the other side are the Earl of Warwick, Sir Thomas Smith, Sir Nathaniel Rich, Sir Henry Mildmay, Alderman Johnson and many more. On Monday they were before the King with their accusations and allegations, where Sir Ed. Sackville carried himself so malapertly and insolently that the King was fain to take him down soundly and roundly.

[434] July 12, 1623: Sir Thomas Roe hath taken great pains and thought he had done a *chef d'oeuvre* in concluding a truce or peace for our merchants with the pirates of Algiers and Tunis. But he is in danger to be disavowed and all this labor lost (howsoever it comes about) and we left to the mercy of those miscreants who have already seven or eight hundred of our able mariners, among whom many gunners and men of best service at sea, who by this treaty should have been delivered. And their wives, kindred, and friends do so importune his Majesty at all turns that he is forced sometimes to give them hard usage both in words and worse.

[435] July 26, 1623: The last week the Earl of Warwick and the Lord Cavendish fell so foul at a Virginia or Bermudas Court that the lie passed and repassed, and they are got over to try their fortune; yet we do not hear that they are met, so that there is hope they may return safe. In the meantime their Ladies forget not their old familiarity but meet daily to lament this misfortune. The factions in those two companies are grown so violent as Guelphs and Ghibellines were not more animated one against the other, and they seldom meet

upon the Exchange or in the streets but they brabble and quarrel; so that if that Society be not dissolved the sooner, or cast in a new mold, worse effects may follow than the whole business is worth.

Our old acquaintance Master Pory is in poor case and in prison at the Terceras, whither he was driven by contrary winds from the north coast of Virginia (where he had been upon some discovery), and upon his arrival was arraigned and in danger to be hanged for a pirate.

Our East India Company was at a low ebb but is now somewhat afloat again by the arrival of three ships richly laden. But I hear a whispering that the Spanish Ambassador hath a meaning to arrest them upon pretense of the business of Ormuz.[14]

[436] August 30, 1623: Here is a rich ship called the Palsgrave arrived from the East Indies laden with pepper, cloves, nutmegs, and other commodities. . . .

Master Pory is come home very poor, and the best help he can get or hope for from his friends is to procure him a protection from his old debts.

[456] August 7, 1624: Our East Indian merchants were somewhat revived the last week by the arrival of the Dolphin, a ship of good burthen laden with silks, indigo, calicoes, and such other commodities. But in the meantime the St. George, one of the best merchant ships of England, of four or five hundred ton with 32 pieces of ordnance, is seized upon at Naples, whither she was fraught by one Richaut, a Stranger that hath all the factory Burlamachi was wont to have, upon pretense that the Marquis Inojosa had bargained with him and bought it at his being here, which he denies. But howsoever they juggle between them, the ship is lost for us, and we, according to the old motto *Video et taceo,* see it and say nothing; as likewise the Dunkirkers rifle our ships at sea as familiarly as if open wars were proclaimed, whiles we protect theirs in the Downs.

---

[14] The East India Company and the Shah of Persia had captured Ormuz from the Portuguese, and the English established a factory there. James made the Company pay £10,000 each to him and Lord Admiral Buckingham as their share of the profits.

XI. Private Lives and Public Service, 1617-1624

WAR IN BOHEMIA,
PARLIAMENTARY HEROES AND SCAPEGOATS

THE *tolerant, eloquent, equivocal figure of Lancelot Andrewes, Bishop of Ely and then of Winchester, dominated the list of Chamberlain's friends during these increasingly lonely years. The continuing warm friendship with Lady Winwood at Ditton and Lady Fanshawe at Ware Park kept alive Chamberlain's habit of a summer "progress." Master William Camden brought weekly news to Paul's until his last illness, and Chamberlain wrote to Isaac Wake in Venice, receiving tuppence-worth of news now and then. He turned to sermons and lectures increasingly for interest. Evidently depressed by the way the world went, he no longer urged (perhaps because he could no longer help) Carleton to seek a Secretaryship, as first Lake and then Naunton fell by the wayside.*

"Tumbling and tossing" the papers and books in the late Secretary's study, Chamberlain and Lady Winwood provide a glimpse of the utterly casual way in which state papers were kept and cared for (witness Sir Walter Cope's promise, when he could not find his key, to make a bonfire of Cecil's correspondence with Carleton in 1612); no ambassador, no secretary of state, yet considered leaving records of negotiations to his successor.

Buckingham consolidated his power over the Howards with surprising ease, much aided by a generation of remarkably silly women. In 1619, he bought out the ancient Lord Admiral and undertook the job of running the Navy himself. Sir Edward Coke, getting a little of his own back, assisted in the overthrow of Lord Chancellor Bacon, and emerged a Parliamentary hero from the debates on monopolies. Meanwhile the beginning of the Thirty Years War in Bohemia, where James's son-in-law had been named King, moved the leader of Protestant Monarchs to send special embassies and

228]

*renew marriage negotiations with Spain, while the City of London
raised money by private subscription, and volunteers went off to
fight under Sir Horace Vere.*

[276] October 31, 1617: Upon the receipt of your letter of the 19th
of this present, I went to the Bishop of Ely,[1] whom I had not seen
long before his going into Scotland, nor since he was Councillor. I
was very welcome to him, and he used me with extraordinary kindness, though he expostulated with me very much for my long absence. I delivered him your proposition and withal (upon long conference) somewhat you had written touching the Arminians' coun-
tenancing themselves with some of his letters. Whereupon he fell
into long speech of a writing that the Archbishop Whitgift got from
him in some parts of that argument, and that he knows not what
became of it for he never gave copy of it but one only to Master
Hooker, who promised to return it but never did. But he expressed
not all the while which opinion he inclined to, but still insisted that
if they had any writing of his they should show it, concluding that I
should assure you that they have no letter of his, and with that
vehemency that he would give me leave to send you his head in a
platter if they could show any letter of his.

He told me further that Grotius, when he was here, dined once
with him and supped another time, but other communication than
passed at table he had none with him, though he understands since
that he gave out and fathered many things upon him that were
neither so nor so. Surely he hath a wonderful memory, for he not
only calls to mind any matter that passed at any time, but the very
time, place, persons, and all other circumstances, which seemed
strange to me in a discourse of almost two hours.

[277] November 8, 1617: The next day after I wrote my last, meeting with your brother Carleton, I conferred with him about his son,[2]
and told him in effect what you had written and what a furtherance

---

[1] Lancelot Andrewes.

[2] Dudley, who Carleton hoped would come as Secretary to his Embassy in
The Hague.

it might be to him every way in mine opinion. But I perceive by him he had written to you already . . . and would not resolve till he heard from you again.

Your brother Harrison is in town likewise, and upon Wednesday came Sir Henry Savile.[3] They do all apprehend how much the Lady Hatton might prevail if she would set her whole mind and strength to it, and I think they have and will find means to put her in remembrance. But the voice goes that the place is not likely to be disposed of in haste, for the King says he was never so well served as when he was his own Secretary, and to that end hath delivered the seals that were belonging to Sir Rafe Winwood to the custody of the Earl of Buckingham; and there perhaps they shall remain till they both grow weary of the trouble.

[278] November 15, 1617: Some whisper that [the Lady Hatton] is already engaged and means to employ her full force, strength and virtue for the Lord Haughton or Holles,[4] who is become her prime privy councillor and doth by all means interest and combine her with the Lady of Suffolk and that house,[5] a man whom Sir Edward Coke can noways endure and from whose company he would fain, but cannot, debar her. The world speaks of large offers made in his behalf, but others say that he which is already in place[6] makes as large to keep him and all others out. Neither is it now so much worth the following, seeing he hath gotten very lately the £1400 a year allowed for intelligence.

[280] December 20, 1617: Your friend Tobie Matthew shall remain here, as it is bruited, and be dispensed withal for taking the oath of allegiance, which, were it not in him, I should think it might prove a case of strange consequence.

His grand friend and protector[7] cannot forbear *pugnare cum*

---

[3] Carleton's father-in-law; Carleton was hoping for Winwood's place as Secretary of State.

[4] John, first Lord Holles of Haughton.

[5] The Howards.

[6] Sir Thomas Lake.

[7] Francis Bacon.

larvis[8] and is still glancing at the memory of our late deceased friend: as lately, in the arguing of the case before him twixt Secretary Lake and the Lord of Exeter and the Lord Burghley about the Lord Roos, he demanding why they had not followed this business sooner, answer was made by the Lord Burghley and his counsel that it was undertaken by a worthy Councillor deceased, who if he had lived till this time was in a way to compound it to the satisfaction of all sides; whereupon he replied, "If you trusted to him, you trusted to a rotten reed who would have failed you in the end. Indeed he had ways of his own, but now he is gone the way of all flesh," etc. This I assure you was much misliked by all or most that were present, and generally by all that have heard of it since. But they say a live dog hath the vantage of a dead lion.

[282] January 10, 1618: The King, before his going to Theobalds on Thursday, made Sir Robert Naunton Secretary, with many good words, saying he had destinated him to it presently upon the decease of Sir Rafe Winwood, though he acquainted nobody with it till now; further, that he did it *motu proprio* and *ex certa scientia*[9] of his sufficiency, without any other mediation, and gave him many good lessons, but specially of agreeing and drawing in one line with his fellow Secretary. . . .

The Earl of Exeter complains very much of the Spanish Ambassador, that he having from time to time afforded him many favors and giving him entertainment both at his house in Northamptonshire, at Wimbledon, and often here in town, upon assurance that he would procure the delivery of Molle[10] out of the Inquisition at Rome, he hath been so far from performing his promise that he hath now lastly seduced his son Roos and sent him to Rome with such recommendation as he is in danger to be utterly deprived of him. Your friend Tobie Matthew is become a great man with that Lady,[11]

---

[8] To compete with the worms.

[9] Of his own impulse and from certain knowledge.

[10] John Molle, tutor to William Cecil, Lord Roos, had been arrested when in Rome with Lord Roos in 1608, because in translating from the works of Duplessis-Mornay he had written of Babylon and Antichrist. He refused conversion and remained in prison for thirty years.

[11] Frances, Countess of Exeter, young step-grandmother of the unfortunate Lord Roos; Roos's venomous wife Anne Lake was about to make libelous accusations about their relationships.

and I heard it now two several ways that he hath perverted her to become a Roman Catholic, which I should be sorry should prove true, or that it should be blazed too far. . . .

I thank you for the French letter, and should have thanked you more if you had sent the determination of the Inquisition in the controversy twixt the Franciscans and Jacobins, which would have been a good errand for me to have visited the Bishop of Ely, who hath kept at home all this Christmas and preached not at Court, being surprised by a sudden surfeit of pork that had almost carried him away; but now he is in a manner recovered and sits up again. Since he was Councillor I come not so much at him as I was wont without some good occasion.

[283] January 17, 1618: Sir Thomas Lake's barony is at a stand, for having obtained the making of one, he found means to name himself, which the King yielded to; but when it was remonstrated to the King how unfit it was that a man of his fashion and education should have precedence of all the barons in England (as by virtue of his office he was to have), the King said that was not his meaning. But because he had promised, he should be a baron if he would, so that he left his office of Secretary; which no doubt he means not to do, unless ambition prevail very much with him and his Lady; who is said to have brought him into a strange labyrinth by accusing the Lady of Exeter of practicing to poison his daughter, the Lady Roos, and sending for a servant of hers by a wile, whom he himself examined and kept prisoner in his own house, which is thought somewhat hard in his own cause.

[285] February 7, 1618: We heard a fortnight since of Sir Henry Wotton's misfortune,[12] but I can hardly conceive how his house could be so wholly consumed. He is in pitiful plight if his case be such as the Venetian Ambassador painted it out to an English gentleman, that he is there *senza robba, senza denari, senza fede.*[13] . . .

---

[12] His house at Venice was burned to the ground.
[13] Without clothing, money or credit.

Yesterday I met Master Tobie Matthew whom I had not seen these six months, since which time to my seeming he is much defeated. He told me he was going to a play at the Blackfriars; but methinks playing and Friday's fasting agree not so well together as praying in a man of so much profession.

[286] February 14, 1618: Your letters of the 3rd of this present were delivered here by Master Baskerville the tenth. I thank you very much for the papers that accompanied them, which I will return when I have thoroughly read and perused them, which I have not yet done by reason of our lectures at Paul's this term time; and after I once go out of doors in the morning, I seldom come home till late at night. You need not misdoubt the passing of them through many hands, for I am now come to that pass that I keep not any company that cares for such matters, or that indeed are capable of them, saving only Master Camden, who makes a journey once a week the more into Paul's to meet and show me such occurrents as he hath from Master Beecher and others out of France, which, together with what I have from you, is now in a manner all the entertainment I have.

I made an errand to Ely House to have showed the Bishop the Pope's determination twixt the Franciscans and Jacobins, if he had not seen it, as likewise what you wrote touching Grotius, to make him at least more wary hereafter, though for aught I ever heard he hath used caution enough that way. But he was at Lambeth, and lies now at Whitehall, where in Secretary Winwood's time I came very seldom and now not at all.

[287] February 21, 1618: I went again this week to my Lord of Ely, and had some speech with him concerning Grotius, from whom he confesses he had a letter lately, and that before Christmas one came to him for an answer, but being presently to preach at Court, and not finding himself well at ease, he made his excuse. But I perceive by this that he holds him for a very learned and able man; yet I doubt not but this little conference will serve him for a caveat here-after. . . .

Master Trumbull is going over again, having obtained double

allowance for his entertainment hereafter, upon the precedent of Master Beecher, and no doubt but Master Wake[14] will follow the example.

[**288**] February 28, 1618: On Sunday the Lady Roos was from the Council table admitted to the custody of the Bishop of London. . . . The business is now in the King's hands, but with this caution from the Earl of Exeter, that he recommends it unto him as to a judge, and a just judge, and not as an arbitrator. Sir Thomas Lake and that side desire to be left to the law and that they may follow it in the Star Chamber, which the Lord of Exeter seeks by all means to avoid, as a dilatory course, and that were like to make an end of him sooner than the cause.

For my part I know not what to conjecture, but it should seem that Sir Thomas Lake and his are fallen into a labyrinth whence they know not how to get out, for it behooves him to make good proofs of so heinous imputations against a lady of her sort, and it stands her upon likewise to clear herself from so foul scandals of precontracts, adultery, incest, murder, poison, and suchlike peccadilloes.

I have gone further in this matter than I meant at first, for it had been better to attend the issue than to write so uncertainly and by guess, but for want of other news I do only tell you what is said in Paul's. The Lady Roos . . . is described and pointed out to be a very pert lady, and is said to *matrissare* right, or rather to domineer as much over her mother as her mother doth over some others.

[**289**] March 7, 1618: Master Wake's three halfpenny-worth of news cost me a whole shilling, but I presume it will be welcome to my Lady, because she is so well acquainted with the place and the persons.

[**290**] March 16, 1618: Harman the post, when he brought your last letters, not finding me at home, left word I should provide you

---

[14] Agents in Brussels, Paris, and Turin respectively.

some flowers; but I, knowing what plenty and variety you have there of tulips and the like, could not conceive what manner of flowers he meant, till he, coming on Friday last to tell me that he was to go towards you this day, spake of wallflowers and primroses, which the Lady Winwood says you may easily have at the milkhouse over against you, where she was wont to provide herself of those sorts, without any trouble or charge of sending so far. But if there be any other kinds here that you desire, both she and the Lady Fanshawe have promised to furnish you with any of their store.

Young Fanshawe is ready to go into France to spend a year in travel, and tarries for nothing but his license, which hath been deferred now this fortnight by reason the Secretaries have little access to the King during his indisposition, but hopes to be presently dispatched now that the King begins to look abroad.

[292] April 1, 1618: Though here be nothing since my last worth the writing, and that my Lady herself be so sufficient a secretary for you and so well stored and furnished with all that is current at Court, yet I must put in my mite, that you may see I would not be sparing if I had more. As far as I see or can gather, her coming may be many ways beneficial to you and not unfruitful to others, for it is generally received and held that her main errand is for money, which no doubt will procure some better course for the entertainment of Ambassadors. And I think your coming over will be no hard matter to compass, which will be a good means for you to discern how matters are likely to pass and to direct your course accordingly. . . . I am not altogether of the opinion of some that look for so sudden alterations, for the world is grown as cunning in countermining as in undermining; but sure this business of the Lady of Exeter will bring forth somewhat.

[294] April 20, 1618: Yesterday I had a sight of my Lady at Mercer's Chapel in company of the Countess of Bedford, who came to hear the Archbishop of Spalato that made a kind of introduction for the new-come Italian preacher.[15]

---

[15] Caesar Calandrini, brother-in-law of the financier Philip Burlamachi; he had been Chamberlain's travelling companion in 1611.

[295] April 29, 1618: I am not so sorry for your stay as glad that you were not in the tempest we had here on Sunday night at northwest, one of the sorest that I have heard, which puts me in remembrance and practice of that we pray for in the procession for all that travel by land or by water; in which number you were in my special memento (by way of provision) if you should need it.

[296] May 5, 1618: Harman the post that brought your letters of the 25th of the last is dispatched back very speedily. . . . I am glad my Lady is not in town, for she would straight apprehend that this his sudden return might be a stay or delay of your coming; for before she went she suspected some working against it, and therefore gave out that she expected you hourly. Secretary Lake hath of late had so many feathers pulled from him that he fears to be left bare, and therefore no doubt doth *omnem movere lapidem*[16] to keep off competitors; and still makes himself strong among the North Britons, for seeing he could hold the Secretaryship of the Latin tongue no longer, he hath brought in one Read, a Scottish man, who is in hand to translate all the King's works into Latin. . . .

I hear no news nor speech of Secretary Naunton, no more in a manner than if there were no such man in *rerum natura,* which is a strange kind of obscurity for a man of his place, to lie so close and hidden that he should scant be seen or heard of at home.

[298] August 13, 1618: I was sorry to understand by your letter from Margate that you found no readier passage,[17] for I know how tedious it is to be wind-bound, specially when business doth press. . . .

The Lady Winwood hath lost her elder daughter Betty, who died of a burning fever on Tuesday last and was brought up the next night to be buried by her father. No doubt it is a great affliction to the good Lady, for this child was her only jewel and she more fond of it than of all the rest.

---

[16] Leave no stone unturned.

[17] Carleton had spent June and July in England.

[300] October 14, 1618: The Lady Winwood hath been dangerously sick at Ditton. She sent me a letter to Ware Park to let her understand when I came to town, for she had promised you certain of her husband's papers, which she would have me choose out for you, though she doubted they would now come out of season because you have stayed for them so long. She is not so well recovered as to come hither yet, but she offered to send me her key. Now I do not well remember what it is you most desire, unless it be some of his books of negotiations, so that if you please to send me word what be the times or the pieces you most desire, I will give her to understand. . . .

The Lady Fanshawe desires to be remembered to you both. Her son is lately come out of Fance, where he was soon weary.

[301] October 24, 1618: About this day sevennight there went a packet to call home Master Beecher, but no passengers permitted to go over, nor any ship to go from any port without special warrant from Secretary Naunton. This course hath held now this full fortnight, which is longer than ever I knew any restraint in that kind, and breeds much speech what the reason should be. But no man I meet withal can make any probable conjecture unless it be that a swarm of priests and Jesuits is said to be lately arrived and crept in among us. Some say the Marquis Buckingham, being newly possessed of the Admiralty, begins this way to show his care and diligence; it is given out that he hath compounded with the old Admiral [18] for a good round sum of ready money and £3000 yearly pension during his life, and after his decease £1000 to his Lady and £500 to his eldest son by her, which must be doubled to him when she is gone.

[303] November 7, 1618: On Wednesday last Sir Richard Wenman married the stale widow[19] in St. Bartholomews, that brags she had the refusal of a White Staff.[20] . . . The best is he takes nothing to heart

---

[18] Charles Howard, Earl of Nottingham, now eighty-two, d. 1624.
[19] Anne, widow of Chamberlain's brother Robert (d. 1607).
[20] I.e., an officer of the King's Household.

but gives himself *buon tempo,* and in company of two Councillors more was seen at an ordinary play at the Blackfriars since this term began. The widow made her capitulations with Sir R. Wenman to live in London all the winter, not to be troubled with his children, to reserve £400 a year for her own maintenance, leaving him £800 a year to dispose of, besides £2000 ready money and other implements that she brings with her.

Your brother Carleton is in town and so is his son, who I think will write to you and inform you of what he knows and hears. For my part, I should not wish you to engage yourself too far as these tickle times stand.

[305] November 21, 1618: This week upon notice from Master Locke[21] that what you wanted of Sir Rafe Winwood's negotiations was from the year 1609 to 1612, I went to the Lady Winwood who was very willing to satisfy you therein and presently carried me into the study where his books and writings were, where she, her gentlewoman and myself, in tumbling and tossing the books and papers all over, could light on none that he wrote since his going into the Low Countries, but only such as concerned his business in France. She was somewhat troubled withal (for she meant to reserve them for her son), but saith she will make a quest of inquiry after them, wherein she requires your assistance; for no doubt they that furnished you with the former can tell what is become of the rest.

Your sister Williams and all her retinue are come to lie in town for this winter, having taken a house, or the best part of a house, not far from Fleet Bridge.

[306] November 28, 1618: Upon receipt of your letter of the 14th of this present, I went to my Lord of Winchester[22] with the printed paper of the Synod, which he was glad to see and took kindly from you, saying withal that he could make shift with the Dutch, and that it was the first general Synod that ever was held with one bishop.

---

[21] Who was now managing Carleton's business affairs in London.
[22] Lancelot Andrewes, promoted Bishop of Winchester. The Synod of Dort was debating the problems raised by Arminian teaching.

Your Commissioners[23] are arrived, but what welcome they shall find I know not. Our people begin to flout them already, saying brawn is like to be good cheap this Christmas, seeing so many boors are come to town.

[314] January 23, 1619: The Commissioners meet at Merchant Tailors' Hall, and I hear our men find your Dutchmen very subtle and cunning. How they will agree in the end I know not, but we hear that hitherto they speak loud on both sides.

[315] January 30, 1619: On Wednesday . . . there was some entrance into the Lady of Exeter's business and order taken to abbreviate and cut off superfluous and impertinent matter and so make it more fit for the King's hearing. . . . The Lady of Exeter went that day to the Star Chamber accompanied by the Countesses of Arundel and Bedford, and a comitiva of I know not how many ladies more, to the number of thirty coaches; but whether she appeared in the Court or no I cannot certainly learn. Secretary Lake and his followers continue still confident, and some say the Lady Roos was there likewise with her little troop. The speech goes that she is to marry[24] with the Lord John Paulet, another grandchild of the Earl of Exeter's and heir apparent to the Marquis of Winchester.

[316] February 6, 1619: [Lady Winwood] hath bestowed her niece on Sir John Trevor's son and heir. I remember I wrote you more than a year and a half since that there was a treaty with Sir John Pakington's son, which came so near to conclusion that all articles were agreed and the wedding clothes made; but when it came to the upshot, the gentlewoman had no manner of liking, nor could by any means be persuaded, which so displeased her uncle that he left her worse by ten thousand pound than he meant to have done, which doth no whit grieve her, in respect that she hath her choice. . . .

---

[23] To negotiate about trade in the East Indies.
[24] William Cecil, Lord Roos, had died in Italy during the summer.

The King sat in the Star Chamber on Wednesday from nine o'clock till past twelve, and yesterday from before eight till almost one. He recommended brevity to the lawyers, and kept them as close to the point as he could. Himself made a short spech the first day in which among other things he compared himself to Solomon that was to judge between two women . . . and to find out the true mother of the child (that is, verity).

[317] February 13, 1619: Your sisters are shut up here in town, the smallpox being come among them, which began with your niece's little daughter not full a fortnight old (a thing I have seldom seen or heard of) and so spread to the other three children, and hitherto gone no further. I never knew them generally so infectious.

The King means to go back toward Newmarket on Monday. Yesterday he went to visit the Queen at Hampton Court. He was in the Star Chamber anon after seven o'clock on Monday, and had the masque that night, that he might be as early there again on Wednesday morning, both which days he held out with great patience till after twelve. . . . There was strange stuff, they say, delivered, and indeed such as was not to be heard in such a presence, insinuated in such manner as was generally understood.

It seems Sir Thomas Lake hath made very great means, for he and his daughter Roos have been twice or thrice at least with the King since Sunday and perhaps since Wednesday; . . . yet if all I heard be true, within these few days the King said he was not for his service that would presume at this time in this cause to write him lies, for whom the Spanish Ambassador had been so importunate a suitor and solicitor, and one that was so devoutly prayed for daily at Brussels, as Trumbull had sent him word. And withal openly in the Star Chamber upon Monday *ex re nata*,[25] he gave an item to all his secretaries or that stood to be secretaries, not to impart matters of state to their wives. . . .

Now upon inquiry I find that Sir Thomas Lake is fined at £5000, his wife at £5000, and the Lady Roos at 10,000 marks, besides £4000 costs to the Lady of Exeter, . . . his son Sir Thomas at

---

[25] Pursuing this train of thought.

500 marks to the King and £1000 to the Lady of Exeter for putting
in a cross, slanderous bill into the Court. Their further sentence is to
make submission in that Court or where the King shall appoint to the
Lady of Exeter; and himself, his Lady, and the Lady Roos to imprisonment in the Tower at their own charge during life; Sara their
maid to pay £100, to be publicly whipped and branded in the face
with F and A for a false accuser. . . . The Lord Digby was somewhat more mild, and would have mollified his offense by the tender
affection he bare to his wife and child . . . but the King willed him
to clear him if he could, or condemn him with the rest. . . .

The King spake long and excellently to every point, comparing
this to the first judgment, Sir Thomas Lake to Adam, his Lady to
Eve, and the Lady Roos to the serpent.

And this is the sum of all I could write you of the King's sitting
five days in the Star Chamber. He spake likewise to the Justices of
Peace and Lieutenants of Shires, to make preparations for musters
and to have all their trained men ready at ten days' warning; as likewise against papists that begin to wax bold upon opinion of a match
with Spain.

[318] February 20, 1619: Sara hath . . . been examined again and
upon confession of the truth promised to be released of her punishment, but hitherto she stands obdurate; and I think is this day to be
first whipped if she redeem not herself, as the Lady Lake wished her
to do at parting with her, upon any conditions, without regarding
them at all: which was a crafty and malicious counsel, howsoever
the matter should fall out. As likewise Sir Thomas Lake wished her
to be constant in the truth, but whether she did or no, she should not
want while he lived.

On Monday toward eight o'clock at night, himself, his Lady, and
the Lady Roos were sent to the Tower in several coaches, and
lodged asunder in several lodgings as close prisoners. . . . They
say she takes this affliction very impatiently, and was fain to be carried as it were by violence into the coach, a thing usual to such
insolent natures that can neither bear prosperity nor adversity.

The King went to Theobalds on Tuesday, but before his going,
Sir George Calvert was sworn Secretary. . . . The night before he

was sworn, the Lord of Buckingham told him the King's resolution, but he disabled himself diverse ways, but specially that he thought himself unworthy to sit in that place so lately possessed by his noble lord and master.[26] The King was well pleased with his answer and modesty, and, sending for him, asked him many questions, most about his wife. His answer was that she was a good woman and had brought him ten children, and would assure his Majesty that she was not a wife with a witness.

This and some other passages of this kind seem to show that the King is in a great vein of taking down highhanded women. And yet the Lady Hatton doth manage her matters so well that she daily wins ground of her husband, holding her great friends still in hope and expectation, who are loath otherwise to exasperate her if they may win her by fair means. I can say nothing more, but seeing she would do you no good in this cause, I pray God she did you no harm.

[319] February 27, 1619: As I wrote the last week, Sara Swarton was in the fair way to be whipped. But when the cart and all other implements were ready to carry her to the pillory at Westminster, where she was expected by great multitudes, her stomach came down and she desired to speak with the Lord Chief Justice, to whom she confessed a great deal of villainy: but specially that she had taken an oath and received the sacrament to keep all close. Yet she freely acknowledged that the imputation of poison and incest laid upon the Lady of Exeter were merely forged and false, as likewise the recognition of the said Lady to the Lady Roos. But she would not confess who wrote it, more than that one led another's hand in writing it. Her confession was likewise large in other points touching the young Lady's behavior, which by report was so filthy as is not to be named, and that incest which they would have imposed upon others returns on their own heads, betwixt her brother Sir Arthur and herself. . . .

It seems to me very strange and yet most true that Sir Thomas Lake should be so absurd and base as, since his imprisonment, to write to the Lord of Exeter and his Lady to remit and forgive the costs and damages awarded them in the Star Chamber.

---

[26] Calvert had been Clerk of the Council.

[320] March 6, 1619: Sir William Cooke, a near kinsman of the Lord Chancellor's, [died] of the smallpox. But Sir Arthur Lake[27] and his wife lie sweating (they say) of another kind, it being yet in question among friends of both sides whither the Lady had them, by his gift or by her own purchase.

[325] April 24, 1619: Your States and other Commissioners here had a great feast made them for a farewell on Monday at Merchant Tailors' Hall, and on Tuesday night our artillerymen made them a great supper there, with a warlike dance or masque of twelve men in complete armor. It seems they are quite broken off about the Moluccas, which may come ill to pass for both sides—but what remedy?

I met the last week with a proposition of yours made there I think in January last, about the defectuosity of these Commissioners' authority and instructions, and about their cunning declining of some other points that were to be cleared, wherein you spake home. But in my poor opinion there would either be more done or less said, for, *verba dum sint*,[28] they will still be the same men.

[332] July 15, 1619: Poor Harry Parker was released on Friday out of the Gatehouse where he had lain five or six weeks. . . . Sir Arthur Lake was delivered somewhat before, and on Saturday the Lady Roos, for her good service, was set at liberty,[29] whiles her father, poor man, passes his time in sawing off billets and giving order to sell land and all his leases. . . .

Upon report of your being so much troubled with the stone, I had some conference this last term with Sir William Borlase, who hath been much afflicted with it heretofore, and presumes this medicine I send here enclosed is a special preservative to prevent it,

---

[27] Son of Sir Thomas.

[28] While words are (only) words.

[29] Parker, deputy Clerk of the Star Chamber, had been "charged by the Lady Roos that for money he had forborne to swear her when she was examined" (Letter 327). On June 19, "the Lady Roos did under her hand acknowledge . . . all the faults and forgeries of that business" (Letter 330) and was pardoned her fines.

having had especial proof of it as well in himself as others. The thing is very safe and easy, which is not the least commendation of a medicine.

[333] July 31, 1619: Your letter of the 16th of this present found me out at Ditton, where I continued ten or twelve days very well used and much made of and yet, I know not how, grew very weary of the country, whether it were that I was somewhat crasie all the while, or that I was seized with the ordinary disease of age: to be nowhere so well as at home. . . .

Sir Harry Wotton is come (they say) in poor plight, having tarried as long as his credit would hold out, and with as little hope to procure his entertainment here, or any tolerable condition.

Sara Swarton is quit by making a public submission on Sunday last at her parish church of St. Martin's in the Field, and acknowledging her faults and forgeries, but afterward (as I hear) in the same place clearing Sir Thomas Lake and his Lady (what she could) and laying all the blame on the Lady Roos. On Thursday Sir Thomas Lake was set at liberty (but his wife lies by it still), and against his coming home the bells were rung and a noise of trumpets ready to receive and welcome him; and all this by order from himself, if it be credible.

[335] August 23, 1619: On Tuesday last I went with the Lady Winwood to render the visit at Ware Park. The young Lady Trevor (her niece) with her husband, Mistress Packer, her eldest son, and her ward Wingfield, were all our company. They found very kind and friendly usage and came away well pleased, but for a mischance that happened to young Bedell, the late bridegroom, who following hard after a buck the Lady Winwood had struck, his horse carried him against a tree, so that with the blow and fall he was sore battered and bruised, and at our coming away we left him in a burning fever. But a physician was presently sent for, and I hope all will be well; else should I be loath to return thither tomorrow for the rest of this summer, as I have purposed and promised if God will. . . .

Yesterday by good hap I lighted on Maurice Abbot, and in conference of East India matters I told him how little you were beholden to them, considering your care and pains in their business. He confessed you were forgotten because you were not in their eye, but he would put some in mind of it that might see it amended. . . . If you hear nothing of them before I return, I will cause Sir Thomas Smith to understand it one way or other.[30]

[336] September 11, 1619: I came from Ware Park on Wednesday morning with the Lady Fanshawe upon a sudden occasion of Sir Christopher Hatton's sickness, who, after all the helps of physic and nature, and many good signs of recovery, left this world yesterday in the afternoon. His disease was altogether after the manner of Secretary Winwood's, so that from the first hour I saw him, for all the physicians' fair promises, I gave him for lost. He hath left a fair estate in lands, but I doubt much encumbered with debts, and his younger children utterly unprovided, for he died intestate; unless the poor Lady, by the administration and the wardship of her son, granted indifferently to her and Sir Thomas Hatton, can find means to raise portions for two daughters and three younger sons, besides the heir.

His death, besides the loss of so good a friend, concerns the Lady Fanshawe and her son very much, for that he was Master of that Office[31] in trust to their use, and now by his death they are driven to sue to the King to have the patent renewed in their own or some other name, which in this catching world may prove a matter both of trouble and charge to them.

[337] October 2, 1619: I came to town on Michaelmas day with the Lady Fanshawe, who follows her business so close that (notwith-

---

[30] Abbot was Director of the East India Company and brother of George Abbot, Archbishop of Canterbury; Smith was Governor of the East India Company. Carleton was feeling put out because the Commissioners had all been given fine presents but himself, "the prime instrument," forgotten.
[31] Remembrancer of the Exchequer, held by Sir Christopher in trust for Lady Fanshawe and her son, Thomas.

standing some rubs) she hath gotten her eldest son sworn Master of the Office since Sir Christopher Hatton's decease; and all things else so well settled as could not be expected in so short time among so many and sudden removes of the Court from place to place, and in vacation time when so many officers were absent through whose hands the business must pass.

I received at Ware Park your letters . . . touching the loss of Sir Christopher Hatton, which his friends bear the more patiently for that in all likelihood, if he had lived long, he would have much weakened, if not ruined, his whole estate, being of so easy and kind nature that he could deny nothing to his friends or kindred, who wrought upon him extraordinarily, and being already entered so far into debt as would in no long time have eaten and consumed as good a living as his.

[349] March 11, 1620: The Bishop of Winchester began Lent with an excellent sermon upon the epistle of the day out of the prophet Joel, and there was the greatest throng that ever I saw at a sermon.

[354] May 27, 1620: Here came a messenger from the Princes of the Union[32] with a short errand (they say) and as short a letter, desiring to know our resolution, for that they could no longer depend upon excuses and distinctions, but must provide for the residue as well as they could. . . .

For all the haste, I do not hear he is yet dispatched, but Sir Henry Wotton must carry the answer and take them in his way to Venice, being to take his leave at Court in the Whitsun holidays. . . .

Sir Thomas Lake kissed the King's hand the last week and is in hope by the good help of his Spanish friends to come to the Council table again, if not further.

[355] June 28, 1620: Sir Henry Wotton is now upon his departure, accompanied as I hear with more than twenty young gentlemen,

---

[32] The Protestant Princes of Germany, wanting help against the Emperor in Bohemia and the Palatinate.

who I presume go most upon their own charge, or else he will not be long able to continue his late confident speech that he doth not now owe one penny in England, which one of his friends, standing by, said would be an excellent epitaph if he could leave it on his monument.

[356] July 8, 1620: Sir Henry Wotton is so confident of himself and his dexterity in managing the business he goes about that he told diverse of our captains he was in hope to effect that they should keep their swords in their scabbards. In the meantime our new levies go on but heavily; and whereas they thought they should have been oppressed with multitudes of followers, they are fain to send far and near into the country to make up their numbers, which if they were once full they would be gone presently this next week.

I am sorry Sir Horace Vere should go so slenderly accompanied as to command but 2000 men, which gives the Spanish Ambassador occasion to break jests, and say he must needs confess we are a very brave nation that dare adventure with 2000 to encounter 10,000.

[358] August 4, 1620: Your cousin Rowland Lytton is coming towards you, and perhaps brings this letter. . . .

Sir George Smith, his brother-in-law, is come to a fair preferment for a man of his rank, to trail a pike in my Lord of Oxford's company, of whom some idle companion hath made a ridiculous rhyme which goes about (but as I am no author, so I would be no spreader of it but to yourself):

> Some say Sir Edward Cecil can
> Do as much as any man.
> But I say No, for Sir Horace Vere
> Hath carried the Earl of Oxford where
> He neither shall have wine nor whore:
> Now Hercules himself could do no more.[33]

---

[33] Sir Horace Vere was Commander-in-Chief of the English volunteer forces. Henry de Vere, 18th Earl of Oxford, held a command under him.

[359] September 9, 1620: I am very glad to see the care you have of those young gentlemen, your kinsmen the Lyttons, that are so careless of themselves (specially Phillip), and it is a worthy part of you, and no doubt propitiatory before God and men to have that regard as well of the dead as of the living. . . .

The Bishop of Winchester went beyond himself in his magnificent entertainment of the King at Farnham Castle, for it is certainly said that in three days (besides presents and other helps) it cost him toward three or four and twenty hundred pound.

[360] September 16, 1620: I am sorry [your Lady] hath so slow success in her business[34] and is still fed with promises. I assure you that (as far as my understanding doth reach) it cannot be imputed to want of care, diligence, nor dexterity, no nor to want of friends, but to some fatal *fénéantise* and barrenness of the time.

[361] October 7, 1620: We have yet no certainty of the people's joining with the Princes, nor have any great hope what good they can do upon such disadvantage. But considering how the case stands, and the time of year, it seems the war will be drawn out in length, and so we and our friends consumed *à petit feu;*[35] which might in all likelihood be prevented if we could be persuaded to strike at the root and not stand lopping off twigs and leaves which will sprout again as fast as they are taken away. . . .

Your Lady hath brought her business to good pass and is in a fair way to obtain the arrearages, if promises, protestations, and Privy Seals be of any force. But matters of payment grow so faulty and fallacious that a man cannot presume of anything till he have it in his hand.

[363] October 28, 1620: We are in suspense whether we shall have a Parliament after Christmas or no. For mine own part I cannot

---

[34] Obtaining payment of Carleton's allowance as ambassador.
[35] By a slow fire.

perceive any good either way, for impositions and patents are grown so grievous that of necessity they must be spoken of, and the prerogative, on the other side, is become so tender that (like a *noli me tangere*[36]) it cannot endure to be touched. . . .

For aught I see you are not like to hear of Phil Lytton, for before his brother Rowland's letter came, he had put himself into the Earl of Salisbury's service. There will be but little miss of him, for as far as I can learn by his friends, *antiquum obtinet*.[37] . . . This week the Lord Chancellor[38] hath set forth his new work called *Instauratio Magna,* or a kind of new organum of all philosophy. In sending it to the King, he wrote that he wished his Majesty might be as long in reading it as he hath been in composing and polishing it, which is well near thirty years. I have read no more than the bare title, and am not greatly encouraged by Master Cuffe's judgment, who having long since perused it gave this censure, that a fool could not have written such a work and a wise man would not.

[364] November 4, 1620: It seems we live of late under some rolling planet, for it is observed that in less than five years most of our principal officers have been displaced or disgraced, as a Lord Chancellor, a Lord Treasurer, a Lord Chamberlain, a Lord Admiral, a Master of the Horse, a Secretary, a Master of the Wards, a Lord Chief Justice, and an Attorney General.[39]

[365] November 9, 1620: Your Lady is in great deliberation and suspense what to do, whether to make towards you by the first occasion, or to expect you here, whereunto she is animated by the

---

[36] Don't tread on me.

[37] His old habit persists.

[38] Francis Bacon.

[39] Respectively, Thomas Egerton, Lord Ellesmere, Viscount Brackley; Thomas Howard, 1st Earl of Suffolk; Robert Carr, Earl of Somerset; Charles Howard, 1st Earl of Nottingham; Theophilus Howard, Lord Walden; Sir Thomas Lake; William Knollys, Viscount Wallingford; Sir Edward Coke; and Sir Henry Yelverton. Egerton died March 10, 1617; Somerset and Lake were disgraced by their women; Coke had dared challenge the royal prerogative; but the Howards, Knollys and Yelverton had all sinned by finding themselves in opposition to Buckingham.

advice of diverse your good and great friends. For mine own part, I know not what to wish, unless I were thoroughly acquainted with all the resorts that pertain to this business; for if the motion proceed from the *primum mobile,*[40] it must be followed, but if from secondary causes and pretenses, it were good to descant upon it . . . unless you bring *aliquid novum aut magnum*[41] that may seem to require your personal presence. In which case likewise I would wish you to have sufficient warrant and not to rely too much upon private letters, for I cannot forget Sir Thomas Bodley that overthrew himself and his fortunes by such overweening. . . .

The King pricked the Sheriffs on Sunday before going from Theobalds. . . . This course of pricking Sheriffs is come to that pass that it is in a manner all one to be presented in the bill or to be out, for there is such canvassing on all sides that whosoever is any way capable of it in any shire must look to himself, whereby great men's followers make a continual rent or contribution of all gentlemen that seek to avoid it.

[**367**] December 22, 1620: Captain Goldwell brought me [your letter] with the news of Sir George Smith's decease, which I did presently impart to your cousin Bess Lytton who lies now at Master Underwood's, a new-married woman to one Master Windham . . . a good match, and I am very glad of her good fortune. . . . Some nine or ten days since, Sir Henry Wallop carried down the Lady Smith and her children to keep Christmas in Hampshire, whither we have sent the sad tidings, and expect her here shortly. In the meantime the Master and other officers of the Court of Wards are made acquainted with the case, and we hope to find favor. And if you have any occasion to write to Sir Benjamin Rudyard, I wish you would be pleased to recommend the cause to him, the rather for that the gentleman went voluntary, and died in the King's service.

[P.S.] I had almost forgot that on Tuesday was sevennight I was invited, by a gentleman sent to my lodging, to dine with the Lord Chancellor, where I was used with much kindness and familiarity— howsoever it came about.

---

[40] Prime mover. I.e., Buckingham.
[41] Something new or great.

[369] January 20, 1621: On Wednesday . . . Secretary Naunton was commanded to keep his chamber or his house and suspended from meddling in any public business. Some add that Secretary Calvert was then sent to search his papers and fetch his seals from him. How far this is true I know not, more than that Secretary Calvert went to him. Many surmises there be touching this alteration, but the most probable in my judgment is that there was some secret intelligence twixt him, the Baron Dohna and others about the business of Bohemia. . . .

Some will needs ascribe this disgrace to the working and potency of the Spanish Ambassador, but it is not likely: unless perhaps Sir Thomas Lake should succeed and be put again in his old remitter, which some harp upon but I cannot believe. Neither will I conceal that the voice and choice runs generally twixt yourself and Master Packer, in which case for my part (as the world goes) I know not what to think nor what to wish, but leave it to His disposition who doth all for the best, to whose holy protection I commend you and my good Lady.

[370] February 3, 1621: On Saturday the Lord Chancellor was created Viscount St. Albans with all the ceremonies of robes and coronet, whereas the rest were only done by patent; and yet for all these special favors the King cannot forbear sometimes, in reading his last book, to say that it is like the Peace of God, that passeth all understanding. . . .

My Lady's daughter Tredway hath found out a good husband, one Stafford, a scholar of Oxford about 17 years old, but of a very good state and towardliness, though the match were made without consent of his friends, he being yet a Ward.

[372] February 17, 1621: As I was closing up this letter by candle-light, an officer of the East India Company brings me commendations from Sir Dudley Digges, with this enclosed letter, and withal delivers me two hundred Jacobus pieces for your use, all sound and good (as he says) which shall continue safe in my custody, God willing, till you send order how to dispose of them. The fellow that brought them

went away as he came, for that I had no commission nor know not how to gratify him.

[374] March 10, 1621: Touching the Parliament, they are very busy about Sir Giles Mompesson[42] and the rest of that crew. . . . But Sir Giles Mompesson . . . fearing himself, yesterday was seven-night at night, under color of finding certain papers in his wife's closet, escaped from the Sergeant who had him in custody and hath showed a fair pair of heels; whereupon the next morning the Nether House had a conference with the Lords, who together with the Prince, promised all manner of assistance for his apprehension. And there the Marquis of Buckingham made a good and honorable speech of his continual carriage in these and the like business, and so washed his hands and cleared himself that he renounced all kind of protection of such persons. . . .

This and the like business hath held the House all this week, and on Thursday . . . they had a conference with the Lords, where the Prince was present as he is likewise almost every day in the Upper House, where they had appointed and made choice of six persons for several parts to show the incredible enormities, abuses, and extortions the realm endured by these people and their courses. Sir Dudley Digges was for the preamble and introduction, which he performed so exceedingly well that he won great approbation; and Sir Ed. Coke yesterday in his report to the House, besides other high praises, said he spake apt, ornate, *perspicue,* and *breviter.* . . .

Sir Ed. Coke's part was to show precedents, what the law and other Parliaments from time to time had done in like cases, which he did so admirably well that he hath won his spurs forever. And they all confess that they could not have missed him, for that he hath so led and directed them all this Parliament that they cannot be satisfied with applauding him both before and behind his back. And indeed he is a happy man if he can leave here, for he hath proceeded hitherto with a great deal of sincerity, temper, and discretion, more than usual in him.

Having written thus far in the morning, all I can learn since dinner

---

[42] A kinsman of Buckingham's, in trouble for raising extortionate sums under his monopoly for licensing inns; James had refused Buckingham's request that he dissolve Parliament, so the Marquis swam with the tide.

is that the King went this day to the Parliament House. . . . Thus much is said, that the precedents and examples produced by the Lord Coke are not liked nor allowed of, as falling out in weak reigns and turbulent times.

[375] March 24, 1621: The Parliament House receives daily very gracious messages from his Majesty, whereby they are much animated . . . ; they ply the business very hard, and for the most part sit both before and after dinner, besides many conferences and committees. For they find it more than Hercules' labor *purgare hoc Stabulum Augiae*[43] of monopolies, patents, and the like.

And they are now fallen into another labyrinth (whence they see no way out) of briberies and extortions in matters of justice, and the first tempest is fallen upon my Lord Chancellor, against whom there come in daily more petitions and accusations than they can overcome, wherein his own friends are made special instruments against him, as Sir George Hastings, Sir Richard Young and others who, being principal brokers, for defense of themselves are forced to accuse him. It were too long to tell you the particulars, but three, four, seven hundred, yea a thousand pieces were but ordinary morsels, and there is a cause yet depending and not finished that hath already yielded him (from both sides) eighteen hundred pound. . . .

Yet seems he doth either dissemble or not feel the ignominy that hangs over him, but carries himself as he was wont. Yet his friends give out that he is very sick, and so would move commiseration. But all men approve the Lord Coke, who upon discovery of these matters exclaimed that a corrupt Judge was the grievance of grievances. For mine own part I assure you I do much lament that a man of so excellent parts should prove so foul and faulty as is pretended.

Diverse Lords do visit him daily, and the Lord of Buckingham more than any, which the world thinks is not without a mystery, and many things are spoken that are not to be written. The Spanish Ambassador was likewise to visit him, but he desired to be excused; yet sending him word withal that he was now nearer to his religion than ever, for that he began to believe and feel a purgatory.

Many indignities are said and done against him, and diverse libels cast abroad to his disgrace not worth the repeating, as savoring of too

---

[43] To purge this Augean Stable.

much malice and scurrility. God send him patience, and that he may make the best use of this affliction.

[376] March 28, 1621: Sir Ed. Coke doth not altogether hold the great applause he had, which was such that (besides every man's particular commendation) the whole House was drawn to give him thanks publicly for his care and diligence, with which being puffed up he became careless what he propounded, and brought forth precedents sometimes misapplied or perverted to a wrong sense; but most men impute this to his age and want of memory, which indeed begins to fail him so far that they are fain to help him in his reports from committees to or from the Higher House. And it seems he overlades himself with too much business, so that they plainly perceive that *aliquando bonus dormitat Homerus.*[44]

The Lord Chancellor stirs not abroad since he wrote to the Lords, which letter contained little of worth either for words or invention, only complaining of want of health and excusing himself from base bribery. . . .

Secretary Naunton hangs still in suspense, only he hath the liberty to graze in St. James's Park.

[378] April 18, 1621: On Tuesday his Lordship [the Bishop of Winchester] sent to me to go with him the next day to Stepney to the warming of his brother Salmon's house, who hath lately bought there as handsome and convenient a house, with fine gardens and orchard, as I have lightly seen. There was a great meeting of all the kindred, where you were often remembered; and in truth you could not have done a favor or kindness to more thankful people, or that would better acknowledge it.[45] My Lord himself drank two several healths to you, which went round.

I was glad to see him so well disposed, and not tie himself to strict diet in respect of his late indisposition, which continued not

---

[44] The good Homer falls asleep now and then.
[45] Carleton had helped Lancelot Andrewes's brother-in-law, Robert Salmon, win a case in The Hague.

long, though he told me he made very hard shift and was put to great pain to preach on Easter Day morning to the Lords and minister the Communion to the King. The sermon is excellently commended, being upon the remainder of his text the last year, but he will not be entreated to let it come abroad unless the King command him, as he did for the copy of that he preached the first day of the Parliament; but what is become of it we cannot learn. . . .

The King was expected yesterday in the Higher House, but he sent them a message by the Lord Treasurer that the Lord Chancellor had been with him overnight and would have resigned the Great Seal, which he would not receive but wished him to clear himself, adding withal that he would have him heard and his excuses admitted with favor, and even his extenuations if they found cause; but if matters proved foul, to proceed as they thought good.

I send you here a psalm or kind of pharisaical prayer of his made since his trouble, which methinks savors little or nothing of true humiliation.

We hear that the Lord Digby is shortly to return to the Archduke's, from thence to the Duke of Lorrain, to the Emperor, thence into Italy and to the Duke of Savoy, and so into Spain, which will be a great expense of time and money . . . so desirous we are to be truly and indeed (as well as in title) *Pacifici,* and to follow that good rule *omnia experiri*[46] before we come to blows.

[380] May 2, 1621: Sir Henry Yelverton was to appear upon Saturday, but hindered by sickness—which was inquired into by five or six sent from the Higher House; so on Monday in the afternoon he came to his answer, which was long and vehement, but little stuff of any moment that I can hear of, save that he endeavored to cast many aspersions upon the Lord of Buckingham and his "regal authority" (as he termed it), and further comparing these times in some sort to those of Edward the Second, wherein the Spensers did so tyrannize and domineer; whereupon the Prince, seeing him so transported with passion, asked leave of the Lords to interrupt him, as not able to endure his father's government to be so paralleled and scandalized, so that he was returned to the Tower close prisoner. . . . Now if

---

[46] To try everything.

Principis ira be *mors,*[47] what a madman is he to run his head thus against the wall. . . .

At a conference with the Lords, the Lord Coke, having occasion to make often mention of the Universities, did ever (as his manner is) name Cambridge first, whereupon some Lords took occasion to remember him that the first place had been given twice or thrice by voices in the House, and in rank in the Subsidy Book, to Oxford. But he continuing in his course, Sir Thomas Edmondes put him still in mind of it; but he answered him somewhat short, that he needed not to trouble himself so much about it, for that he belonged to neither.

[381] May 5, 1621: On Thursday the Lower House was called up by the Lords to assist and be pesent at the sentence pronounced against the late Lord Chancellor, which was to this effect: that he is fined at £40,000, to be imprisoned in the Tower during the King's pleasure, disabled ever to bear office in the Court or Commonwealth, to have no voice in Parliament, not to come within the verge (or twelve miles) of the Court. He scaped degrading very narrowly, for the Prince, all the Prelates, the Lord of Buckingham (with his party, and diverse proxies of those that were absent) overswayed the other side by only two voices, and so is it set down in the record. . . .

There is some distaste . . . in the Higher House about Sir Henry Yelverton, who being committed by them a kind of close prisoner, the King hath laid a more strict commandment upon him, and makes show that he will take that matter into his own hands, which the House seems to take as some disgrace and discouragement, and tomorrow in the afternoon desire to have access to his Majesty about it.

I did always fear that those fair and plausible beginnings of the Parliament would not have so fair an end; and if these fractions be not soldered and made up the sooner, I doubt it will not continue long.

---

[47] If the anger of the Prince be death. Yelverton was called in for allowing, as Attorney General, the issue of the offending patents for the licensing of inns and the manufacture of gold and silver thread. Yelverton had already had the worst of a four-year feud with Buckingham and saw no point in sparing the favorite, but soon lost his nerve.

[382] May 19, 1621: The question . . . about taking Sir Henry Yelverton's cause out of the Lords' hands was soon decided by the King's voluntary remitting him to them. But as it falls out, he was not worth the contesting, for whereas much was expected at his hands, and his brave words made show as if he would bind bears, when he came to answer and explain himself he did it so weakly and poorly, and with so many tears and protestations . . . that his very friends were ashamed of him, and his inconstant baseness and boldness to undertake matters he was noways able to prove or perform. Whereupon the Lords, in reparation of the King's honor, proceeded to censure him at 10,000 marks, to imprisonment in the Tower during the King's pleasure, and to make his acknowledgement and submission at that bar; and to do the like to the Lord of Buckingham . . . which sentence, for as much as pertained to him, the Lord of Buckingham presently forgave and remitted.

Thus we see that great men weakly opposed thereby become the stronger; and it is no small comfort to him and his (as he professes) that he is found Parliament-proof.

[383] June 2, 1621: The Lord Chancellor went to the Tower in the beginning of the week, where he must attend the good time. His man Sherburn is in hard case, for being arrested for some of his debts, and finding no relief at his hands, he is fain to hide himself, as being engaged for him more than he is worth.

[384] June 9, 1621: I know not whether I wrote to you that the Lady of Doncaster was gone to the Spa . . . and that her Lord had delivered her £5000 for her ordinary expenses, of £10,000 he had lately given him; as likewise the Marquis Hamilton is to have as much for his journey into Scotland toward the Parliament there. But the greatest sum is gone with the Lord Digby,[48] which rises daily in re-

---

[48] John, first Lord Digby, Ambassador to Spain, was to negotiate again about the Spanish marriage, this time hoping to exchange Prince Charles's hand for the promise that Spain would guarantee the return of the Palatinate to Palsgrave Frederick.

port by those that take upon them to know the particular payments.

God send he may perform *aliquid dignum tanto hiatu*.[49] But the world looks for little good that way, seeing he hath taken Tobie Matthew and Gage for his principal agents and assistants. God knows how it comes to pass, but sure men's hearts begin to sink and fear that religion is in hard case, as well at home as abroad; and for France, great multitudes of those poor souls flock over daily, as well hither as all along our western coast to save themselves from the storm that threatens them and withal to implore our promised aid in this distress. But though we give good words yet there is no preparation nor sign of succor.

[385] June 23, 1621: The late Lord Chancellor hath lain now a good while at Fulham in what was Sir Thomas Smith's house, but is gone this day (as I hear) to his own house at Gorhambury, having, as should seem, no manner of feeling of his fall but continuing as vain and idle in all his humors as when he was at highest, and his fine of £ 40,000 to the King is so far from hurting him that it serves for a bulwark and protection against his creditors. . . .

Master Bell, meeting me yesterday, wished me to advertise your Lordship that, upon the opening of the East India business this last week at the Council table, most of the Lords thought you had not pressed it there in time, else had it not come to this pass. For besides the wrongs and indignity, their trifling is no longer to be endured. . . .

Sir Dudley Digges hath told me once or twice that he thinks it long since he heard from you, having written so often, and as it should seem begins to suspect your affection towards him upon some sinister information maybe given you from hence. . . . I would not wish you should take notice of anything from me, for he useth me kindly, and is in a fair way to some preferment, being greatly favored by the Lord of Buckingham and the Prince, and indeed he gained a great deal of credit upon the closing of the Parliament, having for some ten or twelve days before so pleased all sides in the greatest difficulties that he had the general applause and approbation.

---

[49] Something worthy of so much longing.

[386] July 14, 1621: The King lay two or three days the last week at Windsor, and there made an atonement and as it were renewed the marriage twixt Sir Edward Coke and his Lady, sending them home to Stoke very lovingly together. Men will not believe but there is some further mystery in this reconciliation (specially being sought by her), or at least that she would provide to save the Lord Holles harmless, who being pursued in the Star Chamber is in danger to be fined at the Lord Coke's suit.

[387] July 21, 1621: [On Wednesday] afternoon, the Earl of Northumberland was released from his long imprisonment in the Tower, whence the Lord of Doncaster went to fetch him, and brought him home to his house with a coach and six horses. It was my chance to see him in Paul's churchyard, and in my judgment he is nothing altered from what he was more than fifteen years ago that he was committed. He hath liberty to lie at Petworth or in any place within thirty miles' compass of it, within which circuit I take Sion to be. The warders of the Tower make great moan that they have lost such a benefactor. . . .

All the lords and great men about this town go to visit and congratulate with the Earl of Northumberland. The Earl of Arundel supped with him the first night and dined there the next day, whither came likewise, unbidden, the Spanish Ambassador, who is grown so affable and familiar that, on Monday, with his whole train he went to a common play at the Fortune in Golding Lane, and the players (not to be overcome with courtesy) made him a banquet when the play was done in the garden adjoining.

[388] July 28, 1621: On Monday my Lord of Winchester sent for me to dine with him and take part of a stag the King had sent him the day before. There was not much company, nor any stranger but Master Selden that was newly delivered.[50]

---

[50] The Earl of Southampton, Sir Edwin Sandys, and John Selden, lawyer and antiquary, had all been imprisoned after Parliament was recessed for the summer, presumably for opposition to Buckingham, although "it is confidently given out that it is not for anything done or said in Parliament."

I asked him in private concerning Master Bell's report. He assured me that to his knowledge there had nothing passed at the Council table to your disadvantage, and that he had been more diligent there of late than he used to be, by reason of his attendance on the Lord of Southampton's business. All he remembered touching that argument was in this manner, that Sir Noel Caron having given the King assurance that the Commissioners or Deputies for the East India affairs should be here before midsummer day,[51] the time being past, the King took it very ill to be so delayed and deluded. . . . And surely I am of opinion that Master Bell was mistaken in his intelligence, for hearing that the Ambassador was blamed about such business at the Council table, he imputed that to your Lordship that pertained to Sir Noel Caron. . . .

This week a great misfortune is befallen the Archbishop of Canterbury, for going into Hampshire to consecrate a chapel at the Lord Zouche's, and being (for pleasure) set up in a stand to shoot at a deer, instead of a buck he hath killed the Keeper.

[389] August 4, 1621: Sir Dudley Digges was in town on Sunday, but his stay was so little that I did not see him. His errand was to condole, and comfort the Lord of Canterbury for that heavy mishap. . . . For aught I can learn there is no more sorrow than needs, and I could wish they were somewhat more sensible of such a disaster; for howsoever mischances may light anywhere, and cannot be prevented, yet what should a man of his place and profession be meddling with such edge-tools. . . . Presently upon the fall of the fellow (who lived not half an hour), he sent away to inform his Majesty, who returned a gracious answer that such an accident might befall any man; that himself had the ill luck once to kill the keeper's horse under him; and that his Queen in like sort killed him the best brach that ever he had: and therefore willed him not to discomfort himself. The keeper and he were both on horseback, and not in a

---

[51] The complicated agreement reached in 1619 for a joint council of defense at Batavia and division of East Indian trade between the two countries had been ignored and flouted by the ruthless Dutch imperialist Coen. The impending negotiations produced no real settlement, and fierce Anglo-Dutch encounters continued in the Far East until England finally declared war on Spain, when the larger alliance solved the more local dispute. Caron was Dutch Agent or Ambassador in London during most of James's reign.

standing, as was reported. It is given out his Lordship will provide for the widow and three children in competent manner.

[391] October 13, 1621: There is a commission . . . to examine the Archbishop of Canterbury's case, and to pronounce whether he stand irregular or no. . . . Some say the Archbishop of York is sent for to succeed him (because Winchester would in no wise accept it) . . . but these, I take it, are but idle surmises, for my Lord of Canterbury continues very confident, not forbearing the Council table, the Star Chamber, nor anything else he was wont to do, wherein I have heard wise men not so much commend him, that he shows no more feeling of so great and heavy a misfortune.[52]

[393] October 27, 1621: Sir Dudley Digges came to town some eight or ten days since, but finding your so-long-promised Commissioners not yet arrived, is returned home till he hear they be certainly come. I imparted your proposition unto him, who approves and commends it very much, only he thinks you are somewhat too mild and mannerly with so unreasonable slow and dull cattle. Surely the more I think of their courses towards us, the more I impute it to some fatal cause that doth thus disunite and sow so many quarrels between us, when there is most need of love and concord; and that among so many, none should . . . perceive that while the frog and the mouse wrestle and wrangle, the kite hovers over them to carry both away.

I know not how it comes to pass, but I have heard diverse men of good judgment of opinion that the Venetians are not so wise, nor have not men of such sufficiency, as in former times. And so, methinks, the States do not ply the Spaniard at sea so well as they might, considering their chief strength and his greatest weakness lies that way; for if they continue to vie and revie with him at land, and suffer him to bring home his treasure in safety, besides all other hazards the charge will soon eat them out. But I take too much upon me to meddle with matters above my reach.

---

[52] But he fasted monthly on the Tuesday of the keeper's death for the rest of his life.

[**394**] November 10, 1621: The King went away on Tuesday about noon toward Newmarket, so that it is doubtful whether he will be here at the beginning of the Parliament. But before his going he absolved the Archbishop of Canterbury *a poena et culpa*,[53] as well from irregularity as scandal. The Commissioners so balanced the matter that they were five to five, the Bishop of Winchester taking part with the four lawyers against the other Bishops, and that with so forcible reasons and arguments that it is thought he chiefly brought weight to the business and swayed it on that side.

[**399**] December 22, 1621: The weather continues still so violent that I am forced to write in my gloves, a thing I never used nor practiced before.

Since my last, the King wrote twice to the Lower House, to have them go on with business . . . to which they made a mannerly answer on Tuesday . . . ; but withal, for fear of surprising, gave order to the Speaker and the whole House to meet at four of the clock, where they conceived, set down, and entered this protestation enclosed. . . . [The Lower House] wanted the assistance of some of their principal members, for Sir Samuel and Sir Edwin Sandys stood mute all this meeting, and our friend Sir D[udley]. D[igge]s. either silent or so little regarded when he spake that he had been better have sat still. In truth I am sorry in his behalf, for he is a proper and, I presume, an honest man, but he hath utterly lost the House, that hath a strong opinion of his halting. And the worst is he may chance hereafter stand straight on neither leg. . . .

On Monday Master Locke brought me your letter with the ill news of Rowland Lytton's death, whose loss I lament with all my heart, for to speak freely my opinion, he was the best that was left of that race. In Lent last . . . both his brother William and Sir Henry Wallop spake to me to furnish him with [£40], upon promise to see me reimbursed within a month, each of them for twenty pounds. Sir Henry Wallop's part I received, but from Master Lytton I have not heard since, though he hath been often in town. . . . I should not say so much for so small a matter, but that I hear he doth many other ways degenerate from so worthy a father and mother.

---

[53] From guilt and punishment.

[402] February 16, 1622: Your nephew came to you so well stored that I doubt not but he hath made a full relation and furnished you with whatever is here stirring. Whiles he was here I was the less diligent, and shall not be very forward hereafter, as being discouraged diverse ways, for the times are dangerous, and the world grows tender and jealous of free speech. . . .

Sir Henry Savile went to Eton on Wednesday, in weak case but well resolved in mind, and willing to depart when it shall please God to call, the rather, he says, for that having lived in good times he doth fear or foresee worse.[54]

[404] March 30, 1622: The late Lord Chancellor hath set out the life or reign of Henry the Seventh. It is pity he should have any other employment. I have not read much of it, but if the rest of our history were answerable to it, I think we should not need to envy any other nation in that kind.

[405] April 13, 1622: The Emperor's Ambassador had audience on Sunday in the Upper House of Parliament, and delivered his message in Dutch, which was for the most part matter of compliment and commendation of our King's carriage in these troubles of Germany. The King went the next day to Theobalds and came to town on Wednesday to give him private audience at Whitehall, and went back the same night. Tomorrow he shall be feasted where he had his first audience, things being so ordered that his entertainment may be *per omnia* equal to that of the Marshal Cadenet, though there be great difference in their outward show and appearance; for this man is but poorly accompanied and as poorly accoutered, saving that he hired a fair jewel to wear in his hat. There is great intercourse twixt him and the Spanish Ambassador, who no doubt doth embouch and tutor him every way. . . .

On Thursday the City mustered and showed 6000 men in the field before St. James, where the Emperor's Ambassador was a good while among them, and perhaps had seldom seen for such a number

---

[54] Savile died February 20.

more likely men nor better armed and appointed. But the Prince, though they were so near, would not vouchsafe them his presence.

[**407**] May 11, 1622: I am sorry you cannot meet with Barclay's *Argenis*,[55] which indeed are somewhat rare here, being printed at Paris, and risen from five shillings they were sold at first to fourteen; but I have taken order to have one if there were any to be had in Frankfort mart. I hear the King hath given order to Ben Jonson to translate it and that it is in good forwardness, but I am deceived if he can reach the language in the original or express himself in that manner, whatsoever he doth in the matter. Besides, there be many covert names shadowed, sometimes in anagrams and sometimes otherwise.

[**408**] June 8, 1622: The Countess of Buckingham hath recanted again and is come home to her mother Church, and goes duly to the sermons in the Chapel. Good Dr. White, our lecturer at Paul's, and the Bishop of St. David's, Dr. Laud, have the honor of reducing her; but the world says the danger of leaving the Court was the greatest and most pregnant motive.

Kit Villiers that was in so fair a way to preferment is said to have marred his marriage and given his cousin Bess Sheldon such earnest that he cannot well forsake the bargain.

The Lord of Purbeck is out of order likewise, for this day sevennight, getting into a room next the street in Wallingford House, he beat down the glass windows with his bare fists, and all bloodied cried out to the people that passed by that he was a Catholic and would spend his blood in the cause, etc. His Lady on Sunday made a petition to the King for alimony or maintenance, which reflecting upon the old Countess, the Lord Marquis that was by very nobly said he would answer the petition and take such order hereafter that she should be furnished to the full and have no more cause to complain.

---

[55] Chamberlain had found John Barclay's *Argenis* "the most delightful fable that ever I met with."

[410] July 1, 1622: The smallpox reign and rage very much, both in city and country. Your Cousin Windham, or Bess Lytton, coming lately to town with her husband in her way to go visit his friends in Somersetshire, was surprised and oppressed by them so that on Wednesday morning last she died, to the great grief and discomfort of her friends, especially of her husband, of whom she was entirely beloved; and not without cause, for she hath left the report and reputation of an excellent wife. This week he carries her down to be buried in Norfolk.

[412] August 10, 1622: I returned from Ditton the 7th of this present, where I had continued almost a whole month. And I stayed somewhat the longer upon notice that the Bishop of Winchester was to preach at Windsor the 5th of August, which he did, taking his text from the 4th to the end of the 7th verse of the 24th chapter of the first book of Samuel. His voice grows very low, but otherwise he did extraordinary well and like himself. I dined with him that day, and could not leave him till half an hour after six o'clock. The weather was very hot, and he so faint and wet that he was fain to go to bed for some little time after he came out of the pulpit.

[413] September 25, 1622: I hear that Tobie Matthew is gone to his father, with recommendation from the King that, as he did discountenance him upon the King's displeasure, so he would now receive him to favor upon his reconciling to his Majesty. His *fidus Achates,* Master Gage, is come from Rome with a copy or draught of the dispensation for the Spanish match, on condition the King carry good respect to the Roman Catholics, which no doubt will be done in good measure like the Spanish pavane: as much forward as backward.

[417] November 4, 1622: Your brother Carleton is in town in some perplexity, for fear of being put into the bill of Sheriffs, and plies all his friends that can any way help to keep him out.

[418] November 16, 1622: [The King] pricked the Sheriffs in such haste that there hath been since great alteration. . . . It is observed this year that many Londoners that have lands in the country are specially picked out, and for the rest, either men of mean account, or such as have been Sheriffs already, or else (for a kind of gentle correction) such as were too forward in the Parliament or too backward in the benevolence. . . .

Sir Edward Conway is thought shall certainly be Secretary, and the delay is no longer than till the Lady Naunton be brought abed; for being a woman of a great spirit, as her husband says, he feared she might take some conceit or apprehension at his remove that might be to her hurt, and therefore desired it might be kept from her till she were well laid and the danger over.

[423] February 10, 1623: The Lord of St. Albans . . . busies himself altogether about books, and hath set out two lately, *Historia Ventorum* and *De Vita et Morte,* with promise of more. I have yet seen neither of them because I have not leisure. But if the Life of Henry the Eighth, which they say he is about, might come out after his own manner, I should find time and means enough to read it. . . .

Sir Isaac Wake hath gotten almost £2000 that was in arrearage and hath leave to come home for a month or twain to settle his affairs and marry his Mistress Bray. . . .

I am earnestly desired by Dieston[56] and diverse of his good friends to entreat your favor for him, and that you would be pleased to afford him the carrying of your packets as occasion serves. Questor hath taken some spleen against him and would hinder him from going to and fro, though he have offered him all the fair conditions he doth demand, and seeks by all means to give him satisfaction. You have good experience of his diligence and honesty, and it lies in your Lordship's power to employ him there, and from hence we doubt not of Secretary Calvert's and Conway's furtherance.

---

[56] Who had been messenger between London and The Hague during the whole of Carleton's embassy there.

[428] April 19, 1623: The Provost of Eton outlived nine days, which is counted the fatal time for those that be cut of the stone, but died two days after, when the canvass for the place began afresh, and Sir Robert Naunton laid in hard for it . . . but the King reserves that and all other matters of grace or favor till the Lord of Buckingham's return.[57]

[429] May 3, 1623: Sir Isaac Wake hath leave to come home and we expected him weekly, but upon the Prince's arrival in Spain, he had order from thence to do somewhat which hath hindered his journey, to the great grief of his sweetheart Mistress Bray, my ancient valentine.

[430] May 17, 1623: Your cousin Will Lytton hath had a good windfall of late by the death of the Lady Weld, his wife's aunt, who made him executor, whereby it is thought he will get four or five thousands at least besides two hundred pound land and great store of good stuff. I should congratulate his good fortune if he were more kind to his sisters.

[431] May 30, 1623: All your affairs here are in good case and prosper, and those clouds and mists removed that threatened foul weather. It cannot be but a great comfort as well to yourself as all your well-wishers to see so many good friends stand so close to you . . . so that there is no doubt but all shall succeed well here-after, and that the white mule[58] will be more tractable.

---

[57] From his adventure in Spain with Prince Charles. Sir Henry Wotton got the post.

[58] Presumably Buckingham. Carleton was again interested in becoming Provost of Eton. He also had the very ticklish job of carrying King James's equivocal and disheartening instructions to his daughter Princess Elizabeth, Electress Palatine, who was by this time in exile in The Hague.

[432] June 14, 1623: Your Lady[59] is well and everywhere welcome and well seen. I dined with her this day, where we had good venison and good company of Master Livingston and his wife. And she is so well stored that, a fresh buck coming in, it pleased her to give me a part, whereof I am very proud being so early, and it will do me much honesty.

[433] June 28, 1623: Before the closing of this letter, going to see if your Lady would command me anything, she told me she would not write till she heard from you or that your nephew had his dispatch, saying he was like St. George on horseback who was ever riding but never removed.

We met yesterday at Sir Horace Vere's, where there was great cheer and good company, specially Low Country captains, no women more than her Ladyship, the Lady Smith, and her sister.

[437] October 11, 1623: My stay in the country[60] was longer than I meant. . . . Finding myself better disposed and more lightsome in body and mind than I had done many a day, I did endeavor to enjoy it to the uttermost, thinking it a good work for an old man *curare valetudinem;* for besides field sports abroad, we had always good company within doors, and such plenty of partridges as I have seldom seen, which is the more to be wondered at, seeing we seek to spoil them in the nest or rather before, when our curiosity and delicacy is of late proceeded so far that in the springtime partridges with eggs is the only dish in request.

[444] January 3, 1624: Before the Parliament was fully agreed, Sir Ed. Coke was sent for to the Council table and told the King had special use of his service in a commission into Ireland, so that he was willed to prepare himself to be gone within forty days. Being sur-

---

[59] Once again in London seeking payment of Carleton's overdue allowance.
[60] At Ware Park.

prised with this sudden alarm, and pausing a while, the Council required his answer, which he gave in few words, that he came not thither to answer but to obey. . . . It was since said that the Prince had labored for his stay and to save him from so hard a journey in respect of his years, being threescore and. fourteen, and of some other construction that may be made of this employment. But for aught I hear, he must go.

[445] January 17, 1624: They have chosen their knights and burgesses already in some places, as in Kent where Sir Nicholas Tufton and Sir Dudley Digges, thinking to carry it without contradiction, when it came to the election, Tufton was chosen, but when it came to Digges, Sir Edwin Sandys . . . carried it, either in truth and number of voices, or by partiality of the Sheriff as is pretended. But if this be a trick of Sandys (as is suspected) to save himself from going into Ireland, it will not serve his turn. . . . Besides . . . the cry of his party that Tufton was a papist and Digges a royalist is very offensive, and is thought will incense the King more toward him, which needs not.

His colleague Sir Edward Coke is likewise chosen for two or three places, as Coventry, Windsor, and I know not where else, but he prepares himself to be gone and took his leave of the King on Monday and kissed his hand. The poor man sets a good face on it and makes show to go cheerfully, but in secret tells his friends he never looks to see them again.

XII. Gazette, 1619-1624

[336] September 11, 1619: We hear the Palsgrave is crowned King of Bohemia, so that there is now no place left for deliberation nor for mediation of peace till one side be utterly ruined. God send him good success, but surely it was a venturous part and like to set all Christendom by the ears. The world thinks it was a plot of the Prince of Orange and the Duke of Bouillon to draw in our King *volens nolens,* but how he is every way provided for such a business you know or may easily guess.

But the best sign I see is that I heard this day that the Lord Digby and Sir Walter Aston are willed to stay their preparations for Spain: this is an excellent and everlasting theme for discoursers, to whom I leave it.

[340] November 13, 1619: There is a late review of old gold plate and jewels in the Tower to be put into coin, for some good purpose as we presume and wish; for seeing the chance is thrown in Bohemia, we think we have all our parts in the success, and sure the most are ready to assist them not only with our prayers but with our purse. . . .

Yesterday a tilt-boat laden with threescore persons going for Gravesend was overrun by a ship or ketch under sail and 40 of the passengers drowned, being most of them as I hear clothiers of Kent that came to an ill market.

[341] November 20, 1619: We have lately lost Samuel Daniel, the poet, Sergeant Chibbon, a great lawyer of Essex, and Sir Edmund Withipole who, being cut of the stone this day sevennight, died within four days after.

270]

[346] January 25, 1620: Yesterday the Bishop of London called together all his clergy about this town and told them he had express commandment from the King to will them to inveigh vehemently and bitterly in their sermons against the insolency of our women and their wearing of broad-brimmed hats, pointed doublets, their hair cut short or shorn, and some of them stilettos or poignards, and such other trinkets of like moment, adding withal that if pulpit admonitions will not reform them he would proceed by another course. The truth is the world is very far out of order, but whether this will mend it God knows.

[347] February 12, 1620: We are here in a strange case to complain of plenty, but so it is that corn beareth so low a price that tenants and farmers are very backward to pay their rents, and in many places plead disability; for remedy the Council have written letters into every shire, and (some say) to every market town, to provide a granary or storehouse with a stock to buy corn and keep it for a dear year; but though this be well advised and make a fair show in speculation, yet the difficulties be so many that it will not be so easy to put it in practice.

Our pulpits ring continually of the insolence and impudence of women; and to help the matter forward, the players have likewise taken them to task, and so do the ballads and ballad singers, so that they can come nowhere but their ears tingle. And if all this will not serve, the King threatens to fall upon their husbands, parents, or friends that have or should have power over them and make them pay for it.

[348] February 26, 1620: One Peacock, sometimes a schoolmaster and a minister (but a very busy-brained fellow) was the last week committed to the Tower for practicing to infatuate the King's judgment by sorcery (they say) in the business of Sir Thomas Lake and the Lady of Exeter. He hath been strictly examined by the Lord Chancellor, the Lord Coke, the Lord Chief Justice, the Attorney, Sollicitor, and others, and on Tuesday was hanged up by the wrists; and though he were very impatient of the torture and swooned once

or twice, yet I cannot learn that they have wrung any great matter out of him. Sir Thomas Lake was confronted with him at the Lord Chancellor's, whereon a suspicion rises that the matter may reach to him or his Lady.

[349] March 11, 1620: The King came hither the Saturday before Shrovetide, and the two days following here was much feasting and jollity, and the Christmas masque repeated on Shrove Tuesday night. On Saturday last the Prince made a ball and a banquet at Denmark House, which he had lost at tennis to the Marquis of Buckingham, who invited thither a number of ladies, mistresses, and valentines, a ceremony come lately in request and grown so costly that it is said he hath cast away this year £2000 that way. . . .

The Dean of Westminster hath been very strict in his church against ladies and gentlewomen about yellow ruffs, and would not suffer them to be admitted into any pew, which being ill taken, and the King moved in it, he is come to disavow him, and says his meaning was not for yellow ruffs but for other manlike and unseemly apparel.

[350] March 20, 1620: The King of Bohemia wrote a letter to the Lord Mayor and his brethren for the loan of £100,000, who imparting it to the King, he said he would neither command them nor entreat them, but if they did anything for his son-in-law he would take it very kindly. Whereupon the Mayor conferring with the Court of Aldermen, they referred the matter to the Common Council, who putting it over to the Wardens and several Companies, received answer that when it should please the King to declare himself, so that things might be lawfully and orderly done, and when they should see what the clergy, nobility, and the rest of the realm would do, they would look into their purses and see what they could do. . . .

Here is great speech and expectation of the King's coming to Paul's Cross on Sunday next, where the Bishop of London should preach his Court sermon in the afternoon. Some surmise that the King will there deliver somewhat touching the matters of Bohemia, others, concerning this intended match with Spain; but if it so fall out that he come, I rather believe it is about the repairing of Paul's, which indeed grows very ruinous.

[351] April 1, 1620: On Sunday in the afternoon the King came in pomp to Paul's Cross, where the Bishop of London preached upon a text given him by the King, being the 13 and 14 verses of the 102 psalm; the better half of the time (being above two hours) he spent in a pathetical speech for the repairing of Paul's. After the sermon the King had a banquet in the Bishop's house, where he moved the Lord Mayor and Aldermen to undertake the work, protesting (as the Bishop had touched in his sermon) that he could be content to fast with bread and water to see it done.

He was received at Temple Bar by the Lord Mayor and Aldermen, who presented him with a purse of gold of 1000 marks and another with £500 for the Prince. The citizens stood by companies with their banners and streamers all along the streets. . . . The King came along in his doublet and hose, and suffered the Prince to ride bareheaded before him all the way, both coming and going. The train was not so great by reason of many disputes among his followers for place and precedence . . . greatest of all . . . noblemen's younger sons with the Councillors *minorum gentium*,[1] which being beforehand decided by the Lords in commission for the office of Earl Marshal, the Knights Councillors appealed to the King, who upon these differences was ready to turn back when he was getting on horseback, but in conclusion he left the matter as he found it with order that none of the arguers on either side should accompany him, whereby he was but slenderly followed. . . .

The Lord Mayor and his brethren are about some course to provide money for Bohemia, and many noblemen make great show of forwardness, among whom the Earl of Dorset is the foreman, having already, they say, disbursed £100 and promised to furnish as much yearly for four years to come if the war last so long. There is a collection likewise among the Clergy, whereof diverse have underwritten bountifully and cheerfully; yet I hear of one about this town that hath subscribed for half a crown.

---

[1] Of the lesser orders of nobility (the knights).

The motion for Paul's comes not very opportunely, for it cannot be but these contributions, coming together, must needs cross one another.

[352] April 29, 1620: We have here a great commission come forth for the business of Paul's comprehending all the Council, diverse Bishops, with the residentiaries of that Church, diverse Aldermen, and other citizens, and for want of better, Master Wymark[2] and myself, that am very unfit for any such employment, and I know not how I came in unless it be for my love to the place. The whole number is 66, and the first day of sitting was this day sevennight, when there was little or nothing done but order taken how to proceed. I have not been among them since, so little joy I take in the office. The King is very earnest to set it forward, and they begin hotly, but I doubt when all is done it will prove (as they say) Paul's work.

[355] June 28, 1620: Our drums beat daily about the streets for the raising of men for this new service, but I hear of no great confluence, it being an unusual thing here to gather men of any good sort by that means. Our 4000 men are fallen to 2000, the rest being to come after by way of supply, and yet for this poor number here is such sharking and shearing, and such a deal of discontent that I can scant promise myself any hope of success. . . .

There was one Maxwell committed to the Tower yesterday, but I cannot learn the cause, more than that some say he hath written somewhat in derogation of the King of Bohemia. The fellow seems to have some scribbling vein, by a book he wrote some years since wherein he paralleled and compared the Howards and the Stuarts.

[356] July 8, 1620. Our new levies go on but heavily, and whereas they thought they should have been oppressed with multitudes of

---

[2] Edward Wymark, one of Chamberlain's chief companions in Paul's-walking, whose account of news Chamberlain did not, however, consider infallible.

followers, they are fain to send far and near into the country to make up their numbers, which if they were once full they would be gone presently this next week. . . .

The world is now much terrified with the Star Chamber, there being not so little an offense against any proclamation but is liable and subject to the censure of that court.

And for proclamations and patents, they are become so ordinary that there is no end, every day bringing forth some new project or other, as within these two days here is one come forth for tobacco, wholly engrossed by Sir Thomas Roe and his partners, which if they can keep and maintain against the general clamor will be a matter of great commodity, unless peradventure indignation (rather than all other reasons) may bring that filthy weed out of use. In truth, the world doth even groan under the burthen of these perpetual patents, which are become so frequent that, whereas at the King's coming in there were complaints of some eight or nine monopolies then in being, they are now said to be multiplied to so many scores. . . .

The Spanish heretic that was condemned three or four years since died lately in Newgate, and although he lived so miserably that he was almost starved, yet there were more than forty good ducats in gold found in his patched rags after his decease.

[357] July 27, 1620: Our commission for Paul's begins very roughly, having taken order that all the houses at the east and west ends shall be pulled down and demolished before the first of September, and those on the south and north sides before Whitsuntide next, which is somewhat a hard case, for more than 2000 souls one and other (as they pretend) to be turned out of house and home upon so short warning, and with so little hope or appearance of recompense, whereupon they made petition to the King at his being here; but he referred them back to the Commissioners, saying that *stat sententia*[3] they must down, but would have some means found to give them satisfaction, which is a matter not so easily done as said, for to begin with all the Commissions are fain to rate themselves at £20 a man to defray the charge of pulling down the houses and filling up the cellars and holes. But for mine own part I must confess I am

---

[3] The decision stands.

so tenderhearted that if I must needs pay this money I had rather it should go *ad aedificationem* than *ad ruinam*.[4]

[358] August 4, 1620: The demolishment of the houses about Paul's is threatened every day, but the people either do not or will not seem to believe it, nor do not remove nor avoid, but some make jests as if it were not meant in earnest, and one in knavery wrote upon his door *stet quaeso candide lector*.[5]

[359] September 9, 1620: This progress is passed over without any memorable matter more than that Kit Villiers and one Sir Robert Dayall, a Scot, upon a very light occasion did beat a gentleman of the Earl of Southampton's followers and spurred him almost to death.

[365] November 9, 1620: One thing I must not forget, that as I wrote you last year that it was strange we should complain of plenty, so now I must tell you that plenty hath made us poor, so far forth that tenants generally cannot pay their rents, and many make suit to give up their leases. The reason we cannot yet reach unto, but that there is a general want of money; but whence that should proceed, let them look to it whom it most concerns. Corn and cattle were never at so low a rate since I can remember, wheat at two shillings a bushel, barley at seven shillings a quarter, *et sic de caeteris*. And yet can they get no riddance at that price, so that land falls everywhere; and if you have money, you may buy good land at thirteen or fourteen years' purchase.

And yet I know three or four noblemen that, within these five days, had letters for a new contribution to the Palatinate, commending their forwardness upon the Baron Dohna's solicitation, before the King had declared himself, whereas now after he had showed himself in the cause it is expected they should show the same zeal and bounty if not more. And the like letters I hear are now come to the

---

[4] For building . . . for destruction.
[5] Prithee honest reader, let it stand.

City, which surely is somewhat unseasonable, having so lately given a benevolence to Bohemia and the Parliament so near at hand that will require more payments. But *necessitas non habet legem.*[6]

I send you the proclamation for the Parliament, penned by the King himself, and would not be entreated by the Lord Chancellor and Lord Chamberlain to leave out the word "wrangling lawyers."

[366] November 17, 1620: With my best wishes for your health and happiness, which God continue and increase to your full content. From London this 17th of November, the happiest day that ever England had to my remembrance.[7]

[367] December 22, 1620: The last week the Bishop of London was willed to call all his clergy before him and to charge them from the King not to meddle in their sermons with the Spanish match nor any other matter of state. But for all that, on Sunday following (whether by chance or otherwise) a young fellow at Paul's Cross, upon his text "Thou shalt not plow with an ox and an ass," spake very freely in general.

The King requires a great loan of money from the City, which they are fain to put off with a voluntary gift of £10,000, meaning to sell part of their plate and forbear their usual feasts and meetings till they have raised that sum; it seeming hard to them (besides the forbearing of a £100,000 for which they have neither had interest nor principal almost these four years, and besides a benevolence this summer to Bohemia, and a Parliament so near at hand) to have this charge laid upon them.

And yet for all this penury there is money given out and preparation made for a masque at Court these holidays.

[368] January 13, 1621: On Monday [the French Ambassadors] were entertained in seeing the Prince, with six or seven noblemen

---

[6] Necessity has no law.
[7] The anniversary of Queen Elizabeth's accession.

more, run at tilt, which the Prince performed very well and gracefully.

That night they were feasted by the Lord of Doncaster at Essex House, with that sumptuous superfluity that the like hath not been seen nor heard in these parts: whereof to give you some taste, it is to be understood that there were more than a 100 cooks (whereof forty were masters) set on work for eight days before; the whole service was but six mess, furnished with 1600 dishes which were neither light nor slight, but twelve pheasants in a dish, four and twenty partridges, twelve dozen of larks, *et sic de caeteris;* and for fish, all that could be found far and near, whole fresh salmons served by two and three in a dish, besides six or seven Muscovy salmons whereof some were above six foot long. It were to no purpose to reckon up the grosser meats, as two swans in a dish, two chines of beef, two pigs, and the like. But it is doubted this excessive spoil will make a dearth of the choicest dainties, when this one supper consumed twelvescore pheasants baked, boiled and roasted.

After supper they had a banquet, then a masque, then a second banquet, so that, the sweetmeats alone rising to £500, the whole charge is said to be above £3000, besides six-pound-weight of ambergris spent in cookery, valued at £300.

The King and Prince were present with the Ambassadors at a table that went cross the upper end of the long table, so that the King, sitting in the midst, had the full view of the whole company and service. They supped in a lower gallery; the masque was in a large room above.

[369] January 20, 1621: I have not heard of any of your posts now a good while, which makes me write by the ordinary conveyance.

The French Ambassador went hence on Sunday morning, having sent away the most part of his train the two days before, being himself such a freshwater soldier that he rather chose to go by coach through all the foul ways than take the benefit of the river to Gravesend, and endures the sea so ill that, at his coming, he lay sick at Dover two days before he could recover himself, and was often heard here to say that he would willing give a 1000 crowns that he were well over. He was followed to Rochester by diverse shopkeepers of the Exchange for satisfaction of wares delivered to some of his followers to the value of £400. How they sped I hear not, but perhaps they thought that might be abated, having bestowed a £1000 to £1200 among them. The Lady of Doncaster presented him with two waistcoats and petticoats for his wife, which are said to be extraordinary fair and rich.

[370] February 3, 1621: The winds have been and are still so contrary, and the weather so extreme cold, that I was hindered from writing the last week, the Thames being now quite frozen over so that people have passed over to and fro these four or five days; but not so freely as in the great frost, for the winds and high tides have so driven the ice on heaps in some places that it lies like rocks and mountains and hath a strange and hideous aspect. It hath been seldom seen that this river should be twice frozen over in one winter, and the watermen are quite undone to lose the benefit of term and Parliament both. . . .

The Parliament began on Tuesday with the greatest concourse and throng of people that hath been seen, so that there was some hurt done by the breaking of two scaffolds and otherwise. The King went on horseback and was very cheerful all the way, and from the church was carried in a chair to the Parliament House, being so weak in his legs and feet that it is doubted he will find little use in them hereafter but be altogether *perdus* that way. His speech lasted above an hour, though he commended brevity very much. . . . We expect it in print, though (by that I have heard) there are diverse passages in it that persuade the contrary, or at least are like to be omitted. Sergeant Richardson was chosen Speaker, but seemed to take it so unwillingly that, seeing no excuse would serve the turn, he wept downright.

[371] February 10, 1621: It is most certain that England was never generally so poor since I was born as it is at this present, insomuch that all complain that they cannot receive their rents; yet is there plenty of all things but money, which is so scant that country people offer corn and cattle or whatsoever they have else in lieu of rent but bring no money. And corn is at so easy rates as I never knew it, wheat at 20 and 22 d. a bushel, barley at ninepence, and yet no

quantity will be taken at that price. So that for all the common opinion of the wealth of England, I fear when it comes to the trial it will prove as some merchants which, having carried a great show a long time, when they are called upon too fast by their creditors are fain to play bankrupt. But the strangeness of it is how this great defect should come and be perceived but within these two or three years at most. Diverse reasons are devised, as some say the money is gone northward, some eastward, and I know not whither; but these and suchlike are delivered in Parliament. . . .

The Spanish Ambassador is not ignorant of the ill affection generally borne him, and therefore being, or seeming to be, afraid, the King's house at Nonesuch is prepared and trimmed up for him, whither he goes this day to avoid the fear and fury of Shrove Tuesday.[8]

[372] February 17, 1621: I had only a sight of Sir Dudley Digges, who delivered me your letter of the 5th of this present and was the next day admitted to his place in Parliament, not without some dispute, by reason he was chosen when he was out of the realm; but by favor he prevailed, and was no sooner set but spake.

They begin there now to follow the business more close and have already granted two whole subsidies, the first to be paid at one entire payment in May next, the other in November and May following, without mention of any fifteens because they lie more heavily upon the meaner people than subsidies do. . . . I am glad this came so frankly and readily from them without stop or contradiction; . . . and it comes well to pass in regard of the opinion abroad, which no doubt will raise the noise more than the wool is worth. . . .

The greatest matter now in hand is about recusants, which being so multiplied by connivance, it is more than time to put the statutes in execution that are already in force, to remove and restrain them from this town during the sitting of this Parliament at least, as likewise to disarm them, with such further restrictions as shall be thought meet. . . .

Yesterday one Shepheard, a lawyer, was thrown out of the House

---

[8] When the apprentices were often disorderly.

and disabled forever being there, for a speech the day before against a bill concerning the Sabbath, wherein girding and glancing at the Puritans and seeking to make them ridiculous, himself grew foolish and profane.

Our new Earl of Berkshire was then likewise committed close prisoner to the Fleet from the Higher House for brabbling with the Lord Scrope that carelessly and unawares stepped in at the door before him. . . .

Now since dinner I understand that the King gave great thanks to the House for their ready contribution, and did accept and acknowledge it so much the more in regard that, both at home and abroad, there was such an opinion of disunion twixt him and his people as if nothing could be expected.

[374] March 10, 1621: We hear that Sir Robert Mansell [9] and his fleet have done just nothing, but negotiated with those of Algiers for certain slaves. And they complain of their usage on the coast of Spain, that they are fain to buy their water, and could not be suffered to carry aboard a thousand ducats they had taken up at Malaga to provide fresh victuals for their sick and weak men, with a number of other discourtesies and indignities. . . .

But it is not good rubbing on that sore, for one Ward, a special preacher of Ipswich, is but newly released out of prison, where he lay a good while for having a picture of the Spanish fleet in '88, with the Gunpowder Treason and some other additions of his own invention and hand (having some delight and skill in limning), which his friends say had lain by him at least seven or eight years and not looked into till now. As likewise another minister (whose name I have forgot) was clapped up for collecting and setting out a treatise of the intermarriages of the House of Austria. And now this week Dr. Everard (reader at St. Martin's in the Field) was sent to the Gatehouse for glancing on Sunday was sevennight at the Spanish match, and deciphering the craft and cruelty of the Spaniards in all places where they come, specially the West Indies; all or most part of what he said cited and taken out of their own authors.

---

[9] Sir Robert Mansell had been sent to subdue the pirates of Algiers and free the English subjects held prisoner there.

[375] March 24, 1621: We look for proclamations this next week touching the subsidy which is to be paid in May next, and to call in and cashier all monopolies, patents, protections, bills of conformity, habeas corpus, and such other gross corruptions crept in against law or conscience. But I doubt we hope for more than we are like to find, though indeed the King be very graciously inclined, and never showed himself more forward to redress what is amiss; but immoderate desires cannot be satisfied, which makes me fear that this fair weather cannot always last.

[376] March 28, 1621: Before their breaking up there was much intercourse and diverse passages of kindness and compliment between both Houses. And indeed all this Parliament they have proceeded with great respect each to other; and that which is best of all, the King hath showed himself very well pleased with all their proceedings, not only in allowing them but animating and commending them . . . protesting that he held and found them a very wise council, and which had discovered that unto him which he should never have known but too late, that his kingdom was like a garden overgrown with weeds, wherein he desired their help to pluck them up by the roots, and cursing them and their memory that had so many times and so many ways diverted him from this course of holding parliaments: promising further so to govern and carry himself hereafter that if the kingdom were elective, they should rather be willing to make choice of him than any man living. . . .

The tilting on Saturday passed with the ordinary show, saving that the Prince and his followers was very rich, and himself ran exceedingly well and absolutely best of the whole troop, which was fourteen, which, together with his affability and courtesy in the Parliament, hath won him great reputation and love. And indeed it seems he is much improved by his diligent frequenting the Parliament House and observing how matters passed, for he could not have lighted on such a school in a whole age to learn experience and try diversity of wits and humors.

[377] April 7, 1621: Upon some slight abuse offered to the Spanish Ambassador and his litter as he passed through the streets on Mon-

day, three young fellows or prentices were whipped at a cart's tail on Wednesday. But the punishment was lightly laid on, as it were *par acquit,* and they yet so pitied that diverse affronts and insolencies were done to those that were overseers of the execution; wherewith the King was so much moved that he came yesterday of purpose from Theobalds to the Guildhall (which was trimmed up with hangings, and a cloth of state and a throne at the upper end) meaning, as was thought, to make some sharp speech against these disorders. But going up first to the Mayor's Court, it seems he was mitigated by the relation of the Recorder and others, who having examined the cause to the full, found it nothing so heinous nor foul as it was painted, nor worth his Majesty's showing himself in it. Whereupon, after some private admonition to the Aldermen to look better to the government, and to see these young fellows with their abettors and rescuers thoroughly punished, he departed without coming to the place where he intended and was expected to speak.

[378] April 18, 1621: After the King's being at Guildhall there came out a proclamation to restrain prentices and other base people from abusing or offering wrong to ambassadors, their followers, Lords, Ladies, gentlewomen, or other persons of quality, in gesture, word, or action; and my Lord Mayor for his part hath set out another to the same effect. And strict order is taken by every Alderman and his deputy by going from house to house, to charge men to look well to their children and servants in that behalf.

[379] April 23, 1621: On Friday after dinner the King made a speech to both Houses in the hall at Court, wishing them more speedy dispatch for that the time and heat of the year grew on, so that they could not sit long, commending their proceedings hitherto, but giving them this caution, that they should not scandalize great persons without pregnant proof; intimating withal that as they had prevented his demand with the free grant of two subsidies (the greatest part whereof was spent already) so they would take further notice of his necessities, which grew daily upon him by the charge of his son and daughter with their five children and his mother, not having

a ridge (or as most say, a furrow) of land left them to live on; yet he was not altogether out of hope to recover the Palatinate by treaty, and for that purpose was sending an ambassador to the Emperor and into Spain.

[380] May 2, 1621: The Nether House sits hard, but we hear of no great dispatch. Nay, it seems they entangle themselves with new and unnecessary business that little belongs to them, though they have more than enough of their own, as going about to overthrow the Baronets, and to intermeddle with the grievances of Ireland, and suchlike, which the King cannot take well though he have hitherto showed a great deal of patience. . . .

This day one Floyd, an obscure lawyer, should, by sentence of the Lower House, have ridden with his face to the horsetail and stood on the pillory for lewd and contemptuous words against the King and Queen of Bohemia and their children spoken in the Fleet where he was prisoner. But he is remitted or respited about the question whether the Lower House can give any sentence of that kind; or rather, as most say, for that the King thinks better to suppress such scandalous speeches than by his punishment to blaze them further abroad.

[391] October 13, 1621: The Parliament is [further] adjourned by proclamation from the 14th of November to the 8th of February, which being counted a kind of dismal day, as well in other respects, as for the rising of the Earl of Essex [in 1601], it is a marvel it was not remembered.

[393] October 27, 1621: We hear of a rich carrack taken by the pirates almost in sight of Lisbon. I had rather the Hollanders had lighted on her, for it would have stood them in better stead.

Here is order for a gathering for the afflicted French church.[10] I doubt it comes somewhat unseasonably and will rise to no great matter so soon after so many payments, of subsidies, for Bohemia,

---

[10] I.e., for relief of the Huguenots.

and the like. And withal I can assure you that money goes here very low and scant, and the opinion of our great wealth is well fallen.

All manner of corn rises daily, and we are in fear of want as well by reason of the ill harvest, whereby much grain in many parts is lost for lack of ripening, as for the bad yield and ill season to sow for the next year.

On Tuesday last here was the highest tide that hath been seen many a year, for it ran all over Westminster Hall and did great harm in Thames Street. . . .

For lack of better news, here is . . . a ballad or song of Ben Jonson's in the play or show at the Lord Marquis' . . . for which and other good service there done, he hath his pension from a 100 marks increased to £200 *per annum,* besides the reversion of the Mastership of the Revels. There were other songs and devices of baser alloy, but because this had the vogue and general applause at Court I was willing to send it.

[394] November 10, 1621: I forbare the last week because here was nothing to write but of my new Lord Mayor's pageants, and the old Mayor's failing, who the night before he should have accompanied his successor to Westminster did *sgombrare,*[11] conveying all of worth out of his house and himself with his wife into some secret corner in the country, where ever since he hath played least in sight. He is one of the Farmers,[12] and always esteemed a man of great wealth. Howsoever, it falls out that he is now *fallito,*[13] and many men like to lose great sums by him.

You may guess in what case we are, and how sound at heart for all our fair shows, when neither Lord Mayor, Aldermen, Farmers, no, nor whole Companies, as the East Indian, Muscovy and others, are not able to hold out and pay their debts.

Yet as hard as the world goes, here was £30,000 taken up the last week for the Palatinate, furnished by Sir Baptist Hicks, Sir William Cockayne, and Peter van Lore ratably, for which service the last was knighted this day sevennight.

On Sunday in the afternoon the Parliament was by proclamation

---

[11] Vanish.
[12] Collectors of customs fees.
[13] Bankrupt.

brought back from the 8th of February to the 20th of this present, which though it be very short warning, yet it seems the urgent necessity will admit no longer delay.

[395] November 17, 1621: We are like to have our new Dean, Dr. Donne, at Paul's, so, as a pleasant companion said, that if Ben Jonson might be made Dean of Westminster, that place, Paul's and Christ Church should be furnished with three very pleasant poetical deans.[14] . . .

Sir Jerome Horsey made a motion they might have a sermon to begin [Parliament] withal, which for aught I hear was not much harkened to. It seems we grow into a superstitious opinion of sermons as the papists do of the mass, that nothing can be done without them, insomuch that an idle custom being lately brought up, that all Cheshire men about this town, Staffordshire men, Northampton, Sussex, Suffolk (*et sic de caeteris*) should have a meeting once a year at some hall, and laying their money together have a feast, it must not be done without a sermon.

[396] November 24, 1621: On Tuesday the Parliament began. There was a sermon prepared but not preached. Their first work was to call in and disannul protections, which were grown to great excess, so that merchants, tradesmen, and all manner unthrifts and debtors walked securely under somebody's name during the Parliament, which was generally misliked and thought a gross error that they, who take upon them to set all straight, should give way to such an abuse; so that henceforward they have taken order to restrain that privilege only to their necessary servants and attendants. But whether the Lords will follow the example is doubted. . . .

The Lord Treasurer spake concerning the state of the treasure and revenues, which he confessed were very poor and bare; that the King had been very bountiful, and twice or thrice repeated that he had been unfortunate in his officers; that this business of Bohemia

---

[14] Richard Corbet was Dean of Christ Church.

since the beginning had cost the King £211,000 and I know not how many odd pounds, shillings and pence out of his own coffers, besides £34,000 from the Nobility and £75,000 from the Commons; that they must consider how blessed we have been under his Majesty's government . . . ; how gracious he had been in taking away at one clap since the last sitting of the Parliament four or five and thirty monopolies worth so many subsidies; how much the realm had been bettered since his time by the settling of trades, improving of lands, by the prices of wool and corn till within these two years; with much more to this purpose—which was thought somewhat strange, when all or most of the hearers knew the realm was never so bare and poor since he was born.

[397] December 1, 1621: The Lower House fell to their business on Monday, and after much debating by Wednesday resolved on a subsidy to be paid in February next, concluding that all recusants (or whose wives, children or servants are so) should pay double and be counted as aliens, and that they should not be rated by the ordinary assessors but by the Commissioners. This is all they can do to show the apprehension and dislike of the incredible increase of that faction by the countenance or connivance that hath been given them of late. . . . There have been many good and free speeches used, and some perhaps more violent than needed, against the Spaniard *rebus sic stantibus*,[15] and much urging for a war of diversion; which indeed for mine own part I did ever think the only way, and not to stand pottering and pelting in the Palatinate only to consume both our men and means. . . .

I have heard extraordinary commendation of a neat speech made by one Pym, a Receiver, wherein he labored to show that the King's piety, clemency, justice, bounty, facility, peaceable disposition, and other his natural virtues were by the adverse party perverted and turned to a quite contrary course; and though he were somewhat long in the explanation of these particulars, yet he had great attention and was exceedingly commended. . . .

It is much marvelled that, so much business being now on foot both at home and abroad, the King should keep still at Newmarket,

---

[15] As matters stood.

where by reason of the foul weather and ways he can take no great pleasure nor have any store of company.

[398] December 15, 1621: The Remonstrance and Petition . . . was a kind of answer to the King's letter that did a little daunt them at first, but they soon recovered their spirits and sent away their messengers. . . . The messengers came back on Thursday, and yesterday made their relation in the House.

It seems they had a favorable reception, and the King played with them in calling for "stools for the Ambassadors to sit down." But in conclusion he read the Remonstrance but would not look on the Petition, and for answer returned his pleasure in writing which was twice read yesterday in the House, containing two sheets of paper at least, the principal points whereof (as far as I have heard) were that he would do his uttermost to recover the Palatinate and that he was not so unnatural as to forsake his children but would adventure all he had to maintain their right; but for the manner of managing that business they must leave that to him. Touching religion, he puts them out of doubt that he stands firm in that wherein he was bred and brought up, and which he hath ever professed, and hopes still to live and die in it, and that he will give way to any good laws they shall make for the establishing and continuance of it. As for the match with Spain, it was so far proceeded in on his part that, if those conditions and covenants he hath propounded may be accepted and kept, there is no more speech to be used in it; and that his dearest son had written unto him how unkindly he took it that they should busy themselves and intermeddle so much in his marriage.

Other things there were sharp enough, which they must digest as they may; but sure there is not that good understanding between the King and them that were to be wished, whilst he is so apprehensive of the least point that may seem to touch his prerogative and they so jealous and careful to preserve their privileges. And withal it is thought some privy whisperers and tale-carriers do misinform his Majesty and so animate him to the prejudice of the House. . . .

On Sunday night here was a great fire at the Fortune in Golding Lane, the fairest playhouse in this town. It was quite burned down in two hours and all their apparel and playbooks lost, whereby those poor companions are quite undone.

[**399**] December 22, 1621: On Thursday about three or four o'clock in the morning a great fire brake out in the six clerks' office in Chancery Lane that burned down that house and four more, besides others quite pulled down. . . . The fire was so vehement that it caught hold of the Rolls on the other side of the street, but by great labor and danger it was quenched, for which service Sir Julius Caesar gave twenty pound among them that best deserved it. There is great store of money said to be lost, besides other things of value; but the loss of rolls, records and writings is irreparable.

[**400**] January 4, 1622: If the Parliament be dissolved, many impute it to some ill-affected about the King. But he is too strong in his own judgment and of too great experience to be led along or rely on private whisperers. Others would lay it (as likewise Sir Ed. Coke's commitment) on Don Gondomar. Indeed, I have not read nor heard of any Ambassador so potent as he is said to be. And it seems to carry no good decorum if the report be true that the States[16] never yet had audience, and their backs no sooner turned, but he had present access to the King's pleasure.

But I hope all will be for the best and these breaches made up sounder than ever twixt the King and the Parliament. Otherwise I see not how the King's wants can be supplied, for that is the only ordinary, ancient, and plain highway, and all other devices and projects are but bypaths that lead to discontent.

[**401**] January 19, 1622: The King went hence to Theobalds the 9th of this present in the morning, and at his going the proclamation for dissolving the Parliament was published. . . . That afternoon he escaped a great danger, for riding in the Park, his horse threw him or fell with him in the midst of Middleton's water, so that if there had not been present help at hand, a miserable mischance might have followed. . . .

The Lords [of the Council] . . . proceed by way of persuading a benevolence, and sending for men of known wealth they deal with

---

[16] The Dutch Commissioners.

them severally, and have hitherto had so good success that they have drawn diverse to give £200 and most £100 . . . but it is thought they must descend to lower sums or else it will prove no benevolence but rather a *volens nolens*.[17]

The willfulness of the Lower House hath brought us to these terms, whereby we may see that *vanae sine viribus irae*,[18] and that there is no disputing nor contesting with supreme authority.

[**404**] March 30, 1622: Within these few days we have had diverse alarms of a great Spanish Armada preparing directly for England, which though it be not very probable, yet coming so many several ways, as from Venice, Rome, Spain, and other places, the Council begin to apprehend it, and to make provision accordingly as well by musters as otherwise. I should rather fear Ireland, where the redshanks belonging to the Earl of Argyll are already entered in great numbers. . . .

There was leave said to be given to the Earl of Argyll to levy a regiment of 4000 English and Scots to serve the Spaniard, but as far as I hear with no great success, for the Spanish Ambassador says he can have a whole regiment of captains but few or no soldiers.

[**410**] July 1, 1622: On the first Sunday of this term, the Bishop of London preached at Paul's Cross, where there was a great assembly but a small auditory, for his voice was so low that I think scant the third part was within hearing.

The chief points of his sermon were touching the benevolence, wherein he would prove that what we have is not our own and what we gave was but rendering and restoring; another part was about the repairing of Paul's; and the largest in confuting Pareus's opinions touching the peoples' authority in some cases over unruly and tyrannical princes, for which heresy of state his books were publically burned there toward the end of the sermon.

That afternoon our Dean[19] made a very good sermon in the Church as he hath done diverse of late, with great concourse.

---

[17] An unwilling gift.
[18] Protests are useless without power.
[19] John Donne.

[412] August 10, 1622: Master Ruthven, the Earl of Gowrie's brother that hath been prisoner in the Tower ever since the King's coming in, was released the first of this month and confined to Cambridge or Oxford with a pension of £500 a year. And now to make a complete jail-delivery, all priests, Jesuits, or other papists imprisoned are set at liberty and are not henceforward to be troubled for saying . . . of mass or refusing the oath of allegiance or supremacy and the like. I have not yet seen the Lord Keeper's letter that goes about, nor the letters patent under the Great Seal to this purpose, that by this example those of our profession shall find more favor in foreign parts.

It is likewise ordered as I hear that none of our preachers under the degree of a Bachelor of Divinity shall meddle with any matter of controversy in the pulpit, and that all lectures shall be put down saving on Sundays. . . .

Barnes and Hull, two mercers in Cheapside of the best account, are driven to get a protection, which is next door to a bankrupting. Two or three of our prime and principal taverns are likewise sunk and shut up.

We have had three new proclamations this week: one against transporting of wools, woolfells, fuller's earth, and the like; another forbidding mariners, seafaring men, shipwrights, or ship carpenters to serve any foreign prince or state without special license; the third against four-wheeled carts or wagons that with their weight mar and tear the highways.

[413] September 25, 1622: On the 15th of this present, the Dean of Paul's preached at the Cross to certify the King's good intention in the late orders concerning preachers and preaching, and of his constancy in the true reformed religion, which the people, as should seem, began to suspect. His text was the 20th verse of the 5th chapter of the book of Judges,[20] somewhat a strange text for such a business, and how he made it hold together I know not, but he gave no great satisfaction—or as some say, spake as if himself were not so well satisfied.

---

[20] From heaven fought the stars, from their courses they fought against Sisera.

[**416**] October 26, 1622: Much consultation hath been about raising of money. . . . The City came in question, but it was remembered how much they were behindhand already since their last loan, and that they are extremely impoverished, as may appear by a list of 1500 houses that stand empty within the Lord Mayor's precincts, whereof 500 bankrupted. And it is a strange sight and not known in this age till within these two or three years to see booksellers, stocking men, haberdashers, pointmakers, and other mean trades crept into the Goldsmith's Row, that was wont to be the beauty and glory of Cheapside.

But in conclusion, after all these devices, none was found to be so fit as the plain, ancient way of Parliament, and so I hear it was certified. But the King is so distasted with their tedious manner of proceeding that he will hardly be drawn unto it, unless matters be so prepared that there be a more quick dispatch. . . .

The King hath lately made Hugh Middleton, a goldsmith, a baronet for his good service in bringing the water to London and finding out the silver mine in Wales.

[**419**] December 7, 1622: Here is a strict proclamation come forth that all Lords spiritual and temporal that are not of the Council, all Lieutenants, Justices of Peace, and gentlemen of quality should repair to their houses and places of abode and there keep hospitality this Christmas . . . which comes ill to pass for diverse of all sorts that were come up with their wives and families to nestle here and are now fain to pack away again, not daring to adventure the penalty.

We have had a very crasie winter hitherto and continues still, so that, here being no infectious sickness spoken of, the bills hold weekly at 270 and 280 buried about this town.

[**420**] December 21, 1622: Now to prevent that the Court be not too thin and bare by the absence of so much nobility and gentry, there is order given that besides the Lords of the Council and others

that attend about the King's and Prince's persons, all the gentlemen of the Privy Chamber and pensioners shall wait and give ordinary attendance all the holidays.

Great complaining here is for want of payments, and indeed there is a general dearth and scarcity of money, and yet, as hard as the world goes, I hear the Lord of Carlisle hath a pension of £2000 for one-and-twenty years in recompense of service. . . .

We hear that Count Gondomar is to return hither shortly because it seems no man knows so well the length of our foot.

[422] January 25, 1623: Here was nothing to write of but dancing and feasting, which was more frequent all this Christmas than ever I knew or remember, and continues ever since till now. . . .

Ben Jonson they say is like to hear of it on both sides of the head for personating George Withers, a poet or poetaster as he terms him, as hunting after fame by being a chronomastix or whipper of the time, which is become so tender an argument that it must not be touched either in jest or earnest. For old Dr. White, our Prebend of Paul's, is commanded to keep his house for that, preaching there on Twelfth Night, he prayed God to preserve the King and Prince from any that should go about to withdraw them from their first love and zeal to religion, which is interpreted as a kind of libel—as if there were some danger of such a matter. . . .

Presently after the holidays our gentlemen, that were as it were banished from hence by the proclamation, came up again thick and threefold and do grumble that they should be confined to their houses; for after most of them were gone, even upon Christmas Eve, came forth another proclamation for their wives and families and widows to be gone likewise, and that henceforward gentlemen should remain here during terms only or other business, without bringing their wives and families—which is *durus sermo*[21] to the women and will hardly be digested. And it falls out by experience that the commandment did little good but rather hurt, for being driven to make their provision in haste, the markets rose so in all places where they came that the poor, instead of relief, found their burden heavier.

---

[21] Hard language.

[**427**] April 5, 1623: The 24th of the last month (the day of the King's inauguration) the Council came to Paul's Cross. . . . One Richardson, a young man of Magdalen College in Oxford, preached, and performed it reasonably well, and the better because he was not long nor immoderate in commendation of the time, but gave Queen Elizabeth her due.

[**429**] May 3, 1623: The King kept St. George's feast at Windsor, where there was no great show nor the knights and procession went not out of their ordinary circuit by reason the King was fain to be carried in a chair, not for any grief or infirmity more than the weakness of his legs. . . . On Monday the King removed to Hampton Court, on Tuesday hither, and on Thursday the first of this month went a-Maying to Theobalds. We had that day a general muster of 6000 men, well armed and appointed. His way lay through the midst of them, so he passed along without any great applause given or received, more than a volley of shot when he was past, which so terrified Secretary Conway's horses that they ran away and threw his coachman down, and without good help himself in danger of a shrewd turn.

[**432**] June 14, 1623: Our Lord Mayor was knighted at Court on Sunday last, where the Recorder made so formal and flattering a speech that the King seemed to surfeit of it and was not pleased. Among other faults he found with the City, the principal was that whereas at his first coming the Goldsmiths' Row in Cheapside was so fair and flourishing, they had now suffered it to be overrun and blemished with poor petty trades which he would have removed and none to nestle or keep shop there but jewellers and goldsmiths. . . .

An unruly son of the Lady Finch's, whom she sent to Virginia to be tamed, within five or six days after his return fell into a drunken quarrel with the Watch, where he was so hurt that he died the next morning and . . . his companion is almost in the same case if he be not dead already.

[**433**] June 28, 1623: The business of making gold thread that was so cried down the last Parliament as a monopoly exceeding prejudicial to the commonwealth, and for which Sir Giles Mompesson, Sir Francis Michell, and others were called in question and diverse others in danger, is now proclaimed and set up again under color of a new corporation.

[**439**] November 8, 1623: The next day after I wrote last [October 25] here fell out a pitiful accident in the Blackfriars, where the papists had hired a house next to the French Ambassador's (that so they might be as it were under his protection) to hold their assemblies, say mass, meet at sermons, and perform all other their exercises and rites after the Romish manner. A great multitude being met there on the 26th of the last month to hear Father Drury, a famous Jesuit among them, preach in an upper room, the floor sunk under them, or rather the beams and joists not able to bear the weight brake in the midst, being otherwise found upon search and view noway faulty or rotten but strong and sound.

Many perished, partly battered and bruised, but most part smothered, for the first floor fell with such violence that it brake down a second under it, though the walls and roof stirred not but stand firm. Besides Father Drury and one Riddiat, another Jesuit, the Lady Webb (sister to Sir Lewis Tresham), Mistress Sommers, and some few young gentlewomen, we hear of none but mean people, to the number of 95 or thereabout, though some speak of more, for in the first confusion many were conveyed away by their friends and said to be concealed. If the day had not been so very foul, many greater persons had been taken in the trap. But God provided better for them, though the papists give out it was a great blessing for them that perished because their dying in this manner is a *supersedeas*[22] from Purgatory, and that they are gone directly to heaven. And their priests will not allow it to be called or thought a judgment, but only a work of God.

A number were hurt, maimed, and lost their limbs which found little help or comfort at first, our people being grown so savage and barbarous that they refused to assist them with drink, *aqua vitae,*

---

[22] Dispensation.

or any other cordials in their necessity, but rather insulted upon them with taunts and gibes in their affliction as they were carried away all that evening and the night following . . . ; and even in Cheapside, where they should be more civil, they were ready to pull and tear them out of the coaches as they passed to their lodgings or to the surgeons. But there was as good order taken as might be on the sudden to repress the insolency and inhumanity of the multitude, and for the relief of the distressed. . . .

Some descant much of the day being their fifth of November,[23] but in my judgment nothing is more remarkable than that this was the first so solemn assembly of theirs that I have known or heard of in England these threescore years and more, and whereby you may see how bold and forward they are upon a little connivance. . . .

I commend our preachers' carriage in this accident, for generally they do not dilate nor aggravate it very much. And for those that I have heard, if they touch it at all, they do it temperately and charitably.

[440] November 15, 1623: We are so daily as it were called upon and visited with new disasters that we should be very dull, or rather in a deadly slumber, if they do not waken us; for on Wednesday last toward eight o'clock at night, a fire brake out at Sir William Cokayne's that terrified all this town, for the wind was so high and sat in such a corner that it threatened much harm, and withal the fire was so furious that the flakes and coals were carried far and near, some into the Thames and some beyond the Cross in Cheap. And surely but for the good order and great care there had been great danger, but by the diligence of good people, whereof diverse were maimed and hurt, there were but three or four besides his own house quite burnt, and some dozen pulled down and defaced.

He had great store of goods and merchandise in his house, whereof though some were saved, yet he lost at least to the value of £10,000, and one Holingshead, a neighbor of his, £6000, besides the housing and a world of household stuff and other goods lost and purloined in that confusion. Among the rest the Lady Raleigh had her house pulled down.

---

[23] Anniversary of the Gunpowder Plot, 1605, by the new Gregorian calendar.

I have seldom known a man less pitied, as well in respect of his great wealth as for his severity, and specially for that business of clothing,[24] wherein all England hath and is like to suffer so much, which was his only plot and project, and procured him many a curse from poor people, which is not to be contemned when it is deserved.

[443] December 20, 1623: The Countess of Sussex died the last week, and her greatest care in leaving the world was that her Lord should not marry his concubine (that was one Shute's widow, and sister to Mistress Meautys that was the Lady Cornwallis). But neither the Lord of Holderness's nor the Lord of Canterbury's diligence in sending of pursuivants could not prevent it, for the next day after his Lady's decease they were married and . . . she is become an indifferent common Countess.

But the strangest match in mine opinion is that Alleyn,[25] the old player, hath lately married a young daughter of the Dean of Paul's, which I doubt will diminish his charity and devotion towards his two hospitals.

[455] July 24, 1624: The case [of Amboyna][26] is much commiserated by all sorts of people and hath so much alienated our affections that we cry out mainly for revenge of such injustice and indignity. And the King takes it so to heart that he speaks somewhat exuberantly, and I could wish he would say less so he would do more.

For my part, I shot my bolt at first, that, if they were no wiser than I, we should stay or arrest the first Indian ship that comes in our way and hang up upon Dover Cliffs as many as we should find faulty or actors in this business and then dispute the matter afterwards, for there is no other course to be held with such manner of

---

[24] Cokayne's plan, 1615, to stop export of undyed cloth.

[25] Edward Alleyn, a famous Elizabethan actor and founder of the College of God's Gift, Dulwich, for six poor brothers, six poor sisters, and twelve poor scholars, married Constance, daughter of John Donne.

[26] Where a number of English merchants had been tortured and killed by Dutch East India Company agents.

men as neither regard law nor justice nor any other respect of equity or humanity, but only make Gain their god.

[464] January 8, 1625: Our soldiers[27] about Dover and in their way thitherward commit many foul outrages and live, as they say, at discretion, and all the way as they passed spoiled as if it had been in an enemy's country, which was not wont to be so; but either our people are grown more barbarous or there is no good order taken to provide for them. Howsoever it be, it shows we are but young warriors, and there goes more to the furnishing and setting out of an army than bare pen and ink.

---

[27] Of the army recruited by the mercenary general Count Mansfeld for the relief of the Palatinate.

XIII. The Spanish Marriage

"JACK *and Tom Smith*" *arrived at Canterbury in February, 1622, their false beards dangling and their gorgeous coats shrieking deception. Giving "some secret satisfaction" to "untwine themselves" from the astonished officials who detained them, they continued to Paris, where the French Court elaborately failed to recognize them, and so on to Spain to be welcomed by Gondomar's "Nunc dimittis." Instead of crowning eight years of negotiation with the success that Gondomar and King James devoutly hoped for, Prince Charles and Buckingham turned a harebrained escapade into a diplomatic fiasco.*

In 1614, Ambassador Diego Sarmiento de Acuña (he was created Count Gondomar in 1618) reopened the project of a Spanish marriage for Prince Charles, without any real hope that the necessary papal dispensation would be forthcoming, but aiming to prevent another Protestant marriage or, even worse, a French one. The game went on until 1618, by which time the players could no longer pretend not to recognize that the complete toleration for Catholics required by the Pope would never be politically acceptable in England. Gondomar departed to claim his well-earned peerage, having stalemated James's policy for nearly five years, as well as having become his best friend.

In September, 1619, James's son-in-law, Frederick, Elector Palatine, flouted the will of the German Emperor Matthias and the advice of all the Electors, including the other two Protestants, and accepted the invitation of the Protestant nobility of Bohemia to become their King. "There is now no place left for deliberation or mediation of peace till one side be utterly ruined," wrote Chamberlain prophetically. But James the Peacemaker did not see it that way.

While a futile embassy under James Hay, Viscount Doncaster, circulated the courts of Europe, a cousin of Philip III of Spain, Ferdinand of Styria, got himself elected Emperor following Matthias, and made plans, not unknown to Spain, to throw Frederick out of Bohemia and to occupy his lands in the Palatinate. Gondomar was rapidly dispatched again to London in March, 1620, to discourage any temptation on James's part to yield to popular and Parliamentary clamor for war.

In April, 1622, Gondomar again left England, having gained two precious years of peace for his new master, young Philip IV. The Pope delayed till June the announcement of the obviously unacceptable terms he would require for the marriage of Prince Charles to the Spanish Infanta. In September Frederick's capital of Heidelberg fell; in October Sir Horace Vere had to surrender Mannheim. Endymion Porter set off in November with an ultimatum from the English Council to Philip IV: Help restore the Palatinate or end negotiations and expect England to join the war in Europe.

Philip found that he could command neither the Emperor nor his aunt, the Archduchess Isabella, Regent in Brussels. Gondomar meantime seems to have become the only Spaniard to believe honestly and sincerely that the marriage of Prince Charles and the Infanta was the best policy for Spain, England, and Europe—and that it could somehow be achieved. Endymion Porter arrived back in London with an amended treaty, and a message from Gondomar to Charles saying that the time had come for his visit to Madrid.

But Gondomar had reckoned without "Tom Smith," Marquis of Buckingham.

[349] March 11, 1620: The Spanish Ambassador came to town on Wednesday, being attended at Dover by Sir Louis Lewknor, with many coaches among which one of the King's best, as likewise at Gravesend by one of the King's best barges, and the Earl of Dorset sent to receive and entertain him. He is lodged at Ely House which is extraordinarily furnished for him, with a rich cloth of estate, a thing more than I remember ever afforded before to any other Ambassador. The chapel is likewise trimmed up with an altar (they say) and other implements. . . . But to welcome him, the next day after his arrival here, drums went about the streets to give notice to all voluntaries that would serve the King of Bohemia to repair to Westminster this next week where they should find good entertainment.

[360] September 16, 1620: We had a short and quick alarm here at the first news of Spinola's entering upon the Palatinate, and it

troubled the King a while; yet the Baron Dohna[1] could not persuade him to intermit his sports and enter into some serious consideration of the business, protesting he did not know whether his master at that hour had one foot of land left in those parts, whereupon they say he received a strange answer. But the Spanish Ambassador, being expostulated withal touching breach of promise in that point, said he was glad of it, and wished Spinola had all the rest, that his Majesty might see his power in having it released and restored.

These proper conceits serve the turn for the time, and set him up so high on his tiptoes that in a late encounter and contestation with Secretary Naunton he carried himself so arrogantly and insolently as if all our Councillors were petty companions in respect of him, the great Ambassador (as he calls himself) of the great King of Spain. In truth he presumes very much every way, and this summer made a solemn progress into Buckinghamshire to the Lady Dormer's, where he had great entertainment, so that she spent more than fifty pounds a meal for five meals he was there. From thence he went into Northamptonshire to the Lady Tresham's, and so up and down the country among that crew, where it is verily thought he negotiated a counter-contribution to Bohemia in behalf of the Emperor.

[379] April 23, 1621: The French Ambassador gives out that the King of Spain on his deathbed bequeathed his daughter to the Emperor's son. But the Lord Digby's advertisements say that (among many other remembrances) he gave special charge to his son[2] and the Council to go on with the match for our Prince, and by all means to continue the peace and good correspondence with this Crown, having found the King so just and punctual in all his words and promises. I see not how this controversy (or rather, contrariety) should be reconciled, seeing they vary in the very letter of the text.

[400] January 4, 1622: We had news this morning out of Spain that the marriage is concluded and the Palatinate to be restored out of

---

[1] Baron Achatius von Dohna, Ambassador from James's son-in-law Frederick, Elector Palatine, who had just been thrown out of his "winter" Kingdom of Bohemia.

[2] Philip IV; Philip III died March 21. The French Ambassador was right.

hand; or in case the Emperor make any difficulty, the Spanish forces there shall turn against him. This bruit is enough to break off the Parliament, which I make no question will be dissolved.

[414] October 5, 1622: It is said the King is much displeased with the business of the Palatinate, and if he receive not shortly better satisfaction from Spain will resent it in another manner than he hath done, and begins to apprehend how much they abuse his patience and long-suffering.

[415] October 12, 1622: Master Cottington relates how much they were troubled and grieved in Spain at the news of the besieging of Heidelberg (for he was dispatched before they heard of the loss), and brings the names of the Commissioners now at last appointed to treat of the match, which are five: Don Balthazar de Zuñiga; Count Gondomar; Rostegney, the principal Secretary; the King's Confessor, a Dominican friar; and the Bishop of Segovia.

[418] November 16, 1622: The news of the rendering of Mannheim is nothing welcome, though I see not how nor to what purpose it should have held out longer; yet because we know not the reasons, and for that all came thence gave out confidently it would endure yet four months, it breeds much discourse, the rather for that it is said there came peremptory command from Spain that Tilly should leave that siege and the Palatinate, or else the Infanta should employ all the Spanish forces to constrain him. . . . If they mean truly, they may as well do it now they have all in their hand as before, or rather better and more to their honor and satisfaction of the world.

[421] January 4, 1623: Endymion Porter arrived here[3] on Thursday with pleasing news, for the King was very merry and jocund that

---

[3] From Spain.

night specially and ever since; it is given out that the match is fully concluded on their parts, and that the Duke of Medina Sidonia is to come shortly to see all things ratified here. And we are so forward that we look for the Infanta in May, because there is order taken for the making ready of ten of the King's ships with all speed. And we say that the Lord Admiral Buckingham shall go to conduct her; and I have it *di buona mano*[4] (and under the rose) that the Prince himself goes in person. In the meantime, Gondomar is to be sent into Germany to see the Palatinate restored. You may believe as much of this as you please.

[**424**] February 22, 1623: On Monday the Prince with the Lord of Buckingham, going from Theobalds and giving out that they went to New Hall, turned down toward the Thames, and coming to Tilbury ferried over to Gravesend, so to Rochester, Canterbury, and Dover, where taking ship on Wednesday morning, it is thought they had a fair passage to Dieppe and so mean to post into Spain. . . . But their fair riding coats and false beards (whereof one fell off at Gravesend) gave suspicion they were no such manner of men, whereupon one was sent to Rochester to have them stayed. But being past, another was dispatched who overtook them not far from Sittingbourne (by reason one of their horses failed), so that they were stayed at Canterbury for that Sir Louis Lewknor, attending the Ambassador[5] and taking them for suspicious persons, had sent notice to the Mayor. How they untwined themselves there I know not; but at Dover they were stayed again till they had given some secret satisfaction.

The news came not abroad, nor the Council knew it not, till Wednesday and then was it in every man's mouth. But few believed it at first because they could not apprehend the reasons of so strange a resolution, as being a mystery of state beyond common capacities. I hear the King sent to the Council two days since that the cause why he imparted it not to them was for that secrecy was the life of the business: that it was the Prince's own desire, that the Marquis had no hand in it but only by his commandment, that by this means he should soon try whether they meant fair dealing; that he would have them

---

[4] From a reliable source.

[5] Lewknor, in charge of Protocol, was awaiting Boiscot, newly arrived from Flanders.

consult what equipage or attendance should follow, and to provide to stay the amazement of the people, which is thought shall be done shortly by some proclamation showing the motives or imposing silence.

Indeed the world talks somewhat freely, as if it were done that they may be married at a mass, which could not so handsomely be done here, or to prevent the difficulties of the Pope's dispensation, seeing it is ordinary with them that *quod fieri non debuit, factum valet.*[6] Others assign other causes, but all concur that it is a very costly and hazardous experiment. . . .

I can hardly conceive how they should pass through France undiscovered, though the ports be shut up here for a time. And I have heard the French Ambassador sent away a post on Monday by the way of Plymouth, which if he find passage will prevent [7] them by many a mile; and no doubt he sent other ways likewise, having gotten notice of it by some means or other. The Earl of Carlisle is to go this day toward France to comply with that King and to excuse the necessity of keeping the journey secret. . . . *Jacta est alea,*[8] and there is no more left but to make the best of it.

[425] March 8, 1623: We have little certainty of the Prince's journey since his going hence, but only that they landed at Boulogne the Wednesday and rode three posts that night. On Friday they came to Paris very weary, and resting there all Saturday, went away early on Sunday morning. Some give out that during their abode there they saw the King at supper, and the Queen practicing a ball with diverse other Ladies, which though it be somewhat confidently affirmed, yet I think it not probable by reason it was their first Saturday in Lent.

We have had since many rumors that they were stayed, but now they talk of a post should come yesternight with news that they are past Bayonne and that my Lord Digby and Gondomar, with I know not how many litters and coaches, were ready at the frontiers to receive them—which sounds as unlikely as most of the rest. . . .

The Sunday after their departure, all the Council about this town came to Paul's Cross, where it was expected somewhat would have

---

[6] What was forbidden succeeds, once done.
[7] Anticipate.
[8] The die is cast.

been said. But the preacher had his lesson *in haec verba,*[9] only to pray for the Prince's prosperous journey and safe return.

[**426**] March 21, 1623: For want of better matter, I send you here certain verses made upon Jack and Tom's journey (for the Prince and Lord Marquis went through Kent under the names of Jack and Tom Smith). They were fathered at first upon the King, but I learn since they were only corrected and amended by him. . . .

The last news we heard of the Prince came this day sevennight by Walsingham Gresley that belongs to the Earl of Bristol. . . . It seems by that he brings and says, that the Prince was not expected there, but that it will be as strange news to them as it was to us, and withal that things are not so forward and ripe there as we take them. But what this noble ingenuity and confidence—to commit and cast himself into their hands—may work is uncertain.

In the meantime, here be two ships making ready with all possible speed, the one at Portsmouth, the other at Plymouth, to carry away his provisions and servants, whereof the Lord Leppington (or Carey) hath the chief charge to see them carry themselves civilly and religiously, and that they go not to mass. . . . There is continual posting likewise through France, which together with the expense that the other must make from the seaside to Madrid will so exhaust our coin (that is so scant already) that it is feared we shall be driven to use black money (as they call it) and is now in a manner altogether current in Spain. And wise men stick not to say that this match one way or other will stand the King and kingdom in as much as she is like to bring, besides whatsoever else may happen.

Many of our churchmen are hardly held in and their tongues itch to be talking, insomuch that Dr. Everard, the preacher at St. Martin's in the Field, is committed for saying somewhat more than he should; and on Sunday last at the parish church next to us, another went so far that the parson of the church caused the clerk to sing him down with a psalm before he had half done.

I had forgot that the Lord of Buckingham went Extraordinary Ambassador, and as prime commissioner with the Lord of Bristol (the Ambassador Resident) and Sir Francis Cottington in the treaty

---

[9] In these words.

of the marriage; and that we hear of a patent gone after him whereby he is made Duke of Buckingham.

[427] April 5, 1623: On Sunday Grimes, Gentleman of the Horse to my Lord of Buckingham, arrived here out of Spain with news of the Prince's wonderful entertainment and kind usage there, a relation whereof they say we shall have next week in print. In the meantime I send you here what is come to my hand.

Gondomar, at the first sight of the Prince, fell down flat before him and would not be raised, but cried out, *"Nunc dimittis,"* as having attained the top of his desire. . . .

The first of this month, by commandment, here was bonfires and ringing of bells for this welcome news of the Prince's safe arrival at Madrid. God send we may praise at parting—which I wish the rather, for that in the midst of all this jollity I hear the Lord Digby writes that, as he pretends no private benefit to himself in the good success of this business, so he desires he may be blameless if, by reason of the Prince's coming, matters fall not out according to expectation. Here is a whispering underhand of no good intelligence twixt him and the Lord of Buckingham.

[428] April 19, 1623: The Prince desires his Majesty to hasten the sending of the fleet, for he hopes to be with his Lady Infanta at the seaside before it arrive. Yet in the meantime the sending for his arms and tilting horse make men doubt all cannot be well done so soon. They are shipped here already, but the wind that should carry them away keeps them in the river, and most men think they are like to serve to little use after so long lying on shipboard and so long a journey by land from the seaside to Madrid, together with so great change of air and diet, and the heat of the year coming on; whereby it will be nothing fit neither for his Highness to use so violent an exercise.

But that which makes men suspect most of all that matters are not so current is that we hear the Marquis of Inojosa, your old acquaintance, is coming hither Ambassador and is to set out thence the first of their May, or rather (as the Spanish Ambassador here gives out), the tenth. The dispensation is not come neither, but they say the Duke of Pastrana is sent to Rome to hasten it. But he goes in a litter, as is given out. . . .

But let men think and talk what they will, the King knows more than we all, who is very confident of the success and joys much to talk of the Prince's journey and all the accidents by the way, whereof he was fully informed by Grimes, and how many falls they had: the Lord Marquis seven, Sir Fra. Cottington twelve, and so of the rest, only the Prince had never a one.

[**429**] May 3, 1623: The dispensation is said to be come, but with what clauses and conditions is not yet published. . . . But at the coming of the Marquis of Inojosa we shall know as well that as the other articles that concern the King of Spain and the Infanta, which are likewise said to be hard enough, as the leaving the Hollanders, the giving license to the Spaniard to bring what number of ships he please into our ports, there to furnish and victual them at reasonable rates, and I know not what else; which I am so far from believing that I cannot persuade myself but the fear is more than the danger.

Now for the Infanta's part, it is said she is to have £8000 jointure for every £100,000 she is to bring, which being given out to be £600,000, it will make a great breach into the Crown land, which hath been so much weakened already. And this must be confirmed by Parliament, with diverse other prerogatives and privileges she is to have, more than ever Queen of England had. The Spanish Ambassador hath been at St. James's and Denmark House to fit and appoint her lodgings with many alterations. Specially there must be a new chapel built in either place, for which order is taken with the Surveyor, Inigo Jones, to have them done out of hand, and yet with great state and costliness. The Savoy chapel likewise shall be converted to the use of her household. . . .

The fleet is preparing with all speed, and the Prince's ship so richly furnished with all manner of bedding, hangings, and the like, as hath not been seen at sea; and all things else are so carried as if we were to receive some Goddess or *numen tutelare*[10] to come amongst us. . . .

---

[10] Divinity for (our) protection.

And there is no greater reason alleged of the hastening of it than the great charge the Prince puts them to there and the penury and dearth of all things there at this time, which those few that come thence deny . . . yet it is thought they have their lesson taught them, an argument whereof is drawn from this: that none of the Prince's servants that were sent for are suffered to go to Madrid, no, not his chaplains. . . . And thus they go up and down like a well with two buckets.

[**430**] May 17, 1623: [The Earl of Carlisle] arrived here on Thursday out of Spain. . . . It was bruited before his coming that he had given small content and carried himself more stiffly in some points than some there saw fit, whereupon as well he as the Earl of Bristol were made strangers to the business. And reports went that the Prince's servants were kept from him, and that all things were managed by himself and the Lord of Buckingham; as likewise that the King keeps all to himself *in crinio pectoris*,[11] and acquaints nobody with anything comes thence, but burns the letters as fast as he reads them.

For my part, I presume these are but discourses of idle brains who had rather make news than want matter to talk. Indeed posts go very fast to and fro, for since this day fortnight that Gresley arrived, here have been two more, whereof one that belongs to Sir John Hippisley came in less than seven days from Madrid, a thing not heard of.

We say here that Sir William Crofts is sent from the Prince upon some message to the Queen of Bohemia.

Here is great haste to set the fleet forward, and Sir Francis Steward is gone already with the patent whereby the Lord Marquis is created Duke of Buckingham and Earl of Coventry. He was willed to make all possible speed, that it might be there before the marriage, for the more grace to his Grace.

Yet all these plain demonstrations cannot beat it into the heads of the vulgar but that there be many rubs yet to be removed before the match be concluded, for they talk of many uncouth and unlikely conditions propounded, as well touching religion as matter of state,

---

[11] In the cupboard of his heart.

specially the committing of Plymouth and some other western haven into the Spaniard's hand till the jointure be assured and other promises performed. But this is so improbable and almost impossible that it cannot but proceed from a vain fear in the people, who the less they know the more they suspect.

[431] May 30, 1623: On Monday, the Duke of Richmond, the Lord Treasurer,[12] Marquis Hamilton, Lord of Arundel, Secretary Calvert, and I know not who else, are to go toward Southampton to set all things in order thereabout for the reception and entertainment of the Infanta, and all westward there is commandment for musters and other provisions if occasion serve.

Yet all this while we have had no news from Spain since I wrote last, which breeds suspicion that there is some stop or restraint in France. The Lord Leppington landed this week and . . . came post from the seaside and delivered all he had to the King. But otherwise he either knows or says little, as likewise the Lord of Carlisle is very silent, yet somewhat breaks out sometimes, as that at his coming away the Infanta gave him leave to kneel to her above an hour, which is thought to be more than needed, either to be given or received; whereupon our great Ladies begin to consult how to demean themselves when she comes, specially the double Duchess,[13] or as some wags call her, the Duchess-cut-upon-Duchess. . . .

In the meantime some mutter that we presume much upon the Spaniard, that we trust him with our only Prince, the principal and richest jewels of the crown, and the best part of our navy all at once, besides so many other men of worth. But it is answered again that for their own interest it stands them upon to keep touch with us, being as it were without all other friends.

We look daily to hear of the solemnization of the marriage.

[432] June 14, 1623: Till yesterday we had no news out of Spain this month or five weeks, for the King had found a way to have ad-

---

[12] Lionel Cranfield, 1st Earl of Middlesex.

[13] Frances, widow of the 1st Earl of Hertford, who had married the Duke of Lennox and Richmond as soon as she decently could in 1621.

vertisement thence without notice of anybody, the packets being sent to our Ambassador in France who sent them away by some servant or messenger of his own and stayed those that brought them till answer came back to dispatch them. But now Sir Francis Cottington and Gresley are come together; . . . the world doth guess there is some difficult point that requires Cottington's coming to the oracle. And withal we hear there is order given for the ships to stay a fortnight.

[435] July 26, 1623: The Lords of the Council were sent for to Theobalds the 16th of this month to be made acquainted with the articles concerning the Spanish match, where it is said there was some sticking upon points of religion, specially by the Scottish Lords; but it was answered that it was not now to be disputed what was of convenience but what of necessity, the Prince being in their hands and the King's children despoiled of their patrimony, which was not to be recovered but by this means or by a bloody and uncertain war, and setting all Christendom together by the ears. So that in effect this was not so much a matter of counsel as a preparative for what they were to do on Sunday, when there was great doings at Whitehall, the Spanish Ambassador being to be feasted and the King took his oath to observe all the articles agreed upon, which were read by Secretary Calvert in Latin and lasted almost an hour.

I have not seen nor heard much of them, but one among the rest, that the Infanta is to be allowed 24 priests which are to have as it were a bishop over them and not to be any way subject to our laws, that she is to have the education of her children till they be ten years old, with many other points concerning her jointure, and favorable toleration toward the Romish Catholics.

But I will not omit one thing told me by three several persons that saw it, that the ceremonies being ended and the anthem sung, when the Bishop began the prayer for the King, the Ambassador's confessor or Jesuit, that stood by him within the traverse, clapped on his hat and so continued all the while, though the King and Ambassador were bare.

The feast was plentiful and the Ambassador as gallant and gaudy as your Venetians, but none of our people made any show saving

Master Gage and the Earl of Carlisle, who had a rich suit of black taffeta with gold pearl. . . .

After dinner all the Council, to the number of 29 as I hear, were sworn to see all those articles performed to the best of their power. . . .

It is given out that the Prince, wearied with so long delay, had packed up and was upon coming away when the King of Spain came to him, and so all controversies were accorded between themselves, insomuch that the King propounded to have all dispatch upon the Prince's own word and promise for performance of all that was agreed. But it was thought better to have a double string and not to neglect our King's oath, for that the Prince might pretend he was not master of himself, being in their power.

[436] August 30, 1623: The 20th of this month the King was aboard the fleet at Portsmouth, and dined in the fairest ship, called the Prince. They went thence this day sevennight toward Plymouth where they are to take in fresh victual, and a number of cooks were sent hence to make a world of baked meats. Yet the ships have order to stay there fifteen days for further command, before which time it is presumed we shall have the long-expected news.

[437] October 11, 1623: On Monday (a very foul and rainy day), the Prince came by Ware but stayed not more than to change his coach. He landed at Portsmouth on Sunday in the afternoon, came that night to the Lord Annandale's by Guildford, and the next morning before eight o'clock hither. He landed at York House, whither he sent for the Council that attended him at Whitehall, and after breakfast went toward Royston, not admitting the Spanish Ambassador's unseasonable demand of audience.

I have not heard of more demonstrations of public joy than were here and everywhere, from the highest to the lowest; such spreading of tables in the streets with all manner of provisions, setting out whole hogsheads of wine and butts of sack, but specially such numbers of bonfires, both here and all along as he went (the marks whereof we found by the way two days after) as is almost incredible; besides what was done elsewhere and all over, insomuch that at Blackheath there was fourteen load of wood in one fire, and the people were so mad with excess of joy that if they met with any cart laden with wood they would take out the horses and set cart and all on fire.

A number of other particulars I could set down too long to relate, but among all there being solemn service in Paul's, the singing of a new anthem was specially observed, the 114th psalm, "When Israel came out of Egypt and the house of Jacob from among the barbarous people." But above all, certain condemned prisoners had the best hap and most cause to rejoice, who being on their way to Tyburn were reprieved by the Prince's coming in the very nick.

I can tell you nothing of their reception at Royston but that the King going down to receive them, they met on the stairs where, the Prince and the Duke being on their knees, the King fell on their necks and they all wept. That night a post was dispatched for the Duchess and Countess of Buckingham and the Lady of Denbigh[14] to come next day to Royston.

The Prince was seventeen days at sea, and in his passage had the fortune to part a fray twixt four Dunkirkers and five Hollanders. . . .

Matters are still kept so secret that we know not what to judge of the match. The King at his last being in town treated alone with the two Spanish Ambassadors more than a whole hour together, nobody being admitted into the room.

The Prince at his coming away bestowed twelve thousand pound upon the officers that attended him, besides jewels presented to the King, Queen, Infanta, and other great men and women of the Court to such a value as I cannot easily subscribe to.

The Duke of Buckingham's carriage in all the business is much applauded and commended, and sure if it were altogether as is reported, it was brave and resolute. The Count Olivarez and he parted but upon indifferent terms, for he only told him that if ever it were his chance to come where he had to do, he would not fail to requite him. The Earl of Bristol and the Spaniards give out that if it had not been for his impatience, the marriage had been consummated before Christmas Day.

---

[14] Wife, mother and sister respectively of the Duke.

[438] October 25, 1623: The King is expected here about Thursday; and the Tuesday after, the Duke of Buckingham feasts the Spanish Ambassador at York House, which is thought to be done rather *pro forma* than *ex animo*.[15] It is said the King himself will be there, which is more honor than any of our Ambassadors or the Prince himself could receive in Spain, so jealous are they of their state and gravity; but sure if there were no wiser than myself, I could wish that we should deal with such supercilious people *lege talonis*,[16] and mete to them in their own measure.

Our courtiers and others that were in Spain begin now to open their mouths and speak liberally of the coarse usage and entertainment, where they found nothing but penury and proud beggary, besides all other discourtesy; insomuch that even the Romish Catholics complain of Gondomar, who was their idol here, that he used them as bad as the best.

And this journey hath wrought one unexpected effect, that whereas it was thought the Spaniards and we should piece and grow together, it seems we are generally more disjointed and farther asunder in affections than ever; besides the good it hath done in religion by laying open their gross ignorance and superstition, not only in their ordinary and public practice but even in those that pretend and would seem learned. And this event might be added to those other examples of Plutarch *de utilitate capienda ex inimicis*.[17]

[441] November 21, 1623: The great feast held at York House on Tuesday night. The King, Prince and Spanish Ambassadors were all present saving the Marquis Inojosa, who would not abate the least punctilio of his pretensions.[18] I hear little of how matters passed there, but only of the superabundant plenty, when twelve pheasants were piled in a dish, that there were forty dozen of partridges, as many quails, *et sic de caeteris* in all kind of provisions, which ostentation of magnificence is to no purpose when it is to so little use, but

---

[15] For form's sake rather than from the heart.
[16] By the law of the jungle.
[17] Of benefits to be gotten from one's enemies.
[18] He claimed precedence over the Ambassador Extraordinary Don Diego de Mendoza who had arrived in England with Prince Charles.

only to bring a scarcity and as it were to trample God's good blessings under foot. The banquet cost three hundred pounds. There was a masque of young Maynard's invention whereof I hear little or no commendation, but rather that the Spaniards took offense at it. The main argument of it was a congratulation for the Prince's return. . . .

The selected Commissioners for Foreign Affairs sit much. I think I forgot to send you their names, as the Lord Keeper, Lord Treasurer, Lord Chamberlain, Lord Marshal, the two Dukes, Marquis Hamilton, Lord of Carlisle, Lord Belfast, Chancellor of the Exchequer, and both the Secretaries, which make a full jury. God send them still to give a just and true verdict.

[**442**] December 6, 1623: Rivas, the Spanish courier, . . . came not till Sunday in the afternoon, with news that the Queen of Spain is brought to bed of a daughter, for which their Ambassadors here made bonfires that night with other demonstrations of joy, as shooting of muskets and showing of lights on the top of their house and at the windows; but the French Ambassador passed it over with a bare bonfire before his door the next day. . . .

Rivas brought likewise some private letters that say the proxy or procuration left with the Lord of Bristol is delivered, and that the espousals were to be performed presently and had been then done but for this accident of the Queen's delivery. This breeds much discourse, but it is not believed for many reasons. . . .

My Lord of Buck. used the principal Walloons of Mexia's[19] train with . . . extraordinary courtesy and favor, soliciting them to discontentment and telling them he marvelled how so brave a nation could endure the Spanish tyranny; but if they would help themselves they should not want other help. . . .

We long to hear out of Spain how matters stand there, for howsoever the balance seems to incline from them, yet the former earnestness and some late speeches (that it should be a match in spite of all the devils in hell and all the Puritans in England) hold us in suspense; though they say a Parliament is assuredly agreed upon twixt this and Easter. How the Lord Digby hath carried himself in

[19] Special Ambassador from the Infanta's aunt, the Archduchess Isabella, in Brussels. As Chamberlain remarked (Letter 437), there were so many ambassadors "it seems they mean to hold a Council table here."

the business I cannot learn, but sure the Duke of Buckingham is much animated against him. . . .

I send you here the inscription of a pillar that is to be set up in the place where the King of Spain and our Prince parted, wherein the Duke of Buck. is quite forgotten, as if he had been none of the company. The masque at York House were not worth the sending but that it is so free from flattery.

[443] December 20, 1623: Peter Killigrew came out of Spain the last week having been but four and twenty days in going and coming, which, the short days and ill ways considered, is thought somewhat extraordinary diligence; yet Gresley that was dispatched after him overtook him within less than three days. They both relate that they came in good time, for the match was in great forwardness and ready to be solemnized, for the scaffolds and other public preparations were set up and in order, so that their coming was taken for a great affront, as if it had been *à point nommé*[20] to forbid the bans.

It is said to be very unwelcome news to the Lord of Bristol, who it seems hath set up his rest upon it. He is daily decried more and more; and here goes up and down a kind of relation made some seven years since, when he went first Extraordinary Ambassador, that discovers him and his vanity more than I could easily have believed of a man esteemed of his wit and judgment, and how many disgraces and indignities he swallowed to bring his own ends about without regard to his master's, his country's or his own honor. It is thought to be written by Sir Robert Phillips, who imparted the substance of it by letters to the last Bishop of Winchester, Montagu, and he to the King. If it had then been believed, it might have saved a great deal of labor and cost that hath been since not so well spent— but for the experience we have had by it, which cannot be too dear.

And surely if things fall out as we expect and hope, God's providence is wonderful over us, to turn that to our good which in all appearance was so contrary both to our religion and state. . . .

We have a whispering that the Junta or Commission for Foreign Affairs shall be somewhat abridged in number, for though they be sworn to secrecy, yet some things are found to be vented and come

---

[20] Done on purpose.

abroad that were better kept close. The appearing of Sir Robert Mansell that hath been long under hatches, the thronging of sea captains to the Court, the sending of Sir Robert Amstrother into Denmark, but specially of the Lord of Kensington into France (though under color of a private compliment), make us suspect there is somewhat abrewing; and withal the papists hanging down their heads that were so brag of late, that the Lord Arundell of Wardour, a busybody, made means to the King that he might be their agent in Court, as those of the religion have theirs in France.

[445] January 17, 1624: Here is a Monsieur come from the French King with a present of fifteen or sixteen cast of hawks, some ten or twelve horses, and as many setting dogs. He made his entry very magnificently, with all this retinue in very good order and with store of torchlight, which gave the more luster to all this long show and to his own bravery, being indeed very rich and gallant. His hawks fly at anything: kites, crows, pies, or whatsoever comes in the way. He is to tarry till he have instructed and inured our men to his kind of falconry, which had not need be long, being so costly; for he and his train stand the King in five and twenty or thirty pound a day. . . .

In two or three days the whole frame of the business suffered great alteration, and the proverb that Tottenham is turned French quite changed into Spanish: for they are said to promise *monts et merveilles*,[21] and make so many fair offers that we know not how to refuse them they come so fast upon us, as first to send the Infanta hither in April upon their own charge with half the dowry in hand and sufficient security for the rest, to leave matters of religion to the King's own disposition, to restore what they have in the Palatinate into the King's hands and to join with him both by treaty or arms to recover the rest; with other advantageous conditions which do so stagger some of the Council that were thought to stand fast, that the sway seems to go on that side. And surely, unless God set to His helping hand, we are like to be carried away by these sirens' songs and suffer shipwreck in calm and fair weather. But *spero meliora*,[22] and I have some reason that I dare not brag of.

---

[21] Mountains and marvels.
[22] I hope for better things.

[446] January 31, 1624: The Junta for Foreign Affairs sat hard all . . . week. . . . It is said that the Prince at the last meeting showed himself very averse from the match, as well in regard of matter of state as of religion. . . . It seems the Duke of Buckingham engrosses the Prince's favor so far as to exclude all others both from the father and son. This is thought to cause some heartburning, and that they aim to take down his greatness, upon which apprehension it is said he stirs not from the King, but keeps close about him to cut off all access.

The last resolution about this great business was carried on Monday to Newmarket by the Duke of Richmond, the Lord of Carlisle, and Secretary Conway. What it was God knows, but here hath been so much variety and uncertainty of reports and surmises now a great while that I find it a pain to be so long in suspense, and therefore resolve to give it over, as a matter that concerns me as little or less than other men in respect both of my orbity[23] and age, and will only wish all well and pray God to turn all to the best. . . .

If I could expect good of parliaments I should hope well of this, because they are more careful than usually they have been in their choice of knights and burgesses, and have not that regard of great ones' letters and recommendations that they were wont.

[457] August 21, 1624: I doubt not but you have heard of our famous play of Gondomar,[24] which hath been followed with extraordinary concourse, and frequented by all sorts of people old and young, rich and poor, masters and servants, papists and puritans, wise men, etc., churchmen and statesmen, as Sir Henry Wotton, Sir Albert Morton, Sir Benjamin Rudyard, Sir Thomas Lake, and a world besides; the Lady Smith would have gone if she could have persuaded me to go with her. I am not so sour nor severe but that I would willingly have attended her, but I could not sit so long, for we must have been there before one o'clock at farthest to find any room. They counterfeited his person to the life, with all his graces and faces, and had gotten (they say) a cast suit of his apparel for the purpose, and his litter, wherein, the world says, lacked nothing

---

[23] Childlessness.
[24] Thomas Middleton's *A Game at Chess*: Gondomar is the Black Knight; the White Courtiers are not heavily disguised.

but a couple of asses to carry it and Sir G. Peter or Sir T. Matthew to bear him company. But the worst is, in playing him they played somebody else, for which they are forbidden to play that or any other play till the King's pleasure be further known; and they may be glad if they can so scape scot-free. The wonder lasted but nine days, for so long they played it.

[462] December 4, 1624: The next day after I wrote last [November 7] we had here great triumph and rejoicing for the good forwardness of the French match, by public commandment: the organs in Paul's played two hours on their loudest pipes, and so began to the bells, the bells to the bonfires, the bonfires to a great peal of ordnance at the Tower. God grant it may prove worth all this noise.

XIV. Last Letters

CHAMBERLAIN'S *brother Richard, with whom he had lived for over twenty years, died in February, 1624, leaving him "alone of all my father's children" and executor of a long-neglected estate. The tone of these letters is understandably forlorn, not cheered by the "sorest winter (every way) that hath been in the memory of man." There are noticeably few of the references to mutual friends that filled the early letters; Chamberlain had survived his contemporaries and no longer tried to keep up with their children and grandchildren. "My many businesses will scant give me leave to listen after that is told me," he writes gloomily—and then goes on for pages that grow more and more cheerful as he indulges the happy habit of decades.*

There were other than personal reasons for gloom, for an observer who grew to manhood in another century under such another monarch. The thirteen months covered by these letters saw vertiginous changes in policy as Buckingham and his young Prince broke off the long negotiations with Spain and rushed into Charles's marriage with the sister of Louis XIII of France. They saw the brief period of Parliamentary optimism over the Prince's deportment change into outright defiance over Buckingham's incredibly irresponsible pursuit of his new policy. Chamberlain sounds very elderly as he writes in sorrow and anger of the massacre of English merchants in Amboyna, one of the Spice Islands, and of the terrible conduct of the mercenary army recruited to recover the Palatinate by the rascal Mansfeld.

And here is the last chapter in the saga of Sir Edward Coke and his Lady Hatton—the disgrace of the spirited daughter they had together sacrificed to the Buckinghams; Lady Hatton's comic if sordid fight with the "double Duchess" over rent; and old Sir Edward's return to Parliament, despite the plan of the previous year to send him off on a Commission to Ireland.

The old King died; the new King took over the royal housekeeping; the young Queen arrived; Buckingham continued, more and more petulantly, to call the tune. The whole summer is clouded by the increasing menace of the plague and by a suspension of action in the midst of the whirlwind realignments and recriminations.

*The last letter finds Carleton's dream of a job in London finally
come true after fifteen years abroad. However, no sooner had he
become Under-Chamberlain of the Household, by Buckingham's
agency, than he was sent off again to Paris to smooth over the
cracks already apparent in the new alliance.*

[**447**] February 21, 1624:

MY VERY GOOD LORD,

The extremity of the weather kept me from writing the last week,
besides another impediment of more consequence (to me), the decease of my brother,[1] who left this world the 10th of this present.
His great age of 76 and many infirmities made his loss the less
lamented, being deprived of his sight, and in a manner of his hearing, feeling, taste, and all other senses save smelling, which with his
memory continued perfect to the last gasp; so that his life was not of
late time *vita vitalis,* and a man might verify in him *Non est vivere
sed valere vita.*[2] Now am I left alone of all my father's children,
omnes composui,[3] the last of eight brothers and sisters, and left to
a troubled estate, not knowing how to wrestle with suits and law
business and such tempestuous courses after so much tranquillity as
I have hitherto lived in, and, which is worst of all, in a weak bottom
—as no other was to be expected from a man that for twelve or
fourteen years never looked to his reckonings, and therefore, according to the proverb, they have looked to themselves and left little or
nothing. But I must pass it over as I may and bid all good days adieu
in this world when I have most need of rest and quiet. This is but
a melancholy discourse, and therefore will dwell no longer upon it,
only adding this, that I doubt I shall not be hereafter at so much
leisure as I have been.

This term brought forth no greater matters than the censuring of
one Moore, an attorney, for speaking very lewdly and scandalously
of Queen Elizabeth and Henry the Eighth. His judgment was to lose
both his ears, imprisonment during the King's pleasure, and other
suchlike punishments, which was executed accordingly this week in
Cheapside, where he laughed all the while. The last day of term,

---

[1] Richard, with whom Chamberlain had lived since c. 1604.
[2] Life is not to live at ease but a leave-taking.
[3] I laid them all to rest.

Sir Fra. Englefield was fined likewise in the Star Chamber at £3000 for touching the Lord Keeper[4] with bribery. It was thought somewhat hard that such a cause should be dispatched by bill and answer in the compass of so short a term, and upon the accusation of one witness, Sir Miles Sandys (for in effect it was no more), Sir John Bennet being already disabled as no competent witness, and withal coming under color of kindness to visit him in the Fleet, and so to draw him to some intemperance of speech.

Here runs up and down a proclamation come out of Ireland against Jesuits and priests to avoid that kingdom within forty days upon pain and peril may fall thereon. It is well said if it may be as well done, but I doubt *sero medicina paratur*.[5] I would have sent it if I had met with a convenient messenger, as likewise Dr. Donne's *Devotions*,[6] in his sickness newly come abroad, wherein are many curious and dainty conceits, not for common capacities, but surely full of piety and true feeling.

The Parliament that should have begun the 12th of this month was put off till the 16th and then, by reason of the Duke of Richmond's death, till the 19th. He died of an apoplexy in his bed on Monday morning. His Lady takes it extreme passionately, cut off her hair that day with diverse other demonstrations of extraordinary grief, as she had good cause, as well in respect of the loss of such a Lord, as for that she foresees the end of her reign.

The King went to the Parliament on Thursday, with greater show and pomp than I have seen to my remembrance. I was so much and so many ways invited that I could not refuse to go, and to say the truth I went specially to see the Prince, who indeed is grown a fine gentleman and beyond the expectation I had of him when I saw him last, which was not these seven years; and indeed I think he never looked nor became himself better in all his life. The King made a very gracious and plausible speech, confessing he had been deluded in the treaty of the match, but referring it now wholly to their consideration whether it should go forward or no, according as they should see cause upon the Prince's and Duke of Buckingham's relation. It may be we shall have it in print; therefore I will leave the rest to the Press or to some other of your friends that can set it down better.

---

[4] Bacon's successor, John Williams, Bishop of Lincoln.
[5] The cure appears too late.
[6] John Donne's *Devotions upon Emergent Occasions*.

Dr. Cary, Bishop of Exeter, preached at Westminster at the Opening of the Parliament, and Dr. Hall yesterday at Paul's to the Convocation. The show of nobility was fair. The youngest baron was Sir . . . Grey that married Sir John Wentworth's daughter, who came newly out of the mint, his patent being scant dry. He was made at the suit of the Duke of Richmond for his brother the Earl of March, but when it came to the payment, Secretary Conway had £4000 of the money till he had found another for himself, and then to repay it. The Earls of Northumberland and Hertford, and Lord Saye and the Lord of St. Albans were not called, or if they had writs *pro forma,* yet they were willed to forbear and absent themselves.

Sir Thomas Crew, the Sergeant, is chosen Speaker, and is to be presented this day to the King. Sir Ed. Coke is of the House, and the first day set them straight in a business wherein they were going awry.

David Cecil your kinsman, presumptive heir to the earldom of Exeter, shall marry Mistress Smith, the Countess of Exeter's daughter, with £3000 present portion and £200 a year till she pay £2000 more.[7] So, with the remembrance of my best service to my good Lady, I commend you to the protection of the Almighty. From London this 21th of February 1623.

Your Lordship's most assuredly at command,
JOHN CHAMBERLAIN

God send us good news from your side, for we have a terrible alarm that you are shrewdly put to, and it cannot be but a great loss every way, and if the enemy should fortify and nestle there, we apprehend extreme danger as the world stands.

[448] March 20, 1624:

MY VERY GOOD LORD,

Sir Edward Conway brought me your letter on Monday last with a great deal of compliment, which is so unfit for me and so un-

---

[7] David Cecil, son of Sir Richard and grandson of Thomas, 1st Earl of Exeter by his first wife; Anne Smith was daughter of Sir Richard's second wife, Frances, widow of Sir Thomas Smith. Lady Hatton, daughter of Lord Thomas, thus David's aunt, squashed the affair (below, Letter 448).

welcome that I grew weary with standing so long bare, and which is worse I got then a cold that I cannot yet be rid of. He sent me likewise a present of handkerchiefs from my Lady Carleton which I cannot but accept with all thankful respect, though I have tasted so much and so many ways of her bounty already that I find myself overcharged as it were, but that I see she will be still like herself in proceeding to works of supererogation.

I hear not yet of the book you mention so that I cannot impart it to Sir Isaac Wake,[8] who doth so ply the Parliament that he is hard to be found, and it stands him upon, for his employment is at the stake to stand or fall as matters pass there, though he have received his letters and instructions, and lords it handsomely already.

I will not take upon me to write news, your nephew[9] being here, and so many other Parliament friends that can furnish you from the fountain; and indeed my many businesses will scant give me leave to listen after that is told me: for what with proving of wills, making of inventories, finding of offices, suing of liveries, procuring of motions, following of lawyers, calling for debts, casting accounts and the like, I have scant time to breathe. And withal I find myself to fail so fast every way (specially one of my legs) that I see not how I shall be able to hold out. But I do what I can, and for assistance (finding housekeeping so chargeable and troublesome), I have called in a nephew to me, one I wish as well to as to any kinsman I have, so that I am now *in statu quo prius,* a sojourner, as ever I have been. Which makes me often remember your story of Sir Matthew Carew's dream when he was young of his wrestling with beggary, for it hath pleased God still so to deal with me and so to temper my fortune that, as I did never abound, so I was never in want; and so He hath sent me now what is sufficient (I hope) and no more, except I should overlive some younger than myself, which is altogether unlikely. And for goods and personal estate, it is so dispersed and in so many fragments, that I fear much of it is in hucksters' hands, and the times and our justice such as I know not what account to make of it. But to what purpose is all this, or (as one says) *quid ad te?* but that you may see how my thoughts are exercised, and that *ex abundantia cordis os loquitur,*[10] or as sick men use to tell their pains and griefs

---

[8] Carleton's former Secretary in Venice, now replacing Sir Henry Wotton as Ambassador there.

[9] Dudley, Carleton's Secretary in The Hague.

[10] The tongue speaks out of the fullness of the heart.

to all that come in their way, as if imparting it to others they did somewhat ease or unlade themselves.

I would fain tell you some good tidings of the Parliament in general, but in truth I know not what to judge, for there be so many Spanish pavanes backward and forward, so many heats and colds, as are rather likely to tire than to keep them in breath. Yet I think there was never Parliament better affected from the highest to the lowest to the good of the King and kingdom. But diverse speeches and answers from the King have been so misunderstood, or so cloudy, that they have had need of interpretations and explanations, which nevertheless are not so satisfactory but that scruples remain, and they are so wary and cautious on all sides as if they were to treat with enemies and in danger to be overreached; which makes me admire the wisdom (or the fortune) of the former time, when all things went fairly on in parliaments without jealousy or diffidence. Where the fault is now I know not, but they are very suspicious; for having made large offers for the maintenance of the war if the King would declare himself, he is not willing to come to that point, but, striking out "war," inserts "for the great business in hand," which is subject to diverse interpretations. Neither will they be led along by their old *duces gregis*[11] Sir Edwin Sandys, Sir Dudley Digges, and Sir Robert Phelips, for they have so little credit among them that, though they speak well and to the purpose sometimes, yet it is not so well taken at their hands, for still they suspect them to prevaricate, and hold them for undertakers. Among some few others, Sir John Savile *antiquum obtinet*[12] and is still the same man.

Here is much muttering of the coming of Padre Maestro,[13] who passed through Paris a week since and comes directly from Rome, where the Pope is said to find great fault with the Spaniard for managing his business no better when the Prince was there and would have the match go on again by all means, in which regard he will be content to dispense with his dispensation, in taking away that clause that the Romish Catholics should have a public church in London or elsewhere, wheresoever the Infanta is to abide. Other offers are spoken of which the Spaniards say are such and so large

---

[11] Leaders of the crowd.
[12] Preserves his old custom.
[13] Fray Diego de Lafuente, confessor to Gondomar in London 1618-1620, had just obtained the Papal dispensation for Prince Charles's marriage to the Infanta.

as cannot be refused. The Spanish Ambassadors presently, upon any show of distraction or difference in these business, frequent the streets from the one end of the town to the other with all their pomp and as it were in triumph, under color of visitations of other Ambassadors and friends. And how truly I know not, but it is said that many letters pass continually twixt them and the Court, by mediation of somebody near about the King, which are thought to hinder or retard many good resolutions. The Marquis is held a cunning negotiator, and *nasutus* enough, though he have little or no nose; and so much maligned that there is a current speech that he hath lost somewhat else of more importance since his coming hither and that made him more man, and they are so confident and precise in it that they name the very time of his circumcision to be the next day after Twelfth Day.

The Countess of Olivarez[14] hath lately sent the Prince a large present of provisions, as 48 gammons of bacon, diverse vessels of great olives, as many of olives without stones, a great quantity of capers and capperons, many frails or tapnets of special figs, many sweet lemons, and 300 weight of dried or candied melocotons, great quantity of other suckets and sweetmeats, besides 48 melons, all which in three carts was conveyed into the riding place or house at St. James's two days agone. The Prince never vouchsafed to see it, but, rewarding the messenger, left it all to the disposing of Sir Francis Cottington. He never misses a day at the Parliament and is so careful to have all things go well that, if any good follow, we shall owe it to his care and solicitation, and to the general good will and approbation of his virtuous disposition, as being noted free from any vicious or scandalous inclination, which makes him every day more gracious and his actions to seem more graceful than was at first expected; and in truth his journey into Spain hath improved him so much that it is a received opinion he concealed himself before.

I understand since this morning that the Lower House hath agreed to pay three subsidies and three fifteens twixt this and November, if the King will declare himself and that they may have the managing of their own finances; but how the King will brook any such restriction is the question. Sir Benjamin Rudyard was the first that brake the ice and being followed by 38 to the same purpose, that it should be employed to assist and support the Hollanders, to furnish out the

---

[14] Wife of Philip IV's Chief Minister.

Navy, to provide for the security of Ireland, to make magazines of arms, powder and other provisions, and collaterally for the recovery of the Palatinate. Sir George Chaworth was of a single and singular opinion to yield the King two subsidies and four fifteens for his own use, without troubling ourselves with the Low Countries, who had subsisted more than forty years of themselves and were like to hold out as much more for aught we saw. This offer is to be presented to the King tomorrow; and withal both Houses are resolved, by the mouth of the Lord Keeper, to clear the Duke of Buckingham of the imputation laid on him by the Spanish Ambassadors in their complaint to the King that he had traduced and spoken scandalously of their master in the grand committee or conference.

I wrote that Davie Cecil should marry the Lady of Exeter's daughter, but that match was marred by the Lady Hatton at the very upshot. Your brother Carleton is in town and all his children saving his son George and his daughter Harrison. They diet, for the little time they have to tarry, with your nephew and his Lady Cotton. I send Dr. Bargrave's sermon, and the little woman's work for my Lady. Dr. Hall's *Concio ad clerum*[15] is for yourself. So with the remembrance of my best service to my good Lady, I commend you to the protection of the Almighty. From London this 20th of March 1623.

Your Lordship's most assuredly at command,
JOHN CHAMBERLAIN

[449] April 10, 1624:

MY VERY GOOD LORD,

We have had here such an Easter that I have seldom known a colder Christmas, which is but a hard conclusion of the sorest winter (every way) that hath been in the memory of man; neither is it yet past, the wind continuing still at northeast, which doth so keep back the spring that we have scant any sign of summer's approach.

The Earl of Dorset, after three or four days' sickness, died on Easter Day of a surfeit of potatoes, leaving no great matter to his successor when his debts and legacies are discharged, which arise almost to £60,000.

---

[15] Joseph Hall's sermon (cf. Letter 447).

The Duke of Richmond's funeral is to be at Westminster the 19th of this month. There hath been a hearse, with his statue on a bed of state, above these six weeks at Hatton House, where there hath been great concourse of all sorts, and all things are and like to be performed with more solemnity and ado than needed, but that it so pleaseth her Grace to honor the memory of so dear a husband, whose loss she takes so impatiently and with so much show of passion that many odd and idle tales are daily reported or invented of her; insomuch that many malicious people impute it as much to the loss of the Court as of her Lord, and will not be persuaded that, having buried two husbands already and being so far past the flower and prime of her youth, she could otherwise be so passionate.

Sir Isaac Wake is not yet gone nor, for aught I see, going. He means not to carry his Lady along with him by reason of her weak constitution and many dangers that may happen in passing the mountains, but she is to follow him in August; and he is very angry with any that argue of the conveniency of her going now, as well in regard of his company as of the charge and season of the year, as if they mistrusted his judgment or affection, or that he knew not what were fitting for her, protesting withal that he will give any man £1500 that would undertake to bring her safe after him to Venice; which methinks (though I be no good majordomo) I could do with a great deal less and yet get well by the bargain if I were but twenty years younger.

All the last week Sir Henry Wotton was said to be Provost of Eton, in relinquishing his reversion of the Rolls, which should be conferred on Sir . . . Heath, the Solicitor, for a certain sum of money, wherewith Sir W. Beecher should be satisfied and contented. But now the cry goes that he is like to be Master of the Wards if the Lord Treasurer[16] sink. He hath set out lately a book of architecture, which I have not leisure to read but hear it reasonably commended, though at first I thought he had busied himself to little purpose to build castles in the air.

Sir Albert Morton is in speech to go Ambassador into France to reside, but I hear withal that he makes courtesy to accept it. I know not his reasons, but I should think somewhat hath some savor, and, though he be a sufficient able gentleman, I should as much marvel at his refusal as at the offer. Sir Edward Herbert is to be Vice-Chamberlain when he comes home, but I shall believe it when I see

---

[16] Lionel Cranfield, first Earl of Middlesex, about to be impeached.

it. The Earl of Carlisle prepares to go thither Extraordinary,[17] and the Lord of Kensington is to be joined in the commission with him.

The King hath been these ten or twelve days at Theobalds. The Spanish Ambassadors were with him in the morning before he went together with Padre Maestro, who was newly arrived and pretends to have lost his commission and instructions that were taken from him in France. The Prince and the Duke of Buckingham were present. But this day sevennight, when the Prince was here and the Duke of Buckingham gone to New Hall, Padre Maestro had a long private audience at Theobalds hand to hand, which is not known to what purpose it can serve but to breed jealousies.

The Parliament goes slowly on by reason of many rubs that come in the way, but they are very careful for the security of religion, and to that purpose have drawn a petition which they sent up to the Lords to join with them, wherein the Prince gave great satisfaction, assuring them that if he did treat of marriage with any of contrary religion, it should be with that caution that there should be no manner of connivance but for herself and her servants strangers.

Now they are entered into a new business that hath held them all this week, of sifting the Lord Treasurer, wherein matters proceed not so clearly that we can make any certain judgment what will become of him; for matters brought against him hitherto (in my conceit) are neither so heavy nor so heinous but with a favorable construction they might pass uncensured; and I think for our time few of his predecessors in that place, if they were as narrowly searched into, but they would be found as faulty. But his harsh and insolent behavior to all, with his inclination to the Spanish match, his entertaining of all projects and devices to raise money by the impoverishing of the realm, his hindering the calling of the Parliament, his plotting the last benevolence and proceeding in it with such violence, hath bred a general distaste; and in particular his facing the Lord of Buckingham and seeking to set up a new idol (his wife's brother) hath procured his hatred; and lastly his unrespective carriage toward the Prince many ways (too long to be related) hath kindled *giusto sdegno*[18] in him and bred deserved indignation: wherein I have marvelled that a man of his wit and experience, and otherwise so wary, should so far forget himself, but that I remember an old saying, that *Perdere quos vult Jupiter prius dementat.*

---

[17] To negotiate the marriage between Prince Charles and Henrietta Maria.
[18] Reasonable irritation.

Yet he continues very confident and doth not forsake himself, but, coming yesterday into the Upper House with his wonted countenance, undaunted made a bold speech that he could not be touched in his faith towards his Master, in his providence in his place of Treasurer, nor in his indifferency betwixt the King and his subjects, and therefore would desire no favor, but justice against his accusers; and withal sent to the Lower House to desire he might be heard there himself or by his counsel, which was granted him and is appointed to be heard there this afternoon.

He was at Theobalds on Wednesday before seven o'clock in the morning with the King in the Park, and though the Duke of Buckingham were there, yet he went away before he could come. It should seem by all we can guess that the King gives only the looking on, and leaves him to his fortune, which he follows with all industry; and when he cannot go himself, sends his Lady great with child to solicit for him.

Gresley[19] was dispatched on Thursday for Spain. We cannot learn yet that his Lord of Bristol is on the way, but I take him too wise to make any great haste home, specially as long as the Parliament sits. So with the remembrance of my best service to my good Lady, I commend you to the protection of the Almighty. From London this 10th of April 1624.

Your Lordship's most assuredly at command,
JOHN CHAMBERLAIN

[452] June 5, 1624:

MY VERY GOOD LORD,

The next day after I came to town I met with your letter of the 19th of the last month, and thereby understood of your nephew's disaster,[20] if I may so call a mischance for which there is no fence; but rather it may *cadere in virum sapientem fortem nobilem*[21] or whomsoever, and therefore he is not to take it too much to heart, but rather as a dodge that could not be avoided. And surely it is a kind

---

[19] Walsingham Gresley, steward to John Digby, first Earl of Bristol, Ambassador to Spain.

[20] Young Dudley Carleton had contracted to marry a Dutch woman named Volbergen, who then jilted him.

[21] Happen to the wise, the brave, the noble.

of good hap that such a natural malignity showed itself now rather than hereafter, and the party better lost than found that would so easily depart from her first love, not regarding her vow, nor the disgrace that would follow in being made *fabula vulgi*[22] and the talk of the town: wherein (if all be true that I have heard) she doth but *matrisare*,[23] and labors of an hereditary disease: wherefore, *computatis computandis*,[24] I am of opinion he is rather to thank God for this accident than any way to grieve or vex himself, and I do not doubt but he will make that use of it in good time, though at first it troubled him. I have not seen him this week, but I hear he is gone down to his father and will be back again this night.

Sir Isaac Wake went away in Whitsun week and had so fair a passage to Bologne that some which accompanied him thither to dinner came back to supper at Dover that night. There is great nearness and dearness twixt him and Count Mansfeld,[25] who (I hear) hath given him a coach and six horses, and they converse with extraordinary freedom and familiarity. He hath left his Lady behind, who tells me she is to follow in August, but pretends such a tenderness of health and disposition that she cannot allow herself less than ten weeks to reach to Turin.

Our Parliament ended on Saturday with the passing of three or four and thirty acts, though diverse were stopped that were much desired. The parting were with no more contentment than needed on neither side. The King spared them not a whit for undertaking more than belonged to them in many matters; and for answer to their grievances, which were presented in two very long and tedious scrolls, he said that having perused them he thanked God with all his heart that they were no worse. He gave them thanks for their care and charge toward his children, but withal told them in a sort that they had given him nothing. And this was the course of his whole speech, to pay them in such coin.

Though he passed the bill for the sale of the Lord of Middlesex's lands toward the payment of his debts and raising of his fine, yet he said he would review their sentence and confirm it as he saw cause;

---

[22] A topic of common gossip.

[23] Take after her mother.

[24] Reckoning one way or another.

[25] Count Ernest von Mansfeld, an unsavory mercenary earlier employed by Frederick, Prince Palatine, and by the Dutch, was being allowed to raise an army in England for a proposed joint effort with France, to invade the Palatinate and relieve the besieged town of Breda.

wherein he made good what he insinuated in a speech he had made in his behalf, that in such cases the Nether House was but as informers, the Lords as the Jury, and himself the Judge, giving them likewise to understand that he took it not well nor would endure it hereafter that they should meddle with his servants, from the highest in place to the lowest scull in the kitchen; but if they had aught against any, they should complain to him, and he would see it redressed according to right.

The Lord of Middlesex was set at liberty out of the Tower on Tuesday and continues yet at Chelsea. Some say he is to be confined to one of his houses in Sussex or Hertfordshire, but there goes a voice that he is in possibility, or rather probability, to be sworn a Gentleman of the Bedchamber, and then the world is well amended. It is given out (how truly I know not) that his delivery out of the Tower stood him in £6000, and that he gave great sums to keep off this tempest, if it might have been.

Here is much canvassing about the making of captains and colonels for these new forces that are to be raised to assist the Low Countries. Sunday last was appointed, and then put off till Tuesday, when, they flocking to Theobalds with great expectation, the King would not vouchsafe to see any of them nor once look out of his chamber till they were all gone, but word was sent they should know his pleasure twixt that and Sunday. The prime competitors are the Earls of Oxford, Essex, and Southampton. The fourth place rests between the Lord Willoughby, the Earl Morton (a Scottish man) and Sir John Borlase. It hath seldom been seen that men of their rank and Privy Councillors should hunt after so mean places in respect of the countenance our ancient nobility was wont to carry, but it is answered they do it to raise the companies of voluntaries by their credit, which I doubt will hardly stretch to furnish 6000 men without pressing, for our people apprehend too much the misery and hard usage of soldiers in these times.

And now in the very nick comes news how barbarously the Hollanders have dealt with our men in the East Indies, in cutting off ten of our principal factors' heads after they had tortured them, upon color of a plot they had to surprise their fort of Amboyna, which whether true or false, they need not to have used them so rigorously, but either have kept or sent them home in chains with their confessions and proofs. The rest of the English there have sent a protest against this manner of proceeding, which doth dishearten their friends and those that otherwise wish them well, that cannot speak nor hear of this their insolence without much indignation.

The King went on Sunday toward evening to Highgate and lay at the Lord of Arundel's to hunt a stag early the next morning in St. John's Wood. The Lord of Buck is at New Hall, whither he went to avoid the importunity of visits that would give him no rest. I do not hear but that he is reasonably well, though the papists give out malicious reports that he should be crased in his brain; but I have learned by them that know that there was no such matter, but that the suspicion grew by reason of his often letting blood. Only they confess he hath a spent body, and not like to hold out long if he do not tend his health very diligently.

There be commissioners appointed for the Earl of Bristol's business, but I cannot name them nor when nor where they are to meet. He carries himself very confidently, they say, and speaks big; but by all I have heard, I cannot conceive how he can clear himself of concealing or conniving at that all the world saw. The Spanish Ambassador Inojosa prepares to be gone on Wednesday by order from the King as I hear, and that without any audience or solemn taking of leave at Court. This week they had news of the arrival of the West Indian fleet (perchance before it be come) wherewith they are all so overjoyed that besides other demonstrations they stripped themselves out of their working-day clothes and put on all their best array.

So with the remembrance of my best service to my good Lady, I commend you to the protection of the Almighty. From London this 5th of June 1624.

Your Lordship's most assuredly at command,
JOHN CHAMBERLAIN

[459] October 9, 1624:

MY VERY GOOD LORD,

I have been airing myself almost these three weeks at Ware Park, and now the term calls me to town sore against my will, for the country is so pleasant and the weather so temperate that the like season hath not been seen many a day, which is the more welcome for that the hot and dry summer had so parched and withered all

things that it is a double pleasure (besides the profit) to see the
later spring more fresh and flourishing than the first: with such plenty
of all manner of fruits, specially quinces (which happens rarely),
that I never knew the like quantity, nor more fair and cheap, for I
myself bought eight for a penny, and the best rate for the fairest is
not above half a crown for an hundred. This advertisement is for my
Lady, that she may imagine what a world of sweetmeats and what
conclusion she might have made and tried if she had been here.

This town continues sickly still, for this week there died 347,
which yet is less by almost an hundred than they were a fortnight
since; but yet in consideration of the danger the Parliament is put off
from the second of November till the 16th of February.

On Monday the Spanish Ambassador Don Carlos Coloma went
hence without kissing the King's hand as he desired, leaving the new
Agent, who is well seen and much made of, whereupon some suspect
that there is a new kind of negotiation on foot, and that somebody by
their will would follow the old bias and look back into Egypt.[26]
But the report goes that matters are well forward in France, and
that the Duke of Buckingham is to go thither shortly, though perhaps
those that be there must give place first, that the honor may be all
his.

The Prince is not yet so fully recovered of his fall but that those
which see him and mark him suspect some secret bruise, which perchance is but out of their abundant care and tenderness towards him,
which appears by the ringing of bells and bonfires the 5th of this
month, as an anniversary remembrance of his happy return the last
year.

Our papists begin to hold up their heads again, for whereas writs
were gone out to inquire o'er their lands and arrearages for not paying according to the statute, letters are gone down to suppress that
course, and, if any have paid, to restore it: it being (as is said) the
first article of this new alliance that no Romish Catholics be troubled
or molested for their conscience in body or goods.

You have Count Mansfeld with you, and we expect him here
again shortly, for they say he is to have hence 8000 English and
4000 Scots under six regiments, whereof the first stands in question
twixt the Earl of Lincoln and the young Lord of Doncaster. The
Lord Cromwell is to have the second, Sir Charles Rich the third

---

[26] I.e., reconsider the proposed Spanish marriage.

(whose lieutenant is to be your acquaintance Master Hopton that married the Lady Lewen). The fourth is allotted to Sir John Burgh; Colonel Gray and one Ramsey are named for the Scots. God speed them well whatsoever they do or wheresoever they go, but it is beyond my experience or reading to have such a body of English committed and commanded by a stranger, to say no more.

On Saturday last one of the Dunkirkers, besieged by the Hollanders in the Downs, suddenly hoisting sail escaped away, but was followed by four or five of the Hollanders. What became of them God knows, for that night fell out the sorest tempest that hath been lightly seen, for the next morning our streets were covered with tiles, and in some places as thick as they used to strew rushes. We hear of great harm done and many ships lost, to the number of three or four and twenty about the Downs; and the Antelope, a ship of the King's, scaped very narrowly and was forced to cut down her mainmast and all her tackling. We hear the rest of the Dunkirkers in this confusion got away, as likewise that diverse coal-ships of Newcastle are lost, and two French ships and two English at Weymouth, beside some loss at Plymouth and other places whereof as yet we have not the certain knowledge.

About a fortnight since, our old friend Sir Michael Dormer died of a fit of his old disease, the palsy. On Monday Sir Robert Naunton had his patent delivered and was sworn Master of the Wards by the Lord Keeper. The Earl of Somerset's pardon was sealed on Thursday[27] in as ample manner as could be devised, and he hath taken a house at Chiswick, but with promise not to look toward the Court. The Earl of Middlesex his fine is now come down to £20,000 which must be paid presently, and so he shall be quit.

The Lord Chief Justice is in speech to be Lord Treasurer, which, if it fall out, he is not like, poor man, to supply the place long, either by reason of age or some other defect. The Lord Zouche hath parted with his place of Lord Warden of the Cinque Ports to the Duke of Buckingham for a £1000 present money and £500 a year during his life, so that Sir John Epsly is like to be Lieutenant of Dover, though Sir Dudley Digges expected it, upon promise or what other reason I know not, but the gentleman though he deserve well hath ill luck that nothing will fall to his lot.

I hear now of more harm done by the late tempest at Portsmouth,

---

[27] Robert Carr, the fallen favorite, in spite of James's vow never to pardon anyone involved in the death of Sir Thomas Overbury.

where the sea brake into the town and hath overthrown two bulwarks and a good part of the rampire that will hardly be repaired with the cost of £12,000. At Plymouth likewise the father, mother and a child were killed in their beds by the fall of a chimney, and the King's ships that brought the jewels out of Spain suffered much and was near lost.

Here hath been a rumor these three or four days that Gondomar is to come hither again, but I cannot believe it unless I see it, for though perhaps they think no man knows the length of our foot so well as he, yet no sufficient provision can be made but will be baffled by the people.

Towards the end of the last month the Lady Wake took her journey for Venice attended by Grace, Faith, and Fortune, her three maids, which is a good omen to be so accompanied. I dealt with her before my going into the country to forbear the voyage till the spring, in regard winter was so nigh, and of her own weakness and tenderness to travel in hard weather; but she was so resolute that she would not be persuaded, but said she would go though she were to die at Dover, for if God took her He should find her in her way, which was a good meditation and worthy of a virtuous wife. In which contemplation I will end, with the remembrance of my best service to my good Lady, and commend you to the protection of the Almighty. From London this 9th of October 1624.

Your Lordship's most assuredly at command,
JOHN CHAMBERLAIN

[463] December 18, 1624:

MY VERY GOOD LORD,

Though the wind continue so constant at west that we have heard nothing from you many a day, yet I will not forbear to advertise that little we have here. The French Ambassadors[28] went hence the last week, the first night to Theobalds, the next to Royston, and so on Thursday sevennight to Cambridge, where they had audience the next day both public and private. The articles were agreed and signed, the King, Prince, Duke of Buckingham, and Secretary Conway only

---

[28] Who were negotiating the marriage of Prince Charles and Henrietta Maria.

present, the rest of the Council (though almost all the great Lords were there) not so much as called or inquired after.

There should have been a comedy, but the shortness of time, the King's indisposition, and their hasting away cut it off. Some disputations in philosophy there were, but of no great fame. Many of the strangers had their grace to proceed *Magistri in Artibus, Doctores Theologiae, et utriusque Juris,*[29] and in the crowd some English, among whom I hear your nephew Dudley is become a new Master of Art. On Sunday the Ambassadors were feasted in the presence by the Prince (for the King kept his bed). The rest of their retinue dined in the great hall at Trinity College (where the King lies) with the Lords and Council.

They came back on Tuesday and supped the next night with the Lord Keeper, where they had great entertainment and choice chamber music, and in the church, where they heard three anthems sung by the best of the chapel and that choir, in rich copes and vestments, wherewith they seemed to be much pleased—till Master Treasurer[30] somewhat unseasonably told them he was glad to see them allow and approve so well of our service, and that upon their Chrismas Day; which put the little monsieur so out of countenance to think that he had committed an error or made some *pas de clerc* that he sat sullen and spake not a word all supper.

On Thursday they were feasted by the Earl of Warwick, and that afternoon visited the Duchess of Richmond, who, to keep her state and grace her audience, assembled all the Ladies of her acquaintance. I cannot forget one good passage of hers (though not at that time) that, in discourse of the Lady of Southampton's loss and how grievously she took it, she used this argument to prove her own grief was the greater: "For," quoth she, "I blasphemed"; a witty speech forsooth, and worthy to be put into the collection of the Lord of St. Albans'[31] *Apothegms,* newly set out this week, but with so little allowance or applause that the world says his wit and judgment begins to draw near the lees. He hath likewise translated some few psalms into verse or rhyme, which shows he grows holy toward his end. If I could meet with a fit messenger, you should have them both.

The King lies still at Cambridge (for aught we hear), pained with

---

[29] Doctors of Theology and of either Law (civil and ecclesiastical).
[30] Sir Thomas Edmondes, Treasurer of the Household.
[31] Francis Bacon.

the gout in his hands and arms. When he removes, it is appointed to Royston and so hitherward.

On Saturday Sir James Ley was made Lord Treasurer, and the Earl of Montgomery and he sworn together of the Council. We hear yet of no great alteration toward, save that he hath changed his grave velvet nightcap into a golden coif. It is observed as a strange thing that we have four Lord Treasurers living at once, four Lord Chamberlains, four Secretaries, three Masters of the Wards, two Keepers or Chancellors, two Admirals (if the Lord of Nottingham be not dead as they say he is) *et sic de caeteris* in several places and offices. . . .

Sir Fulke Conway (brother to Master Secretary), having his house in Ireland burned about his ears by negligence in taking tobacco, and escaping the first fury of the fire, would needs adventure in again to save certain writings or papers, but came back so singed and stifled with the smoke that he died presently, leaving better than two thousand pound land a year in that country, to descend to Master Secretary for aught we know.

The Lady Purbeck [32] is sick of the smallpox, and her husband is so kind that he stirs not from her bed's feet. I hear of a suit in Chancery twixt the Duke of Buckingham and his two brothers about certain lands of the Lord Grey made over to them in trust (as he says) but they understand it otherwise.

The Lord North's daughter is to be married to the Lord Dacre, which is no great fortune nor preferment for so fine a gentlewoman to have a widower with two or three sons at least.

We hear of great entertainment at Turin made to the Lady Wake, set down to an inch, being such as have been seldom or never afforded to one of her quality, but we must believe the last to be the best.

Our soldiers are marching on all sides to Dover. God send them good shipping and good success, but such a rabble of raw and poor rascals have not lightly been seen, and go so unwillingly that they must rather be driven than led. You may guess how base we are grown when one that was pressed hung himself for fear or cursed heart, another ran into the Thames, and after much debating with the constable and officers, when he could not be dismissed, drowned

---

[32] Frances, daughter of Sir Edward Coke and the Lady Hatton, wife of the feeble John Villiers, Buckingham's elder brother.

himself. Another cut off all his fingers of one hand, and another put out his own eyes with salt. Sir William Bronker hath a difference with Count Mansfeld, whereupon he forsakes the service and speaks not the best of him.

So with the remembrance of my best service to my good Lady, I commend you to the protection of the Almighty. From London this 18th of December 1624.

Your Lordship's most assuredly at command,
JOHN CHAMBERLAIN

[465] February 11, 1625:

MY VERY GOOD LORD,

I presume this gentleman shall not need much recommendation, when you understand him to be Henry Fanshawe, whom you have known almost from his childhood at Ware Park. He is fallen into an humor of following the wars, being before settled in a quiet course of life and in a good place belonging to his late father's, and now his brother's, office. Withal he is yet his brother's heir, who hath neither wife nor child; but neither present possession nor possibilities will keep him from being a soldier, nor preferring *arma togae*.[33] He had a great mind to go with Count Mansfeld, but his mother and other friends, being loath he should run such a desperate course, have rather persuaded him to begin his first lesson in a more orderly discipline which they conceive and hope, by my Lord General Vere's favor and your Lordship's good counsel and advice, may be more for his good. My Lady Fanshawe hath a great confidence in your Lordship's favor and good will towards her and hers, which was a principal motive for her to bend and direct him this way.

To describe him in a word, he hath good parts and much good nature, and no manner of harm I protest to my knowledge, but a little youthful levity and aptness to be led by company. Because he goes not directly to The Hague but to the camp, I will not charge this letter with more than concerns this business, meaning to write, God willing, tomorrow; which may find more speedy passage than yours I received the last week of the 6th of January. So with the remembrance of my best service to my good Lady I commend you

---

[33] Preferring arms to the toga (Cicero).

to the protection of the Almighty. From London this 11th of Febru. 1624.

Your Lordship's most assuredly at command,
JOHN CHAMBERLAIN

[**466**] February 12, 1625:

MY VERY GOOD LORD,

I have been somewhat slack and not written since the 8th of January upon diverse reasons and considerations, as first that your nephew being here and conversing so much at Court may so plentifully furnish you that there could be nothing left for me to relate. Besides, matters for the most part go here so untowardly that I take no pleasure in the remembrance, much less in the blazing them abroad or continual complaining, which might seem to savor of some malignant humor or of a malcontent. But the main hindrance indeed was the continual care and travail I took in following a suit in the Chancery, which had almost wearied my body, my mind, my purse, and my friends. But I thank God I had a final end of it this day sevennight, which, though it were not altogether as I wished, yet it was such as I will not greatly complain of, seeing I am rid and released from a great deal of trouble with so little loss, as for £567 to go away with £400; and I do bear it the better because I observed the course of that Court to be seldom to give any man all his pretensions and demands. And in truth I am so little partial to myself or mine own cause that I found it in mine own judgment *cas pour ami*[34] (as Montaigne speaks), so as my Lord might have leaned to either side with equal show of reason and equity, the rather because it had been foiled with ill handling, so as I account it won out of the fire.

I doubt not but you have heard of the Lady Purbeck and her fair issue, which business hath exercised this whole town now a good while and will pose them all that deal in it, if she stick still to her tackling and maintain her ground that it is her husband's, specially if he continue to avow it, as they say he doth. There be many passages too long to recite, but this must not be omitted, that the Lady of Suffolk gives out her son Robert (the reputed father) to be in-

---

[34] Suit for an ally.

sufficient and so not liable to such a scandal. The young lady is kept somewhat straitly so that none of her friends or acquaintance come near her, yet she carries herself with such resolution that she shows herself to be her mother's own daughter.

The Lord President's son, young Montagu, hath buried his wife who hath left him a little daughter. The Lady Cope is become a widow again by the death of Sir Thomas Fowler, but whether she hath gained or lost by the bargain I cannot learn. Sir William Clarke is gone at last, though at great leisure. I hear not of any great legacies but left all in a manner to his son Will, that is out of danger of being a Ward. Would you think that in his greatest weakness, means was made with some importunity that he should marry the French Lady Carew? But he had the grace to hold out, *et ut vixit sic morixit.*[35] . . .

Secretary Conway is here in town and hath not been at Court since the King went, whatsoever the matter is; they say he shall shortly be made a Lord or a Viscount or more. Sir Albert Morton is not yet returned from Newmarket, though I hear he be sworn and hath the seals delivered him by Sir George Calvert, who had £3000 of him, and is to have as much more somewhere, besides an Irish barony, for himself or where he list to bestow it for his benefit. Young Hungerford is made a Baron *en payant;* for this is the true golden age: no penny, no paternoster.

Your brother Carleton hath been in town this fortnight. He hath an inkling that his son's lady is with child. We hear nothing of your nephew Dudley since his going to Newmarket the second of this month. So with the remembrance of my best service to my good Lady, I commend you to the protection of the Almighty. From London this 12th of February, 1624.

> Your Lordship's most assuredly at command,
> JOHN CHAMBERLAIN

[467] February 26, 1625:

MY VERY GOOD LORD,

Your letter of the 11th of this present was left here on Thursday by my Lord General Vere's man, who went presently towards the Court, but I hear nothing of that you sent by the Secretary of the

---

[35] As he lived, so he died.

Muscovy Company, unless it were that of the 6th of January, which are all I have had since the 16th of November. My last was of the 12th of this present, the day before the Lord Belfast died, who hath left a great estate of lands and goods in Ireland and here, to Sir Edward Chichester, his younger brother. His government with one of his companies of horse and foot are given to one Hamilton, a Scottish man, his other company of horse to a young son of the Lord Deputy's, whereas such charges were more fit for men of service and experience in a kingdom so tickle and ready to revolt. Yet it seems we hope better of them if it be true (that is said) that the Viscount Rochford is named to succeed the now Lord Deputy.

The Lady Purbeck with her young son and Sir Robert Howard [36] are committed to the custody of several Aldermen, Barkham and Freeman, to be close kept. When she was carried to Sergeants' Inn to be examined by the new Lord Chief Justice and others, she said she marvelled what those poor old cuckolds had to say to her. There is an imputation laid on her that with powders and potions she did intoxicate her husband's brains, and practiced somewhat in that kind upon the Duke of Buckingham. This (they say) is confessed by one Lambe, a notorious old rascal that was condemned the last summer at the King's Bench for a rape, and arraigned some year or two before at Worcester for bewitching my Lord Windsor's implement. I see not what the fellow can gain by this confession but to be hanged the sooner.

Would you think the Lady Hatton's stomach could stoop to go seek her Lord Coke at Stoke for his counsel and assistance in this business? She hath another cross likewise of late, that upon her continual clamor and complaint how she was straitened in her lodgings at Hatton House, and what a bargain the Duchess of Richmond had of it with offer to take it again: the Duchess taking her at her word hath left it on her hand, whereby she loseth £1500 a year during her life, besides £6000 the Duchess pretends to have of her, which was given for a fine, and bestowed in walls, walks, and other reparations.

We hear that Mansfeld's troops are almost half starved. If it be so, *maius peccatum habent* [37] that should have made better provision and taken better order for them. It will quite discourage our people

---

[36] Sir Robert was the presumed father of the child.

[37] Theirs is the greater fault. This shockingly mismanaged expedition was refused landing by the French. When it finally landed at Flushing, only 3000 men survived of 12,000 who set out.

to be thus sent to the slaughter, or rather to famine and pestilence. The time hath been when so many English as have been sent into those parts within these six or eight months would have done somewhat, and made the world talk of them; but I know not how we, that have been esteemed in that kind more than other nations, do begin to grow by degrees less than the least, when the basest of people in matter of courage dare brave and trample upon us. I have known the time when they durst not have offered the least of those indignities we have lately swallowed and endured. But they presume upon our patience and somewhat else, otherwise they would have showed some resentment, or given some sign of their dislike of such barbarous cruelty by some notorious example upon the authors and actors, and not suffer the chief instrument, the Fiscal, to walk up and down Amsterdam untouched, without anything said to him, as we hear he doth, and turn us over for satisfaction till the return of I know not whom out of the Indies God knows when. But they are every way too cunning for us, and know that *chi ha tempo ha vita,*[38] and understand every way to the wood.

But now forsooth here be letters of mart given out against the East Indian Company, but I doubt our ships will see them and not see them, and upon farfetched considerations forbear. But *fiat justitia et ruat mundus:*[39] I am the longer in this and more earnest for more reasons than one, specially (which I cannot dissemble) that you are taxed to be somewhat *tepido* in the business: and withal for that I see they have almost lost the hearts of their best friends here, which their countrymen here perceive well enough and apprehend too much, so far forth as to fear some ill May Day (which God forbid), and therefore informed the Council the last week of diverse ill presages, among the rest of a sermon newly printed, but made long since, by one Wilkinson, which I know not what relation it can have to this late accident (for I have not read it), but the epistle or preface made by a minister is bitter enough; then of a play or representation of all the business of Amboyna ready to be acted; and of a large picture made for our East Indian Company describing the whole action in manner and form. Whereupon the Council gave order the picture should be suppressed, the play forbidden, and the book called in, and withal for a strong watch of 800 men extraordinary against Shrove Tuesday to see the city be kept quiet.

---

[38] Who gains time saves his life.
[39] Let justice be done and the world fall in ruins.

When I had written thus far comes the Muscovy Secretary with your letter of the 4th of this present. He tells me he lay long at the Brill for a wind, and in the end was fain to come for Zeeland. Indeed your magnifico of Venice doth *star sopra di se*[40] and sends you great news of his reception, as much as if I should dilate to you the Lord Mayor's going to Paul's with his torches on Candlemas Day. Such another piece of work I have from him of his grace, wherein there is not a word of his wife, my ancient valentine, which I will take leisure to answer.

Our Parliament is like to hold the 15th of the next month. Sir George Calvert, or Lord Baltimore, which is now his title, is gone into the North with Sir Tobie Matthew, which confirms the opinion that he is a bird of that feather.[41] On Thursday Sir Thomas Wentworth of Yorkshire married the younger daughter of the Earl of Clare.

We hear that Gondomar hath lately sent a man of his own with a packet to the King, who they say of late receiveth and readeth all dispatches from abroad. The Earl of Bristol comes to town this night, having taken Sir Thomas Watson's house at Westminster, though the common voice assigned him another lodging;[42] but it is said now the King will have him shortly reconciled to the Prince and Duke of Buckingham without any repetition of former matters.

Posts run continually betwixt us and France, but no further conclusion hitherto than was almost four months since, the reason whereof is said to be for that the dispensation is clogged with unreasonable conditions, and withal the French would have the King and Council all sworn to observe all articles. God send all for the best, but *vix Helena tanti,*[43] and I should be sorry to see us brought so low as to accept whatever is imposed.

I come now from meeting your nephew Dudley in Paul's, who came yesternight from Newmarket, where he hath been almost this month. He puts me in hope we shall see you shortly, which I shall be as glad of as any poor friend you have. So with the remembrance of my best service to my good Lady, I commend you to the protection of the Almighty. From London this 26th of February 1624.

Your Lordship's most assuredly at command,
JOHN CHAMBERLAIN

---

[40] Sir Isaac Wake was "getting above himself."
[41] Catholic.
[42] Prison, for falling foul of Buckingham over the Spanish marriage.
[43] Helen was hardly worth so much.

I had almost forgotten that John West gives your Lordship many thanks for your great kindness showed to his kinsman, and though I presume he writes himself, yet he entreats me in no wise to omit it.

[**468**] March 12, 1625:

MY VERY GOOD LORD,

I have not heard of your nephew Dudley[44] since Sunday was sevennight that he went to Moor Park to the Lady of Bedford's, and thence was to go the next day to Theobalds for his dispatch, which should seem is long adoing, but I marvel the more that, the Duke of Buckingham having been here in town twice or thrice in this space, he hath not appeared, nor any word of him.

The day I wrote last, being the 26th of February, Will Murray of the Prince's Bedchamber and Sir Humphrey Tufton going into the field upon some light quarrel, Murray and Gibson, his second, upon words between themselves, fell foul one upon another, so that Gibson was left dead in the place, and Murray lightly hurt in the head. The Scottish men held Gibson for the best cannoneer in Christendom, and he had the reversion of the Master Gunner's office. The worst is they give out he was in drink when this mischance befell him.

The same day here happened a greater disaster, by reason of the highest tide that hath been known in the memory of man, which did great harm in Thames Street and all along the riverside, insomuch that Westminster Hall was full three foot deep in water all over; but the greatest loss we hear of is the drowning of the marshes and overthrowing the walls in Kent, Essex, Lincolnshire, Yorkshire, and other places near the sea, to an exceeding hindrance and desolation, which had been more if it had fallen out in the night as it did in the daytime, whereby they had means to save their cattle and much other goods.

The Marquis Hamilton died on Ash Wednesday morning of a pestilent fever as is supposed, though some suspect poison because he swelled unmeasurably after he was dead in his body, but specially his head. Upon the opening of both, the physicians saw no signs of any such suspicion, but ascribe the swelling to some malign or venomous humor of the smallpox or suchlike that might lie hid. Two nights

---

[44] He had been back in England, as Clerk of the Council, since August, 1623.

afterwards his body was carried with much company and torchlight to Fisher's Folly, his house without Bishopsgate, thence to be conveyed into Scotland. He is much lamented as a very noble gentleman and the flower of that nation. The papists will needs have him one of theirs, which neither appeared in his life nor in his death that we can any way learn, but it is no new thing with them to raise such scandals and slanders. The Council table will have a miss of him and the Lord Belfast, who went cheerfully away and said he was never more willing to live than he was now to die, as foreseeing a ruin not to be avoided but by miracle. This hath been a dismal year to great men, by the loss of two Dukes, four Earls, and I know not how many Lords, besides a number of our citizens of the best rank.

The Duchess of Richmond is retired from Hatton House to the other part of Ely House, where she hath her Lenten sermon as orderly thrice a week as they are at Whitehall, and with as much variety of preachers.

The Lady Purbeck's business is come to this pass, that all matters of sorcery, witchcraft, and the like being let fall, she is only prosecuted for incontinency in the Spiritual Court and High Commission, where she hath taken her oath to answer certain articles, but Sir [Robert] Howard would by no means be induced to swear, whereupon he was committed close prisoner to the Fleet. On Thursday they were both convented again before the Commissioners at Lambeth, where Sir Robert persisted in his former resolution and withal claimed the privilege of a Parliament man, which I think was yielded to. She was willed to put in bail or go to prison, for that Alderman Barkham desired to be rid of his charge. She answered that if he were weary of her, she was not weary of him where she found so good usage. But for putting in of bail, she knew not how to do it, her friends having so forsaken her that she doubted they would do it. Then she desired she might have counsel, which being granted, she required the Lord of Buckingham would give her money to fee them, for she had nothing nor knew where to have any. This was the sum of what passed then, and they were to appear there again as this day. I doubt she hath a hard task in hand, and that she shall find *summum jus,*[45] though they give her good words to draw her to conformity. . . .

The French match is still *in nubibus,*[46] and few or none know yet

---

[45] The full measure of the law.
[46] In the clouds.

what to judge of it, for our great Ambassadors themselves are said to write contradictories. In the meantime they lay it on, and we as idle in expense as if we were Lords of the Indies, or as if the cause were to be won or outvied by bravery. Ville-aux-Clercs that was lately here is said to do ill offices and to press points that amount to a toleration, in confidence that we are so far engaged that we must yield to anything. Once Wat Montagu is sent away with some resolution, which what effect it will produce we shall see hereafter; but sure the proceeding grows cold after so many bonfires, unless Gondomar's coming quicken the business. A ship of the King's and a pinnace are making ready to fetch him at St. Sebastian's, and there is a whispering that he comes not unwelcome or unsent-for.

Secretary Conway is somewhat off the hooks, as the voice goes, and will shortly retire to his government in the Isle of Wight, with a title of Viscount Newport: or as some say to be Deputy of Ireland; and Sir John Coke is in speech to succeed him. But these are idle rumors that run up and down, with little or no ground; yet if it should so fall out, these sudden preferments would be held but slippery places.

The King was overtaken on Sunday with a tertian ague which continues yet, but without any manner of danger if he would suffer himself to be ordered and governed by physical rules.

I send here a rhyme made by one of King's College in Cambridge upon a play presented lately at Newmarket by his neighbors of Queen's College. If you have not seen it already, you will think it worth the reading. So with remembrance of my best service to my good Lady, I commend you to the protection of the Almighty. From London this 12 of March 1624.

Your Lordship's most assuredly at command,
JOHN CHAMBERLAIN

[470] April 9, 1625:

MY VERY GOOD LORD,

Your nephew came to you so full fraught with whatsoever was here to be had that it is needless to add to your store, specially Sir Henry Vane being ready to be dispatched to the Queen of Bohemia,[47] who can supply what is wanting. The manner of King James his death with all circumstances are better known to them than to me, so that I will not touch it, because I presume we shall hear all at the funeral where the Lord Keeper preaches, who was present for four or five days before his decease, because the Bishop of Winchester (whom the King called much after), by reason of a sore fit of the stone and gout at the same time, could not attend.

The corpse was brought from Theobalds on Monday night and passed through Smithfield about nine o'clock, so through Holborn, Chancery Lane, and the Strand, to Denmark House, where it reposes till the tenth of the next month appointed for the funeral. The convoy was well accompanied by all the nobility about the town, the pensioners, officers, and Household servants, besides the Lord Mayor and Aldermen. The show would have been solemn but that it was marred by foul weather, so that there was nothing to be seen but coaches and torch.

The King came to Whitehall to the sermon on Tuesday and there continues settling his Household and seeking to bring it to the ancient form, whiles all the late King's menials, servants and officers are commanded to attend the body at Denmark House; but being apprehensive that by their absence they might be dispossessed of their places and lodgings, they made a petition to be continued in both. The King's answer was that he would do them all right, but it were hard if the rising of the master should be the fall and ruin of his servants and followers. Yet all continues *in statu quo prius,*[48] with very little addition or alteration, only Sir Humphrey May was sworn of the Council with the rest that would swear, for the Lord Baltimore —or Sir G. Calvert—asked time to deliberate whether he might take the oath of allegiance, wherein he is since satisfied, for on Wednesday order was given for the Earls of Suffolk, Middlesex, and Bristol, the Viscounts Wallingford and St. Albans, the Lords Wotton and Baltimore not to take the oath, and so are discharged from the Council.[49]

The number of Bedchamber men are abridged, for I hear but of

---

[47] Charles, upon succeeding to the throne, wanted to assure his sister Elizabeth, in exile at The Hague, that he would do all he could to help her.

[48] As before.

[49] Suffolk, Wallingford and Wotton had all been cashiered by Buckingham for maladministration of King James's household; Lionel Cranfield, Earl of Middlesex, and Francis Bacon, Viscount St. Albans, had been sacrificed to Parliament seeking scapegoats; Bristol and Baltimore took exception to Buckingham's new foreign policy.

six, all or most such as were about him in the same place when he was Prince. It was said the Duke of Buckingham was only sworn Gentleman of the Bedchamber, but I can learn no certainty of it. He hath been lately much troubled with an impostume that brake in his head, and is yet somewhat crasie, but he continues in wonted favor and greatness.

The King shows himself every way very gracious and affable, but the Court is kept more strait and private than in the former time. He is very attentive and devout at prayers and sermons, gracing the preachers and assembly with amiable and cheerful countenance, which gives much satisfaction; and there is great hope conceived that the world will every way amend, if the necessity of the time constrain not the contrary now at the first.

Sir George Goring came out of France on Saturday last before the King's death was known. What he brought is kept close, as likewise what message or instructions Wat Montagu carried who was dispatched thither this week. Sir Walter Aston came out of Spain toward the end of the King's sickness with some new propositions (as is said) from the King of Spain. He left his Lady there, but whether he be to return I hear not.

We have ill news of 311 men going for Ireland cast away about the Isle of Anglesey. Most of them were of Sir Robert Yaxeley's company. The Lord Berkeley's young Lady is said to be distracted, and her sister the Lady Fitzwalter is or hath been little better, both proceeding from the same cause of jealousy. Three or four days before the King's decease, Secretary Conway was made Lord Conway of Ragley, his house in Warwickshire. We hear the King was proclaimed in Edinburgh the Wednesday after he was proclaimed here in London.

I wrote some eight weeks since by Master Henry Fanshawe, of whom we hear no certain word since he went, but here was a flying tale that he should be dead at Flushing presently after his arrival there; but there be so many improbabilities in the report that there is no credit in it. Yet his mother and other friends are much afflicted with the rumor, so that if you could learn any certainty of him we should be glad to hear it, though his own negligence and idleness be much to be condemned for not writing all this time.

One Roberts of Bristol, burying his father (who was my old acquaintance), gave mourning cloaks to certain of his friends and familiars, with a proviso to have them again after the solemnity ended, which is the argument of the letter and ballad enclosed, which will make you laugh if you be in a good mood. And so I leave with the remembrance of my best service to my good Lady, and commend you to the protection of the Almighty. From London this 9th of April 1625.

Your Lordship's most assuredly at command,
JOHN CHAMBERLAIN

The Lord of Leppington looks higher than the Vice-Chamberlainship[50] which I hear was proffered him. This week the Lord Coke, with his gloves on, touched and kissed the King's hand, but whether he be confirmed a Councillor or cashiered I cannot yet learn.

[473] May 14, 1625:

MY VERY GOOD LORD,

Since I wrote the day before the funeral by your man, I have received yours of the 30 of the last month, wherein you give a touch at my longer silence than usual. I know not what passage my letters may find, but I keep my wont once in fourteen days at least, or oftener, as I have matter or occasion.

The great funeral was the 7th of this month, the greatest indeed that ever was known in England, there being blacks distributed for above 9000 persons, the hearse likewise being the fairest and best-fashioned that hath been seen, wherein Inigo Jones, the Surveyor, did his part. The King himself was chief mourner, and followed on foot from Denmark House to Westminster church, where it was five o'clock stricken before all was entered, and the Lord Keeper took up two hours in the sermon (which they say we shall shortly have out in print), so that it was very late before the offering and all other ceremonies were ended; in sum, all was performed with great magnificence, but the order was very confused and disorderly. The whole charge is said to arise to above £50,000.

Sir John Garret, our eldest Alderman, died two days since. The sickness begins to show itself and to spead in diverse places, having

---

[50] Carleton was also interested in the Vice-Chamberlainship of the Household, a post which John Digby, 1st Earl of Bristol, continued to hold. Carleton got the job later in the year, having made himself *persona grata* to Buckingham when that great diplomatist came to The Hague to try to negotiate an alliance with Holland, Denmark and Sweden.

already infected 13 parishes. Our whole number this week was 332, of the plague 45; whereupon the Parliament that should begin on Tuesday next is yet in suspense, and we hear yet of no resolution whether it shall hold or be put off for a time.

Much ado there hath been and is still for places. Sir Henry Wotton is chosen for Sandwich where Sir Edwin Sandys missed his hold and his hope, as likewise at Maidstone.

The Dunkirkers are very busy, and within these three weeks have taken sixteen sail one and other, whereof four or five English. Our fleet is in good forwardness, and is to be augmented with some merchants' ships and twenty colliers more. We are now pressing 10,000 men for land service, of which number Sir Ed. Cecil, Sir John Ogle, Sir William St. Leger, Sir Henry Power, Viscount of Valentia, and I know not who else are named to have regiments.

But our greatest news is that on Wednesday morning the Duke of Buckingham went for France, accompanied only with the Earl of Montgomery, Secretary Morton, Sir George Goring, Sir Thomas Badger, and Wat Montagu. What the reason should be of so sudden, *non si penetra*[51]: some say to salute the Queen and carry a fair present of jewels, but most think *aliquid latet*[52] that her setting forth is so long and often deferred, and that somewhat more is to be performed for the Catholic cause before we shall see her, and then we are fallen out of the frying pan into the fire. I would be sorry we should be so overreached; but if it be the fortune of our forwardness, who can do withal? She was prayed for last week in the King's chapel by the name of Queen Henry, for Henriette, but since the style is changed everywhere to Queen Marie.

On Thursday Sir John Walter was made Lord Chief Baron, Sir Thomas Trevor a Baron of the Exchequer, and Sir Henry Yelverton a Judge of the Common Pleas. Your nephew Carleton[53] is in town with his Lady great with child, and means to continue here till the end of term. So with the remembrance of my best service to my good Lady I commend you to the protection of the Almighty. From London this 14th of May 1625.

> Your Lordship's most assuredly at command,
> JOHN CHAMBERLAIN

---

[51] We cannot fathom.

[52] There is some hidden reason. Buckingham was seeking help for a war against the Emperor or the King of Spain. He also behaved outrageously, supplying a fair amount of the plot for Dumas's *The Three Musketeers*.

[53] John Carleton.

Among many epitaphs and funeral elegies set out by Cambridge and Oxford and other choice wits upon the late King's death, I send you this short one, which I take to be Sir Isaac Wake's, for it came thence in his hand.

Q. Can a king die and we no comet see?
   Tell me, Astrologers, how can this be?
A. Heaven's beacons burn but to give alarm
   Unto a State of some ensuing harm.
   The Angels carrying up our blessed King
   Did still with music his sweet requiem sing.
   No innovation being to be heard,
   Why should Heaven summon men unto their guard?
   His spirit was redoubled on his son,
   And that was seen at his assumption.

To the right honorable Sir Dudley Carleton, Lord Ambassador for his Majesty at The Hague.

[**476**] London, June 12, 1625:

MY VERY GOOD LORD,

We hear the ill news of the Earl of Oxford's decease, which is the more lamented for that he was the only hope and support of so ancient and noble a house, which is like to go to ruin, his successor[54] (they say) being a man of mean worth or regard. But this is the common fate of all worldly honor, to fade and fail.

We do or say little here, but expect the Queen's coming, and marvel it is so long deferred. It should seem we have poor intelligence when the King posted hence the last of May to meet her, and the Lords and Ladies were sent somewhat before to attend her coming at Canterbury, where they have tarried ever since, to their great trouble and charge; but the King cheers them up almost every day with messages from Dover and persuades them to patience. On Whitsun Eve he dined aboard the Prince Royal, and visited two or three of his ships more that lay in the road, but that evening there fell out such a storm that made them fall foul one upon another and did much harm.

---

[54] Robert de Vere, his second cousin.

The cause of the Queen's stay is said to be her mother's sickness on the way, and if all be true that is reported, they can make no great haste, being to march with a little army of 4000 at least, whereof the Duke of Chevreuse and his followers make up 300 and 60 that belong to his kitchen. He and his Lady are to be lodged at Denmark House, where she is to lie in, and their allowance from our King is £200 a day, besides £100 for Ville-aux-Clercs and his consorts. But they come in an ill time, for the sickness increaseth and is spread far and near, so that 25 parishes in this town are infected already, and this week's bill ariseth to 434 in all, of the plague 92; so that if God be not merciful to us, this town is like to suffer much and be half undone. And that which makes us the more afraid is that the sickness increaseth so fast when we have had for a month together the extremest cold weather that ever I knew in this season. What are we then to look for when heats come on and fruits grow ripe?

I purpose (God willing) to go to Ware Park this next week. Your brother Williams and his retinue are already at Gilston. Orlando Gibbons, the Organist of the Chapel (that had the best hand in England) died the last week at Canterbury, not without suspicion of the sickness. Our Parliament should begin on Monday, but no doubt it will be put off again, which makes the knights and burgesses complain that they are kept here with so much danger and expense to so little purpose, for there is no likelihood they can sit here long, if at all.

The Earl of Montgomery, the Earl of Carlisle, and Secretary Morton are come out of France, where they and the rest were dismissed with bountiful presents. The Duke of Buckingham himself wrote to the King that he had already to the value of £80,000, the Earl of Carlisle to 22,000 crowns, the Earl of Holland to 20,000 crowns, Secretary Morton to £2000; Sir George Goring had a diamond from the King of £1000, from the Queen Mother one of £300, and curious plate to the value of £1200, as likewise Sir Fra. Nethersole, the same quantity of plate. How much or how little of this is true I cannot affirm, having *nihil praeter auditum*.[55]

We hear that the Great Mogul hath imprisoned all our men and seized their goods at Surat, by practice of the Hollanders as is thought, which if it prove true, *actum est de amicitia*.[56]

Three posts arrived within these two days out of Scotland with

---

[55] Having it only by hearsay.
[56] It is done out of (false) friendship.

news that the Earl of Argyll is come thither with forces to trouble that country or Ireland, to which he is a near neighbor. Surely we have small advertisement that could not discover nor prevent such a practice.

Sir John Bennet hath lately penned and printed certain meditations upon the 51th penitential or psalm of mercy. It seems *afflictio dat intellectum,*[57] and that he hath made the best use of it.

At the closing of this letter I hear the Queen came to Boulogne on Thursday, and may by this time be got over, if the northerly wind that hath reigned yesterday and today do not hinder her; and likewise that the sickness is come into the Lord Mayor's house, so that he is driven to shut up his doors, to forsake the town, and hath left Sir Thomas Bennet his deputy. So with my best wishes for your health and happiness, and the remembrance of my service to my good Lady I commend you both to the protection of the Almighty. From London this 12th of June 1625.

Your Lordship's most assuredly at command,
JOHN CHAMBERLAIN

To the right honorable Sir Dudley Carleton, Knight, Lord Ambassador for his Majesty at The Hague.

[**477**] June 25, 1625:

MY VERY GOOD LORD,

John West is so thankful a man for your favors showed to his kinsman that he doth nothing but load me with courtesies and compliments, that I am driven to tell him that I must not with the Bergamask take upon me to be the organist when I am but blower of the bellows; and his nephew Captain Sibthorpe is not behind hand in making profession how far he is bound to you and my Lady and how much at your service. Harry Fanshawe is likewise come home as wise as he went, but yet as welcome to his friends as the prodigal child, in whose behalf I must present his mother's thankful acknowledgment.

Though the sickness increase shrewdly upon us, so that this week died 640 in all, of the plague 239, and though this term be abridged to the three first days and to the three last, yet we cannot find in our

---

[57] Affliction yields discernment.

hearts to leave this town as long as here is such doings by reason of the Queen's arrival and the sitting of the Parliament.

The feast that should have been on Sunday (by occasion of the Queen's indisposition or that all was not ready) was deferred till Tuesday, when the publication and confirmation of the articles was solemnized in the great room at Whitehall, where all the Ambassadors and all the French were then feasted, but neither King nor Queen present, nor likewise the next night at York House, whither they were all invited by the Duke of Buckingham and entertained with such magnificence and prodigal plenty, both for curious cheer and banquet, that the like hath not been seen nor known in these parts. One rare dish came by mere chance: a sturgeon of full six foot long that afternoon not far from the place, leaping into a sculler's boat, was served in at supper. In all these shows and feastings here hath been such excessive bravery on all sides as bred rather a surfeit than any delight in them that saw it, and it were more fit and would better become us to compare and dispute with such pompous kind of people in iron and steel than in gold and jewels, wherein we come not near them.

The Queen hath brought, they say, such a poor, pitiful sort of women that there is not one worth the looking after saving herself and the Duchess of Chevreuse, who, though she be fair, yet paints foully. Among her priests you would little look for Monsieur Sancy that went Ambassador to Constantinople when we were at Venice, and is become a *padre del Oratorio*. I doubted poverty or desperation had driven him to it, but they say he is rich and hath good means.

Sixscore thousand pound of her dower is come along with the Queen, which will work no great effect if it be true that fifty thousand pound of it be allotted to the Earls of Carlisle and Holland for their service, and that she require thirty thousand to distribute among her servants. We were in hope the best part of them would have been packing away the next week, but she hath persuaded and prevailed with the Duke and his Lady that she should lie in here, which cannot be but to our great charge and incommodity.

In the meantime there is much urging and spurring the Parliament for supply and expedition, in both which I fear they will prove somewhat resty,[58] though there be great cause and almost necessity

---

[58] Slow, inert.

for both. It began the 18th of this month. The King's speech was short, and the Lord Keeper's not long. Among other things he told them they had drawn him into a war and they must find the means to maintain it, and that they need not doubt nor suspect his religion, seeing he was brought up at the feet of Gamaliel. At the presenting of their Speaker, Sergeant Crew, on Monday, he was answered by the Lord Keeper to his motion touching Jesuits, priests, and recusants, that they must leave that wholly to the King's direction, both for matter, manner, and time.

Since, they have busied themselves much about a fast and appointing three preachers for it against this day. How it goes on I know not, but yesterday they were with the King about it, who told them they should hear very shortly from him. They begin to mutter about matters of religion, that the King promised them when he was Prince that he would never contract any marriage with conditions derogatory to that we profess. They desire to understand what hath passed in that point, and the keeping of them close makes them suspect the more; some spare not to say there that all goes backward since this connivance in religion came in, both in our wealth, valor, honor, and reputation, and that it is visibly seen that God blesses nothing we take in hand, whereas in Queen Elizabeth's time, who stood firm in God's cause, all things did flourish. Others complain that matters are ill managed, and call for an account of the moneys and men that have been already employed; and it seems they glance and aim at somebody[59] for misleading and carrying his rider awry.

Your Dutch Ambassadors are come and have had audience. They lodge all with the Lieger who hath hired Sir Ed. Cecil's house for £140 a year, and Sir Ed. lies at an apothecary's over the way. A lioness hath whelped in the Tower, which some take as a presage that all things are like to succeed as in the former time, the beginnings of both in many circumstances concurring and jumping so just.

So with the remembrance of my best service to my good Lady I commend you to the protection of the Almighty. From London this 25th of June 1625.

Your Lordship's most assuredly at command,
JOHN CHAMBERLAIN

---

[59] Buckingham.

[478] January 19, 1626:

MY VERY GOOD LORD,

I was glad to understand by your letter of the 13th of this present of your safe arrival at Paris,[60] but should have been more glad to have been at hand to congratulate your first coming after so long absence. I came to town the day of the date of your letter, and was welcomed with a sad accident, for that morning our house was on fire by the negligence of servants, but thanks be to God, though there were great fear and danger, yet there was no great loss more than the breaking up of chimneys and floors, whereby my lodging is defaced for the time, and I confined to a narrower circuit. I have not seen my Lady Carleton, but sent the next day after my coming to present my service. My man brought word she is not in town, nor Master Locke who is with her at Imworth. I shall be willing to wait upon her when she returns, though I know not well how to do it, being altogether unable to go so far on foot or in coach by reason of my infirmity.

Neither indeed do I take any pleasure in going abroad to see the decay and desolation of this town, without hope almost in my time to see it better. The coronation holds on Candlemas Day, but private, without any show or feast, at Westminster Hall. The late Lord Keeper (as Dean of Westminster), being to perform certain ceremonies at that solemnity, is commanded to substitute the Bishop of St. David's for his deputy. The Queen's Bishop pretended and stood to have the crowning of her, but the Lord of Canterbury not permitting it, he is gone over to learn how he shall carry himself, or to get a dispensation for his presence.

Some ten days since, the Queen went publicly through this town in a rich embroidered caroche accompanied only with five other coaches from Westminster to the Tower, where she had a banquet, and so with a peal of ordnance came back the same way. This passage was thought might excuse the solemn entry, but that is put off till May, when the King means to go into Scotland to be crowned, and makes account to dispatch that journey in twenty days if it be possible. Great store of Scottish nobility is now at Court, and they say have offered in the name of that Kingdom to

---

[60] Having finally obtained a post in London, Carleton was immediately sent to Paris on a diplomatic mission.

maintain 5000 men for the recovery of the Palatinate, but they will have the paying and disposing of themselves.

We talk of great preparations to sea. God send better success than we have had hitherto. Some lay the blame on the design or counsel, the soldiers on their general, Viscount Sitstill[61] (as they now style him), he on the seamen, but most on his Grace,[62] and he on Sir Thomas Love, and so from post to pillar.

Here be daily proclamations come forth, one strict enough against papists and recusants, if it may be duly executed; but it is thought to look toward the Parliament which is to begin the 6th of February. For my part, I look for no good of this Parliament, the world being so far out of tune every way. Here is a rumor that Sir Ed. Coke is chosen Knight of the Shire for Norfolk and Burgess for Coventry and another place, that Sir Robert Phelips and Sir Francis Seymour are returned for several counties; but the King says he will not dispense with their oath whereby they are tied during the time of their office not to be absent or leave their shire without his license.

The Lord Chamberlain is like to be Lord Steward this Parliament *pro tempore,* or further as he shall carry himself and give cause. The Lord Hobart's place[63] is still in question, but it is thought Sir John Walter shall carry it, and Sir George Croke or Sir Thomas Trevor to be Lord Chief Baron in his room. All I send is taken up upon credit and such use you must make of it. So wishing you all health and a happy return I commend you to the protection of the Almighty. From London this 19th of January 1625.

Your Lordship's most assuredly at command,
JOHN CHAMBERLAIN

To the right honorable Sir Dudley Carleton, Lord Ambassador for his Majesty at the French Court.

[**479**] March 7, 1626:

MY VERY GOOD LORD,

On Sunday I received your letter without date, which was the more welcome, bringing so much hope of a good conclusion, which

---

61 Edward Cecil, Viscount Wimbledon.
62 Buckingham.
63 Chief Justice of Common Pleas; Sir Henry Hobart died December 25, 1625.

hath been since seconded by a general report that all is well agreed, wherein I cannot but congratulate your good success in so difficult and knotty a business.

Our Parliament talks much but doth little, yet they are now entered into deep points and have called the Council of War to account for their proceedings and issuing the moneys otherwise than was prescribed them. They took time till this day to answer. What is passed I know not, for I have kept house these two days and taken a little physic, more than I have done in a dozen years before. But I presume the matter will be pacified, as well as that other yesterday, for having called for the Duke of Buckingham to answer for the managing of these French affairs, the Upper House not allowing so peremptory summons (which, upon better advice, was disavowed by themselves and the fault laid on their Clerk), would not suffer him to go in person, so that he sent the Attorney with another lawyer to plead and justify his manner of proceeding; who, after many arguments and reasons, made this small conclusion, that what he had done was by the King's direct commandment. The disorderly and untoward courses have been taken, make them catch at anything, but when all is done I think they will find want of counsel and good conduct rather than of integrity and good meaning; though it be no small fault for men of mean experience to undertake so much above their reach, and to think their own single capacity sufficient to compare with the strongest and soundest wits of all Christendom together.

Glanville came to the Court on Sunday out of Ireland and Viscount Wimbledon the day before from the Downs. What they say I hear not, but only that the Marshal discharges himself upon Sir William St. Leger that had a counter or controlling commission (as he says) above his. Indeed at his first coming home, St. Leger was ill seen and the Duke gave him no countenance, but within four or five days they grew as great as ever. But by all circumstances, it doth plainly appear this enterprise had no certain design, but left to follow their fortune *avant le vent*.[64]

The last week the Duke had one feather plucked from his wing in the Upper House in the matter of proxies of those that be absent, whereof he having eleven, it was thought inconvenient that one or two men by that means might sway the House. It was much disputed, but in the end overruled, that none should have more than one

---

[64] Before the wind.

besides his own, wherein the Lord Chamberlain showed himself so indifferent that, having eight proxies, he gave four one way and four the other, but his brother Montgomery went directly with the Duke.

About a fortnight since, the widow Countess of Exeter made a great feast for the marriage of two of her servants, whither the greatest part of the nobility about this town were invited. The Duke (by whose advice I know not) went through the streets carried on men's shoulders in a Spanish chair or hand litter, to the great wonderment of a rabble of boys that followed; this was much spoken of and thought more than needed, as likewise that that Lady should make such a pompous feast so soon after the funeral of her only son.

On Shrove Tuesday the Queen and her women had a masque or pastoral play at Somerset House, wherein herself acted a part, and some of the rest were disguised like men with beards. I have known the time when this would have seemed a strange sight, to see a Queen act in a play, but *tempora mutantur et nos*.[65]

There hath been some brabbling once or twice of late with the French Ambassador about apprehending of certain coming from mass at his house. I know not the man, but by that I have heard of him, he seems fitter to be a *boute-feu* than a peacemaker. But he stands firm upon his justification that he hath received many wrongs and affronts, and that all he doth is mistaken and misconstrued many ways.

Our Low-Country captains are called over upon pain of cashiering, so that they complain of their hard case if they can neither find pay or entertainment here nor suffered to go where it is.

Dr. Prideaux, Vice-Chancellor of Oxford, is sent for by the Parliament to answer his partial dealing in returning Master Treasurer Sir Thomas Edmondes for the University, whereas it is pretended Sir Francis Steward had more than double so many voices, as the scholars themselves offer to prove and make good.

Here is a Persian ambassador that had audience yesterday and should have had it a fortnight since, but for an accident twixt him and Sir Robert Sherley who, coming to visit him accompanied with the Earl of Cleveland and others, after some few words the Persian fell upon him in a barbarous fashion and so beat him that he had almost worried[66] him. The reason of this outrage he says to be for

---

[65] Times change and so do we.
[66] Killed.

that he is an impostor and abuses his Prince's name; how it will fall out we shall see hereafter, but in the meantime most of our courtiers favor and run with Sir Robert Sherley.

On Sunday the Earl of Arundel was committed to the Tower for a match made by his son Lord Maltravers with the Duchess of Lennox's daughter, which Lady the King had designed to the Earl of Argyll's son for many important considerations, and was gone so far that in a manner all articles and conditions were agreed upon and nothing wanted but consummation; yet the young couple by prevention were wedded and bedded on Friday. Though the Earl disclaims to have any hand in it, as likewise the Duchess, yet the King understands it not so, but hath confined the Duchess to Sir . . . Kitterminster's house in Langley Park, the Countess of Arundel to the Earl's mother at Horsley in Surrey, the bride and bridegroom to the custody of the Archbishop of Canterbury, and some say the Duchess of Richmond (as having a finger in it at least) to her own house.

I send weekly to Westminster to hear of my Lady Carleton, but she hath not been in town now a good while, nor I think will not appear till your return, which I should be glad to hear of for many good reasons. Among the rest, I have a little commodity of white muscatel, which I would be sorry should decay in color or taste by long lying; I have given notice of it to my Lady to know how she would have it disposed of, but have not yet heard from her. So wishing all health and happiness to your Lordship, I commend you to the protection of the Almighty. From London this 7th of March 1625.

> Your Lordship's most assuredly at command,
> JOHN CHAMBERLAIN

To the right honorable Sir Dudley Carleton, Lord Ambassador for his Majesty at the French Court.

Postscript

We never learn what happened to the muscatel. Chamberlain may have seen more of Carleton during his last two years than he had for the previous fifteen, despite several excessively frustrating missions on which Carleton was employed by his weathercock patron.

Chamberlain lived to see Carleton raised to the peerage in May, 1626, as Lord Carleton of Imbercourt. By the end of June, Carleton was paying for his peerage with a particularly nasty embassy to Paris. Charles chose his most discreet professional to soothe Louis XIII's reception of the news that his sister Henrietta Maria's servants and clergy had been thrown out of England. Carleton's reception was cold.

Lady Carleton died in April, 1627. She had been entirely devoted and a substantial help to him; their children all died in infancy. He was not given long to mourn. Back he went to The Hague as Ambassador Extraordinary—to justify to the understandably nervous Dutch Buckingham's latest policy, war with France; to protest the building of French ships in Dutch ports; to demand belated compensation for the outrage at Amboyna; and to conceal the fact that none of the promised money for Mansfeld's army or for the Princess Elizabeth's debts was forthcoming.

Carleton was allowed to leave The Hague after a miserable year, probably not in time to bid farewell to John Chamberlain, who died in March, 1628. Carleton himself had only four years left to live, during which he reached the top of his profession but can hardly have felt much personal satisfaction in his success. On July 25, 1628, he was created Viscount Dorchester, and in December he became Secretary of State, as the posthumous candidate of his assassinated patron.

In August, 1628, while Buckingham was busy fitting out his expedition to relieve the French Protestants at La Rochelle, Carleton received a visit from Contarini, the Venetian Ambassador in London, who brought, via the Venetian Ambassador in Paris, a proposal for peace between France and England. It was following a meeting arranged by Carleton between Buckingham and Contarini that the frustrated soldier Felton struck his blow against the egregious Duke. Carleton himself helped prevent the crowd from lynching Felton when the assassin calmly revealed himself.

At fifty-six, Carleton decided to try again to provide himself with an heir. His new wife, widow of the first Viscount Bayning, presented him two years later with a posthumous daughter. His nephew, Sir Dudley, inherited his title and an estate valued, after twenty years of rigorous service, at £700 per year.

Yet had he lived to reap further royal rewards, Dudley Carleton, Lord Dorchester, the objective professional trained to defend the tortuous turns of Stuart policy, might well have found himself sharing the harsher fate of Strafford and Laud.

Index of Proper Names

(Index of Subjects follows)

Abbot, George, Archbishop, 72, 102, 110, 111, 115, 190; kills keeper, 260-2, 297, 356, 360

Andrewes, Lancelot, Bishop of Chichester, Ely and Winchester, 51, 78, 86, 110, 115, 133, (228), 229, 232, 233, 238, 246, 248, 254-5, 259, 262, 265, 347

Anne of Denmark, wife of James I, 69-70, 72-4, 77, 78, 87, 92, 121, 134, 144, 149, 152-3, 172, 177, 180-1, 190, 201

Arundel (title), *see* Howard

Backhouse, Samuel, of Swallowfield, Berkshire, Sheriff, 47, 175

Bacon, Sir Francis, Lord Verulam, Viscount St. Alban, 2, 25, 70, 130; masque *Thames and Rhine,* 75-6; Attorney, 100-1; Somersets, 102; Parliament 1614, 105; health, 147, 181; (155-6); Council, 171; Coke, 174, 176; Lord Keeper 180; Winwood, 184-188, 230-31; 186; Sherburn, 188, 257; 203, (228), *Instauratio Magna* 249, 251; Viscount, 251; impeachment, 253-58; Henry VII, 263; 265, 322, 336, 347

Bainham, Sir Edmund, 19, 23, 37, 58

Barclay, John, *Argenis,* 264

Bedford (title), *see* Russell

Beeston, Sir Hugh, 4, 51, 200-201

Bennet, Sir John, 96, 179, 180, 321, 353

Bodley, Sir Thomas, 21, 46, 66n., 93, 96-98; 250

Burghley (title), *see* Cecil

Brooke, Henry, 8th Lord Cobham, 7, 24, 194

Buckingham (title), *see* Villiers, Compton

Caesar, Sir Julius, 64, 91, 93-94; 115, 142, 289

Calvert, Sir George, first Lord Baltimore, 241, 251, 309-310, 340, 343, 347

Camden, William, Clarenceux King-of-Arms, *Annales* quoted, 5n.; 49, 63, 86-87; *Annales* published, 166; 233; letter to, 222

Carleton, Alice, letters to, 102, 116, 131, 157, 162, 165; (X), 100, 179

Carleton (b. Gerrard) (Tredway) Anne Lady, (44), 186-7, 235-6, 248-50, 251, 268, 323, 333, 356, 360, (361)

Carleton, Sir Dudley, first Viscount Dorchester, (2), (44-5); Paris 50-53; Norris 57; Gunpowder plot, 57-8, 62, 66, 84-5; job-hunting, 60-66; in *1617,* 230, 242; in *1620,* 250; in Venice 66, 89, 90-91, 99-100; unpaid, 85, 87, 100, 248; papers, 95, 237; transfer to Hague, 159, 160-1, 167; Winwood and Somerset 158, 166-7, 169-70, 165; at The Hague 178, 267, 353; Dutch Commissioners, 243; East India Company, 245, 251, 258, 260, (319), 342; London, 349n.; Paris, 356-8; (361-2)

Carleton, Sir Dudley the younger, 188, 263, 268, 323, 329-30, 336, 340, 343-4, (362)

Carleton, George, 6, 16, 46, 48, 55, 57; his lazy son 99; 174, 180, 188, 229, 238, 265, 326, 340

Carleton, John, 99, 174, 180, 188, 350

Carleton, sisters' catholicism, 52-6

Carr (b. Howard) (Devereux) Frances, Countess of Somerset; 102; divorce, 113-6; wedding, 116-7; trial 118-120; Tower, 121-3; 172

Carr, Sir Robert, Viscount Rochester, Earl of Somerset, 90, 91, 126; marriage 102-3; Winwood 103; Overbury, 112; gift to King 113; 114, 116, 119, 165-6; trial 119-20; Garter 121, 171; 122, 123, 194, 334

Cecil (b. Lake) Anne, Lady Roos, 231n., 232, 234, 239-44

Cecil, Sir Edward, Viscount Wimbledon 46, 350, 355, 357-8

Cecil (b. Brydges) (Smith) Frances, Countess of Exeter, 231-2, 234, 239-42, 322, 359

Cecil, Robert, Viscount Cranborne, 1st Earl of Salisbury, 2, 3, 4, 5, 7, 10, 14, 16; Essex' trial 18; 33; Gunpowder Plot 58; Garnet, 38; 40, 61; Parliament 1610, 42; Carleton, 45, 51, 60, 83-85; Cope, 54, 60; Winwood, 49, 54; Chamberlain, 84; illness, 87-90; posthumous reputation, 92, 94, 125

Cecil, Thomas, 2nd Lord Burghley, first Earl of Exeter, 231, 234, 239

Cecil, William, 1st Lord Burghley, (2), 4; funeral, 6-7

Cecil, William, Viscount Cranborne, 2nd Earl of Salisbury, 61, 90, 111; 137; 168

Cecil, William, Lord Roos, grandson of 2nd Lord Burghley, 169, 185, 197, 231

Chamberlain: hates haste 6; speaks freely, 10; in militia, 13; moves house, 17; needs satin, 26; advises Carleton 50-51, 53-5, 90, 160, 165-7, 250; mermaid, 55; escort, 59; brothers' deaths, 63, 168, 320, 323, 339; Cope, 60-66; travels, 80-83; Cecil, 84; illness, 86, 98, 358; death of Winwood, 191; less travel 167-244; to lectures at Paul's, 233; dines with Bacon, 250; happy summer, 268; sad about policy, 316-7, 342; Conway's compliments, 322-3; Sir Isaac Wake 327; fire at home, 356; muscatel, 360

Charles, Prince of Wales, Charles I, King of England, 71, 74, 76-8; created Prince of Wales 174; 263, 269, 277, 282; in House of Lords 1621, 255, 282, 321, 325; to Spain 303-311; return, 311-13; 316, (319), 325, 333; King, 347-8, 351-6

Cobham (title), *see* Brooke

Cockayne, Sir William, (205), 285, 296-7

Coke, Sir Edward, marriage, 9; 18;

Chief Justice 100-1; Privy Councillor 101; 132, 142-3; vs Chancery, 138; disfavor, 170-6; Villiers marriage, 176-7, 182-4, 187, (228), 341; Parliament 1621, 252-4, 256, 259; 1623, 268-9; (319), 322, 349, 357

Coke (b. Cecil) (Hatton) Elizabeth Lady, Carleton, 85, 191; Villiers marriage, 172, 175-6, 182-4, 187, 230; 242; 259; (319), 322n., 326, 341

Compton (b. Beaumont) (Villiers) (Raynes) Mary, Countess of Buckingham 143, 153, 172, 183-4, 264, 312

Conway, Sir Edward, 1st Viscount, 266, 322-3, 340, 346, 348

Cope Castle, Kensington, later Holland House, 64, 70, 87, 93, 160

Cope (b. Grenville) Dorothy Lady, 59, 64, 65, 85, 88; widow 160, 163-164, 340

Cope, Sir Walter, 44, 50-51, 54, 57, 60, 61, 64-6, 70, 83-4, 85, 88; Cecil's illness and death, 89-93; Sir Julius Caesar, 93-4; Master of Wards, 94-5, 106; death, 159; 160, 211 (228)

Cranborne (title), *see* Cecil

Cranfield, Sir Lionel, 1st Earl of Middlesex, 107, 150, 286-7, 328-331, 334, 347

Devereux, Frances (b. Walsingham) (Sidney) widow of Essex, 26

Devereux, Robert, 2nd Earl of Essex, 2, 4, 5; out of favor, 6; 8, 9, 10; prepares for Ireland, 9, 10, 12; in Ireland 15; new knights 16; rebellion 17-19; (192), 200, 284

Devereux, Robert, 3rd Earl of Essex, 26, 111, 113-116, 120, 331

Digby, Sir John, 1st Lord, 1st Earl of Bristol, Ambassador to Spain, 189, 221, 255, 270, 304, 308, 312, 314-5, 329, 332, 343

Digges, Sir Dudley, 88, 109, 208, 251-2, 258, 260-1, 262, 269, 280, 324, 334

Ditton Park, Bucks, home of Sir Ralph Winwood 167, 184, 244, 265

Donne, John, sermons, 141, 290, 291;

Ph.D., 164-5; daughter 297; *Devotions,* 321

Dormer, Sir Michael, of Ascott, Oxfordshire, 4, 48, 56, 334

Edmondes, Sir Thomas, 54, 55, 65, 104, 110, 155, 161, 166, 177, 181, 336, 359

Elizabeth, Princess, 69-76, 126, 267n., 308, 346

Elizabeth, Queen of England, conspiracies against 5, 9; Essex, 6, 8, 9, 10, 12, 17-19; dances, 10, 29; progresses, *1601,* 47, *1602,* 21; 15, 29, 33, 37, 46, 55; death 22, 23; funeral, 25; 141, (192), 277, 294, 320, 355

Essex (title), *see* Devereux

Fanshawe (b. Smith), Elizabeth Lady, 62, 64, 100, 142, 162, 169, (228), 235, 237, 245-6; 338

Fanshawe, Sir Henry, of Ware Park, Hertfordshire, 93, 110, 168

Fanshawe, Henry, 338, 348, 353

Frederick V, Elector Palatine, 68-77, 88, 98, (228), 257n., 270, 272, (299)

Gent, William, 52, 55, 96, 98

Gondomar (title), *see* Sarmiento

Grotius, Hugo, 178, 229, 233

Harington, John, 1st Lord Harington of Exton, and Lady Harington, guardians of Princess Elizabeth, 72, 77; farthings 126; 194

Hatton, Sir Christopher, cousin of Queen Elizabeth's Lord Chancellor, 110, 168, 245-6

Hatton, Elizabeth Lady (b. Cecil), *see* Coke

Hay, James, Viscount Doncaster, first Earl of Carlisle, 40; courtship 122, 178, 186; to France, 169, 171-3, 178; 257, 278, 293, (299), 304, 308-10, 352, 354

Henrietta Maria, wife of Charles I, 350-4, 356, 359 (361)

Henry, Prince of Wales, 26, 42, 43, 68; patron 91; vast projects 71, 77; illness and death, 69, 78, 195

Herbert, Philip, 1st Earl of Montgomery, 4th Earl of Pembroke, 40, 177, 337, 350, 359

Howard (b. Talbot) Aletheia, Countess of Arundel and Surrey, 77; Italian feast, 142; 163, 181, 239, 360

Howard, Charles, Earl of Nottingham, Lord Admiral, (2), 10, 13; gifts to the Queen, 33; on Garnet, 38; (45); bogus gift from Spain, 117, (228); bought out by Buckingham, 237

Howard, Henry, Earl of Northampton, 2, 24, 74, 90, 109, 111, 116; death 118

Howard, Thomas, 2nd Earl of Arundel and Surrey, 125, 138-139, 148, 259, 332, 360

Howard, Thomas, Lord Howard de Walden, 1st Earl of Suffolk, 2, 4, 14, 90; family: Frances, 113-4, 121; Elizabeth & Thomas, 123; son feuds 137-8; sons at Paul's, 151; Robert & Frances Coke 183, 339-41, 345; hospitality at Cambridge 163; in disgrace, 347

Inojosa, Marquis St. Germain, 306-7, 310, 311-313, 332

James I, King of England, 5n., 11, 20; proclaimed King, 23-5; 38-9, 40, 87, 126, 130, 137, 153, 273, 289; on religion, 35-6; coronation delayed 57; hunting 34, 37, 62, 147, 332; Progress, 1608, 40-41; to Scotland, 140-2; Parliament 1610, 42; 1621, 253-8, 279-84, 287-9; 164, 321, 325-6, 330; Secretaryship, 91, 95, 230; Coke 100, 170-79; Winwood 183, 190; Lake, 232, 241; Abbot, 260; Lady Exeter's case, 234, 239-41; high-handed women, 241-2; Trade, (205), 215, 217, 222, 226; War, 1619, 270; 1620, 276-7, 300-1; 1622, 301-2; Prince Charles' marriage, 301-15, 316-7, 343; illnesses, 96, 151-2, 294, 336; death, 346-7, 349, 351; also chapters IV, VI and IX passim.

Jones, Inigo, 149, 307

Jonson, Ben, 264, 285, 293

Knebworth, Hertfordshire, home of Sir Rowland Lytton, 2, 19, 20-21, 46, 47, 49, 53, 56, 63, 95

Lake, Sir Thomas, 23, 70, 71, 88, 104, 107, 133, 169, 230, 232, 234, 236, 239-44, 246
Lake (b. Ryder), Mary Lady, 104, 241-4
Laud, William, 264, 356
Lennox (title), *see* Stuart
Lisle (title), *see* Sidney
Lytton, Sir Rowland, of Knebworth, Hertfordshire, 2, 6, 12, 13, 19, 45, 46, 48-49, 51, 53, 54, 56, 59, 61, 62, 63, 99, 157, 158, 162, 166, 169, 180; Anne Lady, 47-8; sons: Philip, 174, 248-9; Rowland, 247, 262; Sir William, 45, 49, 61, 99, 168, 211, 262, 267

Mansell, Sir Robert, 20, 21, 73, 225, 281, 316
Mansfeld, Pierre Ernest, Count of, 298n., 330, 333, 338, 341
Matthew, Sir Tobie, 24, 182, 186, 188, 230-33, 258, 265, 343
Montgomery (title), *see* Herbert
Morton, Sir Albert, 317, 327, 340, 350

Naunton, Sir Robert, 201, 203, 231, 236-7, 251, 254, 266-7, 301, 304
Neville, Sir Henry, 17, 25, 46, 47, 88, 91, 101, 196, 210
Norris, Sir Edward, Governor of Ostend, (2), 45, 48, 53, 55
Norris, Francis, 2nd Lord, 1st Earl of Berkshire, 44-45, 57, 59, 63, 281
Northampton (title), *see* Howard
Northumberland (title), *see* Percy
Nottingham (title), *see* Howard

O'Neill, Hugh, second Earl of Tyrone, 7, 14, 20, 22, 26
Overbury, Sir Thomas, 91, 102, 111, 112-113; death, 115-116, 118
Oxford (title), *see* Vere

Parry, Sir Thomas, (2), (44), 46, 49-50, 106
Percy, Henry, ninth Earl of Northumberland, (2), 13, 14, (44), 54, 57-8, 60, 62, 66, 83-5, 121-2, 128, 259, 322
Pory, John, 86, 99, 219, 222, 227

Raleigh, Sir Walter, (2), 4, 5, 14, 118, 192-203; Lady, 296
Rich, Sir Henry, Lord Kensington, 1st Earl of Holland, 89, 130, 160, 354
Rich (b. Cope), Isobel, Countess of Holland, 59, 64, 76, 89
Roe, Sir Thomas, East India Company, 195, 213, 220, 226, 274
Roos (title), *see* Cecil
Russell (b. Harington), Lucy, Countess of Bedford, 128, 154, 235, 239, 344

Sackville, Richard, 3rd Earl of Dorset, 41, 326
St. Alban (title), *see* Bacon
Sandys, Sir Edwin, 108-9, 259n., 262, 269, 324, 350
Sarmiento, Diego Sarmiento de Acuña, Count Gondomar, 162, 189, 196, 247, 251, 253, 259, 289, (299-300), 300-1, 303, 304, 306; parodied, 317-8; 335, 343, 346
Savile, Sir Henry, 44, 55, 96-8, 196, 230, 263; Lady Savile, 97
Sidney, Sir Robert, Viscount Lisle, 2nd Earl of Leicester, 5, 46, 97, 121
Smith (b. Lytton), Judith Lady, 157, 250, 268, 317; Sir George, 247, 250
Southampton (title), *see* Wriothesley
Stuart, Lady Arabella, 25, 174
Stuart (b. Howard) (Pranell) (Seymour) Frances, Duchess of Lennox and Richmond, 309, 321, 327, 336, 341, 345, 360
Stuart, Ludovic, 2nd Duke of Lennox, 1st Duke of Richmond, 20, 148, 309, 321, 327
Suffolk (title), *see* Howard
Sutton, Thomas, founds Charterhouse, 43

Tyrone (title), *see* O'Neill

Vere, Henry, 18th Earl of Oxford, 247, 351
Vere, Sir Horace, 181, 229, 247, 268, 338

Villiers (b. Coke), Frances, Viscountess Purbeck, 182-4, 187, (319), 337, 339-41, 345

Villiers, Sir Christopher, 178; courtships, 153, 264; 276

Villiers, Sir George, Marquis, first Duke of Buckingham, rise, 119, 121, 123, 130, 134, 177-8, 308; family, 143, 177-8, 184, 223, 227, (228), 229, 337, 345; sides form, 132-3; proclamations, 150; Lord Admiral, 237; "rolling planet" patronage, 249, 267, 334, 337, 347; Parliament 1621, 252-7; of 1626, 358-9; in Spain, (299-300), 302-12, 315; managing policy, 313-8, (319), 326, 328, 332-3, 335, 350, 351, 354-5; unnecessary grandeur, 358-9, (361-2)

Villiers, Sir John, Viscount Purbeck, 177-9, 187, 282-4, 264

Wake, Sir Isaac, 157, 159; letters to, 159, 212; 234, 266-7, 323, 327, 330; his Lady's journey, 335, 337; 343, 351

Wallop, Sir Henry, of Farleigh, Hampshire, 47, 63, 66, 106, 250, 262

Ware Park, Hertfordshire, home of Sir Henry Fanshawe, 62; gardening, 61-2, 99, 157; hospitality, 93, 100, 167, 244, 268; 322, 352

Wentworth, Sir Thomas, 1st Earl of Strafford, 1614, 108, 109; 343

Williams, Alexander and Elizabeth (Carleton), 46, 52, 62, 87, 106, 157, 161, 169, 179, 238, 352

Winwood, Sir Ralph, Paris, 24, 46, 49, 53-4; marriage, 56; son, 59; Hague, 65, 87; seeks Secretaryship, 91-2, 102-4; Principal Secretary, 104, 105-9, 155, 110, 112, 132-3, (156), 162, 167, 173, 180-3, 187; friendship with Chamberlain, 44, 48, 55, 56, 66n., 101, 106, (155), 181; Bodley, 96; Carleton, 106, 155, 158, 161, 169-70, 173, 177; Fanshawe, 168; Coke, 171; Bacon, 185, 188, 230-1; Roos, 185; Raleigh, (193), 196; illness & death, 189-91

Winwood (b. Ball), Elizabeth Lady, 104, 120, 157, 162-3, (228), 235-7, 239, 244

Wotton, Sir Edward, 1st Lord, 13, 33, 46, 74

Wotton, Sir Henry, 44, 65, 69, 84, 88-9, 91-2, 208; ill-fated epigram, 94; 99, 107, 158, 161, 166-7, 185-6, 232, 244, 246-7, 317, 327, 350

Wriothesley, Henry, 3rd Earl of Southampton, 4, 8; trial, 18-19, 25, 30; & Virginia Company, 222-3, 226; 259n., 331; widow, 336

Wymark, Edward, 138, 172, 201, 274

Yelverton, Sir Henry, 101, 102, 203, 255-7, 350

Index of Subjects

Ambassadors, from Barbary, 28, 45; Emperor, 263; Savoy, 128; gifts to Turkey, 12; Savoy, from Muscovy, 28-9, 142-3; Great Mogul, 222; English unpaid, 101, 110, 161, 177, 248; Intelligence, 304, 309; incidents, 86, 125, 282-3, 313, 314, 359; see Carleton, Edmondes, Hay, Inojosa, Sarmiento, Wake, Wotton

Bermudas, 209, 211-12, 215

Cambridge University, Bacon, 102; entertains royalty, 76-7, 132-3, 163-5, 335-6; Donne's degree, 164-5, 346

Catholics (priests, papists, recusants), 5, 10, 22, 23, 34; James' position, 35-6; 39, 52; Montague, 74, 124; Rutland, 119; 124; Arundel, 139; T. Matthew, 182 etc.; Raleigh, 201-2; Roos, 231; fear of, *1613*, 126; 129, 135, 136; fear of, *1621*, 280; 287; amnesty, 291; accident in

Blackfriars, 295-6; marriage politics, 241, 304, 316, 328, 333, 350; recusants *1626*, 355; see Jesuits

Censorship, toleration, 127; 141, 195, 274, 277; Spain, 281; 304-5, 315, 318, 320, 342

Courts, Chancery, 138, 337, 339; Circuit, 137; Common pleas, 101, 137; King's Bench, 119-21, 138, 199; Star Chamber, 31, 34, 36, 147, 181, 239-40, 275, 321; Wards, 7, 8, 42, (155), 169, 245-6, 250, 334, 340; House of Lords, 256

Crime and punishments, 5, 30-31, 34, 36-7, 39; Censorship, 127; 131, 135, 137; Shrove Tuesday, 139-40, 143; coiners, 145; Great Seal, 146; 149; deer stealers, 154; sorcery, 271-2, 341; amnesty, 291; 312, 320-1

Diseases and Doctoring, 6, 326; ague, 69, 125, 136; gangrene, 118, 131; plague, 40, 56-7, 80, 349-50, 352-3; smallpox, 21, 95, 146-7, 150, 154, 240, 243, 265, 344; scurvy, 89, 134; stone, 151, 180, 270; prayer therapy, 129; sick seasons, 129, 136, 292; Prince Henry, 69-70, 195; Winwood, 190, 245; Chamberlain, 86, 88, 127

East India, trade, 208-9, 210, 212, 214, 217, 222, 224-7; Amboyna, 297-8, 331-2, 342; Company, 213, 216, 217-8, 220, 227n., 251, 285, 342; negotiations, 239-43, 355

Economic depressions, *1610*, 42; *1620* ff., 220, 271, 276-9, 284-5, 287, 291; measures against, 291-3; scarcity in Spain, 305, 307-8

Fashions, in dress, 39, 74, 75, 99, 102, 133, 141, 153, 172, 271-2; make-up, 128; feasts, 142, 147, 179, 186, 272, 354; Venetian glass, 162; city travel, 356, 359; funerals, 63, 118, 135, 148, 150-2, 348

Fights and duels, 5-6, 27-8, 126-7, 129-30; duels condemned, 130; 137, 138, 154, 226-7, 281, 344, 359

France, Henry IV, 4, 5, 12, 29; peace, 5; trade, 12; character, 31, 42, 178-9; marriage politics, 301, 304, 309, 316-8, 327-8, 333, 335-6, 343, 345-6, 350-4

Gardens and gardening, 61, 62, 93; fruit, 135, 136; plants from Italy, 157, to The Hague, 235; 184

Gunpowder plot, 37-8, (44-5), 57-8, 84-5

Holland, 3, 5, 7, 15, 21, 24, 45, 194, 207; Commerce, (204), 211, 212, 220, 224-5, 239, 243, 260, 355; East Indies, 220, 222, 224, 252, 297-8, 331-2, 342; War, 261, 325, 331, (361); see Merchant Adventurers, Pirates, Thirty Years War

Inns of Court, 30, 32, 34, 74-6, 126

Ireland, 3, 5, 7, 8, 10, 12, 14, 17, 19, 22; parody, 117; 206; plantation, 207; 284, 321, 326, 341, 348, 353, 358; see Essex, Tyrone, Spain

Italy, taxes, 107; mercenaries, 206; embargo in Florence, 12; ship held in Naples, 227; Venetian character, 261, 310

Jesuits, vs. Elizabeth, 9; vs. James, 11, 185-7; Garnet, 37-8; 39, 51, 55, 129, 224, 295-6, 310, 326

London I, building regulations, 31, 146, 150; buildings collapse, 16, 28, 295; fires, 57, 146; Whitehall, 148-9; 289, 296, 337; Depression, *1622*, 292, 294; desolation (plague), *1626*, 356; St. Paul's Cathedral, Paul's-walking, (1), 54, 233; scenes and sermons, 15, 151, 153, 233, 312, 318; repairs, 272-6; Thames, defense of, 14; frozen, 40, 279; travel on, 43, 270; pageants, 72-5; water conduit, 292

London II, City Companies and Government, loans, 7, 10, 13, 140; (no feasts), 277; ships, 9; social duties, 15, 16, 45, 117, 153; Bourse, 40; police, 73, 342; discipline, 145-6; Dutch commissioners, 242-3; Thirty Years War, 263, 272-3; Lord Mayor bankrupt, 285; repair of St. Paul's, 273; King on poverty, 294

London III, Parades and Processions, Reception of King, 39; Prince from Richmond, 78; King to Parliament, 104, 279; Somersets to Merchant Taylors' Hall, 117; Inns of Court Masquers to Whitehall, 74-5; Garter Knights to Windsor, 132-3; King to Whitehall, 153; Bacon to Westminster, 180; King to St. Paul's, 273; King's funeral, 347-9; Queen Henrietta, 356

London IV, Scenes, Invasion fear, 1599, 15; Guy Fawkes, 58; Whitehall bride, 73-4; priests at Tyburn, 123; Bath Knights at Drapers' Hall, 137; footrace, 144; Queen at Exchange, 144; Hyde Park poachers, 154; Sion House, 186; Dutch at Merchant Taylors' Hall, 243; Northumberland leaves Tower, 259; Banquet, Essex House, 278; Gondomar, Ely House, 300; Prince Charles' return, 311-2; Henrietta at York House, 354

Marriage arrangements, Savile rejects a Lord, 97; Mary Fanshawe, 169; Coke-Villiers, 179; Wenman-Chamberlain, 237-8, 239; Lady Carleton's daughter, 251; Sussex', 294; 337, 340
Merchant Adventurers (cloth industry), (204-5), 212-20
Militia, 13-15, 126, 168, 241, 263, 294; beacons, 151
Money and Prices I, domestic: bankrupt mercer, 31; funeral, 63; suit of clothes, 102; rents, 104, 166, 355; seat at a trial, 120; grain, 279; fruit, 333; storm damages, 129; Cope's estate, 129; Coke's marriage settlement, 179; Court: gambling, 42, 144; fancy cloth, 74; gifts, 72, 117; loan to Prince, 94; masques, 102, 130; banquets, 163, 179-81, 278, 313-4; royal wedding, 76; Queen's holiday, 77; King to Scotland, 140; at Farnham, 248; Lady Doncaster, 257; Queen Henrietta, 352; cf Burghley, 6-7
Money and Prices II, Crown revenues, sale of land, 13; 1610 proposals, 42; sale of titles, 131, 133-4, 173, 322,

430; of coats of Arms, 132; of pardons, 133; benevolences, 110, 113, 289-90; forced loan, 216-7; Merchants Strangers fines, 221; Queen's estate, 151; Parliament "the only plain highway," 289
Money and Prices III, money supply, farthings and Burgundy plate, 126; ship carrying coin, 214; Merchants Strangers, (204), 221-2; Reform, 220; Tower treasure, 270; see Economic Depressions
Monopolies, impositions, patents, 107, 223, 252, 275, 282, 295
Muscovy, 6, 7, 24; students, 31-2; ambassadors, 28-9, 142-3; great plans for trade, 209-10; Company, 211, 216, 218, 285; Greenland whaling, 211, 215

Navy, 1597, 3; 1599, 14-15; 1601, 16, 23, 206; wedding, 72-3, 77; pirates, 224-5; Buckingham, 237; 1621, 224; Charles in Spain, 307-9, 311, 316; 1625-6, 325-6, 350, 357
North-west passage, 88, 206, 208

Oxford University, commencement 1602, 21; 30; sleeping preacher, 36; new buildings (Wadham and Merton), 93; Bodley's bequest (Library and Merton), 97-8; M.P., 359

Parliament: 1601, 20; 1605, 35; 1607, 63; 1610, 42; comments on, 1612, 70, 91; 1614, 103-10; elections, 130; 1620-21, 248-9, 252-7, 262, 277, 279-84, 285-8; 1623, 268-9; 1624, 314, 317, 321, 324, 325-6, 328-30; 1625, 345-6, 354-5; 1626, 357
People (Chamberlain's human-interest stories), "Sebastian, King of Portugal," 11; 32, 39, 40; impersonating Prince, 71; Lady Webb, 95; attack "Lady Somerset," 121; 124, 135, 136, 138, 143, 148; debtors, 149-50; 152, 153; Spanish heretic, 275
Plays, players, playhouses, prank, 32; Tragedy of Gowrie, 34; 69; masques by Inns of Court, 74-6; for Somersets, 101, 117; Globe burns, 128; Ignoramus, 132; apprentices wreck

Queen's players, 140; Burbage dead, 150; new Globe, 157; Gondomar at the Fortune, 259; fire, 288; Alleyn, 297; Masques, *1623-5*, 314-15, 359; Middleton's *Game at Chess*, 317; 342; see Cambridge

Pirates and Privateers, English, 12, 20, 34, 124, 205-7; Embargo, 12; Dutch, 312, 334; Dunkirkers, 17, 24, 207, 227, 312, 334; 350; Barbary, 212-13, 224-6, 281, 284

Postal service, 53, 139, 157, 161, 174, 233, 234-5, 266, 278, 340-1

Religion, Arminians, 89, 143, 178, 229, 238n.; Brownists, 146; Church of England, 35; *1614*, 107; no simony, 145; King's constancy, *1622*, 291; Hugenots, 284, (361); Puritans, 35-6, 281; Sectarian fanatic, 143; see Catholics, Jesuits

Signs, Wonders and Curiosities, 31, 35, 36, 41, 70, 125, 147, 249

Sheriffs, 47, 175, 250, 265-6

Spain, War, 3-5, 11, 13-5; navy reform, 16; 205-6; peace, 194, (204); help to Irish, 17, 19, 206, 290; popular feeling against, 145, 207, 280-3, 308-9, 313, 335; oppose Virginia colony, 209, 212; and exploration, 196-7, 201, 221-4; Ormuz, 227; incidents, 214, 240, 281, 290, 332; Philip III, (3), 11, 12, 301; Philip IV, marriage politics, 301-15, 324-5, 333, 348; Olivarez, 312, 325

Spanish Netherlands, Antwerp, 14; 24; Ostend, 45; 126, 314; Spinola, 21, 24, 300-1; see Pirates (Dunkirkers)

Thirty Years War, *1619*, 270; *1620*, 246-8; loan, 272; subscriptions, 273, 276, 285; King's role, 255, 263, 287, 301; volunteers, 274-5, 300, 331, 359; Mansfeld and impressment, 298, 333-4, 337-8, 341-2, 350; Scots, 356-7; casualties, 250, 262, 336, 351; marriage politics, 222, 301-2, 310, 316; defeats, 300-2; see Parliament, esp. *1624-5*

Travel, in England, 43, 142, 162, 167, 270; Bermuda, 215; South Seas, 28, 33; Virginia, 218; to and from Continent, 4-5, 56, 68, 236, 304, 306, 308, 315, 330, 343; Chamberlain's journey, 80-3; ill winds, 215, 236

Virginia, *1608*, 40; investment, (ix), 208, 214; suffering, 209; Pocahontas, 210-11; 215, 218, 219, 222, 223; population, 146, 218; Indian attack, 225-6; 294

Virginia Company, 211, 216, 222, 226

Wagers and dares, 30, 33, 40, 41, 144; King wins a feast, 76; Prince loses Denmark House, 272

Weather, frost, 40, 147, 262, 279, 326; later summer, 333; drought, 134-5; storms, 129, 334-5; high tides, 285, 334; winds, 139, 215; fire, 125